9/5/06

Concert Lighting

Concert Lighting

Techniques, Art, and Business
Second Edition

James L. Moody

Focal Press

Amsterdam   Boston   Heidelberg   London   New York   Oxford
Paris   San Diego   San Francisco   Singapore   Sydney   Tokyo

Focal Press is an imprint of Elsevier.

Permissions may be sought directly from Elsevier's Science & Technology Rights Department in Oxford, UK: phone: (+44) 1865 843830, fax: (+44) 1865 853333, e-mail: permissions@elsevier.co.uk. You may also complete your request on-line via the Elsevier Science homepage (http://www.elsevier.com), by selecting 'Customer Support' and then 'Obtaining Permissions'.

This book is printed on acid-free paper.

Library of Congress Cataloging-in-Publication Data
Moody, James L.
   Concert lighting: techniques, art, and business /
by James L. Moody.—2nd ed.
    p.   cm.
   Includes bibliographical references (p. 265) and index.
   ISBN 0-240-80293-4 (alk. paper)
   1.   Music-halls—Lighting. 2. Lighting—Special effects. 3. Stage lighting. I. Title.
TK4399.T6M66 1997
792,7'025—dc21   9721517
                                CIP

British Library Cataloguing-in-Publication Data
A catalogue record for this book is available from the British Library.

The publisher offers special discounts on bulk orders of this book.
For information, please contact:
Manager of Special Sales
Elsevier Science
200 Wheeler Road
Burlington, MA 01803
Tel: 781-313-4700
Fax: 781-313-4802

For information on all Focal Press publications available, contact our World Wide Web homepage at http://www.focalpress.com

10 9 8 7 6 5 4
Printed in the United States of America

In all of life there is nothing better than to be free to do the things you love. I have been blessed to have not one but several things that have truly made life a joy—my career in theatrical lighting, teaching, and the love of Trudie Helene Sullivan.

My deepest thanks to all those who contributed to this expanded second edition, especially the other designers: Peter Morse, Jeff Ravitz, and Willie Williams. And to my partners and associates, especially Jeremy Windle, at M/R/H Lighting Design, Inc., who helped in so many ways. Thank you all.

Contents

Contents

Foreword

With the virtual explosion of new lighting technology, which brings innovation and change to this field almost weekly, this second edition of *Concert Lighting* by Jim Moody comes at a perfect time. Concert tours may be the fastest growing facet of the lighting industry, both in the United States and especially abroad, and Jim knows the field as well as anyone.

This book builds on the foundation that the first edition established eight years ago and covers much more than concert and tour lighting. As I travel, I hear often of the value of the first edition, so I am pleased to tell these colleagues and friends that *the* expert has updated and expanded the "bible." Whether you're into bus and truck, part of a permanent staff in a tour venue or theatre, or a television designer, this is the guide you need.

As the late Lee Watson intimated in his foreword to the first edition, Jim Moody merges art and the craft in this book. He shows you with practical examples and illustrations how to do it, but he also helps you get inside the designer's head to see *why* designers make decisions on placement, color, and movement. He builds on the history of the art form to help you understand the evolution of lighting control and equipment. This benefits you as you confront older equipment on tour and provides you with a sense of appreciation of new technology.

I have favorite sections, especially those relating to designers' perspectives on lighting and the international touring section. Given the cross-over work of lighting designers, Jim has wisely included sections on television, live theatre, and film, and we gain from his wealth of experience in each. I had the pleasure of collaborating with Jim a few years ago and can hear his "voice" in this book. He writes as he speaks—a practical, sensible approach to the artistry of the business. Jim is a great "teacher," and this book is a great tool.

Dick Durst
Dean of Fine and Performing Arts
University of Nebraska—Lincoln
President, International Association of Designers,
    Theater Architects, and Technicians (OISTAT)
Lincoln, Nebraska
April 1997

Foreword to the First Edition

Jim Moody is the ideal person to write about concert business and lighting. He is one of the entrepreneurs in this new lighting industry, and he writes with great clarity, organization, and readable simplicity. Jim's specialized knowledge of lighting for the concert field embraces the technical and the artistic, as well as pragmatic organizational knowhow. With a solid background in theatre lighting, degrees from Southern Illinois University and UCLA, he moved into concert lighting. He has been a leading advocate for fusion of the innovations and techniques of concert lighting into other production forms.

Jim was honored in 1980 with the first Lighting Designer of the Year Award presented by *Performance* magazine, the leading publication on concert touring. The award was based on a readers' poll of concert industry contemporaries. Jim has also received awards in television and theatre.

Those who are specialists in other lighting design areas—drama, musicals, opera, dance, television, amusement parks, landscape, and architectural lighting, and educators in these fields—will profit from reading this volume carefully. Nowadays almost all working lighting designers cross over into all areas of design use in light. Jim Moody is in a unique position to contribute to our knowledge by sharing his experience and insight into concert lighting. We are fortunate that he has done so in this volume.

Lee Watson
Purdue University
West Lafayette, Indiana

Preface: The Full Circle

Now that concert lighting has had more than 35 years of phenomenal growth, it has finally been accepted by the wider group of theatrical practitioners. I use the word *theatrical* to encompass theatre (spelled as such throughout the book unless referring to a movie theater), dance, television, film, audiovisual, and corporate media, as well as the fringe design media, such as architectural and display lighting.

Experimental years produced many useful techniques for all of the other theatrical lighting media. The developers of concert lighting were interested not only in new technology but also in the adaptation of older techniques from other media. They recognized that the past is often a greater teacher than the future and that it can be used to solve problems. This is well documented with what the early concert designers did to bring about this new art form. Theatre has traditionally borrowed from other fields. In its early days, television used many standards already set by the film industry. Now all of these disciplines can gain from the innovations developed in this newest design field.

While introducing the reader to concert lighting, I also show techniques that have application in legitimate theatre and dance, television, film, and other nontraditional media. However, I can present only the tip of the iceberg. Your individual needs and facilities very likely require expansion or even totally new approaches to be tailored to your needs. I can only hope that this book will open the door to experimentation based on the concert lighting experiences I and those who contributed to this book have had as outlined in the following pages. You will also find examples of how the techniques have been used in some of these other media.

In creating a new theatrical form, there had to be a base, a starting place. Much of it came from traditional theatre lighting. Theatre had the general form and style desired by the beginning concert designer. It was the greatest exponent in the use of color media, an important objective for Rock and Roll designers. One great contribution, the PAR-64 fixture, came from film. Television was still heavily relying on film instrumentation when concert lighting began, so it contributed very little else. As you will see, live video has become a big part of concerts, and therefore the need to understand video is a must for the concert designer.

Concert lighting grabbed onto the principle of psychovisual relations, the emotional impact of how people react to colored light, and expanded our use of its ability to influence the audience. The use of color became an art form unto itself. Whereas pastels and lightly tinted colors (no-colors) were the generally accepted rule in theatre, concert designers went for heavily saturated colors: bold, eye-catching, primary colors. Theatre textbooks on color do give the lighting designer the basic principles from which to start, and you should study them before attempting to read this book. After all, we cannot change the laws of physics; we can just give the audience new visual priorities.

The Broadway musical comes closest to what the concert lighting designer was looking for within the live theatre genre. The follow spot as a key source of light was the primary front light, but ratio and relation between side and back light took on new importance. Back light with heavily saturated primary colors became the dominant source for mood and area lighting.

The available theatrical lighting fixtures in the mid 1960s were the problem for concert lighting designers. The glass lenses did not troupe well, they were heavy, broke easily, and their lumen-per-watt ratio was poor. (That term is used to give the designer or electrician a scale for determining the efficiency of the fixture in relation to other fixtures from which the designer has to choose for the job at hand.) Power availability was a concern in the "found space" to which concerts were relegated. These spaces usually lacked the facilities for a normal theatre or studio setup. A more efficient light source was critical if the limited power resource was to be used.

The development of portable lighting structures may ultimately be the greatest single non-lighting contribution concert lighting makes to other lighting fields. Large spanning structures to mount portable lighting were virtually undeveloped in theatre, film, or television. The highly flexible trussing used in concert work have become part of television studios at several large facilities. Facility planners of the future should take advantage of this basic research and hundreds of thousands of hours of on-the-job trial and error.

The truss developed by concert lighting designers should be viewed not as a classic engineering model, but as a practical, everyday, structural concept that has now been time tested. The size and weight-bearing factors change with application, but the surprisingly utilitarian construction of the devices must be studied and refined if we are to continue to develop new staging techniques no matter what the field of use.

In the final analysis, what we do in any theatrical form is attempt to use light to influence the viewers' perception of the scene, whether we are making a highly dramatic statement or simply providing enough illumination for the viewer to interpret the action. I still go by a saying I heard when I was in college: *It's not where you put the light, it's where you don't put the light that makes for good theatrical lighting.*

That line has always been a guidepost for me in my design for any project, no matter what the media. The absence of light is largely perceived as the dramatic key to the theatricality of creative lighting. It is what separates it from the illumination we find in our everyday lives.

It is incorrect to think that television lighting is nothing more than a technical function of the camera. The need for lighting to create mood and texture is very important. Beyond these, the need to create depth of field and contrast must always be considered. Chapter 22 explains in detail the parameters for video and film reproduction. As with many points in the rest of the book, it is worth keeping these needs in mind for any theatrical lighting design.

The sum total of our experiences contributes to how we use lighting equipment in our various design applications. With the new experiences of concert lighting from which to draw, the answer to a problem may be closer. A solution may be suggested in the following pages that will be of help sometime in the future.

This book presents new lighting concepts. It is an introduction for students and others wishing to learn about concert lighting as a potential vocation. It is also a guide for working designers and technicians in other fields. Those already involved with concert production will find this a useful source. Understanding how concert lighting techniques were developed and how they can be applied in other media can expand any designer's horizons. To enrich your creativity, you must look outside your limited experiences to the loosely connected media in which a theatrical approach to lighting is used.

Concert lighting has often been considered unconventional, but a definition of unconventional use of lighting should not be limited to the use of "nontheatrical fixtures" such as neon, arc, or fluorescent sources. All theatrical lighting elements have unconventional applications if we think about a problem only in the broader context. Do not be limited by how someone tells you to use something or how it was used in the past. Take the situation at hand and solve the problem with whatever means it takes. Theatrical lighting is a creative technology, not an exacting science.

In the following chapters I use the experiences I have had during my 25 years in the concert lighting field. This book is meant to be not the definitive work on the subject but a highly personal view of a few of my designs and my involvement in concert lighting as well as other media. How I have mixed them all together to develop unconventional approaches and methods in lighting is a big part of my technique. This practical, hands-on approach has been uppermost in my mind while I have been writing, and for this reason some reiteration may be evident from time to time. This is intentional, for it is sometimes tedious to have to refer to previous pages. Furthermore, if the basic ideas are restated in several places, it will help you to remember them, and their paramount importance becomes more evident.

Some new terms may not be followed by definitions (check the Glossary). I am assuming that the reader has already obtained a basic knowledge of lighting before reading this volume.

Accept my ideas in the spirit in which they were written, simply as a new way to see things. "Use the good ideas found in life and discard the bad" has always been my philosophy. Make it yours, turn it around, and look at it in new and different ways. Make your own analysis, then push forward and develop innovations of your own.

I have included several chapters that on first glance may seem unrelated to the specific job of lighting a concert. It takes more than a knowledge of lumens and color charts to be a professional designer. Ours is a collaborative art and knowledge of the inner workings of the entire production as they relate to your specific job is essential. Because the concert media has not been written about extensively, I felt I had to spend a portion of this book putting the field into perspective for the reader. Read these chapters as if they were the key to the outer door. You cannot get into the inner sanctum without it.

Acknowledgments

I am indebted to the past and present publishers of *Lighting Dimensions*, Fred Weller and Patricia McKay, editors Arnold Aronson and David Rogers of *Theatre Design and Technology*, and Patricia McKay as editor and publisher of *Theatre Crafts*, for their courteous permission to use material that appeared in articles I contributed to those periodicals.

James L. Moody
Los Angeles, California
January 1997

I

The Concert
Lighting Field

1

The Birth of Rock and the Rise of the Concert Lighting Designer

It is difficult to pinpoint the actual beginning of concert lighting as we think of it today. Certainly the Grand Tour could be seen as having been the byproduct of opera in the mid nineteenth century. The term often was given to a star's travels through Europe presenting solo programs in the European cultural capitals. Later, the Grand Tour came to the Americas. Through the years it also came to include the popular figures of show business, encompassing not only opera but also the stars of dance halls, vaudeville, and the circus. In the late nineteenth century, despite their isolated locations, even small Nevada gold rush towns had an opera house to show the world how "cultured" they had become.

The swing bands of the 1920s and 1930s brought a big change to popular music and, some believe, sounded the first notes that would ultimately be recognized as Rock and Roll. Led by such greats as Duke Ellington, Count Basie, and Paul Whiteman, these bands emphasized instrumental solos—riffing, the playing of a short phrase over and over, which is now considered a key ingredient of Rock and Roll.

Another milestone was the entrance of the pop idol. Although Benny Goodman is widely credited for igniting the first "teen hysteria" in 1938 at a Carnegie Hall concert, it would later be a teenager from Hoboken, New Jersey, Francis Albert Sinatra, who would sustain a legion of young teenage girls screaming during his performances.

Enter the baby boom of the 1940s. Postwar American prosperity saw many cultural changes. An avalanche of consumer products became available to the average family. Money to buy these products also was available in the boom of the postwar years. Men's ability to have total purchasing power also changed. Before World War II, the head of the household made the purchase decisions for the family. But by the early 1950s, manufacturers finally realized the growing financial power of the teen market. Teenagers had allowances, and it was estimated in a 1951 survey that they had $4.5 billion dollars to spend. It was estimated that $75 million of that was spent on 45 r.p.m. single records. In the early 1960s a large number of these war babies, who were 16 to 19 years of age, married, and their buying power increased even more. Producers and manufacturers were eager to listen to this emerging class of purchasers.

3

Teens' listening tastes were having a decided impact on the music business. Disc jockeys could play a tremendous part in record sales. But it still was unclear what teens wanted. Stations relegated blues and country music to times when fewer adults listened. These listeners became known as the "late people." To be a disc jockey you simply needed a sponsor, no experience required. One of those early late-night programs was called "King Biscuit Time" and aired on KFFA in Helena, Arkansas. A disc jockey calling himself Howlin' Wolf had a show on KWEM in West Memphis, Arkansas. Both played blues and some country artists. Because this music was not mainstream, the shows aired between 5 A.M. and 6 A.M.[1]

It may have been more than luck that these programs aired on what were called 50,000 watt "clear-channel" stations. With that kind of power and the phenomenon of AM signal skip due to the ozone, on a clear night, when the conditions in the ionosphere were right, you could hear stations that had "skipped" thousands of miles. Teens in Arizona might hear their first Mississippi Delta Blues from a station in Tennessee, or a group of teens in Wisconsin could tune in to hear young country singers like Carl Perkins or Buddy Holly.

Although blacks owned no radio stations, these few disc jockeys opened the doors to what was almost a secret society of "black music" and culture. Admittedly it was a forced secret because of racism and segregation, but it was a distinct musical style that appealed to white teens who had money to spend.

In Los Angeles, one of the most popular programs was called "Huntin' with Hunter" on KGFJ featuring Hunter Hancock. His style was to mix blues, jazz, and spirituals with rhythm and blues. He was good friends with Johnny Otis, who owned a club called The Barrel House in Watts. Teens began to flock to the club, white as well as black. Hancock's machine-gun delivery, growling, use of hip slang, and general carrying on like a madman caught on. Before long Hancock's program was transcribed to stations across the country. Hancock emphasized that he was bringing listeners the latest and greatest Negro performers. Although everyone assumed he was black, Hancock kept himself out of public view—he was white.

Wolfman Jack later adopted Hancock's style and for many years broadcast from a 50,000 watt station in Mexico without being seen in public. He had a tremendous influence on taste in teen music in the 1960s. In his early days many people also thought Wolfman Jack to be black. He created a mystique and even portrayed himself in the classic George Lucas movie, *American Graffiti*.

The melding of country music and regional sounds such as rhythm and blues had been building until in 1951 a disc jockey named Alan Freed started the "Moondog Show" on WJW radio in Cleveland. The name came from a tune by Todd Rhodes called "Blues for Moondog" and contained a wailing saxophone solo that Freed adopted as his theme song. He'd leave the microphone open and howl like a coyote. It was demented and near anarchy, but it was what teens had been waiting to hear. In 1954 the name was changed to "The Rock and Roll Show." *Rolling Stone* magazine later wrote that the term was perfect because "It was a way of distinguishing the new rhythm and blues

---

1. Ed Ward, Geoffrey Stokes, and Ken Tucker. *Rock of Ages: The Rolling Stone History of Rock and Roll* (New York: Rolling Stone Press, 1986), 68–70.

from just plain blues and the old corny Mills Brothers style. After all, Rock and Roll didn't fit into any of the old categories."[2]

The benchmark of modern concert touring was set in the mid 1950s by the independent record companies in an effort to exploit the fledgling Rock and Roll recording artists. The tours were not a radical departure from what swing bands and orchestras had been doing in the 1930s, 1940s, and 1950s; that is, playing dances in every town that had a community hall or theater. After all, this was the way most musicians made a living—playing live dances. But now the pop singer was not just a member of the band; the singer, rather than the bandleader, came to front the band. Another change was that rather than getting work through a booking agent separate from their manager, pop singers were promoted by an independent record producer, who also controlled the record, or sometimes an independent entrepreneur like Alan Freed. That way the record company made money not only from ticket sales but also, more important, by stimulating record sales. Many artists signed away their publishing rights for a small, onetime fee or were lied to by the record companies concerning a record's earnings.

Concert Lighting Begins in the United States

Lighting did not come into a prominent position until after sound reinforcement made the first inroads around 1960. The inadequate sound systems in most buildings could not handle the demands of recording artists who had come to expect studio-quality sound (not to mention the new electronic effects necessary to make them sound like the record). After an artist became used to absorbing the expense of carrying sound equipment from city to city, lighting was soon to follow.

One of the first artists to carry lighting equipment was Harry Belafonte in the mid 1960s. He had come on the record scene in 1957 from his home in Jamaica and was truly ahead of his time. Chip Monck got his start with Harry. Generally, MOR (middle-of-the-road or light rock) and country-and-western artists were the last to see the value of building a production around their music. For some reason, folk acts like the Chad Mitchell Trio, the Kingston Trio, and Peter, Paul, and Mary took notice of the added value special lighting gave to the show and started hiring companies like McManus Enterprises in Philadelphia to provide lighting for their college dates.

The San Francisco Light Shows

What became known as 1960's acid rock was spearheaded by bands such as Big Brother and the Holding Company, Jefferson Airplane, Warlock, Grace Slick and the Great Society, and Quicksilver Messenger Service. All were based in San Francisco. Actually it was a nonmusical group, San Francisco Mime Troupe, at the close of 1965, who unwittingly created the first light show. Bill Graham, who was their manager, said that people would show up and ask if they could hang sheets on the walls and he'd ask, "What are you talking about?" "My screens, I'm a liquid projectionist," was the answer. Light shows were not planned and they were not even paid. They were just part of what came together spontaneously.

---

2. *Rock of Ages*, 96–97.

"Happenings" could include films, dance, music, mime, painting, and just about anything else people wanted to do, all going on at once.

Bill Graham was brought in to produce the now famous Trips Festival at the Longshoremen's Hall in January of 1966. Later that year, he proudly rented the Fillmore Auditorium on Fillmore and Geary from Charles Sullivan, who was a black man, to put on the second Mime Troupe benefit. But this one was billed as a "Dance Concert." After that Graham could see live Rock and Roll music as the main attraction. He split from the Mime Troupe and started promoting musical groups on his own. Graham arranged concerts that featured individual bands as the main attraction without ancillary features. Films, however, were shown during the set changes to keep the audience occupied.

When he started formally promoting concerts, Bill Graham continued to welcome the light shows and eventually started paying for in-house light shows that he could control. They were a visual explosion of color and design. The shows were based on liquid light projection, strobe lights, black light, and effect lighting to create a visual mood as an environment into which band as well as audience was immersed. The liquid light projector was nothing fancier than the opaque projector your grade school teacher used to show photos and charts from books. Only in place of the book was a pan with oil or water into which paints were pushed, splashed, and injected. The pan was vibrated or tilted to add even more movement to the everchanging patterns that this mixture created.

Graham was not interested specifically in advancing lighting or film or anything in particular, but he was a bulldog when it came to his belief about how the audience should be treated. His background and training in New York theatre gave Graham a belief that with music alone he could create an art form. He wanted the audience to have a great experience. He felt he was the only person looking out for the audience. The bands often didn't care if there even was an audience. If a good experience for the audience meant better lighting and sound, he encouraged and supported it. Graham provided a space for many early lighting designers to push their limits and experiment. He was known for treating the people around him as family. That included yelling at them when he felt it was necessary. Graham would conduct regular meetings before a show for everyone involved, including the ushers.

Lighting was not important in those early concerts because people came more to "make the scene" than to listen to any one band. As band followings grew and Graham encouraged expansion of production values as part of a better experience for the audience, lighting moved beyond the mask of the light show.

Other Cities and Venues

This is not to say that concert lighting did not exist outside of San Francisco. There were other venues at about the same time that received national attention. The Electric Factory in Philadelphia, circa 1967, was one. A very young Bill McManus fell into being the lighting guru by accident. A mistake by a receptionist sent a call meant for McManus's boss, MacAvoy, who was often called Mac, to a 19-year-old working in the shop of a theatrical lighting rental company. Bill "Mac" McManus saw an opportunity and met with a man who said he wanted to open "one of them psychedelic things." He had an old factory on 22nd and Arch and asked if Mac could come look at what it needed for lighting.

Before the Electric Factory opened, the largest live concert venue in town was the Latin Casino, which held about 3,500 persons. The Electric Factory was to hold 5,000, an unheard of size for its day. Fieldhouses at universities held in the 5,000 to 6,000 range, and only a handful of artists dared perform in them. The Electric Factory was so successful that it was turning over the house (audience) two and three times a night.

Because of its experiences at the Fillmore, The Grateful Dead was one of the bands that encouraged light shows and film projection at its other gigs. There quickly developed a "family" around the band. "People just started doing things. We just played and things happened. If it felt good we'd say do it next time," said Jerry Garcia in Graham's autobiography, *Bill Graham Presents*. Josh White noted, "Kip Cohen always said that the reason the light show worked so well was that musicians didn't realize that people had eyes as well as ears. . . . Jefferson Airplane would do twenty minute songs in the darkness in their street clothes with their backs to the audience."[3]

Fillmore East

Bob See recalls that while he was a student at New York University in the School of the Arts Theatre Program, he just happened to walk through an open door with a group of friends into an abandoned movie house near campus. There were Chip Monck and some of the people with Joshua Light Show on the stage trying to put things together:

> We just kind of got involved. Because this was a real event, a real happening. From the standpoint that they were trying things that no one had ever tried before. It was the era of the 60s. So we started working there, Chris Langheart, Bob Gaddard and John Chester. And as the place evolved we sort of took on jobs, I became the technical director and did lighting stuff with Chip Monck (Bob See, personal interview, 1996).

The Fillmore East opened in 1968 in the Commodore Theater. It was at the last minute that the venue took that name. It was to have been called the Village Theatre, but because of a legal threat, the name was changed to Fillmore East after the handbills had been printed. The Fillmore East opened March 8, 1968, featuring Big Brother and the Holding Company with Janis Joplin, Tim Buckley, and Albert King, recalls Josh White. Across the street at the Anderson Theatre, Gladys Knight performed with Pablo's Lights.[4]

Fledgling Lighting in England

While all this was happening in the United States, England was experiencing a blues explosion. Bands devoured any records they could get of Muddy Waters, Lightning Hopkins, B. B. King, and many others. There was a club scene. The Marquee Club in London and the Red Car Jazz Club, which was really a Rock and Roll club, were the places to play. The Round House, another club, catered to visiting American bands

---

3. Bill Graham and Robert Greenfield, *Bill Graham Presents* (New York: Doubleday, 1992), 259.

4. Graham and Greenfield, *Bill Graham Presents*, 232.

like The Doors during the early 1960s. Ian Peacock said, "I remember it was more of a place to hang out than to hear the bands" (personal interview, 1996). Because they were more sophisticated in their equipment, would-be designers came to see and hear what these clubs were doing.

Most often the British bands found themselves playing in community halls and school assembly rooms where there was no stage lighting. Follow spots were even rarer. The British bands were hearing and sometimes seeing what the Americans were doing in a few spots like the Fillmores, but the British lighting industry did not have equipment available to meet the needs of these new media. Consequently, many early systems were designed around American fixtures. It was up to people like Michael Tait to invent what they needed.

Tait was one of the early people to build lighting systems around the specific needs of a band. He started with YES in 1968. Tait had worked at a nightclub and somehow ended up driving the band somewhere. Tait says he just fell into the job. He started by doing anything the band needed. At first that was setting up their small public address system. In those days bands used only vocal microphones. No one thought of miking the drums or guitars. Each band had its own sound system, so the crew completely changed that as well as the band gear after each set.

Tait remembers that the second show he worked was on a bill with The Who, Small Faces, Arthur Brown and the Mind Benders, and YES at the bottom of the bill. The show was in Newcastle, England, in the town hall. There might have been some white light above the stage, but that was all. Tim Murch, who currently works out of the Newberry Park, California office of Light & Sound Design, remembers seeing Black Sabbath in a South Hampton Guild Hall with house lights on circa 1970.

Things developed slowly in England because the size of the audience for most bands did not bring in enough money to support the band, let alone buy lighting. A few bands, like The Who and Pink Floyd, were interested in production. But there still wasn't a lot to spend, nor was the equipment available to spend it on.

Other early British innovators were Jonathan Smeeton and Graham Flemming. Michael Tait says, and it is echoed by Ian Peacock, that people mostly showed up and someone said, "OK, who's doing sound, who's doing lights tonight?" But soon, as in America, people gravitated to what they did best. No formal training, just desire and drive. "We were taking light bulbs and putting them in coffee cans," says Tait. He talks about getting 12 automobile fog lamps, attaching them to a piece of pipe, and connecting them to wirewound potentiometers to make mini-dimmers. "They worked for a few months, but they kept melting. But they had the desired effect, you got a narrow beam of light across the front of the stage," says Tait. "In the beginning I didn't realize you need back light and side light. I had them out front, but it looked flat and horrible. Then one day I couldn't find a place to attach my lights out front and hung them on the side. That's when I realized that side and back light was what it was all about."

Tait's first "go" at lighting was at the Marque Club, which had a red light and a blue light above the stage with switches on the wall. YES's music had a staccato effect and lent itself to the flashing of these lights in time with the music. People went wild. But Tait still didn't consider lighting his skill: "YES first toured America as the opening act for Jethro Tull. I forgot where the first gig was but somebody said, well who's going to call the follow spots? Well, we never had any, so I was the one messing with lights, so it had to be me." He went on to say, "But I found I could do it. I found that I could cue four lights and that I knew what I wanted to do. It was just something that I just naturally could do." (All quotes from personal interviews, 1996.)

Move to Larger Venues

Although these early converted night clubs, auditoriums, and factories got concert lighting off the ground, they were short lived. The Fillmore was open from December 10, 1965, to the end of June 1968. The Fillmore East in the old Carousel Ballroom lasted from July 1968 until September 1971. Winterland became a Bill Graham venue before the Fillmore was closed so that he could promote bands that demanded more money. It held 5,400 people and had been built as a skating arena. It went on for seven more years.

Don Law, a promoter in Boston, was using the old Boston Garden to put on concerts at about the same time as the Electric Factory opened in Philadelphia. Both had about 5,000 seats. The Spectrum (a basketball arena) opened in Philadelphia in 1969 and drew the big acts away from the Electric Factory. All this was significant to concert lighting because these new buildings were not full-time clubs or venues designed for music. Most of them were sports arenas. They were a hostile environment; bad acoustics, no permanent stages, no theatrical lighting, and no intercoms. They needed portable lighting and sound systems. Local and regional lighting and sound companies started to grow because of the larger fees they could charge. Some of the early companies were McManus Enterprises in Philadelphia, Sundance Lighting in Los Angeles, TFA in Boston, and See-Factor in New York. Two of those are still in operation; the other two were sold to larger companies the following decade.

The End of the Fillmores

Bob See recalls Bill Graham calling all the staff together—it was very much a family organization. Graham announced he was closing the Fillmore East even though every show was selling out. He said he just had too many irons in the fire. That was 1971, See said. The Fillmore East held 2,700 people. Acts were playing Madison Square Garden and making four times what they could at the Fillmore; greed had set in. It all came down to dollars. Actually all this didn't just happen. The Monterey Festival took place in 1967 and Woodstock in 1969. Promoters had seen that 50,000 people would come to hear Rock and Roll music. Bill Graham closed the Fillmore East and went back to San Francisco and closed the Fillmore West. That last week in New York, Bob See recounts doing 28 shows in 27 days. The era of the concert hall as an ongoing venue was dying.

Bill Graham went on to promote and/or act as production manager for several national tours with the Rolling Stones, George Harrison, and Crosby, Stills, Nash, and Young, as well as Bob Dylan and the Band. To all those productions he brought his sense of theatricality, production values, and total dedication to making the event an experience for the public. Graham is quoted as follows in his autobiography:

> The greatest compliment I was ever given was at the Fillmore. . . . Two guys looked straight ahead and one said, "Oh, shit, man. I forgot. Who's playing

here tonight?" Without batting an eyelash, the other guy said, "I don't know, man. What's the difference? It's the Fillmore."[5]

Bill Graham died in a helicopter crash on October 25, 1991, returning from a Huey Lewis and the News show at Concord Pavilion. His efforts to promote great shows and his undaunted belief that the public deserved the best show possible gave encouragement to many who worked directly with him or for his shows. Graham wanted bands to give their audience a total experience. He encouraged people to try new things and opened the door for many of those who started this special form of lighting. Bands wanted bigger and more, more, more. To attract a paying audience to large venues meant you had to give them a show. The shows had to go on the road.

Melding Forms

Concerts moved from light shows to more traditional music hall lighting simply because certain performers began to emerge from these groups and gain star status. With this came audience recognition. I believe that the artist's ego was responsible for a move toward the more conventional musical comedy lighting techniques. Artists wanted to be in the spotlight, the traditional symbol of the star.

As with any melding of old and new, especially in light of the youth revolt of the 1960s, recording artists started altering the rules. There wasn't a comedian or animal act to separate the musical presentations as was common in music halls or vaudeville. This was to be a show of solid music that lasted several hours. Lighting began to take on a more important role.

The greatest differences in concert lighting from traditional theatrical lighting are the use of vivid colors; heavy use of back light; and absolute use of follow spots instead of balcony rail, torms, or front-of-house washes. The greatest advances have been in portable lighting structures, the PAR-64 fixture, and computerized moving lights.

The Concert Lighting Designer/Director

The position of a concert lighting designer/director differs from that of his or her theatrical or television counterpart. The main difference is responsibilities. A concert lighting designer is often the only design artist associated with the production. Only the larger concerts can afford a separate scenic artist, so the lighting designer is usually consulted for all visual concepts. Second, there is rarely an extended rehearsal schedule. Often a lighting designer has only one day with the lighting rig. No thought is given to a stop-and-go technical rehearsal.

Concert lighting designers must have a highly developed musical sense. Although many are not skilled musicians, they have a natural aptitude for musical interpretation. Because of everchanging venues and artists' needs, most lighting designers go on the road with the shows they design. A few do leave the show in the hands of a board operator, but I find most designers stay and personally run the console and call their own cues throughout the tour.

---

5. Graham and Greenfield, *Bill Graham Presents*, 181.

This style of lighting design is an art of immediacy. You are not an artist who can put paint on canvas or chip a piece of stone and then stand back to think about your next move for an hour, a day, or a week. You must react instantly. Often there is no time to document what you did.

Concert lighting design is an intuitive art, never to be exactly reproduced again. There are no cue sheets or scripts on which to make notations. Ways of noting lighting cues have been developed but in a much different form than the standard theatrical method. Chapter 6 details one such method. Preparation is the key. Every day brings new locations and, therefore, a new set of problems to solve. Adaptability is a must. One of the most important lessons to learn is: *There is no such thing as a bad decision; the only wrong decision is to make no decision.* If you are prepared for all conceivable problems, you can deal logically and calmly with everyday disasters. Although many innovations have been tried in the last 20 or so years of concert lighting, the techniques are still evolving. Just when we feel the size of the lighting rigs has been pushed to the limit, a new idea is tried that pushes the physical resources of the media, particularly the physical structure of buildings, as well as our imaginations.

I do not believe in an analytical approach—in this business it takes one-fourth art, one-fourth science, one-fourth intuition, and one-fourth adaptability. Teaching by doing, experimenting, and by seeing what others have tried is of the greatest value. That is why this book is presented in four parts. Part I deals with what you should understand about the work: the business and the physical side as well as the creativity it takes to succeed. I have a very strong conviction that designers need to be well versed in business to get ahead in the real world. Part II shows some of the tools being used. Part III is a look at some of my own designs. They reflect what I did to solve both the creative and business needs of the specific tour. These needs are, in my view, inseparable. It also presents opinions from three other concert lighting designers and an overview of overseas touring. Part IV shows how I have used these techniques and other ideas gained in my years of touring to cross over into other media.

2

Tour Personnel and Unions

Anyone who follows the business of Rock and Roll touring has probably become familiar with the term *roadie*. I would like to counter the stereotype that this term has established and discourage its use in the future. The term *roadie* carries a certain degrading connotation, having its roots in the tradition that spawned another infamous Rock and Roll term—*groupie*. Many road crew members in the early years may have been little more than male groupies (family and friends of band members) who simply wanted to hang around with the band, but the industry and its requirements have changed a great deal in the past decade. Rock and Roll as a whole has become more sophisticated and technically more complex. As a result, the persons charged with the care and handling of equipment have become highly important to the success of a tour.

Although people like Michael Tait in England and Chip Monck in the United States could start very successful careers in the 1960s without theatrical training, it is much less likely today. Road crew members have evolved into trained technicians with specific expertise in electronics, musical instrument repair, lighting, sound, and the allied theatrical arts. The untrained hanger-on of the early years has been replaced by the dedicated, trained touring professional. Call them *equipment manager*, *technician*, or *manager*. The explosion in technology for both sound and computer lighting means that the people on the road today have had to have extensive training, usually by the rental equipment company, before they can go on the road. You can't just pick up someone off the street anymore; there just isn't any place for "grunt" labor anymore.

But sadly even after 35 years, there are few standards or formulas in this business. Crew size, wages, titles, responsibilities, and equipment complexity are variable factors that depend on the nature of the show, the whims of the artists and their management, and the financial limits of the tour. The titles and duties listed herein are general definitions as applied to Rock and Roll touring and are subject to adaptation.

Road Crew Duties

A touring artist usually has a manager, a road manager, one or more truck drivers, band technicians, and lighting and sound technicians. As an artist's earning power increases, the production becomes more elaborate and the technical staffs increase in size. In addition to the aforementioned basic staff and security personnel, a touring act may also have a production manager, pyrotechnician, rigger, audiovisual specialist, set designer, audio designer, staging company, tour accountant, costumer, carpenter, production secretary, or any of the other standard theatrical titles. As shows become more complex or egos grow, the crew starts to become top heavy with "manager" titles. Dan Wohleen, production manager for the Greek Theatre in Los Angeles, related one tour roster that had the following:

Tour Director
Tour Manager
Road Manager
Production Manager
Stage Manager

Dan said that he sees fewer tours with a stage manager. The tour manager has become the title of power. A road manager has less and less to do with the production side but does maintain a position close to the band members. A look at Figure 2–1 confirms how many positions may have to be filled to put a tour on the road. That particular Metallica tour in mid 1996 through the summer of 1997 listed no fewer than 90 people on the road.

Figure 2–1 Metallica tour personnel.

(From *Performance* magazine, 20 September 1996, 26. Reproduced by permission of *Performance* magazine.)

BACKSTAGE

METALLICA

Touring: June 27-Aug. 4 (Lollapalooza);
Europe: Sept. 6-Oct. 3; U.K.: Oct. 5-16;
Europe: Oct. 18-Nov. 27; U.S. mid-December-summer '97

Artist Management
Q Prime Inc..
729 7th Ave., 14th fl.
New York, NY 10019
Peter Mensch, Cliff Burnstein
Tony DiCioccio, Sue Tropio
Brian Celler

Tour Manager
Tony Smith

Assistant Tour Manager
Patrick Ledwith

Tour Accountant
Kenny Silva

Production Manager
Dan Braun

Stage Manager
Gary Perkins

Production Assistant
Helen Campbell

Booking Agency
QBQ, Fair Warning-Wasted Talent

Agents
Dennis Arfa, Adam Kornfeld
John Jackson

Drums
Lars Ulrich

Vocals/Guitar
James Hetfield

Guitar
Kirk Hammett

Bass
Jason Newsted

Bass Tech/Equipment Manager
Zach Harmon

Guitar Techs
Andy Battye, Justin Crew

Drum Tech
Flemming Larsen

Sound Company
db Sound (U.S.), SSE Hire (U.K.)

House Soundmixer
Big Mick Hughes

Stage Monitor Mixer
Paul Owen

FOH Sound System Tech
Tom Abraham

Monitor Sound System Tech
Jim Homan

Sound Crew Chief
Bruce Judd

Sound Crew
Roy Parrot, Steve Dando
Niall Slevin, Steve Steiner
Chris Gilpin

Lighting Company
The Obie Company

Automated Lighting
Studio Color

Lighting Designer
John Broderick

Lighting Crew Chief
Ian Cameron

Lighting Crew
Steve Roman, Storm Sollars
Jeff Gregos, Mike Hanson
Terry Smith, Frank Mirabal
John Duncan, Gary Waldie
Jeff Wilson

Status Que Programmer
Ben Richard

Generators
Showpower

Showpower Crew Chief
Carlos Oldigs

Showpower Crew
Ian Smith, Joel Richards

Pyrotechnics
Pyrotek Special Effects Inc.

Pryro Techs
Doug Adams

Pryrotek Crew
John Arrowsmith, Phil Dibello

Set Design
Mark Fisher

Set Construction
Tait Towers

Faulty Towers (U.K.)
Brilliant Stages

Head Riggers
Scott Ward, Bobby Savage

Riggers
Ken Mitchell, Michael Gomez
Chuck Melton

Stage Carpenters
Joe Campbell, Kendall Carter

Freight Forwarding
Rock-It Cargo

Bussing
Senator Coaches
Phoenix Bussing Service (U.K.)

Bus Drivers
John Curtis, Robin Painter
Micky Byers, Gary Wright

Trucking
Upstaging
Transam Trucking Ltd. (U.K.)

Truck Drivers
Martin Ford (lead), Kevin Barnes
Ted Horner, Gordon Brackenridge
Ken Scott, Peter Cook, Alister
Brackenridge, Rod Wilson, Allan
Kearsely, Dale Cole, Davy Jones
Steve Young, Martin Wright, Steve
Dawson, Simon Couldry, Richard
Rivert, Matt Clark, Chris Harte

Air Charter
Platinum Tours

Flight Crew
Jack Roman, captain
Dan Miller, captain
Lisa Mooney, flight attendant
Bill Moody, flight attendant

Band Security
Gio Gasparetti, Graham Court

Venue Security
Bob Bender

Tour Pass Security
PERRi Entertainment

Accounting
Siegel, Feldstein, Duffin &
Vuylsteke

Radios
AAA Communications

Onstage Wireless Systems
Showcom

Director of Hospitality
Janine Vogrin

Administrator
Eric Colby

Dressing Room Executive CEO
Allie Amato

Met Club Schmooz
Mike Davis

Tour Book Itinerary
Smart Art

Catering
Snakatak

Caterers
Frank Cribley, Glynn Bramhall
Mairead De Barra
Dawn Harris, Paul Matthews
Mick Thorton, Anne Crawford

Travel Agency
Traveltech/Richard Joseph
Trinifold Travel/Dave Brock (U.K.)

Record Label
Elektra

Merchandising
Giant Merchandising/Bruce Melick
Andrew Scott, Amir Butt

Manager

Like their counterparts in the theatre, managers are closest to the performers, often handling their contracts, bookings, and money as well as acting as the performer's confidant in personal matters. Managers seem to come in an endless variety of styles: some are deeply concerned with the physical production, some are happy only if the artist is happy, others don't want to spend any money but still demand a top-notch production. Luckily, this combination computer and surrogate mother is usually too busy in the office or managing other artists to tour with the show. You don't want him or her on the road, believe me! They are tough enough to deal with during the hiring phase, when they always have an opinion even though they probably do not know what they are talking about. They are numbers people. If the band makes a lot of money, this type of manager wants to be sure they keep a lot of money, end of story.

Road Manager

The road manager is a position in flux. Although the person in this position may carry the weight of the group's manager's representative on the road, he or she deals more and more in the limited area of seeing to it that the artist's personal needs are met. The road manager may still be in charge of the tour in the hierarchy of the management company, but if there are any sizable production values to the show, other people handle the day to day production needs.

The primary responsibilities of the road manager are to keep the artists happy, functional, and performing; to see that the show goes on no matter what; and, on all but the big tours, to settle the box office and carry cash for the expenses. Many road managers have hopes of becoming managers someday, having worked their way up from crew positions. Road managers are heavily involved in the pretour planning of schedules and tour arrangements and might even have final approval in hiring road crew members.

Tour Accountant

A tour accountant, a relatively new face on tours starting in the 1980s, is now a fixture on almost every tour. This person has an accounting background and has been trained in box office settlement. The accountant also monitors the highly lucrative concession business the venue does each night. There is so much money to be made in T-shirts, hats, and other merchandise that one band in 1996 added $16.00 per person in merchandise sales, more than half of the gross ticket price. The monies involved in an arena-type show and the complicated splits of gross almost dictate the need for full-time specialist on the road just to deal with the house settlement. Dan Wohleen said the following:

> The increasing complexity of the building deals: percentages below a break even for the house, added percentages at 80% and sell-out. There are many areas the band can have monies taken away: catering, overages on the house crew, Union meal penalty, extra security, band demands for more tickets, extra limos, etc.

There was a time when the bands thought that all the little things like limos, gifts, and special meals, were the result of the local promoter's being a nice guy. The truth is that all those costs come out of the artist's pocket in the settlement. There are so many ways to split the take—minimum guarantees, promotional tickets, additional advertising, complimentary tickets, catering costs, extra ushers or security, the list goes on—that box office settlement is a definite, specialized skill. Dan Wohleen said that even the best of tour accountants is not in control of the settlement, because the house, as in Las Vegas, always has the advantage.

Tour Director

Tour director, a rather new position, is similar to the position of production stage manager of a theatrical road company. The tour director, although found only on Mega-tours, maintains the artistic quality of the production. He or she also is involved in any changes the band desires.

Production Manager

Production manager is a logistic position, a hands-on position. The production manager comes in with the crew in the morning and leaves when the last truck is loaded. The production manager handles minute to minute crises, such as replacing something that breaks or finding a doctor in the event of crew illness. The production manager keeps the production running on schedule.

Stage Manager

When the production is highly intricate, involving pyrotechnic effects, moving staging cues, and other special effects, the position of stage manager probably is filled. But as a rule, it is not.

Security

As the title implies, security personnel protect the artist, and keep unknown or unwanted persons off the stage and out of the backstage areas. Most bodyguards are very personable and act more like valets than anything else. Few carry guns, but most are expert in the martial arts. Frankly, everyone feels a little safer with these people around. It is an unfortunate fact that there are a few persons out there who want to harm performers. There is tremendous investment in the artist, and a lot of people are counting on the artist's ability to perform to secure their own livelihoods. Therefore, it is in all the crews' best interest to keep the artist safe, happy, and secure.

Public Relations

Often the public relations (PR) or press agent works for an outside firm hired by the artist or record company to handle publicity. PR people are most concerned with image and publicity. The performer's need to keep in the public eye makes it essential that a coordinated effort be made to ensure not only that members of the local press have the artist's name on their lips but also that the performer's image is positive so that "good press" is the result. While these people are a pain in the neck to the crew, again, the artist's image and, therefore, bank account depend on them.

Truck Driver

Many drivers and trucking companies used in touring specialize in hauling for concert tours. The drivers live by one rule: Get the equipment to the next hall no matter what! They are usually young and nonunion, carrying the necessary Class-A driver's license for tractor-trailer rigs. They may or may not help with the load-out each night. Good truck drivers are highly valued, because if the trucks are late to a hall many crew hours are wasted. In the worst case, a delayed truck can cause the show to be canceled. A switch has occurred here. When I wrote the first edition of this book, there was a norm that the sound or lighting company supplied the trucking. In the late 1990s market, that is no longer true. Most lighting and sound companies have relieved themselves of the burden. There are companies specialized in this field; RoadShow, Upstaging, S.O.S., and Janco are just a few trucking companies dedicated to the concert industry. Some bands who tour consistently keep the same drivers on a retainer. Because a retainer is rare for the sound and lighting crew, this shows just how valuable truck drivers are to a tour.

Lighting Designer/Director

The touring lighting designer (LD) strives to meet all of the usual demands of creative lighting but with an added twist: unlike theatre, which offers a script and a directorial concept for guidance, rock acts rarely have a concept, a program, or a director. At best, the director is the artist, whose onstage point of view offers little in the way of objectivity. The LD often runs the control console personally and may be involved in the physical work of erecting the lighting rig during setup. Rehearsal time before leaving town is limited, and more often nonexistent, so the LD must be able to improvise at the first few shows. While trying to second-guess the act about the song to be played next and preset the two-scene or memory console, the LD must cue the follow spot operators, who have never seen the show and, in worst case theory, may not be very cooperative.

Over the years the position of LD has changed. There was a period in the 1980s when the LD became a "briefcase" designer. He or she did not perform physical labor and was not around for the load-in or strike. There seems to be a backlash here. In general, a tour performing at 5,000-seat venues has a working LD. One who is part of the day to day working crew.

However, there has developed a select group of *lighting designers* who do not tour at all but hand the show over to a *lighting director* who tours with the group, calls the cues, calls follow spot cues, and may operate one of the consoles. This is the situation with very large tours, but there are a few exceptions. Willie Williams kept up active participation in his touring with U2. Other designers, like Patrick Woodroffe, Peter Morse, Marc Brickman, Roy Bennett, and Jeff Ravitz, are in such demand that they move from tour design to tour design.

Lighting Technician

The lighting technician is an electrician who does the physical work of assembling the lighting rig, hooking up to house power (only if no house electrician is available), focusing the instruments, and maintaining the dimmers. Although the barriers between the tour staff and the house union crews seems to have dropped, touring technicians must be diplomatic and clear in their instructions.

Moving Light Operator

Moving light operator is a position that has come about since the advent of automated lights. Because of the technical complexity of the fixtures and a need for people who have been trained to run the computer consoles, the position of moving light operator is a highly skilled one. Some operators move on to become LDs in their own right. A twist that has come about in the last couple of years is that designers are no longer satisfied with one kind of moving light but may have three or more types on the rig. This has made a consolidation of systems desirable in an attempt to keep the number of crew members down and has made skilled operators even more valuable. This is a great position to springboard onto LD.

Sound Mixer

The sound mixer is often quite like the LD. The sound mixer may or may not be involved with assembling the sound system during the setup but does run the console. He or she may be an actual studio-trained mixer with many recording credits who has been pirated away by the artist or simply a road sound technician with a good ear and a deft touch at the controls who has moved up the ladder. The age of computers has entered this area, so the mixer may be called on to run not only the mix console but also a MIDI playback or DAT and ADAT systems. ADAT is a system that is essentially videotape that records on eight channels. Dan Wohleen said, "Three times this past season I had groups come in with ADAT of forty channels. You could actually take that tape to a studio and produce a full album. So a house sound mixer can be a recording engineer as well."

Sound Technician

Like the lighting technicians, sound technicians do the physical work, in this case assembling and maintaining the sound system.

Equipment Manager

The equipment managers handle the basic band gear, set up the amplifiers, drums, keyboards, and other instruments, and remain ready during performances to deal with a broken drum head or guitar string and generally aid the band. The guitar and keyboard technician has evolved into a highly skilled computer specialist. So many keyboards use sophisticated computers and MIDI controls that most of these positions require a very extensive knowledge of specialized electronic components. Although lighting and sound personnel may work for companies contracted to the artist, equipment managers are individuals who generally work directly for the band and are not under outside contract to any company.

Pyrotechnician

The pyrotechnician is an experienced technician, usually required to be licensed by the state in which the show is playing, who handles flash pots, smoke, explosives, and similar effects. Local ordinances are usually very strict about the use of such effects. Although a few acts with especially heavy effects carry their own pyrotechnician, most acts have the promoter hire someone who is locally licensed.

Rigger

The human fly called a *rigger* ascends the heights inside fieldhouses, ice rinks, and anywhere else necessary to secure hanging points for flown lighting and sound systems. The best riggers come from ice shows and circuses and find that the fast pace and reduced setup time of concert tours offer a unique challenge to their daring abilities. Because almost all lighting rigs now are being flown, this position is essential. The safety of the artists and others is at stake. Even very skilled house riggers do not know the exact weights and balance of the touring trusses. It is essential to have someone on the tour with this knowledge.

Audiovisual Specialist, Cameraperson, Video Director

Multiple-screen slide, film, and video projection is used on a large percentage of tours. This has created a need for a separate specialist who sets up, maintains, and operates the audiovisual equipment on the tour. Almost all artists who perform outdoor concerts travel with a video crew to provide large-screen video magnification of the performance. Some indoor-arena shows also have added this element. U2 took this to a higher plane with its Zoo TV Tour. That tour used a very complex system of television screens, live satellite uplinks, and playback systems.

Scenic and Costume Designers

As more rock acts recognize the value of an interesting set, scenic designers are finding more work in Rock and Roll touring. Durability and ease of assembly are prime considerations for touring sets. Although most sets are fairly simple, supermega acts stage an elaborate production that requires a great deal of scenery. This is an area of design held tightly by a very small group of designers. The stakes are so high that it is difficult to enter this arena without credit on another Mega-tour.

Most artists today do not need costumers. One very good area for costume work is with Las Vegas style performers. Disco, funk, and heavy metal acts also go in for exotic costumes, but the general apparel worn on stage by many rock performers is less than a coordinated ensemble. There is a need for a wardrobe supervisor, however. The care and cleaning of stage clothing is a necessity just as it is in the theatre. In some cases the wardrobe supervisor is the companion of another crew member and not specifically trained in wardrobe.

Laserist

The laserist operates and maintains laser equipment, which is used frequently on tours for special effects. The facility has to provide some special requirements such as a constant water supply required for most high-power lasers. These requirements must be clearly spelled out in a contract rider. Local laws may require inspection by a health and safety officer before the performance, and the inspection takes time to arrange.

Other Positions

When the show expands, more positions are added, such as a hospitality director who takes care of the band's dressing rooms. This staff member makes sure the band has what it wants and that preparations are made for the band's arrival. Some bands have been know to carry their own dressing room furniture! A still photographer or videographer may take behind the scenes shots and footage. Personal fitness trainers and massage therapists have been known to travel with a band, as have medical doctors.

The Question of Unions

Road technicians generally range in age from 21 to 30 years, but a growing number of old-line technicians from the legitimate theatre are being drawn into touring by the high wages and relatively steady employment. There are those people who are simply attracted to the excitement of big time Rock and Roll. These workers are often 40 years old or older. Riggers in particular seem to be older men who have the training and years of experience required for competency in their field. It is also true that as many superstars are turning 40 and 50, so are the long-time touring personnel who started in the early days and have stayed with it.

I am aware of no rock acts staffed by union stagehands. The large sound and lighting companies that provide road technicians are not unionized at this time. A very high-level International Alliance of Theatrical Stage Employees (IA) union official recently told me that the union has dropped the ball and has come to a live-and-let-live position. Union members believe they are secure in their positions within the venues and believe they can find a balanced plan that works for both sides. They are not actively looking to unionize road crews on a national level. Would they like to? Yes, and committees within the IA are working on this issue. But it is not a front-burner union-organizing issue as of this writing.

What concerns the unions is the erosion of jobs because of touring techniques and because tour-based equipment companies are moving into event production and corporate presentations.

Although my discussions with several owners and managers of concert lighting equipment companies brought up their objection to the unions, it was not over issues I expected. Their concern was that managers who are buying their services and the budgets within which they must work do not allow for "cost of doing business" increases. The manager demands that the company provide a skilled and competent crew for the tour. But management does not want to hear about having to increase costs because of the supplier's union overhead. The equipment owners said they would love to give crews the kinds of benefits unions provide, but they cannot afford to take money from shrinking profits in the face of stiff competition from other vendors.

There are, of course, objections other than wage scales. No one can be sure just how the unionization issue will be resolved. A few companies in the 1970s tried to work with the IA and were issued Associated Crafts and Technicians (ACT) cards for their employees by the IA international office in New York. Pensions and other privileges were extended to ACT cardbearers but not membership in a specific local. The card basically allowed concert technicians to work in halls with union jurisdiction. Some locals did not taken kindly to the ACT plan, believing that their members should be hired before persons who did not belong to a local. This attitude varies around the United States, of course, from local to local and from east to west. I have had crews work this way, and they generally have been treated very well by the local crews. However, it seems that in the late 1990s this program is dead, and a live-and-let-live atmosphere exists between the road crews and the house IA crews.

Dan Wohleen said he has tremendous respect for his house union crew. They jointly go over the riders of the bands that are coming into their facility. If the crew request seems short or if a problem unique to the Greek Theatre facility is detected, Dan said he has full trust in the judgment of the IA steward to ask for additional crew only when necessary. Dan believes the skills of the union crews rival any road crew that has come through the facility in the three years he has been there. They know the types of equipment the tours use and how to assemble it efficiently. They also make a real effort to be friendly and helpful to the road crew. Yes, IA members do come through as part of a tour crew on occasion, but not under full Yellow Card show status.

The United Scenic Artists (USA), the union that generally represents the interests of theatrical designers in the United States, has not made any real effort to be involved specifically with concert touring. The average Rock and Roll lighting design fee is far above the USA minimum scale. Because many designers also go on the tour and work the actual show, wages have to be arranged on an individual basis. There is no current fixed fee schedule to cover this type of work.

3

Business

It is relatively easy to get a group to say, "Okay, do our lights!" It is not so easy to keep from being ripped off. One problem is that most designers go into a meeting eager to show the group how much they know, so they spill their creative guts. Do not be so naive as to think a manager is not mentally taking down every concept you throw out, even if orally he or she reacts differently. All too often your ideas show up on stage, but you do not!

This is an old story. Because it really does happen, the United Scenic Artists (USA) and the International Alliance of Theatrical Stage Employees (IA) unions have specific rules that no member puts pen to paper or presents an idea to a prospective client until a contract is signed. Excellent rule, but you need two sides to play the game. Rock and Roll has only one side, the manager or producer of the artist. The other side does not exist. Sure, the USA and IA would love to have designers work under their banners, but frankly, they did not realize the economic potential to their members. They were not alone; most of the adult world felt that Rock and Roll was just a fad. A plan geared to Rock and Roll designers' needs and the setting of industry standards is a long way from being a reality.

What are the economics of Rock and Roll touring? Who makes the money and how much? Should you work for a company or an artist or be independent (freelance)—which is best? These are questions that you should consider before you walk into that first meeting.

Because there is no governing body to set fee standards in Rock and Roll, there is a wide range of fees. They appeared static throughout the 1980s because of an increase in the supply of people wanting to enter the business. The 1990s have seen a widening gulf between the fees paid to the few Mega-tour designers and the average touring lighting designer (LD). The economics are such that it is all relative to how much you are in demand as a designer. The idea is to create the demand so you can get paid whatever you want. One old adage still rings true: It takes work to get work. Actors know this, singers know it too. When you are out of the circle of people who can hire you, you are quickly forgotten.

Freelance

There are three roads to follow to lead you to work. The first, the independent or freelance way, is simple. All you have to do is find a client and persuade the artist, road manager, companion, manager, accountant, business affairs manager, and several close friends of the artist that you can do a great job. Realistically, there is a step before this—how do you get past the secretary in the first place? A good test when I was starting was to try and reach one of the top managers on the telephone. If you accomplish this, maybe you should go directly to the presidency of a record company; why stop at being a mere lighting designer!

After you have set up a meeting, the question is: How much do you charge, and where do you get the equipment? It is rare that a group will hire you to design a show without asking you to estimate a budget for the equipment it will take to carry out your design. Therefore, you must convince an equipment rental company that you have a client on the hook and you need the company's best price. Cross your fingers that the company does not go directly to the artist's manager and cut you out. I am not implying that this is a regular occurrence, but it has happened. Some of the things the rental company needs to know beyond how many dimmers, lamps, and trusses you will want are the length of the tour, personnel requirements, who will be responsible for deposits, and the payment method.

The Company Way

There was a period of about ten years when managers did not want to be bothered with payments to multiple companies or to a large number of individuals. The package approach was hot. The company that could supply sound, lights, trucks, travel arrangements, and other services was in a very strong position. Often they sold their services like packaged stereos: good speakers, bad amplifier, okay turntable. The trend went bust in the 1990s. As management companies brought in "tour consultants" or accountants to oversee the finances of the touring portion of their artists' lives, those people had to justify their jobs. Writing one check was not going to do it. Quite as expected, the LDs, scenic designers, tour managers, all of whom had a vested interest in sending work to "friendly" companies, were in support of the breakup.

Herein lies one of the reasons for a designer to hook up with an equipment supplier. Actually, there are two excellent reasons:

1. Accessibility. The company has been at this game a while and already has clients. It can get you past the first steps outlined for an independent; then you can get down to work.

2. Designing for Rock and Roll is a new ball game to most college-trained technicians. Although your education is a good base, you still are not ready to design for Madonna or Prince. The best way to learn the ropes is to work for a company already in the business. Working for someone else might not be your goal, but it can help you get your feet wet while you get a paid introduction to the field.

You lose some freedom when you join a company because there are rules and procedures, and a boss who may appear to interfere with your creativity. That is, if you get any creativity. At first you'll haul cable around the shop and fix connectors and, dare I say it . . . sweep up. But most of these companies do small local shows, and there is where you get your first chance to design. Take it. It may be a fashion show or a college dance, but it is experience in the professional world. The other big advantage is that your management and sales responsibilities are eliminated (two things we will discuss in more detail later in this chapter), and this is a big relief for a new designer.

Direct Contact

The third method of employment is to work directly for the group or artist. Although the trend of groups owning their own equipment has faded, Supertramp's equipment spawned Delicate Productions. The Grateful Dead was one of the last holdouts in equipment ownership. Working directly for an artist does have advantages, but in the long run, you can go stale creatively. You could also become involved in the infighting that plagues so many artists' organizations. Still, this way you do receive a weekly check, and if you are into hanging out with a star—we call them *paid friends*—you have that opportunity. It is still my least favorite option for starting in the field.

Pay and Per Diem

Because there are no union guidelines, your income range is wide. I sent a survey to 50 concert touring rental companies and freelance designers in June of 1987 that became the basis of the figures I used in the first edition. I compared them with the figures I received in my 1996 survey. I was not surprised that the figures had increased on the bottom end, but the gulf had widened on the top end.

If you work for one of the large concert lighting companies, you can expect a salary of about $600 to $900 per week while on the road, depending on your position on the crew. That is only a $100 per week raise in ten years. That is, about a 16 percent increase. In the same period union wages rose 22 percent. In addition, union members receive health and welfare benefits, something most tour companies provide only at the legal minimum. Back in the shop between tours the pay is usually less. Most people are amazed to learn that the IA road contract asks for an amount that falls just above what the nonunion workers are being paid, and in many cases even less. But that does not include the health and welfare plus vacation pay required by the IA to be paid in addition to salary. A good head electrician earns $1,000 to $1,500 a week, but this takes some climbing up the ladder. "Working" concert lighting directors can and do make more, $1,500 to $2,500 a week, but I caution, what people say they get and what is the truth is hard to know. In addition to road pay, designers earn a flat fee of $5,000 to $10,000 up front for the pre-production meetings and design time they invest in a tour. This has not changed over the years and, in fact, has become more and more difficult to justify to the bean counters.

Then there are the Mega-tours. The design fees for the few who can get these jobs can run upward of $50,000 per design. In addition, they are paid a per day rate during rehearsal and to check out the production on the road. They do not call the show themselves. Rather they have a working lighting director or two who know how these LDs like their shows run and who are then generally contracted directly by the artist as part of the tour crew.

As a designer, you must also be a good salesperson. Your product is your design ability. Your ability to push your fee as hard as possible and not give in to a low-ball mentality is sorely tested. Just remember: *There is no loyalty to anyone, and everyone eventually loses.*

You can also expect a minimum of $30 per day as per diem, but the average is $35 per day. This is now often considered taxable as income by the Internal Revenue Service. The tax exempt status is used to allow for food and expenses for each day spent away from home on business. The 1996 legal deductible limit was $50 per day plus hotel and travel. Most accountants advise that if you receive $25 or more per day, you must keep receipts. Consult a tax expert about exactly what you need to do to preserve the tax-free status of this money. Yearly tax changes can eliminate many deductions, so keep informed each year to take advantage of whatever tax breaks there are.

Besides these monies, your hotel and travel should be covered by your employer or the artist. Some companies and artists try to work deals whereby you receive a flat amount per day but you must cover your own hotel. This is a common practice on theatrical bus and truck road shows. I am against this practice for one-night tours. Your day is already too busy to try to make such arrangements, and you are forced to stay at cheap hotels while the band is probably staying at a first-class hotel. I do not believe that the technical crew should be treated like second-class citizens, and neither do most artists. It is only accountants and business managers who don't understand the rigors of touring; they are just looking at numbers.

Equipment Costs

I sometimes believe the saying, "There is always someone else who can do it a nickel cheaper!" was originated in Rock and Roll. When I speak to a prospective client, or even some old clients, this occasionally comes up. There is no question that there is always someone out there who is hungrier. I also hear this over and over again from tour service companies. Because accountants now control the budgets, the ability to keep a client because of friendship with or loyalty from a band or artists is virtually nonexistent. Tim Murch of Light and Sound Design put it this way: "When it comes to putting a tour together, the lighting is the last to know. The lighting designer can't do his job until the scenic elements are together." Even if a budget is known, specific elements are rarely computed accurately. Tim continued,

> Then when the costs of the scenic construction come in and trucking and crew is added in, the lighting gets what's left over. The accountants don't have a clue what we do and nine times out of ten, they push the lighting service company to cut their rates rather than kill the LD's creative input.

Spy Matthews of Delicate Productions said,

> All of a sudden a client we have worked with for years hires a new attorney and a new nine page rider shows up at the office just days before the tour is to leave. We are expected to sign it and get it back to them in 24 hours. Hardly enough time to read it, let alone get any legal advice of our own. We are totally screwed.

Like salaries and fees, there are no official guidelines to equipment costs. A company can be paid $20,000 a night for a tour (the Mega-tours do not follow any formula) while another is paid only $10,000 for a similar-sized system and crew. Although I cannot be sure that what the companies tell is always the truth, and trying to account for the bragging rights factor, the following figures represent norms set this past decade that are not likely to change well into the next millennium:

4 Genie tower systems	$650 to $800 per show
1 truss, 2 Genie towers	$800 to $1250 per show
2 trusses (90 lamps)	$1250 to $1400 per show
2 trusses (120 lamps)	$1500 to $2000 per show
Truss grid (150 to 250 lamps)	$2250 to $3750 per show

All figures are based on a guaranteed five shows per week.

These figures are difficult to come up with, because even small tours now demand some moving lights. Therefore you must add a premium. As an example, you would probably add a cost of $2,500 for ten Intellabeams and operator for one week.

Contracts

Because the USA and IA standard contract forms do not normally apply, you are left to your own devices. I had a $20,000 lesson in contract writing in my early days. I persuaded a group to use my services, so I wrote up what I thought covered all the points of our agreement, and a representative of the group signed it. Troubles developed within the group and they broke up. It took more than three years to collect my money and lawyers' fees (which had come out of my pocket).

The answer is not necessarily a long legal contract. Part of the problem comes from the extremely fast pace at which this work is done. On an average, a group finally gives you the go-ahead three or four weeks before the start of the tour. If you use a lawyer to draw up a contract, you can wait at least a week or two for the finished document to be delivered to you. After the contract is presented to the group, it goes to their lawyers, and the process starts over again, which could mean the tour is over before the contract is signed!

I have found a happy medium by using letters of agreement. These look rather informal, no whereases, just plain language that tells all the details and duties of each of the parties. But even this informal paper must contain the basic components of a legal contract to be valid. The best thing to do is to confer with an attorney, who will give you a list of things that must be covered to protect you properly. I have devised a checklist of points that must be covered in all letters of agreement. Do not use this as a legal reference, because each state has conditions that should be verified by an attorney. The following will help you understand the basics.

Who Are the Parties Involved?

It is not as easy as it might appear to get into writing the responsible parties. Often the person with whom you have negotiated the agreement has no legal standing or power to execute a contract on behalf of the party you want to be responsible for your payment.

What Are You Going to Do for Them?

You must write a job description. Be specific and include even things you assume the other party should know you would do as a designer, such as provide plans and color charts, call the cues, and travel with the show.

What Are They Going to Do for You?

You want the client to pay you, of course. But how much, how often, and in cash or by check? Are they paying travel expenses? All of these things must be spelled out clearly if you do not want to have them come up later in court. Payment schedules that are simple and straight-forward are best. Accountants and tour managers like amounts that get paid regularly rather than many add-on charges that cannot be determined before the tour starts. Remember to ask for program or air credit for yourself if shots are used of your show design for a television special or music video. Asking to be paid additional fees for such use of your tour design will not go over well and could be a deal breaking point. Most managers will not sign such a clause; they believe it puts them in a bad negotiating position. You will most likely get credit, but they will not want it to be locked into a written contract.

What Are You Providing?

You provide yourself, a staff, and equipment. Explain exactly what, in detail, you plan to give them for their money.

When Will the Tour Begin and End?

You need in writing the starting date of rehearsal and the dates of the first and last shows, so that if the tour is canceled, you have justification for a claim for loss of income.

An Optional Paragraph

Your final paragraph can include the standard legal line about suing the other party if he or she does not live up to the agreement and that it is at their sole cost and expense for any legal fees. Actually the expense is set by the court and does not come close to today's high legal fees. It does show, however, that you do know something about the law, and it should keep the other party on his or her toes.

Authorized Representative

Finally, have the authorized representative sign a copy and date it. Make sure the person signs "On behalf of XYZ Productions" and returns a dated copy to you. Because the Uniform Commercial Code has not been adopted in all states, there are many variations and degrees of force with which the courts will hold a letter of agreement as legally binding in this simplest of forms. Consult an attorney in your own state to set up a personal legal plan for your specific situation and needs. The expense may seem high, but not as high as the expense of a lengthy court battle.

If there is a single area in which most designers fail, it is business. Read some books on contract law, business law, and accounting. It can save you great expense and trouble later on. Do not try to be your own attorney or accountant. These are areas in which a little knowledge is very dangerous. There is just too much to deal with and it takes years of training to become an expert. Because most people are eager to work, they tend to jump in with both feet before they take a look under the water. Even if you are going to work directly for the artist or the production company, get an agreement in writing that spells out these simple points. You will not be sorry and the time you spend will be worth it.

The Contract Rider

As theatre, film, or television LDs, normally we do not become involved in the stagehands' contractual part of the production. In theatre, a union head electrician is hired for the show and assists the union in arranging with the producer for the crew. Concert tours take a slightly different road: virtually none of the shows have the traditional unionized road crews, so there are no department heads to discuss crew needs in the pre-production meeting. You will find the artist's manager looking to you to know how long the setup will take and how many local stage hands it will require. Actually, the crewing, physical stage needs, and other items to be supplied in each city in which the concert plays are usually determined jointly by the lighting director, audio engineer, and production manager.

So how do you get your requirements for stagehands known in the different towns? The contract rider.

For a concert appearance, the booking agent sends a general contract, which states the flat performance fee or percentage splits of gate, deposit, billing, and other financial conditions, as well as date and time of show, length of performance, and other details, to the talent buyer or promoter, who signs and returns it. The rider, which covers the specific performance needs of the artist, is usually put together by the tour manager after consulting the lighting and sound directors who are doing the show.

The contract rider is usually considered a supplementary agreement. It is based on the original contract and is incorporated into the original contract by reference to it. The problem is that if it is not part of the original agreement, it is, in effect, a new contract. Therefore there must be a separate and distinct passage of consideration from the offeree. What is it that the artist offers the promoter to accept the rider?

The law considers something called *trade usage* or *custom*. This means that if you can prove in court that it is a widely used and generally common practice in your business to send riders that contain certain information and demands for equipment and services, after the original contract has been signed, a court could accept the rider as a valid part of the agreement.

If you are in a position to send a rider to promoters, send it registered mail, return receipt, so you know they received it. At the very least, send it via an overnight service such as FedEx or UPS. People tend to take this form of delivery as more important than a regular airmail letter and usually see that it gets to the addressee as soon as possible.

Follow-Up

The main problem is not what to put into the rider and in what degree of detail, but will it get to the right people in time? This is why a follow-up or hall advance should be made in conjunction with the rider. Dan Wohleen, production manager at the Greek Theatre in Los Angeles, said this is still a big issue. He finds that he still has to track down the road crew to obtain updated information. He said it is pretty silly when you think that by contacting the venue in advance you are helping to ensure that things are ready for your arrival.

After making sure that each promoter gets the newest, most accurate rider, it is very important to follow up to see that the promoter gets it to the person whose job it is to arrange for the things the rider requires. If your artist is not making his or her first headline appearance, there is already a rider floating around out there. Because it is usually not attached to the contract, it is probably the old one. Good follow-up can take care of this.

Your problems are not over. Chances are that you will get the rider back with changes, deletions, and notations. At that time, check with the booking agency and the artist's management to make sure they are aware of any changes or deletions. Often, a booking agent receives a modified rider, signs it, and sends it back to the promoter, and never tells the road crew. Producing your best effort if the stage is five feet too narrow for the ground-supported truss or if there is only one follow spot instead of the four you had planned in the design takes a lot of physical as well as mental adjustment.

Rider Items

Three general areas must be covered in the rider, as follows:

1. Artist's requirements
   A. Piano, tuned to A440; specify size of piano
   B. Piano tuner to tune piano before sound check and be available after sound check for touch-up
   C. Amplifiers, organ B-3 with one or two Leslies, electronic keyboards
   D. Dressing room needs; how many people in each
   E. Limousines required; airport and hotel pickups
2. Food
   A. Coffee, tea, and soft drinks for crew during setup
   B. Breakfast (if early load-in), lunch, and dinner for crew Include a menu, a couple of different main courses per day so the crew doesn't end up with lasagna three nights in a row
   C. Food trays in dressing rooms for artist; with cheese tray and fruit and possibly liquor and beer; many artists specify brand names
3. Stage requirements
   A. Time of load-in
   B. Number of stagehands required; break down duties clearly, particularly truck loaders required
   C. Number and type of follow spots, possibly position (front, rear, side)
   D. Power requirements for lighting, sound, and band
   E. Stage size
   F. Rigging requirements
   G. Special needs; if any aspect of the production needs special consideration, be it crew, safety, or unusual complexity, don't keep it a secret

In addition to this basic group of items, the rider must include the specifics that pertain to the actual production. These include any items that can incur cost to the promoter or personnel or services expected to be provided, such as balloons or a seamstress. Special note should be given to alert the promoter if truss-mounted follow spots are to be used. Some stagehands will not operate them, and a half hour before the show is no time to find out someone will not do the job.

Remember, all these requests of the promoter *will* come out of the band's settlement. So make sure management is well aware that the band may be incurring hidden costs.

Mark Hogue, who has been a production manager for Chicago, and is a 16-year veteran of the concert wars, has one of the cleanest, clearest examples of a rider I have seen. He used it on the band's 1995 tour. Figure 3–1 shows sample pages from that rider. Hogue said, "I write the tour book so that a novice in the business can get it right. That is not a put down, but when you cover every detail you are insuring your show's quality." That he writes so well may come from the fact that he was theatre trained and was an Equity stage manager for the earlier part of his career.

The Promoter-Facility View

Interviews with several promoters and house production managers revealed their feelings about the contract riders they received. Their

Figure 3–1A Chicago '95 Production Information. Manpower requirements.
(Reproduced by permission of the author, Mark Hogue.)

Chicago '95
Production Information

MANPOWER REQUIREMENTS

A. <u>CREW REQUIREMENTS:</u> All calls to be verified and/or amended by Production Manager five (5) days prior to show date. Please note the staff will be at the engagement site at least 12 hours prior to show time for technical set-up; the following staff will be necessary:

B. <u>CALLS:</u>   <u>1st Stage Call: 9:00 a.m.</u>
        2 riggers 1 groundman
        1 electrician
        1 forklift w/operator (if needed)
        4 loaders
        6 stagehands

        <u>2nd Stage Call: 10:00 a.m.</u>
        6 stagehands
        Additional loaders (if required for 2 trucks)

        <u>Show Call:</u>   Spotlight meeting 30 min.prior to show time.
        4 stagehands on deck
        6 house spot operators
        1 electrician, house-lights
        1 forklift(if needed)

        <u>Out Call: 11:00 p.m.</u>
        2 riggers
        1 groundman
        4 loaders
        1 electrician
        1 forklifts
        14 stagehands

C. <u>RUNNER:</u> One runner will be required from load-in thru load-out. They must have reliable transportation. Knowledge of the locality is a plus, as well as an I.Q. above 10.

Figure 3–1B Chicago '95 Production Information.
House equipment.
(Reproduced by permission of the author, Mark Hogue.)

Chicago '95
Production Information

HOUSE EQUIPMENT

A. SPOTLIGHTS: Six (6) Super Trouper Carbon Arc or Xenon in PERFECT
WORKING ORDER are required. All spotlights must be matched, that is
all carbons, or all Xenon. Any units found not to be satisfactory will
not be excepted as a show expense. Positioning of these spots shall be
determined on day of show. Each lamp must have its own power supply
and be separate from other lamps. Spare lamps must be available.

B. STAGE LIGHTS: To be supplied by Production, or be mutually acceptable and discussed in
advance.

C. SOUND: To be supplied by production, or be mutually acceptable, and discussed in
advance. Please refer to sound specifications addendum.

D. POWER: Completely stable power sources are required at the following increments and
locations:
  1. Lighting -- Two 600 amp/3 phase.Service shall be within 75'of upstage center.
  2. Sound --- One 200 amp/3 phase with a "Bonded Neutral".Service shall
     be within 75' of upstage center.
  3. Generators - Please see OUTDOOR VENUE PRODUCTIONS

E. FORKLIFTS: One (1) forklift w/3000 lb. capacity and a minimum of 10' lift is required.
Fork- lift must be available until the end of the load-out and must not be shared
with any of the facility's movements.

F. CABLE COVERS: If snake cables or any other cables are required to be covered or taped
down, the promoter or venue must supply said covers and required tape.

G. INTERCOM: A fourteen station intercom must be available short notice.
We do carry an intercom system.

H. WORK LIGHTS: Work lighting must be provided for the load out. This lighting must
illuminate all areas where the crew will be working. This includes the
mixing and loading areas.

views were summed up by Dan Wohleen. Out-of-date riders are still a problem, but it is conceded that it is also up to the house to follow through and make sure they have the best information possible. Dan and his assistant work hard to make contact at least two weeks before the scheduled performance. He said that on the whole riders are better than they were ten years ago. When it comes to complex stage and truss designs, a drawing, preferably an AutoCAD drawing of the ground plan and sectional, are helpful for the house crew to understand what is coming. Only Styx came with drawings produced by LD Jeff Ravitz that provided a complete set of plans, including sectional, with its rider this past summer. It allowed the band and the facility to talk in advance and work out some problems that would not have been apparent without the drawings. "We were able to suggest changes that allowed the band to keep some elements that they were willing to drop because they didn't know we could handle it," concluded Dan.

From the promoter's standpoint, essential information that needs to be covered in the rider is stage size, power requirements, number of fol-

Figure 3–1C Chicago '95 Production Information.
Catering requirements.
(Reproduced by permission of the author, Mark Hogue.)

Chicago '95
Production Information

CATERING REQUIREMENTS

<u>BREAKFAST (CONT.)</u>

11) (3) doz. Fresh AA eggs
12) (3) lbs. Fresh Lean Bacon
13) (1) Box assorted Quaker Oats, instant oatmeal
14)   Potatoes: Home fries, or Hash Browns
15)   Fresh Butter and a Soft-Spread Noncholesterol Low-Fat Margarine
16)   Jams or Preserves (Not Jelly)
17) (1) Electric Fry Pan, if self service is required.
18) (1) Four (4) Slice Toaster
19) (2) copies of USA Today
20) (2) Local Newspapers

C. <u>LUNCH:</u> Time to be determined. Meal should serve
       18 people, including 6 strict vegetarians
       2 vegetarians are strict no-dairy
Deli-tray with assorted cold cuts: Including Ham, Turkey, Roast Beef, Corned Beef,
       Chicken salad. American, Monterey Jack, Cheddar, and Provolone cheeses.
       Iceberg lettuce, fresh sliced tomatoes, and fresh sliced yellow or Bermuda onions.
And...
1) Bread: White, Whole Wheat, and Rye w/seeds
2) Hot soup:
       One Broth-type (chicken or beef base) and/or one vegetarian soup
3) Tuna Salad. Made with solid white fancy albacore packed in spring water, and well
       drained. (NO TUNA SOUP)
4) Assorted Salads: (Pick three) Pasta, Potato, 3-Bean, Wild Rice, Cobb, Caesar,
       Waldorf, Fruit, Shrimp, Crab,Cucumber, Lobster, Artichoke, Avocado,
       Salmon, Marinated Tomato or Red pepper, etc.
5) Assorted Munchies: Potato Chips, Nacho Doritos, Tortilla Chips,Pretzels,etc.
6) Hot Salsa: Fresh or Pace Brand, picante medium

low spots, security needs, and band equipment not being provided by the artist. Asked what is most often left off the rider, they specify keyboards, which the artist expects the promoter to rent for the performance, and requests that a piano tuner be there.

Dan still receives poor riders, either confusingly written, heavily photocopied to the point of being unreadable, or simply not complete. "Riders are still coming from booking agents. And that is the worst possible person. . . . They couldn't give a damn," he said, and went on, "I look for dates on pages, time stamps, or look at catering, that changes most frequently, to give me an idea of if the rider is current." Asked if he was finding that the road crews made an attempt to make sure he had the latest rider, he said, "The good ones do. The bad ones will show up and scream about it. The other thing is that groups need to realize that just because it is in the rider doesn't mean they are going to get it." What he is referring to often happens when a rider demands six follow spots and the facility has three. Who pays for the others? Can they be fitted into the facility? That is why advance contact with the facility's production manager is so important. Sure the days are long on the road, but people make their lives even harder trying to put out fires that they started themselves!

Many promoters complain about catering requirements. They believe artists insist on too much food and beverage. But now it comes out of the artist's pocket, says Dan Wohleen. What the business has come to is that facilities write into the contract a set amount they will pay for stagehands, catering, and other services. If the band wants more, it pays for it.

It was also pointed out that although most riders make clear how many stagehands are needed, they do not break down the time, such as four hours to set up, two hours for sound checks, and three hours to strike and load out the show. Because some union fees have different rates for these periods, it helps if the rider gives the average time required for each part of the day's activities.

In summary, the promoter wants clarity, reasonable requirements, and up-to-date riders. Too often the rider contains more verbiage about frills than on services required to put on a good show. Requests for pool tables backstage and limo pickup for girlfriends and boyfriends can mean the difference between the production's having a fourth follow spot or not. Dan Wohleen said, "I've gotten riders that want underwear, socks, boxes of condoms, cases of cigarettes. Excuse me, learn to do your own laundry. I've gotten requests for Sunday papers, paperback books with specific authors. The answer is NO, NO, and NO."

Although not actually part of the rider, insurance is a large expense for a promoter. The fees are based on the history of all the shows the promoter has done. That means that the promoter must split the cost among the shows being promoted that year. Some artists have begun to take out their own insurance because of their past good record, obtaining lower rates if they have not had problems with equipment or, more important, audiences. This is no small sum. On a per show basis, the fee can run $4,000 to $18,000 for liability insurance on a concert. If the promoter has to pay the premium it adds 32 cents to 39 cents to the cost of a ticket. A band can save a lot by having its own policy and adding the house as *additionally insured* for that date. The promoter now has more money to put into the physical production. Thus the show benefits.

Small Production, Low Budget

What about an artist who does not carry lights or sound on the road? This is usually a new artist or possibly an artist trying to re-start a career after having dropped off the charts. This also includes many Vegas-type acts as well as many jazz and country performers. These artists, however, are becoming more and more aware of the need for production values, and they are being brought into the Rock and Roll mode of production.

The rider must be written so that it can be understood by the electrician or promoter's representative who will be given the paperwork to prepare the show. Make a drawing and patch sheet that is very clear. Do not be fooled; the standard theatrical template may not be universally understood as you have been led to believe. Somehow you must produce a light plot that it is reasonable to believe the promoter and facility can re-create. Just leave enough leeway so that you can be flexible when it comes to the physical limitations of the facility.

If you do not carry the lighting equipment, it is best to give colors in general terms, light red and moonlit blue, rather than to specify a #821 Roscolene, because there are several very good color media available. Sometimes not all brands are available in every town. The same holds true for instrumentation. Will you get all PAR-64s when you needed an ellipsoidal spotlight? Try to make clear the area each lamp is to cover and its function, so if a substitution has to be made, the local supplier or electrician can give you something that comes as close to your needs as possible. Make sure you specify a working intercom between follow spots, house lights, light board, and you. Although good intercoms are the rule in the 1990s, I still specify as follows:

> The intercom shall be of the proximity-boom-mike and double-headset type and shall talk back at all positions. No hand microphones or telephone operator sets shall be acceptable.

The actual form of the rider need not be drawn up by a lawyer. But good English and clear presentation of your needs are a must. After the rider is completed, your job is only one-third over. The remainder of the work is follow-up. Of that, one-half is tracking down the person who should have the rider for each venue, and the other half is explaining and working out the compromises. By covering all the bases, you should improve your chances for success. You could say that the contract rider is a waste of time, if in fact you need to work out all these compromises. But, it is still better than starting with nothing. Dan Wohleen made one last point: "Listen to the house guy, he knows the limitations of the facility and he wants to help."

Ideally, for the production crew, a single promoter will be doing the whole tour (it is happening with more and more frequency on Mega-tours, less on arena tours, and almost not at all on theatre or college tours) and then you can get everything set once and not worry—much.

The Yellow Card

A yellow card show is one that is negotiated with the IA local, usually in the town in which the show rehearses or previews. The local works out the needs for all the road and local crew in advance. The form that is sent to each IA local happens to be yellow, thus the name commonly used. The form specifies how many persons in each department—props, carpentry, electrics (sound is still considered part of the electrical department in theatre)—are required for load-in, setup, show run, and strike. The IA local's business agent then sets the calls for members according to these requirements. The card also shows how many people in each department are traveling with the show. You can be sure the business agent of the local will check to make sure each road crew member listed on the yellow card has a valid IA yellow card and a pink contract (a road contract issued by his or her local).

I mention the yellow card even though to my knowledge no concert tour in the past few years has used this agreement. However, because more than half of designers and lighting service companies work in corporate and special projects markets, there is potential that this system will be used.

A yellow card cannot be issued unless all road personnel are IA members and hold valid yellow cards and pink contracts. Just because someone holds an IA card does not mean he or she can obtain a road contract—requirements must be met. So make sure, if you are in a position to hire, that you ask the applicant if he or she can obtain a contract to go on the road, not simply "Do you have a union card?"

None of the large sound companies is currently unionized. This effectively blocks the issuance of the yellow card, even if the lighting companies' employees and the carpenters and riggers are union members. So why even tell you about the yellow card if it is not possible to obtain one?

There are always exceptions to the rules. Besides, I still harbor the hope that tours will become organized. Without going into a long discussion, just remember what I said at the opening of this chapter—you need two sides to play the game and as now constituted, we only have management. Designers still have no way to find a benchmark by which to judge rates. That, of course, is only one part of the problem. The real issue is longevity and what happens to a road technician after many years of service. Neither I nor my associates can name any band that currently has a full-time health and retirement plan for its road crew. Neil Diamond has kept key crew members on retainer for years, but I was unable to find out if they have a paid health plan. Take this warning seriously. You have to look to your own future early in your career to be protected.

The Importance of the Rider

Write everything into the rider and be as clear as you can, because if you believe that everyone knows that you need power on stage to do the show—guess again! People with money promote concerts, not necessarily people who know what it takes to mount a production. It can happen that the promoter is extremely naive and so taken with "show biz" that he or she believes everything is magic, including how a show is set up.

The first reason I place so much importance on the rider is that it shows the promoter that competent production personnel are important to the show and gives a sense of security that the coming production is together. Confidence is half the battle. Second, it helps you get your act together. By taking the time to write a clear, full, and accurate rider, you do your homework, and that helps to anticipate problems before you hit the road. There is no substitute for good planning. If there is ever a time that Murphy's law comes into effect, it is on a concert tour of one-night stands. You cannot avoid problems completely, but you can be prepared if you have spent time in the pre-production stage.

4

Pre-Production

Before you can start a light plot, even for a play, you need to know the physical criteria of the locations. For the concert lighting designer (LD) there are some added twists. It is impractical to look over floor plans for the forty or more facilities in which the artist will perform on a tour. Because facilities vary in width, height, and power availability, it is difficult to design without this information. Where do you obtain your facts? Usually it is the road manager or on a large tour possibly the production coordinator.

The chances are slim that a city-by-city, hall-by-hall schedule will be available a month or two before the show hits the road. The schedule usually arrives a week or less before the first show, if then. So we must deal in broader classifications, that is, theatres, arenas, college gymnasiums, outdoor festivals, racetracks.

A checklist of the basic information needed includes the following:

1. Type of halls to be played (theatre, arena, outdoor)
2. Budget (per show or weekly, and what it must cover)
3. Artist's requirements
4. Stage limitations
5. Crewing
6. Opening acts
7. Prep time available (pre-tour and on the road)
8. Rehearsal time available (before tour with lights)
9. Contract rider, as it existed on the last tour (see chapter 3)

Types of Halls

If the manager can at least tell you the type of halls to be booked, you have the most important piece of information. This becomes clear to you only after you have played a variety of buildings. You must use your own judgment in limiting your staging, basing it on general categories such as theatre or arena, knowing full well the variables from structure to structure are great even within these groups. The type of performance spaces artists play range from arenas to clubs, rodeos, grass fields and college basketball arenas, and anything in between.

Some reference books are available (see the list in this chapter). *Performance* is a weekly trade publication. Its main editorial policy is to list tour schedules (Figure 4–1). Each issue also lists upcoming tours (Figure 4–2). Another feature is the spotlight on a road crew (see Figure 2–1). From time to time, it also spotlights facilities, which makes it a good

ITINERARIES

PERFORMANCE Itineraries include all dates in our database scheduled for an artist starting with the issue date. Changes in the itinerary from the last time it was published are in bold face type. Itineraries that are not updated during a two-week period will not be printed until updates are received by *PERFORMANCE*.

DIRECTORY OF MAJOR AGENCIES WITH OFFICES IN MORE THAN ONE CITY

AGENCY FOR THE PERFORMING ARTS (APA): New York (212) 582-1500; Los Angeles (310) 273-0744; Nashville (615) 297-0100
THE AGENCY GROUP: London (44-171) 278-3331; New York: (212) 581-3100; Toronto (416) 534-4778
S.L. FELDMAN & ASSOCIATES: Toronto (416) 598-0067; Vancouver (604) 734-5945
CREATIVE ARTISTS AGENCY (CAA): Los Angeles (310) 288-4545; Nashville (615) 383-8787
INTERNATIONAL CREATIVE MANAGEMENT (ICM): New York (212) 556-5600; Los Angeles (310) 550-4000
WILLIAM MORRIS AGENCY: New York (212) 586-5100; Los Angeles (310) 859-4000; Nashville (615) 963-3000

New Itineraries This Week

A Tribe Called Quest
Lynn Anderson
Carolyn Arends
Audio Adrenaline
Bad Wrench
Biohazard
Bloodloss
Bouncing Souls w/ Face to Face
JJ Cale
Steven Curtis Chapman
Chum
Edith's Wish
Elcka (Europe)
John Entwhistle
Fat Paw
Ferron
Robert Forster (Europe)
Guy Forsyth w/ Teddy Morgan & Candye Kane
Furnaceface
Gathering Fields
Gene (Europe)
Girls Against Boys
Jerry Granelli
Patty Griffin
James Hall
Ben Harper
Heavy Metal Horns
The Honeydogs
Hubinger Street
Al Jarreau (Japan)
Jason & The Schorchers
Jimmy's Chicken Shack
Michael Johnson
The Joykiller
The Killjoys w/ Limblifter & Starkicker
Kool & The Gang (Europe)
Lifter
John Lurie (Europe)
Ashley MacIsaac
Mango Jam
Me'Shell Ngedeocello
The Melvins
Mephiskapheles
Mighty Joe Plum
Gracie Moon
MU330 w/ Mustard Plug, Slapstick & Skankin Pickle
New Kingdom w/ Red Aunts
Daron Norwood
Psychotica w/ Impotent Sea Snakes
Jerry Reed
Royal Crown Revue
Rufus & The Technorazins
Screeming Trees w/ 54-50 & Solution A.D. (Canada)
Sloan (Canada)
Space (Europe)
Stabbing Westward w/ Sponge
Super Furry Animals (Europe)
The Temptations
Thermadore
Too Skinnee J's
Uisce Betha (Canada)
Voodoo Glow Skulls
Monster Mike Welch
Junior Wells
Paul Westerberg
Lavell White (Europe)
The Who's Quadrophenia
Webb Wilder
Bob Wiseman (Canada)
You Am I (Europe)
Martin Zellar
Zumpano (Canada)

A

A TRIBE CALLED QUEST — (Jive)
BA: CAA*; ITB (44-171) 379-1313
NJ Montclair, St Univ....Oct. 2
VA Harrisonburg, James Madison Univ....Oct. 4
NC Winston-Salem, Lawrence Joel Mem Col....Oct. 5
DC Washington, Capitol Ballroom....Oct. 6
ME Lewiston, Bates College....Oct. 11
NY New York, World Famous Apollo Thr....Oct. 12
FL Gainesville, Florida Thr....Oct. 16
GA Atlanta, College....Oct. 18
PA Bethlehem, Lehigh Univ....Oct. 20
VA Williamsburg, William....Oct. 25
MI Ypsilanti, Fieldhouse....Oct. 26
PA Univ Park, Penn St Univ....Oct. 27
NC Greensboro, Univ....Nov. 2

A.F.I. — (Nitro)
BA: Leave Home Booking (213) 856-9082
TX Denton, Argo....Sept. 20
AR Little Rock, Vino's....Sept. 21
MO St. Louis, Hi-Point....Sept. 23
KS Lawrence, Replay Lounge....Sept. 24
SD Sioux Falls, Pk....Sept. 25
MN Northfield, Key....Sept. 26
ND West Fargo, Elmwood Pk....Sept. 27
MB Winnipeg, Pyramid Cabaret....Sept. 28
SK Moose Jaw, Eagle's Hall....Sept. 29
SK Saskatoon, Shelter....Sept. 30
AB Edmonton, Eastwood Thr....Oct. 2
AB Calgary, Union Hall....Oct. 3
BC Kelowna, Comm Arts Center....Oct. 4
BC Vancouver, TBA....Oct. 5
WA Seattle, TBA....Oct. 6
OR Portland, Stage 4....Oct. 8
OR Eugene, TBA....Oct. 9

AC/DC — (EastWest)
BA: CAA*
Op. act: The Poor
AUS Perth, Burswood Dome....Nov. 2
AUS Adelaide, Ent Center....Nov. 5
AUS Melbourne, Pk....Nov. 7-9
AUS Brisbane, Ent Centre....Nov. 11
AUS Sydney, Ent Centre....Nov. 13-15
AUS Sydney, Ent Centre....Nov. 17
AUS Brisbane, Ent Centre....Nov. 18
AUS Darwin, Football Pk Darwin....Nov. 21
AUS Cairns, Fair....Nov. 24
NWZ Auckland, Ericsson Stad....Nov. 27
AUS Christchurch, Fair....Nov. 30

ACUMEN — (Holographic)
BA: Backstreet Booking (513) 542-9544
KY Newport, York St....Sept. 26
KY Lexington, Area 51....Sept. 28
OH Toledo, Whit's End....Oct. 5
OH Cleveland, Peabody's....(t) Oct. 12
OH Akron, Brewski's....Oct. 18
OH Columbus, Bernie's....Oct. 23
KY Lexington, Area 51....Oct. 24
MO St. Louis, Kennedy's....Oct. 26

TRACE ADKINS — (Capitol)
BA: William Morris Agency*
MI Waynesville, Dugout....Sept. 21
AL Point Clear, Paw's Barn....Sept. 22
TX Three Rivers, Silver Dollar Club....Sept. 26
TX Nacogdoches, Jitterbugs....Sept. 27
TX Pasadena, Livestock Show....Sept. 28
TN Nashville, Wildhorse Saloon....Oct. 4
MD Glen Burnie, Marley's....Oct. 11
VA Richmond, TBA....Oct. 19
GA Lawrenceville, Fair....Nov. 9
TX Arlington, Cowboy's....Nov. 22

ALL MIGHTY SENATORS — (Fowl)
BA: E-Flat Productions (410) 793-3893
NC Raleigh, Davidson College....Sept. 20
NC Winston-Salem, Ziggy's....Sept. 21
VA Virginia Beach, Phil's Grill....Sept. 22
WV Morgantown, Sunnyside Music Garden....Sept. 25
MD Baltimore, Fletcher's....Sept. 26
VA Fairfax, Planet Nova....Sept. 27
VA Richmond, Alley Cats....Sept. 29

TORI AMOS— (Atlantic)
BA: CAA*; ITB (44-171) 379-1313
Op. act: Josh Clayton-Felt
IL Rockford, Coronado Thr....Sept. 20
WI Green Bay, Weidner Center....Sept. 22
WI Madison, Oscar Meyer Thr....Sept. 23
IL Normal, Braden Aud....Sept. 24
MI East Lansing, Wharton Center....Sept. 26
MI Ann Arbor, Hill Aud....Sept. 27
IL Chicago, Arie Crown Thr....Sept. 28
MD Baltimore, Lyric Thr....Sept. 30
PA Williamsport, Comm Arts Center....Oct. 5
SC Charleston, Gallard Aud....Oct. 9
VA Roanoke, CC....Oct. 11
AR Little Rock, Robinson Center....Oct. 13
LA Lafayette, Heymann Performing Arts....Oct. 14
LA New Orleans, Saenger Thr....Oct. 16

ERIC ANDERSEN
BA: Skyline Music (603) 586-7171
MD Timonium, Coffeehouse at Mary's Chapel....Sept. 20
PA Philadelphia, Tin Angel....Sept. 21
NY Pawling, Towne Crier....Sept. 22
MA Cambridge, Passim....Sept. 26
NY Piedmont, Turning Point....Sept. 27
NY Genesee Depot, Comm College....Sept. 28
PA Malvern, Bonnington's....Sept. 29
NY New York, Bottom Line....Oct. 2
ME Blue Hill, Left Bank Cafe....Oct. 3
MA Framingham, Coffeehouse....Oct. 4
CA San Francisco, Great Amer....Oct. 12
CA Santa Monica, Ash Grove....Oct. 13

BILL ANDERSON — (Warner Bros.)
BA: Third Coast Talent (615) 952-3181
GA Atlanta, Music Awards....Sept. 28
GA Hiawassee, Anderson....Oct. 5
NE Emerson, HS....Oct. 7
MN St. Cloud, CC....Oct. 11
MN Cambridge, Middle School....Oct. 12
SD Wagner, Ft. Randall Casino....Oct. 14-15
NE Emerson, HS....Nov. 3
AL Birmingham, Fair....Nov. 7
IA Marquette, Miss Marquette Casino....Nov. 21
WV Wheeling, Capitol....Dec. 14

JOHN ANDERSON — (BNA)
BA: Bobby Roberts Company (615) 859-8899
GA Augusta, Dog Days....Sept. 20
NC Greensboro, Col....Sept. 21
KY Lexington, Fasit Tipton Sales Pavilion....Sept. 24
SC Anderson, Cty Fair....Sept. 26
VA Richmond, Virginia St Fair....Sept. 27
PA Bloomsburg, Fair....Sept. 28
NY Olean, St. Bonaventure Univ....Sept. 29
IN Nashville, Little Nashville Opry....Oct. 5
AR Little Rock, AR St Fair....Oct. 18
IL Taylorville, Nashville North....Oct. 19
NC Raleigh, North Carolina St Fair....Oct. 24
FL Pensacola, Interstate Fair....Oct. 26
KY Louisville, Gardens Arena....Nov. 8
WI Madison, Dane Cty Expo Center....Nov. 9
MI Saginaw, CC-Wendler Arena....Nov. 10
GA Kennesaw, Cowboy's....Nov. 14
FL Fort Lauderdale, Swap Shop....Nov. 24

LYNN ANDERSON
BA: Buddy Lee Attractions (615) 244-4336
TX Plano, C....Sept. 26
NV Reno, Silver Legacy Hotel& Casino....Nov. 8
MS Biloxi, President Casino....Nov. 15-16
NE Valentine, Rosebud Casino....Nov. 26
NV Las Vegas, Showboat Casino....Dec. 10
NV Las Vegas, Showboat Casino....Dec. 15

CAROLYN ARENDS — (Reunion)
BA: William Morris Agency*
ON London, Centennial Hall....Sept. 27
ON Toronto, Massey Hall....Sept. 28
ON Ottawa, Natl Arts Centre....Sept. 29
ON Thunder Bay, Comm Aud....Oct. 2
MB Winnipeg, Walker Thr....Oct. 3
SK Regina, Agridome....Oct. 5
AB Edmonton, Jubilee Aud....Oct. 6
SK Saskatoon, Centennial Aud....Oct. 7
AB Calgary, Jubilee Aud....Oct. 8
BC Vancouver, Jubilee Aud....Oct. 10
WA Yakima, Valley SunDome....Oct. 31
NV Las Vegas, Thomas....Nov. 2
TX Waco, Ferrell Center....Nov. 5
TX Amarillo, CC....Nov. 7
NM Albuquerque, Tingley Col....Nov. 8
TX Abilene, Moody Col....Nov. 9
TX Beaumont, Montagne Center....Nov. 10
TN Chattanooga, Univ....Nov. 14
NC Winston-Salem, TBA....Nov. 15
VA Fairfax, Patriot Center....Nov. 16
TN Johnson City, Freedom Hall CC....Nov. 17
IN Fort Wayne, Mem Aud....Nov. 21
MO St. Louis, Kiel Center....Nov. 22
IL Rockford, Metro....Nov. 23
MI Saginaw, CC-Wendler Arena....Nov. 24
PA Hershey, Arena....Nov. 26
AL Birmingham, Civic Arena....Nov. 29
KY Louisville, Gardens Thr....Nov. 30
OH Dayton, Arena....Dec. 1
AL Mobile, CC....Dec. 3
FL Fort Myers, Lee CC....Dec. 5
FL West Palm Beach, Arena....Dec. 6
FL Lakeland, Carpenter's Home Church....Dec. 7

ASLEEP AT THE WHEEL — (Capitol)
BA: Buddy Lee Attractions (615) 244-4336
TX Bowie, Chisolm Trail Saloon....Sept. 20
TX Arlington, Music Mill Amph....Sept. 21-22
NV Las Vegas, Tropicana Resort....Sept. 27-28
CA Indio, Spotlight 29 Casino....Sept. 29
CA Santa Ana, Crazyhorse Steakhouse....Sept. 30
TX Stamford, Stage Coach....Oct. 5
TX Austin, TBA....Oct. 6
TX Helotes, Floores Country Store....Oct. 12
TX Round Rock, TBA....Oct. 19
OK Geary, Rodeo Joe's Nightclub....Oct. 26
NY Buffalo, Marquee At The Trail....Nov. 1
NY Middletown, Paramount Thr....Nov. 2
MD Hagerstown, Maryland Thr....Nov. 3
GA Smyrna, Buckboard....Nov. 7
FL Orlando, Central Florida Fair....Nov. 9
FL Polk City, Wing's....Nov. 10
TX Beaumont, Plum Nearly Ranch....Nov. 16
CA Anaheim, Disneyland....Nov. 22
NV Las Vegas, Arizona Charlies....Dec. 5
NV Las Vegas, Arizona Charlies....Dec. 7
MO Kansas City, Hotel....Dec. 31

ASS PONYS — ((A&M))
BA: Billions Corp. (312) 997-9999
App. with: Possum Dixon
MA Boston, Middle East Cafe....Oct. 3
NY New York, Brownies....Oct. 4
ME Portland, Bad Habits Live/Zootz....Oct. 5
VT Burlington, Toast....Oct. 6
OH Cleveland, Grog Shop....Oct. 12
IL Chicago, Empty Bottle....Oct. 18

AUDIO ADRENALINE — (ForeFront)
BA: William Morris Agency*
ON Kitchener, Aud....Sept. 21
MI Sandusky, HS....Sept. 22
CA Valencia, Magic Mountain....Sept. 27
CA Santa Clara, Great America....Sept. 28
VA Arlington, HS....Oct. 5
WA Yakima, Valley SunDome....Oct. 31
NV Las Vegas, Thomas....Nov. 2
TX Waco, Ferrell Center....Nov. 5
TX Amarillo, CC....Nov. 7
NM Albuquerque, Tingley Col....Nov. 8
TX Abilene, Moody Col....Nov. 9
TX Beaumont, Montagne Center....Nov. 10
TN Chattanooga, Univ....Nov. 14
NC Winston-Salem, TBA....Nov. 15
VA Fairfax, Patriot Center....Nov. 16
TN Johnson City, Freedom Hall CC....Nov. 17
IN Fort Wayne, Mem Aud....Nov. 21
MO St. Louis, Kiel Center....Nov. 22
IL Rockford, Metro....Nov. 23
MI Saginaw, CC-Wendler Arena....Nov. 24
PA Hershey, Arena....Nov. 26
AL Birmingham, Civic Arena....Nov. 29
KY Louisville, Gardens Thr....Nov. 30
OH Dayton, Arena....Dec. 1
AL Mobile, CC....Dec. 3
FL Fort Myers, Lee CC....Dec. 5
FL West Palm Beach, Arena....Dec. 6
FL Lakeland, Carpenter's Home Church....Dec. 7

AVERAGE WHITE BAND
BA: William Morris Agency*
App. with: Tower of Power 9/25-28,10/1-13
TX Houston, Rockefeller's....Sept. 20
TX Fort Worth, Caravan Of Dreams....Sept. 21
TX Austin, La Zona Rosa....Sept. 22
NM Albuquerque, El Rey Thr....Sept. 24
AZ Phoenix, Celeb Thr....Sept. 25
AZ Tucson, Outback....Sept. 26
CA San Diego, Humphrey's Concerts....Sept. 27
CA Ventura, Thr....Sept. 28
CA Riverside, Amph....Sept. 29
CA West Hollywood, House of Blues....Oct. 1-2
CA Fresno, Paul Paul Thr....Oct. 3
CA Bakersfield, Kern Cty Fair....Oct. 4
CA San Francisco, Fillmore....Oct. 5
NV Las Vegas, Arizona Charlies....Oct. 8-9
NV Reno, Flamingo Hilton Hotel....Oct. 11-12
CA Kelseyville, Konocti Harbor Resort....Oct. 13

THE AWARE TOUR
BA: PGA (615) 377-0201
Feat: Stir, Farmer, Athanaeum, Vertical Horizon, Dead City Radio, Cresta
MO St. Louis, Mississippi Nights....Sept. 20
IL Chicago, Cubby Bear....Sept. 21
MI Kalamazoo, Club Soda....Sept. 23
MI Grand Rapids, Sluggos Down Under....Sept. 24
MI Ann Arbor, Rick's Amer Cafe....Sept. 25
OH Cleveland, Peabody's Down Under....Sept. 26
PA Philadelphia, Middle East....Sept. 27
MA Boston, Mama Kin....Sept. 28
VT Burlington, Toast....Sept. 29
NY New York, Wetlands Perserve....Oct. 2
DC Washington, Bayou....Oct. 3
NC Winston-Salem, Ziggy's....Oct. 4
NC Raleigh, Lake Boone Country Club....Oct. 5
SC Columbia, Elbow Room....Oct. 8
SC Charleston, Music Farm....Oct. 9
GA Athens, GA Thr....Oct. 10
AL Birmingham, Sloss Furnaces....Oct. 11
GA Atlanta, Chameleon Club....Oct. 12
LA New Orleans, Tipitina's....Oct. 15
TX Houston, Satellite Lounge....Oct. 16
TX Austin, Stubbs BBQ....Oct. 17
TX Dallas, Trees....Oct. 18
TX College Station, Dixie Thr....Oct. 19

Figure 4–1 Itineraries.
(From *Performance* 20 September 1996, 34. Reproduced by permission of *Performance* magazine.)

Figure 4–2 Upcoming tours.
(From *Performance* 5 July 1996, 22. Reproduced by permission of *Performance* magazine.)

UPCOMING TOURS

Aerosmith
BA: Monterey Peninsula Artists
Phone: (408) 375-4889
PM: Collins Management
Phone: (617) 868-3100
RC: Geffen
Anticipated Dates: Fall

China Drum
BA: ICM
Phone: (310) 550-4000
PM: Phil Barton Mangement
Phone: (44-181) 673-0567
RC: MCA
Anticipated Dates: mid-July

GWAR
BA: Monster Talent
Phone: (818) 787-9282
PM: Slave Pit Management
Phone: (804) 321-1015
RC: Metal Blade
Anticipated Dates: October-December

Nina Hagen
BA: Monster Talent
Phone: (818) 787-9282
PM: N/A
RC: RCA
Anticipated Dates: Fall

Eric Johnson
BA: Entourage Talent
Phone: (212) 997-1900
PM: Joe Priesnitz Artist Management
Phone: (512) 472-5435
RC: Capitol
Anticipated Dates: Fall/Winter

Howard Jones
BA: Entourage Talent
Phone: (212) 997-1900
PM: Friars Management
Phone: (44-129) 434-7316
RC: Elektra
Anticipated Dates: Fall

Lemonheads
BA: ICM
Phone: (310) 550-4000

PM: Gold Mountain Entertainment
Phone: (213) 850-5660
RC: Atlantic
Anticipated Dates: Fall

Amanda Marshall
BA: William Morris Agency
Phone: (310) 859-4000
PM: Forte Records & Productions
Phone: (416) 323-3864
RC: Epic
Anticipated Dates: mid-July/August

Metallica
BA: QBQ Entertainment
Phone: (212) 949-6900
PM: Q Prime
Phone: (212) 302-9790
RC: Elektra
Anticipated Dates: Winter
/Spring 1997

Peter Murphy
BA: F.B.I.
Phone: (213) 850-5373
PM: Rockmasters Group Ltd.
Phone: (44-171) 727-8636
Anticipated Dates: Summer

Neurotic Outsiders
BA: Artists & Audience
Phone: (212) 721-2400
PM: Big FD Managment
Phone: (310) 441-2484
RC: Maverick
Anticipated Dates: Summer/Fall

New Edition
BA: William Morris Agency
Phone: (310) 859-4000
PM: 617 Mangement
Phone: (213) 436-0544
RC: MCA
Anticipated Dates: October

No Doubt
BA: The M.O.B. Agency
Phone: (213) 653-0427

PM: Tom Atencio & Associates
Phone: (213) 468-0105
RC: Trauma
Anticipated Dates: October-December

Linda Perry
BA: Premier Talent Agency
Phone: (212) 758-4900
PM: Gerard Mangement
Phone: (415) 495-2873
RC: Rockmaster Records
Anticipated Dates: Fall

Slayer
BA: ICM
Phone: (212) 556-5600
PM: Rick Sales Management
Phone: (213) 874-0071
RC: American Recordings
Anticipated Dates: Fall

Supernova
BA: Creature Booking
Phone: (612) 925-6011
PM: 103 Degrees Management
Phone: (619) 235-9404
RC: Amphetamine Reptile
Anticipated Dates: Late summer/Fall

Thinking Fellers Union Local #282
BA:/PM: Creature Booking
Phone: (612) 925-6011
Anticipated Dates: Fall/Winter

Youth Brigade
BA: Monster Talent
Phone: (818) 787-9282
PM: BYO
Phone: (310) 301-6333
RC: BYO
Anticipated Dates: Starts August

The Upcoming Tours column is intended for national tours by major artists, and the column will only list upcoming tours. Send upcoming tour information to *PERFORMANCE*, Attention: Upcoming Tours, or call Tiffany Buchanan at (817) 338-9444; FAX: (817) 877-4273.

source for learning about new venues and what they offer in the way of size and other qualities. *Performance* is responsible for the only formal awards recognition of tour designers and technicians by means of its annual readers' poll.

Pollstar is a newer weekly publication that follows generally the same format as *Performance*. Although the box office receipts, album retail sales, air play, and "Route Booking" sections are great, they do not run as much production-crew information as *Performance*.

Both publications produce special annual supplements that list service companies such as trucking, bus, lighting, sound, and staging companies and agent rosters. These are excellent reference books.

A publication called *AudArena Stadium Guide* is published annually by Billboard. It does not give as much technical detail as it does staff, cost of rentals, and services available. It is only one of several reference guides that Billboard publishes throughout the year.

One helpful organization, the International Association of Auditorium Managers, provides a guide to venues, the *IAAM Journal*. It is probably the most complete listing of stadiums, auditoriums, arenas, and theatres. It is designed primarily to provide a listing of hall and facility contacts for ticket sales, catering, and building services. Although the *IAAM Journal* lacks detailed technical data, it does give hall type, floor or stage size, seating capacity, and other general details, as well as names and telephone contacts at the venues.

The legitimate theatres have a degree of uniformity, because road companies of Broadway plays and musicals are planned around this cadre of known facilities. This uniformity, however, is limited to some 30 or 40 houses across the country. A concert tour plays everything from an old movie house to a symphony hall, and it is still called a theatre tour. A theatre tour for a rock band could go from the Capital Theatre (an old movie house) in Passaic, New Jersey, to the Minneapolis Symphony Hall (no overhead pipes), to the Arie Crown Theatre, Chicago (very deep stage with excellent grid system), to Constitution Hall in Washington, D.C. (a domed stage, no grid), to the Pine Knob Music Center outside Detroit (a covered stage with open-air lawn seating). This is why trusses and other structures are trouped by concert artists even when they do a theatre tour.

When we talk about arena tours, we can expect even less in the way of theatrical facilities, that is, counterweighted pipes and stage. Arenas for the most part are simply large airplane hangars with seating. There has been a trend the past ten years for arena managers and owners to admit that the income from concerts far outstrips that from a sporting event. But they are still reluctant to do much to cater to the concert market.

A most promising resource is the Internet. There are sites that are used by stage managers, other theatre and concert designers, and technicians. At a conference of the United States Institute for Theatre Technology (USITT) a couple of years ago I listened to stage managers talk about tracking dance and road companies by means of the Internet. They were able to obtain up-to-date information and changes about the production that helped them provide what was needed and not waste time. It is possible to obtain ground plans sent via the Internet. Some facilities have made such information available on their Web sites.

At a few exceptionally well-equipped theatres around the country, the house staff cannot understand why we do not use their fixtures and counterweight systems. What they do not understand is that the elements of timing, consistency, and repeatability are the keys to a good concert. A theatre production usually rehearses in each new town, so there is time to make adjustments in hanging positions, focus, and dimmer levels. A touring concert has less than 12 hours from load-in to curtain. The concert designer, as well as the artist, must be assured of what is to be seen during the performance.

Publications that List Tours and Venue Facts

AudArena Stadium Guide
Billboard Publishing
Box 24970
Nashville, TN 37202

IAAM Journal
International Association of Auditorium Managers
500 N. Michigan Ave.
Chicago, IL 60611

Performance
Performance, Inc.
1101 University, Suite 108
Ft. Worth, TX 76107-4273

Pollstar
4697 W. Jacquelyn
Fresno, CA 93722

Budget

Some designers refuse to let budget restrictions encumber their creativity. They prefer to obtain as much information as is available and prepare the design the way they believe it should look. They then present the design to the artist and try to persuade management that the idea is worth any expense.

Maybe I am too much of a realist, but I like knowing at least the approximate budget. Designers who develop the budget after the design is submitted are, on the whole, name designers. They have sold themselves with the understanding that they will have a blank check. Let us consider the other 99.5% of us who must justify our cost to management.

It is wise to ask for a budget when you first talk about the project. Likely as not, you will receive blank looks because a budget has not even been considered, or they will throw it back to you in an attempt to see if you can provide figures lower than the artist paid last time. One way to obtain a rough figure is to give a range per show and observe the manager's reaction. This is not to say that if you return with a terrific idea that will cost more than the budget, you will not be able to talk artist and management into using it. The budget should simply be a median point to use as a guide; you can come in under budget or even over budget if you believe the effort is worth the expense.

Artists' Requirements

The initial meeting should be with the artist. The only way to learn how artists want to look is through meeting them, not the management. You are creating something that affects the performance substantially, and you must be in tune with the artist. Concerns such as stage movement and placement of band equipment must be discussed.

One of my first clients was Billy Preston. I was called in at the last minute to do his tour. At the time I had met only the road manager, not Billy. The road manager assured me he had been with the artist so long that he knew his every move and requirement. The first show looked like I had designed the lighting for Joan Baez when the design was supposed to be for Kiss!

A rapport with the artist must be established. Confidence in you as another creative person who wants to make the artist appear in the best light (no pun) is essential. It is the equivalent of the theatre designer's relationship with the director.

Stage Limitations

Many physical limitations must be considered in the mounting of a show. Ask yourself questions such as the following: Is a backdrop being used that must be lit? In arenas, is there seating in the rear? In outdoor shows, does the wind factor preclude backdrops and some scenic devices? What are the sight lines and width of the stage? Dan Wohleen relates some stories: "An artist had changed from rear to front projection after the tour started and had not informed us. I lost 800 seats to the change and it came out of the artist's pocket." In another case the booking agent had sold the act with 270-degree seating availability to the promoters. When Dan got the rider it was quite clear that there were only 210 degrees of availability. Dan contacted the tour production manager and was told that someone had not informed the booker of the change. Luckily this was discovered before seats went on sale.

What do you do when the band shows up and says it has decided to let someone videotape the performance? Ignore for a moment the additional costs this will incur; what about that "little" five foot platform they need for a camera placed dead in the center of the expensive seats? "It wiped out 120 seats. People were mad at the house, not the band," Dan related.

Because you cannot control the performance spaces in so many locations, the design must anticipate physical staging problems before they develop. Once on the road, it is difficult to keep changing things to meet day-to-day problems. Time is a constant devil, so preplanning and forethought about possible solutions to every conceivable staging question must be considered in advance.

Crewing

Will you hire the crew personally or be contracting a lighting company for personnel and equipment? How many technicians are to be on the lighting crew? How much time is available for setup? How many local stagehands will be hired to help out? If required, are riggers to be provided by the promoter, or are you taking a head rigger or full rigging crew with you on tour?

Crewing is vital. You can design the most spectacular show in the world and it will have been for naught if it is not ready by 8:00 P.M. Remember that time is the unrelenting demon of touring. A touring lighting crew of two technicians is normal; three, four, or more can be found on medium-size shows. Arena and stadium shows have much larger crews (see Figure 2–1). The lighting usually is done with the assistance of four to six local stagehands. However, a large number of special effects take time to set up and can slow things down, as do heavy scenic elements.

A new element has entered the scene in a big way. Moving lights were a novelty in 1985. In 1997 they are almost a necessity. As the PAR lamp became the signature fixture in early concert design, the moving light has taken on the status of king of the hill. However, this wonderfully versatile fixture carries with it a great deal of baggage. Technical support is one problem. The lighting technician really must be a technician. The electronics of these units requires much more maintenance than does a PAR can. Although many manufacturers have worked hard to make them bullet proof and easily serviced, weather, heat, and rain can damage moving lights. They are still the temperamental artists of the road. Another fact is that although they appear to reduce the size of many lighting rigs, moving lights take far longer to program in rehearsal. They also may require an additional crew member, who also operates the computer console, increasing the size of the lighting crew, not reducing it. So the efficiency of having one source of light is reduced by the heavy backup and personnel needed to keep it on the road.

Who handles the road supervision and repair of the set, scrims, drapery, and such? A road carpenter is still rare on a Rock and Roll tour. As the designer you are likely to be responsible for all these elements. That is not to say that you personally have to take hammer and nail to a broken flat, but you will probably need to make sure everything is kept in working order.

Opening Acts

The opening act is often slighted; in the vernacular they are the bottom of the food chain, most of the time. Little consideration usually is given to their need for stage space or lighting. The headline band's equipment technicians usually refuse to move one piece of their stage gear. This is often out of spite, because it was done to them before they became headliners. But it is a fact of the business that you must deal with.

Opening acts with the same management company as the main artist probably receive more consideration, but not always. Stars' egos can be enormous, and artists quickly forget how it was when they were beginning. Do not take for granted that the opening act will be given carte blanche to add special lighting even if they pay for it. In fact, do not agree to allow any equipment to be added to your rig until you have had it cleared with management in writing. If the opening act is permitted anything, you may still want to place restrictions on the extent to which it can use your design.

There is a growing tendency to package a single opening act with the tour. In theatre we look at the show and how its parts are integrated into the whole. In concert touring, 99 percent of the time we design for one element of the show only. Keep the perspective of whom you work for and do not try to be a good guy to the other artists; you could lose your job for that effort. You'd be surprised at what artists are vindictive and downright nasty to opening acts. Even though they were opening acts only a year or two ago themselves. It is payback time in their minds somehow, and you can become caught in the middle if you are not careful.

Prep Time

The first consideration in prep time is the time before the tour allotted to design and physically put the equipment together, check it out, and be ready to rehearse and hit the road. If you are going to use one of the companies in the business of supplying tour lighting, the time required can be cut to a couple weeks, or in a pinch much less, because they have much of the equipment already packaged and are geared to prepare it quickly. A substantial delay occurs when the trussing must be fabricated. If time is tight, do yourself a favor by checking out truss plans that can be realized with in-stock pieces. Also remember that how busy the shop is will be a determining factor in preparation time and very possibly in cost.

The second area to consider for preparation is the time allocated each day to load in and prepare for the sound check. A show that takes a long time to load in, hang, and focus must be planned well in advance.

This is so the promoter can provide adequate assistance. Local stage-hands must be hired and access to the hall must be arranged for as many hours as it takes to accomplish all these things. Planning takes on more importance with the new Mega-tours, such as the Michael Jackson, Madonna, Rolling Stones, and David Bowie tours, which take two to three days to load in.

Ability to judge the setup time is an acquired skill. You can consult with the lighting company in the early stages to talk over your concepts and let them give you their ideas about crew and setup requirements. It takes time to move equipment from one city to the next. A tour that is booked with 600-mile jumps between shows will never make a 9:00 A.M. stage call. Figure on one hour driving time per 50 miles of travel. In areas of the country where superhighways are not the rule, however, travel takes longer, as does travel through large cities to reach a venue, such as Madison Square Garden in New York. The time of year, for instance winter in the Midwest, also is a factor. Unfortunately, booking agents are notorious for their complete lack of consideration of this point.

There have been innovations in the past few years to assist designers in rehearsal. Computer programs such as LuxArt (see chapter 10) can be used to create cues and even color print outs of looks you want to achieve. There are also programs such as WYSIWYG (What You See Is What You Get), a three-dimensional, real-time programming tool that allows you to write cues and download them directly into the tour lighting console. Another recent innovation comes from Strand. Two consoles can be programmed separately and the cues joined for play-back. A conventional console can be set up and cues designed while a moving light operator programs cues that become a part of the program. Later the two programs can be joined, and only one operator is needed.

A unique idea was the FOUR TO ONE scale design stage that Patrick Woodroffe built in London in 1990. It consisted of a miniature stage, set, and miniature lights that could plug into a touring console. While listening to the music, the LD then programs the tour. This is an expensive method, but one that has been very successfully used. Recently relocated to Cologne, Germany, inside the television studio complex of the Magic Media Company, the company is now called Institute for Lighting and Stage Simulation. Its owners believe the FOUR TO ONE stage is a very valuable tool, citing disadvantages and shortcomings in virtual animation and traditional model-building. The system is complete with fourth scale trusses, follow spots, effects units, color scrollers, and musical instruments, including a complete four-to-one scale band, props, and costumes. The computer-based programs are discussed later in the book, but you must consider these as potential tools to make the schedule work.

Rehearsal Time

A few top acts stage a full production (Prince and David Bowie, for example) and approach the tour as if it were a true theatrical show. The more rehearsal time available, the tighter the first show. However, a long rehearsal with lights is rare and becoming rarer. For some reason management believes that spending more money on computer-controlled lighting saves time in rehearsal. Nothing is farther from the truth. To plot each point of movement of each moving light is time-intensive. Jeff Ravitz has even gone to the point of having an assistant keep time. He allocates a certain number of minutes to each song. When time is up, it's up, and he moves on to another song. If not, the tour can open and have great looks for the first six songs, but then the stage goes dark. Computerized lighting is not like manual board lighting, with which you can somehow build a look instantly. The shell of the song must be completed before the tour starts. Jeff said, "I often go into the first city with only a basic look and the absolutely necessary cues within the song, then over the next day or two I fill in the holes. There just isn't enough time allotted by the management anymore. They think it's magic!"

The reality is that the band rehearses in a small room for a week or two, at which time you should be finding places in the music (solos, accents, stage movement, and so on) for lighting changes. But the availability of large stages and the very high cost to the artist of a lengthy full rehearsal place limitations on this phase of preparation. Here is where your planning and ability to make quick decisions are put to the test. Rock bands are not actors who know how to freeze while a light cue is set and then pick up the action again. They play through the song, and possibly repeat it if they want. I cannot emphasize enough that a true rehearsal such as theatre companies enjoy is nonexistent in a touring rock show.

Variety of Venues and Artistic Styles

A career in concert lighting does not limit you to one type of music. A great variety of artistic styles are performing in concert venues throughout the country each day. There were more than 600 musical artists and bands on the road the first week of November 1996, according to *Performance* magazine's listings. This is a relatively inactive time of the year. The peak seasons are April–May, July–August, and October–November. If you break down the more than 600 tours, only four to six involve superstars. About 40 of these acts constitute extra large tours, and about 50 to 100 use touring lights and sound. Another 150 to 200 are gaining a foothold and may hire a designer and rent equipment locally or regionally. Another 30 or 40 are casino circuit acts playing Las Vegas, Reno, Lake Tahoe, Atlantic City, and some large clubs. This circuit can provide for some very creative designing, so do not brush off Las Vegas or Atlantic City. The facilities are extremely well equipped and they are always looking for something new. The rest of the touring acts are playing as opening acts or simply cannot afford or do not care about lights and sound.

The range of places used as performance areas is vast and creates wonderful yet frightening challenges for a designer. Once the aforementioned areas are covered—type of hall, budget, artist's needs, staging, crew, opening act, preparation time, and rehearsal time—you can sit down, listen to the music, and start to rough out a lighting plot. The frustration caused by designing before you know most of this information is utterly debilitating. Learn as many facts as possible and be positive in your concepts but be prepared for changes. This is a known: there will be changes!

5

The Design Stage

Your first concert design will probably be for a local promoter, a college, or a local band. This stage of building a reputation, and more important, building confidence in yourself, usually puts you into the type of show in which the artist has no touring equipment and probably has a very sketchy rider that gives a stage plan (probably nothing like what he or she is currently using), and maybe a basic color chart. You may not even be allowed to "call" the headliner, only the opening act.

So what are you to do? First, go to the promoter and find out how much can be spent on equipment rental. Second, consider the facility in which you are to do the show. Are there the required (or hoped for) number of follow spots? If not, it takes a large chunk out of your budget to rent them and pay the operators.

The best design for a show like this is a very general one; it may also be the safest, but that is secondary. Three or four colors for each of back light and side light circuits may seem too easy, but that is what 80 percent of the local concerts use. If you are sure the star will stay at the microphone, add some back light specials to separate and bring him or her out from the band. (Later I discuss a basic plan for most back truss and side Genie tower type lighting rigs that would tour with a jazz or country artist, even many rock bands. I have seen many such simple plans used very creatively on the road.)

The truth is, subdued colors and tints are not what we are after. Concert lighting is bold. Use primary colors to make a statement. If you pick colors correctly, you can mix them and obtain almost any color you desire. The next stage is to add specials as needed, money or dimming permitting. Too often designers become so involved with *big* that they forget clarity in design. In addition, a wide range of special effects and projections can be added, but these are beyond the type of show we are discussing here.

Fixtures

Your first consideration for light fixtures is general coverage. The parabolic aluminum reflector (PAR-64) medium flood (M) lamp is best for general washes. The channel that you want to give tighter focus is the same PAR-64 but with a narrow (N) or very narrow spot (VNSP) lamp. A fourth lens, wide (W), now is available. The PAR-64 and the less-used but valuable family of PAR fixtures (Figure 5–1) are the workhorses of concert lighting. Being relatively trouble-free and devoid of parts to jam or break, the units have the most effective, dimmable light source available among the standard theatrical-film fixtures. For 30 years the PAR lamp has continued to be the most reliable source for "punch" lighting.

Figure 5–1   The parabolic aluminum reflector (PAR) family of lamps ranges in size from a PAR-16 to the more familiar PAR-64.
(Photo by James Thomas Engineering, Ltd.)

Chip Monck, it is generally agreed, brought the PAR-64 lamp to the concert field. How and where he first saw them I am not sure, but he knew that they were being used in film. Colortran, Inc., had been mounting the PAR-64 family of lamps in a unit they called The Cine Queen. Chip's innovation was to put strong, vibrant colored gels in front of the Cine Queen, but halfway through the show the color burnt out. Bill McManus had seen the lamps and went to Ronnie Altman at Altman Stage Lighting in New York. McManus gave Altman a sketch and asked him to build 500 with the company's stock crinkled finish. The housing was simple, no moving parts, and it had a gel frame holder out front to keep the color away from the hot lamp. "There were no porcelain caps back then and the wiring left a lot to be desired," said Bill. But it worked. He used the 500 Altman built for him on Jethro Tull's Passion Play tour in late 1971. What he didn't know at the time was that Altman had also run 500 more of the design and sold most to Bob See at See-Factor. "I was so impressed that Chip Monck had picked a bottle that had so much punch over anything on the market, but it just wouldn't hold color," Bill told me. On that Jethro Tull tour people went nuts. "We had 250 of the new PAR cans in a box beam truss supported with inverted CM chain hoists. It was the first tour to fly the whole system. The Stones had used Gallaway rams from the floor as support," Bill went on to say.

The efficiency and type of beam spreads available with the PAR-64 family should be viewed in different ways. There seems to be a preoccupation with efficiency because power availability is often a problem. If you are going into an old theatre or college gym, access to auxiliary power can be a headache. Consequently, you want as much light as you can get for as little power draw as possible. The PAR lamp fits this bill best of all. The sealed-beam lamps offer a range of beam spreads that give coverage from very narrow to wide flood fields. These lamps can give you concentrated beams of light that project even the most dense color media. For example, we can compare the beam spread at a 30-foot throw between the very narrow lamp—3.7 × 6.4 feet—and the medium flood lamp—6.5 × 15.5 feet—as measured at 50 percent of intensity. While we are on the subject, those same 1,000 watt (1 kW) lamps produce 560 fc and 150 fc respectively at that distance, compared with a 1 kW Fresnel, which can produce only 195 fc at spot and 40 fc at flood focus at the same distance.

The real lighting effect for many concertgoers is seeing the colored light beams stabbing toward the stage. Often referred to as *air light*, these beam patterns are created simply as a design element and may not even be focused on the artist. They become a large part of the overall design of many tours. Sometimes these patterns are more interesting than the artist's music.

Other available choices are ellipsoidal (leko) and Fresnel, besides the various types of striplights and fixtures designed around multiple PAR lamps such as the PAR-36.

Computer-controlled moving lights are everywhere. They have been so successful that there are third and fourth generations of designs out on the market. They have had substantial impact on concert design (see chapter 14).

The ellipsoidal fixture has not been given the status it enjoys in the theatre, but more and more it is being used for concert lighting. Some designers consider me to be the biggest booster of this fixture. I have lit concerts with well over 180 ellipsoidal and only four PAR-64 fixtures. There is no doubt they require a high degree of maintenance if you use them, but the tight control and ability to shape the beam is a highly desirable quality. New technology in the design of the reflector and lamp by E.T.C., Inc., has brought this style of fixture to the forefront once again. If you use ellipsoidal fixtures to throw patterns on the floor or cyc, they cannot be beat for clarity of image. To use them to light talent is tricky. Use them only when you have a show in which you are confident the talent will stand on the rehearsed marks. Artists who cannot hit marks do more than hurt your design; they waste their own money. If the effect canot be seen because of an artist's inability to be consistent in his or her movements, then the fixtures are not needed and are excess baggage.

The Fresnel fixture has little favor in the concert market because of its weight and limited efficiency. Other fixtures such as the film Mini-Brute, an early application of the PAR lamp designed for broad fill lighting on film and television location, and metal halide (HMI) lamps do find special uses from time to time. Concert manufacturers generally have produced their own designs for grouping PAR-36 in a single fixture (Figure 5–2). They are usually used as audience lights.

Virtually any fixture can be used if the designer has the vision to see the effect it will produce and to use it accordingly. Always keep in mind that the effect and the fixture must work night after night. Nothing is worse than when an effect the artist comes to expect does not work.

Figure 5–2 PAR-36 spot bank. This idea was designed with concert lighting in mind. Groups of four, six, or eight are used.
(Photo by James Thomas Engineering, Ltd.)

Placement of Fixtures

There is a reversal of basic light direction in concert lighting from traditional theatrical lighting. Whereas theatre puts great importance on front light and minimal importance on back light, concerts completely reverse this concept. Two factors are responsible for this. First, there was little or no possibility of consistently finding a balcony or front-of-house position in the 30 or 40 found spaces (spaces not specifically designed as performance areas) used for early concert tours. Second, the lighting of concerts is viewed as effect and accent rather than as the traditional theatrical function of visibility. The concept therefore was to produce all the front light with one or two follow spots and concentrate the fixed lighting effects as back light to surround the singer or players with color.

This is known as *accent lighting* to differentiate it from the theatrical style. Light is concentrated at strategic points on the stage to punctuate the music with heavy colors. This method of lighting truly fits the maxim: *It's not where you put the light, it's where you don't put the light that counts.*

Used as an objective for your designing, this maxim serves you well to keep you from overdoing the design. Too many shows load in 200 fixtures when 100 will do. I had a problem with a group that wanted me to add more lights to the tour because they were cutting back on the set. The logic was that if they had less scenery, more lights would fill in the void. Wrong. You cannot light what is not there, except when using air light. I already had an adequate plot and didn't desire anything more except effects and projections. They had just eliminated the objects I needed as surfaces for projection.

The quantity and placement of fixtures must be directly related to the placement of band and vocalist. It is unreasonable for a manager to request 80 lamps, or 200 lamps, for a client; my reply is, "Okay, I will use that for the budget figure, but I must know more about the act before I can say if that is a correct number of fixtures for the artist's needs." I see no point in renting 80 (or 200) lamps and then trying to figure out what to do with them, although I admit to being put in this position on several occasions.

One of the most effective lighting designs I have seen was for Bruce Springsteen's tour in 1980. His designer at that time, Mark Brickman, had at best 60 lights, but he used them effectively. I am sure that to the audience, it appeared as a much bigger system. Good design in any field is not based on quantity.

Color

I think in terms of colors, not quantity of fixtures, before I begin to draw a plot. What I am trying to picture in my mind are *looks*, planned patterns of light and color to be used one or more times during the show. *Looks* is a television lighting term, and most theatre designers avoid it, but it really is the best way to describe our concerns once the focus of the lighting is finished.

Primary and secondary colors are generally best. For a general plot, try for four colors as side light and five colors plus white for back light on the lead artist. Bands usually use four colors for back washes and three colors for side light, plus two back specials—one warm and one cool color, such as Lee filters #105 (orange) and #137 (special lavender)—to accent their solos. I prefer not to use a follow spot every time a short guitar break is played. A nice hot back light while the follow spot on the singer is doused can be very effective. When I am able to put front specials into the design, I add a warm special and a cool special to each solo player, plus at least two general front or top band washes.

The color medium used today is much more durable than the material Chip Monck tried to use with the first PAR-64 lamps. The formulation of the material to which the color is bonded makes the color part of the structure rather than something that lies on the surface. Virtually all the manufacturers of color work with this method. However, some have found better ways to keep heat from fading the color. Run tests of several manufacturers' products in your favorite colors before you make a large order for the tour.

Three other ways to produce color in light have to be discussed when the topic of color arises. First, the method that Vari-Lite, Inc., uses on its moving light fixtures is a process of sending light at 5,600 degrees Kelvin (daylight) through a series of dichroic prisms, which gives selective refraction; the beam separating components gives a viable rainbow of color. There are also systems that use a series of color wheels that can be rotated into a beam of light and produce color by blocking the unwanted portion of the spectrum. Last, dichroic filters have been used. This method of color selection is produced by means of rotating the dichroic lens and stopping at the color desired.

All these methods are far more complicated than I have stated them. There is neither time nor space for a complete discussion of the psychology of color in this book. I strongly recommend you read any of the number of good theatrical lighting textbooks available for a full discussion of light and the human eye. My favorite book on the subject is *The Beauty of Light* by Ben Bova, but it is currently out of print (see Bibliography).

Circuiting and Dimming

The fixture complement is tied to the dimming available (except in some HMI source moving lights). It is fashionable not to concern oneself with such trivial matters. After all, you were probably taught to leave that to your master electrician or gaffer. However, reality dictates that availability of equipment most often forces you to pick from a choice of dimmer packages, usually in groups of six channels of a particular wattage: 2.4 kW or 6 kW. Not many 3.6 kW, 8 kW, or 12 kW dimmers are found on the road. The 1 kW dimmers are usually packaged in larger groups, a common quantity being 72 per rack.

Always leave some dimmers with unused capacity so that if you have a failure you can gang channels. Better yet, leave two of your largest capacity dimmers as spares in the first place.

Layering

Besides basic position and angle, I look to another idea for most of my visuals: *layering*. This is the process by which one creates depth and separation by using different shades or saturations of a single color. Except for effects, I rarely bathe the stage in a single color. That gives no visual depth. With a conscious consideration of color, coupled with intensity, you not only direct viewers to the part of the stage on which you want them to focus, but you also put the total stage into perspective. Too often I see shows that rely totally on the follow spot, with its dramatic shaft of bright light, to accomplish this task. That is the easy, boring way out. Not only is the source of light important, but also the hue and tone of the colors used on stage create a good design. It seems simple, yet many readers see this and believe it means putting a lot of different colors on the stage all at once. You can layer in a single color by means of hue variation. And do not forget that the absence of light also contributes to this theory.

I first realized how important this idea can be on my early television lighting assignments. In video, the camera cannot show depth; lighting directors must accentuate depth by means of back light and intensity between the foreground and the background. That same approach can be applied to concerts, at which some in the audience are 150 feet away from the stage. In theatre layering has application when used to subtly draw attention to a particular part of the stage. There again, not only the equipment but also the mix of colors you use can make a better, clearer design.

Layout and Symbols

Lest anyone believe that with the drawing of the light plot the design is finished, let me talk about the next step in my approach to design. I have often marveled at beautifully drawn light plots only to be disappointed in the execution of the show. On the other hand, I have often seen light plots scribbled on graph paper or the proverbial envelope that are tastefully executed. I do not defend this method, however, even when circumstances have made proper preparation impossible. The effort and wasted time spent in explanation necessitated by such a crudely drawn plot cannot be defended. The designer owes it to the technicians to give clearly understood and accurate instructions, and they are best conveyed with a properly drawn light plot.

As you study theatrical lighting, it will become apparent that there are several schools of technique. Some styles are created by teachers at a particular institution of learning, or you will be taught the so-called Broadway method perpetuated by the United Scenic Artists (USA) union examination. The Broadway style prevails, but some West Coast designers have made changes that reflect newer thinking. (Keep in mind that if you do wish to practice your craft on Broadway you will need to learn it as required for the exam.) Add in the distinctive style of the British school of design that has been injected into the United States and you have an evolving system on which no one agrees. The United States Institute for Theatre Technology (USITT) took years to agree on standard symbols for lighting instruments; even so, these are still not widely seen on concert designers' plots.

Concert designers have a style all their own. Partly because a large portion of them are not formally trained and because of a heavy British influence, they tend to simplify the plot so that anyone can understand the color, circuit, and control channels at a glance. The main differences between the two styles of drawing (the traditional versus the modern) comprise three areas:

1. *Templates* The traditional method entails both top and side silhouettes; a concert designer uses only top silhouettes or even simple circles.

2. *Electrical hookup chart* Traditional charts are similar to electrical engineering drawings, on which a line is drawn joining all fixtures of a circuit. Concert designers tend to use a number inside a symbol to represent the patching.

3. *Presentation* The East Coast or more traditional method entails use of separate sheets of paper for many different details needed to complete the design. The concert and Las Vegas approach is to have all the information on one sheet.

The light plot shown in Figure 5–3 has all the information needed to complete the color and hanging of a show. Adapting a tour plot to a Las Vegas venue, such as this one for the Aladdin Hotel, generally allows greater individual lamp control and variety of mounting positions than are normally available on tour. The house fly system allows for the addition of drapery and set pieces not always practical for the road. You can see from the lamp symbols (in the key) that the types of fixtures used are a combination of concert PAR-64s and straight theatre fixtures. This works best in this environment. Because the light plot in Figure 5–3 was originally drawn at a scale of $1/_2$ inch to 1 foot there was no room for the circuit chart to be on the same page. The graph sheet (Figure 5–4) makes it easy for the electrician to patch the dimmers and assign the

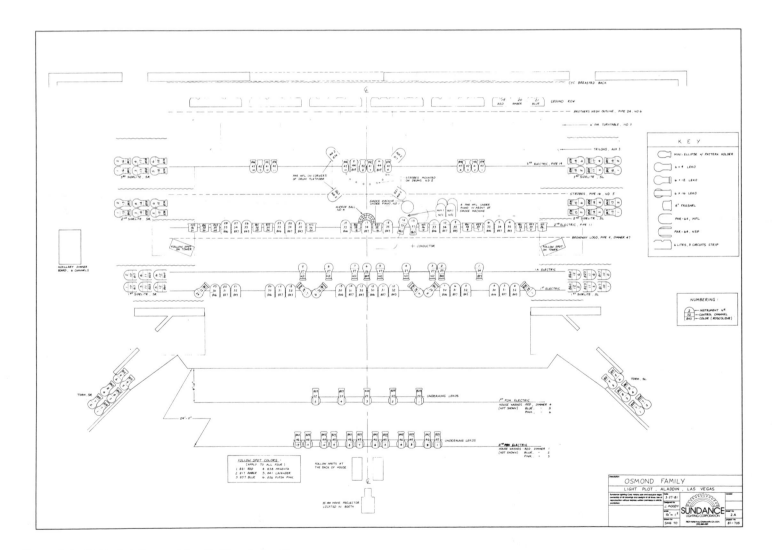

Figure 5–3   Light plot, Osmond Family Show in Las Vegas.
(Designed by James Moody.)

DIMMER		INSTRUMENTS			LOCATION	DESCRIPTION	FOCUS	COLOR		NOTES
N°	CAP	TYPE	AMT	NUMBERS				DESCRIPTION	N°	
1		HOUSE FIXTURE			2ND FOH ELECTRIC	HOUSE WASH	WASH	RED		
2								BLUE		
3								PINK		
4					1ST FOH ELECTRIC			RED		
5								BLUE		
6								PINK		
7	4K	6x9 LEKO	4	1,2/1,2	TORM SR/SL	SIDELITE		BRIGHT ROSE	829	
8				3,4/3,4				SP LAVENDER	842	
9				5,6/5,6				GOLDEN AMBER	815	
10		PAR MFL	4	1,2/1,2	1ST SIDELITE SR/SL			DARK AMBER	817	
11				3,4/3,4				MED. RED	823	
12				5,6/5,6				BRIGHT BLUE	860	
13		6x9 LEKO	4	1,2/1,2	2ND SIDELITE SR/SL			MED. LAVENDER	843	
14				3,4/3,4				LT. GREENBLUE	858	
15				5,6/5,6				MED. GREEN	874	
16		6x9 LEKO	4	1,2/1,2	3RD SIDELITE SR/SL			MED. LAVENDER	843	
17				3,4/3,4				LT. GREENBLUE	858	
18				5,6/5,6				MED. GREEN	874	
19	6K	STRIPLITE	6		GROUND ROW	CYC WASH	CYC	RED		
20								AMBER		
21								BLUE		
22	4K	6x16 LEKO	4	1,2,4,5	1ST FOH ELECTRIC	FRONT LITE	BROTHER	N/C PINK	825	
23	1K	"	1	3		"	DONNY			
24	1K	6x12 LEKO	1	1	1A ELECTRIC	BACKLITE	BROADWAY SP.	MED. BLUE	857	
25			1	2			DONNY, MEMORY	SP. LAVENDER	842	
26			1	6			MARIE SPECIAL	STRAW	809	
27	6K		6	3,4,5,7,8,9			FAMILY	N/C	—	
28	3K	6x12 LEKO	3	1,9,17	1ST ELECTRIC	CROSSING WASH	CHIFFON DRAPE	DK MAGENTA	838	
29	"	"		8,16,24				SURPRISE BLUE	861	
30	6K	PAR MFL	6	4,7,12,15,20,23		BACK WASH	DOWNSTAGE	MED. LEMON	806	
31				3,6,11,14,19,22				MED. BLUE	857	
32				2,5,10,13,18,21				MED. LAVENDER	843	
33	5K	PAR MFL	5	6,11,19,23,28	2ND ELECTRIC		MID STAGE	MED. LEMON	806	
34				5,10,17,22,27				MED. BLUE	857	
35				4,9,15,21,26				MED. LAVENDER	843	

DIMMER		INSTRUMENTS			LOCATION	DESCRIPTION	FOCUS	COLOR		NOTES
N°	CAP	TYPE	AMT	NUMBERS				DESCRIPTION	N°	
36	4K	8" FRESNEL	4	1,12,20,31	2ND ELECTRIC	FRONT LITE	COLUMN	N/C	—	
37	2K	6x9 LEKO	2	13,14		BACK LITE	CONDUCTOR	MED. BLUE	863	
38	5K	8" FRESNEL	5	3,8,18,25,30		FRONT WASH	ORCHESTRA	SURPRISE BLUE	861	
39	"	"	"	2,7,16,24,29				MED. RED	823	
40	15K	MINI ELLIPSE	3	1,5,11	3RD ELECTRIC	PATTERNS	CYC	MED GREEN	874	#235 – RADIAL LINES
41				2,7,12				N/C	—	#232 – STYLISED STARS
42				3,8,13				ASSORTED RED GREEN AMBER		#270 – FIREWORKS
43				4,10,14				MED. LEMON	806	#302 – MUSICAL NOTES
44	2K	PAR NSP	2	6,9		DOWN LITE	DRUMS	STRAW	809	
45	6K	6x16 LEKO	6	1,3,5,7,9,11	2ND FOH ELECTRIC	FRONT LITE	FAMILY	MED PINK	825	
46	"	"	"	2,4,6,8,10,12		"	"	SP LAVENDER	842	
47		BROADWAY LOGO			PIPE 9		SPECIAL			
AUX 1	4K	PAR MFL	4			UNDER SL PIANO	SPECIAL	N/C	—	
AUX 2	4K	PAR MFL	4			ON DRUM PLATFORM	"	DRUMMER	SEE NOTES	← 863, 821, 817, 874
AUX 3		TRILON LITES				TUF TABLES (4)	"	"		
AUX 4		TRILON LITES				"	"			
AUX 5		TRILON LITES				"	"			
ND 1		SMOKE MACHINE				UNDER SL PIANO				
ND 2		DRUM STROBES				DRUMS				
ND 3		TRILON MOTORS				UPSTAGE				
ND 4		MIRROR BALL				CENTER MIDSTAGE				
ND 5		STROBE CURTAIN				PIPE 16				
ND 6		BROTHERS NEON				PIPE 24				

Figure 5–4   Circuit chart, Osmond Family Show in Las Vegas.
(Designed by James Moody.)

control channels. Whenever possible I have the light plot and circuit chart appear on a single sheet.

Over the years I evolved my own method. I have always had trouble printing numbers clearly on drawings, especially when trying to get the color number, circuit number, and control channel number all into the same space. The idea of adding more symbols to the drawing is founded on an idea used by Len Rader, for many years head electrician at the MGM Grand Hotel in Las Vegas. Every light plot that came to him was different, and he said a great deal of time was wasted trying to get the crew to understand what the plot was trying to represent. So Rader started redrawing the plots and keeping them on file so that when the artist returned the load-in was much simpler. On one sheet he had the circuits, dimmer assignments, and color in a form that everyone on his crew understood. I adapted the form (Figure 5–5) and find it easy to understand, having used it all over the world with great success.

In Figure 5–5 the rectangle (symbol for circuit number) behind the fixture symbol is blank. Existing house circuits are assigned by the staff electrician to best facilitate the hang in the particular house. Fixtures also are pointed in the desired direction of focus rather than straight side-by-side as in the traditional method. The five-foot marks allow for a quick reference to fixture placement along the pipe.

Now comes a whole new way of plotting. *Computer-aided design (CAD)* is a generic term or CADD can be used to mean computer-aided design and drafting. Many programs are available. Some are designed specifically for theatre and others for concerts; most CAD programs, however, are used in architecture and manufacturing. CAD provides consistency and clarity of drawing. Although each of us has a favorite, all programs have a common link. That is, they can be changed time and time again without starting over. This has been a boon to designers who need to make several versions of a tour plot. CAD is discussed in chapter 10.

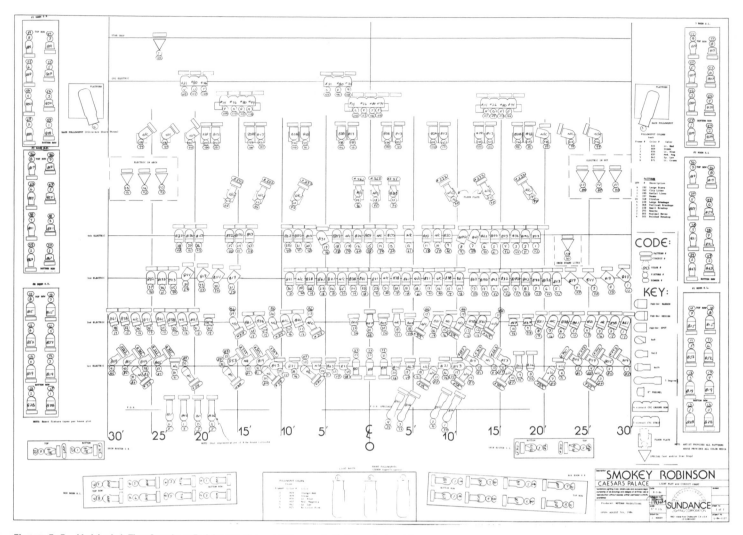

Figure 5–5   Light plot, The Smokey Robinson show at Caesar's Palace in Las Vegas.
(Designed by James Moody.)

The Hang

The final step in your design is deciding whether to mount the fixtures on a pipe or on a pre-rigged truss. What looked good on paper may be junk in the air. As the designer you must not only work closely with suppliers to ensure accurate reproduction of the design, but you must also be open to their suggestions concerning changes that help the repeatability, packaging, and focus of the touring system. If it is a one-time concert, the access to fixtures can be a problem because of scenery or band placement. It might be wise to use a truss so that fixtures can be focused by someone walking or crawling on it. Restrictions in circuit availability, drapery obstruction, and trim height must be considered. I never leave the theatre during load-in on a one-nighter. Designers not attentive during rigging do a great disservice to the crew and show a lack of respect for its efforts on behalf of the production.

Often the house stagehands have suggestions that help simplify the rigging and focus. It is like hunting or fishing: the locals know the woods and the best fishing holes. The designer must keep an open mind to suggestions and not become defensive. It not only helps to have the crew feel part of the show because you listen to their ideas, but it also shows your good sense to know that someone else can look at the problem and possibly come up with a better solution.

Sample Light Plot

The light plot shown in Figure 5–6 illustrates a typical rock band setup. Replace the keyboards with a steel guitar and you have a country band. This can even be a jazz group. The back truss and side light tree design form the basis for all concert design. Heavy back light is the mark of concert lighting.

The band back light washes can be split so that the drummer is separated, because he or she has no back light specials. Some designers split the side light left and right so they can have, for example, a red side light from stage left and an amber from stage right. The real controlling factor is the number of dimmers.

Ideal control of these lamps would be:

4 band back light washes (4 lamps each)
4 drummer specials (1 lamp each)
6 band specials (1 lamp each)

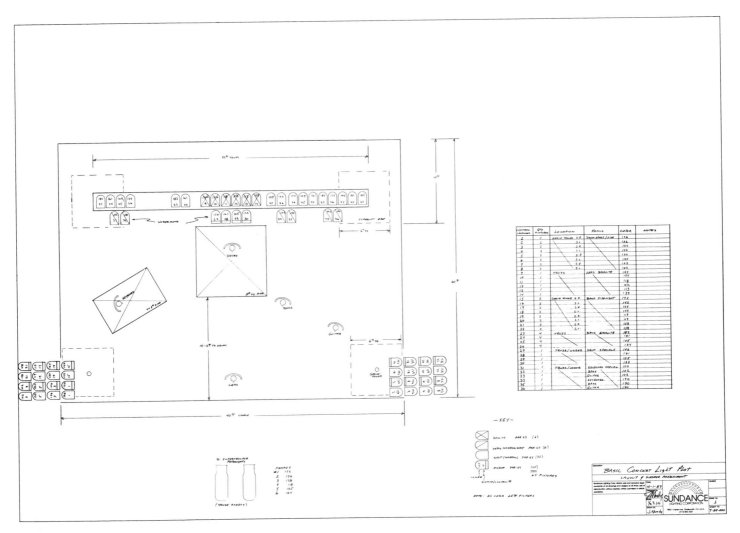

Figure 5–6 Basic concert light plot.
(Designed by James Moody.)

6 lead singer back light specials (1 lamp each)
8 band side light washes (2 lamps each)
8 lead singer side light washes (2 lamps each)
36 channels of control

That quantity hits the nail on the head. Most consoles come in 24, 36, 48, 60, 72, or 96 channels of control. However, I insist on spare dimmers and control channels on the road. That way you can adjust at the last minute if a failure or other loss of dimmer or control should occur. I also make sure I have firmly fixed in my mind, well in advance of the tour, what control I can give up to solve the problem. Preparation is paramount. Using this plot, first I would give up side light circuits, second I would add drummer back light to band washes. In either case, the dimmer capacity must be high enough to accept this additional load, and planning can cover that point. Always have a few dimmers that can accept additional loads.

The colors I select change depending on whether the lead singer is male or female and even whether their skin is black, brown, or white. Without going into the basic theory of color as it applies to theatrical lighting, it should be easily understood that any color (actually the absence of a portion of the visible light spectrum) projected onto a color affects how the human eye perceives that color. Therefore, the designer must be sensitive to skin tone to most effectively illuminate the artist. The following color chart would be an acceptable beginning for most acts. Note that I have not designated a specific color medium. At this point we are more concerned with the broader picture; exact color numbers are not yet important.

Band and drum back light	Red
	Blue
	Lemon
	Green
Band back light specials	Light pink or lemon
	Lavender or sunrise pink
Band side light	Amber
	Blue
	Blue-green
	Lavender
Lead singer back light	Red
	Lemon
	Light blue
	Lavender
	Magenta
	No color
Lead singer side light	Red
	Amber
	Blue
	No color
	Lavender

Color Scrollers and Effects

A few color scrollers (the scrolling-type design gives more colors) can make even the simple plot in Figure 5–6 a very flexible design for a more advanced designer. (Color scrollers are discussed in chapter 10.) The possible combinations that this multiplicity of color brings to the design would be much more advantageous on the road than the increased quantity of fixtures and dimming that would be required to equal the looks they can create. Remember that shipping space is critical.

Moving lights and truss-mounted follow spots can add to the flexibility of the system in Figure 5–6 without increasing the physical truss configuration. The pizzazz that is possible from even a simple layout can be used over and over again. Add the "toys" only after you have mastered the straightforward plot, or you can get in over your head. Complexity can harm you more quickly than anything else.

Variables

Lighting fascinates me because it never looks the same way twice, even when you are using a computer. The atmosphere of the room changes from hall to hall, and your perception is slightly altered. Smoke in a nightclub or at concerts makes the light stand out more. Light from exit signs or candles on the tables changes the darkness level (black level, in television parlance) from show to show.

Other variables are voltage to the lamps and changes in position and elevation. When you move the system from one hall to another, the voltage changes. Not many halls have exactly 120 volts at the input service—it varies between 108 and 123—and then when dimmers are put in line voltage drops another 2 to 4 volts on the output side. String 50 to 100 feet of cable to the lamp, and it is rare to have 120 volts at the lamp filament. Therefore the color temperature changes each day and the color won't be exactly as planned. With many gels, this means visibly altered colors.

Moving the trusses or truss upstage or downstage a couple of feet makes a difference in the angle at which the light strikes the performers; this alters the shading and contrast of the lighting. Another variable is the follow spot positions from hall to hall. Are they straight-on or at a 45-degree angle to the artist? Every variable makes a difference from show to show and must be considered.

Twelve designers can take the example in Figure 5–6 and make 100 looks with no two designs exactly alike. That excites me, and I believe concert lighting releases the same creative imagination as theatre; we must take 50 artists all of whom perform with similar staging and make the work look different.

One final word of advice: experiment, experiment, experiment. I do, even with a show that is already touring. If I am running the board, I try things. Sometimes, it is better, sometimes it is a toss-up, and often it is worse than my first idea. But I still try and will keep on trying to bring clarity and definition to my design.

More Complex Designs

After you become proficient at a simple, straightforward plot, you can press on to some grandiose designs. This field of design loves the outrageous. Freedom in creativity starts with the structures you design. Trusses come in all lengths, shapes, and load capacities. At this point, simply think of geometric patterns and designs (Figure 5–7). The examples are only a few basic ideas for possible grids. More than making a pretty design, the object is to choose light angles that create mood and drama.

Figure 5–7 Examples of truss layouts.

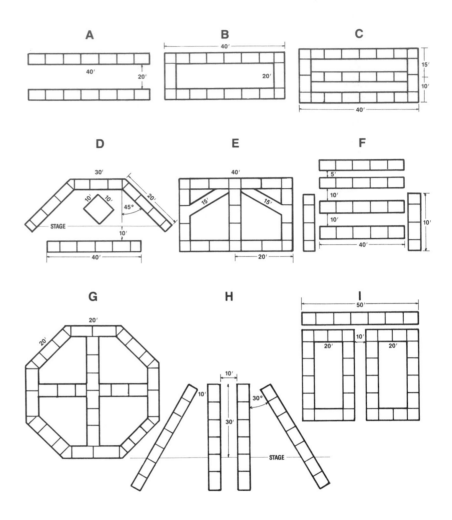

Although there is the practical limitation of load capacity, I have seen trusses that defy structural logic. Chapter 12 provides the technical information you need to decide on a final truss layout. However, at this "pure design" phase of our discussion, you can see how the structures become a real element of the design. Keep in mind that in almost all of the touring systems, the structures are in view of the audience. The layout of the structures can be both a functional and an aesthetic element of your show.

6

Cuing the Music

While preparing a layout and color chart, you must be thinking ahead to how the cues will work with your plan. Does the layout give you the degree of flexibility you want? Does the color chart work as a palette in harmony with the music? A separate design criterion enters the picture. The designer must take the raw data from the mechanical drawing and make it come to life in the same way a musician does with notes in the score.

I know that there are things that we do unconsciously. Someone asks us how we learned to do something and our answer is, "I didn't realize I had done that," or "I don't know how I did that." The fact is we did do it and we somehow learned to do it somewhere, sometime. One of the unconscious things good concert designers seem to do well is analyze music.

From the first time you hear the artist's music, you should be mentally planning the choreography of your lighting, breaking down the music into cue points. The analysis helps determine the type of lighting console you need. Manual consoles were used on most tours up until the mid 1980s. In the case of the John Denver tour, however, there were more than 250 cues in the show. I determined early on that a computer was correct for the job because I wanted smooth, subtle cues that were repeatable. The computer allowed me to design each look and write my cues directly into the memory.

My years of experience allow me to take a few shortcuts, but I am sure I still take the following steps subconsciously:

1. Listen to the song; try to pick up a lyric, a musical phrase, or the dynamics that make the general statement of the song.
2. Translate the song into a primary color.
3. Find the high point of the song (it may not be the end).
4. Find the repeating portions of the music, such as the choruses and verses.

This process will probably lead to four or five looks: the opening, the chorus, the verse, the solo spot, and the end. Changes between verse and chorus may be repeated several times. A cue also may occur at the turnaround, a musical device found in most pop music that allows the songwriter to repeat a melody by interjecting another musical phrase between the similar themes. Are the cues going to be bumps or slow fades? It does not matter what they are. What is important is that each acts as musical punctuation, not simply flashing lights.

After doing this for all songs, look at the song order, or *set* as it is often called in music. See if you have the same color patterns for songs that are back to back. I do not hesitate to change the colors to ensure that a look is not repeated in consecutive songs. Certainly, a look can be repeated later in the set. If the color simply must be used again, try to change the position from which the color comes. For example, when amber back light is used in the first song try using an amber side light or amber follow spot in the next song and possibly use white as a back light. You'd be surprised how different the looks can become with a simple shift in direction or decrease in the intensity of the color to create a new shade.

How do you remember where the cues go? They are not scripted like a play or opera score. Some lighting designers, especially Las Vegas designers, use lyric sheets (Figure 6–1) in much the same way a play is cued by a stage manager. This is a theatrical form rarely used in concert touring but sometimes handy in longer running shows. Although it is not general practice in Las Vegas for the lighting director to leave after a day or two, the board operator can follow the lyrics and call the follow spots and execute the board cues from those notations. I have done this on two occasions where shows were on long, open-ended runs and it worked.

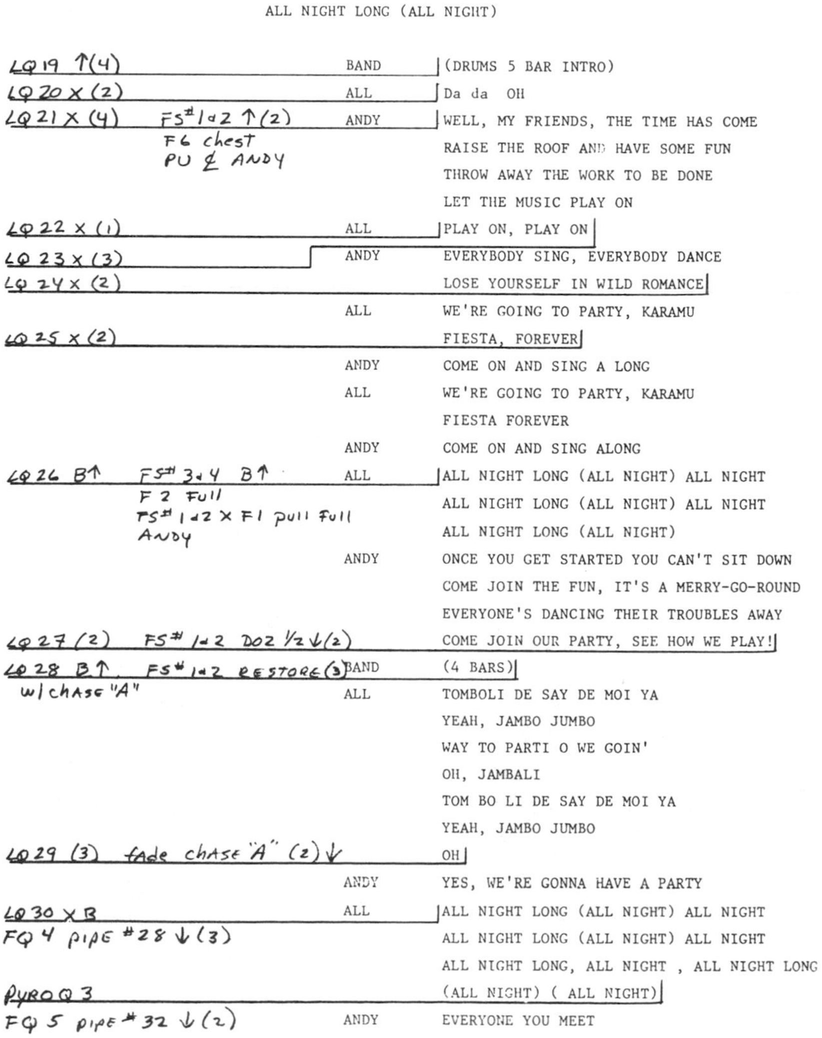

Figure 6–1 Lyric cue sheet. A method for noting lighting, fly, and other cues when lyrics to the songs are available.

ALL NIGHT LONG (ALL NIGHT)

LQ 19 ↑(4)		BAND	(DRUMS 5 BAR INTRO)
LQ 20 X (2)		ALL	Da da OH
LQ 21 X (4)	FS# 1+2 ↑(2)	ANDY	WELL, MY FRIENDS, THE TIME HAS COME
	F 6 chest		RAISE THE ROOF AND HAVE SOME FUN
	PU ♀ ANDY		THROW AWAY THE WORK TO BE DONE
			LET THE MUSIC PLAY ON
LQ 22 X (1)		ALL	PLAY ON, PLAY ON
LQ 23 X (3)		ANDY	EVERYBODY SING, EVERYBODY DANCE
LQ 24 X (2)			LOSE YOURSELF IN WILD ROMANCE
		ALL	WE'RE GOING TO PARTY, KARAMU
LQ 25 X (2)			FIESTA, FOREVER
		ANDY	COME ON AND SING A LONG
		ALL	WE'RE GOING TO PARTY, KARAMU
			FIESTA FOREVER
		ANDY	COME ON AND SING ALONG
LQ 26 B↑	FS# 3+4 B↑	ALL	ALL NIGHT LONG (ALL NIGHT) ALL NIGHT
	F 2 Full		ALL NIGHT LONG (ALL NIGHT) ALL NIGHT
	FS# 1+2 X F1 pull full		ALL NIGHT LONG (ALL NIGHT)
	ANDY	ANDY	ONCE YOU GET STARTED YOU CAN'T SIT DOWN
			COME JOIN THE FUN, IT'S A MERRY-GO-ROUND
			EVERYONE'S DANCING THEIR TROUBLES AWAY
LQ 27 (2)	FS# 1+2 DO2 ½ ↓(2)		COME JOIN OUR PARTY, SEE HOW WE PLAY!
LQ 28 B↑	FS# 1+2 RESTORE (3)	BAND	(4 BARS)
w/ CHASE "A"		ALL	TOMBOLI DE SAY DE MOI YA
			YEAH, JAMBO JUMBO
			WAY TO PARTI O WE GOIN'
			OH, JAMBALI
			TOM BO LI DE SAY DE MOI YA
			YEAH, JAMBO JUMBO
LQ 29 (3)	fade CHASE "A" (2) ↓		OH
		ANDY	YES, WE'RE GONNA HAVE A PARTY
LQ 30 X B		ALL	ALL NIGHT LONG (ALL NIGHT) ALL NIGHT
FQ 4 pipe #28 ↓(3)			ALL NIGHT LONG (ALL NIGHT) ALL NIGHT
			ALL NIGHT LONG, ALL NIGHT , ALL NIGHT LONG
PYRO Q 3			(ALL NIGHT) (ALL NIGHT)
FQ 5 pipe #32 ↓(2)		ANDY	EVERYONE YOU MEET

One-night touring is different. Usually the lighting designer runs the console, but if not, the lighting director traveling with the show is as familiar with the cues as is the designer. If the designer is with the show and should know the music inside out, why bother with a formal cuing method? There are two good reasons: the possibility of illness or accident and the fact that the designer is most likely working for several clients, and without total recall, it is difficult to remember all the cues for each show. Also, after a few years of touring with an artist, a designer builds up an extensive repertoire of songs not in the current show. As the tour goes on old songs are substituted or new songs are tried out. It takes a lot of mental agility to be on top of all that music. John Denver had more than 50 songs the band could play, and he often substituted without warning.

Another method that gives a visual plan of a song is to count out and note each eight bars, just as a choreographer counts out the measures, 1 and 2 and 3 and 4. . . . Then write the numbers down and mark any musical change where they go. Jeff Ravitz, designer for Bruce Springsteen, Styx, John Mellencamp, and many others, uses this method. Take a sheet of paper and listen to the song. Count out each eight bars and then strike a line, put another line after the next eight bars and so on. If something changes before you get to your count of eight, strike a line and insert the number of bars above it, for example, three (Figure 6–2). This way, even if you must call the cues after months or years, you can still count out the measures and get things right. It is also handy for knowing when the end of a solo that does not present a nice clean tag is coming to an end. That is, if the artists always plays the song the same way! In any event, it is a method for you to use in jogging your memory and helps you visualize the song.

Forms

I use a 4 × 5 index card as a form (Figure 6–3). Full-size 8 $^{1}/_{2}$ × 11 pages are too large to place conveniently on the console and scan quickly. The kind of information you place on the card is the trick. I have used the same format with a few variations for many years. Figures 6–4 and 6–5 illustrate two forms. Although there may not seem to be much difference in the two forms, the detail in the preset column (column 4) is simpler for a computer, whereas a total breakdown of dimmer numbers and intensity is required for a manual board.

Notations

Cue Number

I use letters instead of numbers for cues so that if I am calling board cues along with follow spots, no one can confuse cue 1 with follow spot 1 or frame 1. I do not believe in consecutively numbering cues straight through the show, because the song order can and often does change during the course of the tour.

Cue

The cue is the downbeat, instrument, lyric, or whatever you use to indicate when the action should take place. Because the shows are not scripted, I use simple cues such as *band starts*, *first lyric*, *sax solo*, *chorus*, *end song*, and *restore*.

Figure 6–2 Eight-bar notation sheet used by Jeff Ravitz, lighting designer for John Mellencamp '94 tour.

(Reproduced by permission of the author, Jeff Ravitz.)

SONG BREAKDOWN   SONG TITLE JACK & DIANE

PROJECT: _____ MELLENCAMP '94
LIGHTING DESIGN: JEFF RAVITZ

1. Intro - DRUM ROLLS
2. DRUMS - ||||~||||
3. GUIT   < DRUM CRASH >
             < CRASH >
             < CRASH >
4. VERSE (1) |||
6. INST LINE - MINDY ACCORDION - [STOP]
7. VERSE (2) |||
8. CHORUS (1) |||
9. GUIT LINE   < DRUM CRASH >
               < CRASH >
10. VERSE (3) |||
11. CHOR (2) |||
12. DRUMS |||| + ROLL
13. BRIDGE |||| ACCENT
14. INST ||||*|||| ACCENT
15. BREAKDOWN |||
16. ANDY + MINDY INST ||
17. CHOR (3) ||||~||||
18. FADE - DRUMS + MIKE |||
    JOHN SINGS LINE || - FADE↓ HOLD....

A. BAND IN GUIT < DRUM CRASH >
   GUIT + FADE↓ |

Figure 6–3 Cue card for John Denver tour.

"To the Wild Country   John Denver Tour
                                         U.S. winter '78

Que #	Que	Action	Pre-set
A	song starts verse	PSO X PS 85	86
B	chorus - singers	PS 85 X PS 86	(M)60 85
C	Jim Horn solo	PS 86 X PS 85 (M) 6%1	
D	solo over - verse	PS 85 (M) 6%↓	86
E	chorus	PS 85 X PS 86	85
F	back down to end	PS 86 X PS 85	
G	song ends	PS 85 fade	

Action

The action notations (under the Time column in Figures 6–4 and 6–5) can change slightly depending on whether you are using a computer or a manual board. A computer board is simply noted, for example, P.S. 11 × 12 (2). That means preset 11 is to cross-fade to preset 12 on a two count (two seconds). A variation can be written: P.S. 10 @ (6) and previous cue @ (10). That means to pile on preset 10 and fade previous preset on a ten count fade. Parentheses, ( ), always indicate time; the number inside indicates seconds. A mark of *B*↑ indicates a bump up, and *B*↓ and *BO* are ways to indicate a blackout. Brackets, [ ], can be added for other notations. It is also possible on a computer board to be using a channel in the manual mode; the indication is M d36/7 (8), meaning: manually add dimmer 36 to a level of 70 percent on an eight count.

On a manual preset board, the notation can be A × B (3), meaning scene A cross-fades to scene B on a three count; or A @ B @ (3), meaning add scene A and fade scene B on a three count. Another action would be A @ (3), meaning add scene A on a three count.

Figure 6–4 4 × 5 cue card for manual board.

Figure 6–5 4 × 5 cue card for computer board.

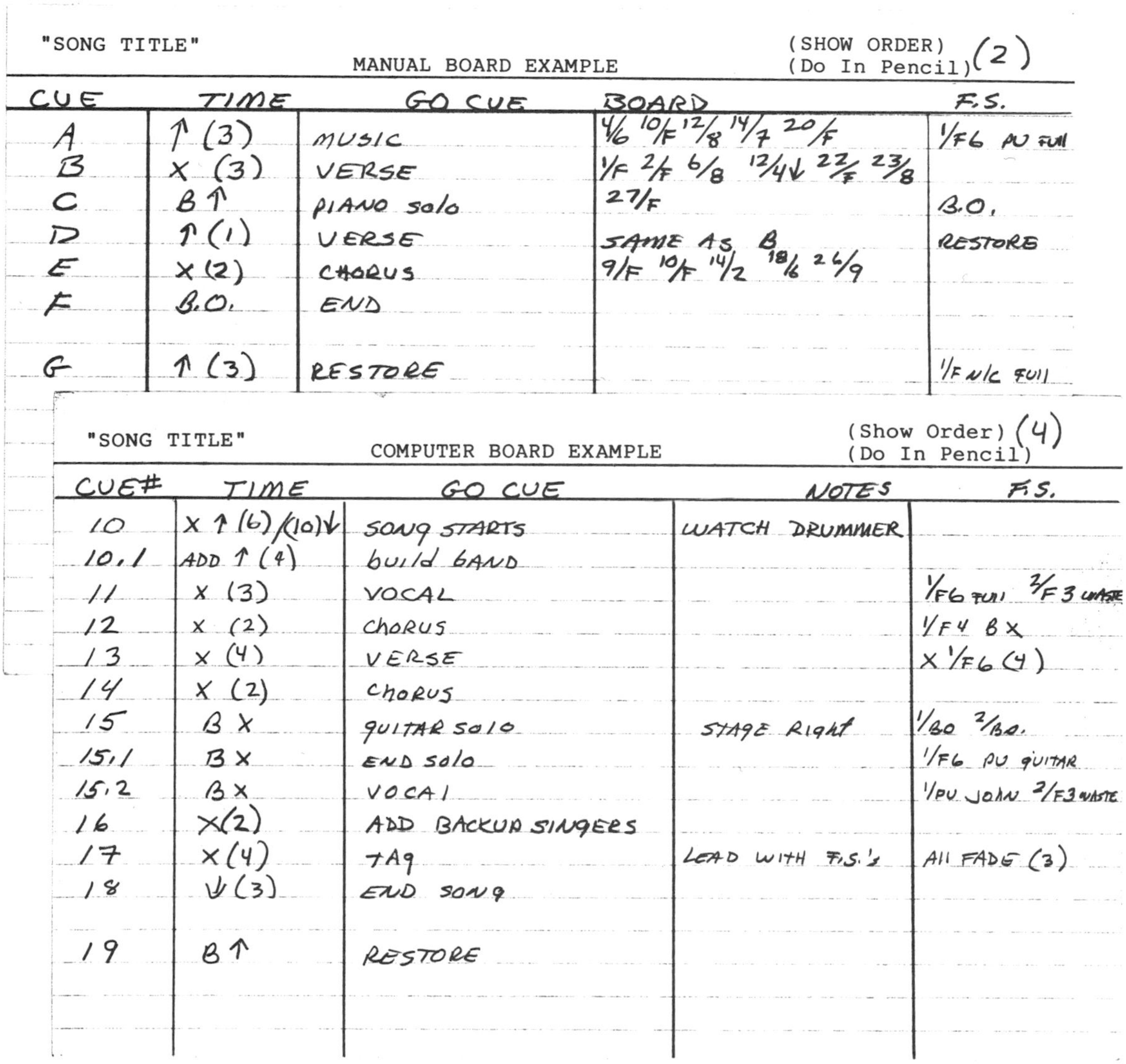

"SONG TITLE" MANUAL BOARD EXAMPLE (SHOW ORDER) (Do In Pencil) (2)

CUE	TIME	GO CUE	BOARD	F.S.
A	↑ (3)	MUSIC	4/6 10/F 12/8 14/7 20/F	1/F6 PU FULL
B	X (3)	VERSE	1/F 2/F 6/8 12/4↓ 22/F 23/8	
C	B↑	PIANO solo	27/F	B.O.
D	↑ (1)	VERSE	SAME AS B	RESTORE
E	X (2)	CHORUS	9/F 10/F 14/2 18/6 26/9	
F	B.O.	END		
G	↑ (3)	RESTORE		1/F N/C FULL

"SONG TITLE" COMPUTER BOARD EXAMPLE (Show Order) (Do In Pencil) (4)

CUE#	TIME	GO CUE	NOTES	F.S.
10	X ↑ (6) (10)↓	SONG STARTS	WATCH DRUMMER	
10.1	ADD ↑ (4)	build BAND		
11	X (3)	VOCAL		1/F6 FULL 2/F 3 WASTE
12	X (2)	ChORUS		1/F 4 B X
13	X (4)	VERSE		X 1/F6 (4)
14	X (2)	ChORUS		
15	B X	GUITAR SOLO	STAGE Right	1/BO 2/BO.
15.1	B X	END solo		1/F6 PU GUITAR
15.2	B X	VOCAL		1/PU JOHN 2/F3 WASTE
16	X (2)	ADD BACKUP SINGERS		
17	X (4)	TAG	LEAD WITH F.S.'s	All FADE (3)
18	↓ (3)	END SONG		
19	B↑	RESTORE		

Preset

The computer uses the column marked Notes (Figure 6–5) as a reference to the action or tools to use to remind you of the purpose of the cue. On a manual board, the Board column (Figure 6–4) indicates each dimmer level specifically, for example, d9/F d10/F d14/2 d18/6 d26/9 × (2), meaning dimmer 9 level full, dimmer 10 level full, dimmer 14 at 20 percent, dimmer 18 to 60 percent and dimmer 26 to 90 percent, cross-fading on a two count. Similarly, d14/3 @ (10) would mean to fade out dimmer 14 on a ten count. This also can be used to lower the dimmer level, for example, d14/3 @ (5), from the previous level to a lower level. Because a fade-out and a change in level look the same in the notes, some designers underline level changes.

Follow Spot

The notations in the follow spot (F.S.) column can be complex if more than one reference must be considered. As a general example, however, a follow spot notation might read "(john) F#6 @ (3)," meaning fade up on John in frame 6, full body on a three count. The use of $B\uparrow$ indicates bump up, and $B\downarrow$ or BO indicates a blackout the same way it does with dimmers. You can develop letter or numerical notes for the size of the circle of light needed; for example, I use $^{1}/_{2}$ for a waist shot, and HS for head and shoulders. You can make up anything that is easy for you to remember when you are looking at your cards.

Miscellaneous

A miscellaneous column can be added for additional notations, such as effects cues, set or curtain cues, and warnings. I do not use colored pencils on my cards, because doing so is time consuming, and the colors are often misread under a red or blue work light. You may have been taught that warnings are one color pencil, goes another, and so on. I do not normally have a script to consult, so this system does not work for me except in Las Vegas venues.

I might add that Jeff Ravitz (see Figure 6–2) uses a full $8^{1}/_{2} \times 11$ sheet of paper to organize this information in a spiral notebook. The eight-bar notation sheet is on the left and the cues on the right. The lettering is much larger and easier to read, and Jeff can add many more notes.

Oral Cuing

I have never seen a theatrical cue light used during a concert. Intercoms have come a long way, and it is reassuring to have a response from the person on the other end. As far as I am concerned, cue lights are a worse means of communication than shouting. I lit one show in which I had no two-way communication, and I can only say that I felt as if I was utterly alone on the ocean calling out for help in the darkness.

The way you communicate to a houselights operator, a board operator, or a follow spot operator directly affects the smoothness of the show and the accuracy of cues. It is truly an art form unto itself. Chip Monck has always been highly regarded for his effective follow spot cuing, especially on the 1972 Rolling Stones tour. He is certainly one of the pioneers in concert lighting and developed many of the cuing techniques still being used.

When I was an air traffic controller, I learned something that is generally overlooked. Speech pattern, meter, and accent are very important. An operator who cannot understand you will not be able to act on a cue. Your diction and local accent can frustrate operators and reduce your comments to unintelligible noise. This is not to denigrate any regional accent; it is a proven fact that how you speak affects the understanding of the listener. The Air Force says that a Midwestern accent can be best understood by every English-speaking person. Meter is important because the speed and inflection you use in your speech affect the operator emotionally. If you are screaming or talking very fast over the intercom, you do great harm, because the operator tunes out. The operator will believe you are not in control, and that is disastrous.

As air traffic controllers, we were taught that 60 words a minute was the speed at which we were to talk, and I still find this a good speed for show cuing. I realize that at times you have a lot to say in a very short time between cues, but take the time to find a way of saying it in fewer words, rather than speeding through to get everything in. After all, if you say it so quickly that no one understands, you might as well not say it at all. All of these points can be worked on in a speech class if you have the opportunity, but you can learn by speaking into a tape recorder, giving cues, then playing the part of the operator. See if you would listen to yourself. Or have a friend who is not in the business listen and try to repeat what you say.

Cuing Follow Spots

I use the key-word method of follow spot cuing. This is a method of calling cues by using words such as *go* or *out* to prompt someone to react as planned, instead of relying on visual or mechanical signaling devices to call the cues.

My pre-show speech to the operators goes as follows:

> Good evening ladies and gentlemen. I'll call the follow spots as Spot 1, Spot 2, and so on. [I indicate the light to which I am referring, for example, northeast corner, left or right of stage, man in red shirt, whatever makes it obvious which spot is which.]
>
> I give all cues as follows: *Ready . . . and . . . Go.* Do nothing until you hear the word *Go*. It will indicate a color change, blackout, fade up, pickup . . . anything else you hear is for information or prepping an upcoming cue. All cue warnings are given as follows: *standby Spot 1 in frame 6 waist on Fred for a three-count fade-up . . . Ready . . . and . . . Go.* The counts are in seconds, and all fades should be evenly executed throughout the numbers. [I count off orally so they hear at what speed I count.]
>
> The stage is set as follows: [Here I lay out the placement of all players, including items that would help operators remember each musician. Some designers use theatrical letters for areas of the stage. If it is necessary because the artist moves around the stage a lot, present such a plan in four or five areas across the stage and two or three areas deep.]
>
> Thank you ladies and gentlemen. I'm looking forward to a great show. Take your color and head for your lights. Check in on the intercom when you are in position.

Although I do not use operators' first names to call cues as many designers do, you should do whatever is most comfortable. Using names makes the work more personal and eliminates one of the many numbers heard by the crew. During a show, I tend to talk to the operators, mainly to give them a feeling that they are part of the show and not treated as robots who turn on and off the lights. If you find that the operators like to chatter, keep up a running dialogue yourself, so you can call a cue anytime it is needed. Be careful not to confuse the operators about what is chatter and what is cue information. I find that better than telling technicians to "shut up." Give the crew members credit for their skills, and they generally respond with their best effort. If operators have a general idea of what is about to happen, they relax, and the tension is relieved. Certainly, this is not always the case, and I have been in positions in which the less said the better. Use your judgment in each show to assess the situation.

Jeff Ravitz draws a plan that numbers all the follow spots and main positions on stage so the operators can have a visual game plan. Jeff also does something I think is quite good. In his talk before the show he not only says most of what I have already mentioned but also gives the operators a plan to follow if the intercom fails. For example, "Spot 1 stay with the lead singer, Spot 2 be on the guitar player."

Summary

Whether you use cue cards or other forms, the important point is clarity and being frugal with cue words and notations. The cards are not designed so that another designer and board operator can walk in and take over right away. The cue cards are a personal preference; they are only there to assist you in running a smooth show. When I use board operators, I do not write cards for them. I use mine to talk them through and let them make their own cue notations.

In the final analysis, the smoothness of your show is directly related to your ability to cue both board and follow spots in time to the music. The aesthetics of your choice of colors and angles affects the audience, but not nearly as memorably as a late or missed cue. The Rock and Roll audience has become very sophisticated and realizes that the lights are an important part of the show. Cue a show well and the artist receives better reviews than if you are lazy and off tempo. The psychology imparted in what we do cannot be underestimated.

7

Road Problems and Scheduling

Timing is the key to the efficient production of a concert tour. Most problems during setup grow to become disasters, not because of faulty equipment or damage that cannot be repaired, but because you only have 15 minutes to an hour to fix them. If that is not bad enough, you are in a strange town, usually close to or after 5:00 P.M. Time is your worst enemy. Effective handling of your setup time gives you more time to find problems and, when needed, obtain parts and make repairs in time for the show.

Time is also the most important factor when a truck is late. A show normally loads in at 10:00 A.M. and has a sound check completed by 6:00 P.M. (on average and depending on production complexity). When the truck doesn't arrive until 4:00 P.M. or 5:00 P.M., can the show be ready? It had better be. Here is where your organizational skills and efficient use of local resources show. In general, problems on the road can be handled on a day-to-day basis if you keep calm and face each one with a mind open to several alternative solutions. Then make the decision quickly. The worst thing to do is delay making a decision. There is no right or wrong, although some decisions are better than others in retrospect. In the end, the show starts at 8:00 P.M., one hopes with sound and at least some lighting. How you accomplish the tasks you are assigned makes you either a successful road designer or a failure.

Power Service

After timing problems, the second most important problem can be finding good power service. This is especially true at colleges. Most schools do not have gyms equipped with a "bull switch" or "main breaker" for use by road companies. Power usually is taken from the houselights panel. This is bad electrical practice and in most instances is a code violation. However, when there is no other power within 400 feet of the stage, you make do. This is an area that needs a discussion all its own. The best answer is to be as knowledgeable as possible: read up, or better yet, talk to a licensed electrician who does temporary service connections for a living. Make it a practice to require a house electrician at load-in. Even though you probably do not need power for an hour or more, it gives you time to discover a problem and then time to solve it without delaying your schedule. If rigging is to be done, the crew needs power for the rigging motors as soon as they start work so as not to delay the load-in.

Follow Spots

Follow spot and operator problems seem to run with power problems. If a facility does not understand your power requirements, it usually does not have good follow spots or operators either.

A good road technician can diagnose what is wrong with a follow spot without being at the light and is able to tell the operator how to correct the problem. Talking operators through the cues is another problem. Because the follow spots are the one lighting element not generally carried with the show (except those mounted on the trusses), the efficiency of the unit is tied to the operator's ability to run it. Unlike Broadway shows, in which several days of rehearsals with follow spot operators are conducted before the show opens for previews, the concert starts with only a brief talk to the operators (see chapter 6). When you give the first cue, you see simultaneously how the operator handles the light and the efficiency of the unit. There is no time to replace or repair the unit. I can safely say that follow spots have caused me more problems than any other element of a show. They are the great unknown factor.

Stages and Ceiling Height

Stages themselves can be a problem. Although size is often unknown before arrival, it is usually the way the stage is built that comes under attack. When the crew arrives to find an unsafe stage, either because it is not braced properly or because it is uneven, the delay in correcting it wastes valuable time. Size variations should be considered in advance so that the set and lights can be adapted—within reason. Large public arenas and auditoriums have sturdy portable stage structures. It is when the stage is built by workers unfamiliar with the devices that are to be placed on it that problems can occur. Concert artists generally bring complete portable lighting systems. If ground supported, these structures add a tremendous weight to the stage. I have actually been told that the house crew thought everything would be okay because the stage had been large enough and strong enough for the "Symphony."

Ceiling height can be a problem. This usually happens in clubs and small facilities designed as multipurpose rooms. The ceiling may be 20 feet high, but put in a 6-foot-high stage and you can place lights only 12 to 14 feet above the stage. You must also consider the composition of the ceiling. Can it take the heat that the lighting fixtures give off? Low ceiling height is an enormous problem for back lighting, because the lamps are at about a 20-degree angle to vertical (normally it should be 35 to 40 degrees). The light spills a considerable distance into the audience, causing concertgoers in the front sections difficulty seeing the performer.

Special Effects

Projected effects or special effects such as smoke, fire, and explosions can cause problems. Projected effects usually require a large, deep stage. What happens when the stage cannot be 40 feet deep, the screen cannot be moved upstage any farther, or the projector cannot be rigged where it is supposed to be placed? The show should carry both rear and front screens for projection. (Actually, a show that carries these effects should have had sense enough to check out these problems in advance.)

Pyrotechnical effects are something else again. Most cities require special licenses or permits to have flash pots or open fire on stage. Some cities flatly forbid the use of fire on stage. Where permitted, these effects must be handled with extreme caution. The best example was seen worldwide during the California Jam at Ontario Motor Speedway in the summer of 1974. The English group Deep Purple used flash pots in its act. The effect was to happen at the end of a guitar solo when the musician was to destroy the guitar and amplifier (fake) with the result being an explosion. After the licensed pyrotechnician had loaded the device with the charge as per regulations set up by the state of California, it was believed, but never proved, that someone with the group decided it was not powerful enough and added more powder to the charge without informing anyone. The result was seen by the quarter of a million fans at the concert and by millions who saw it in a television special. The stage caught on fire; men with fire extinguishers could be seen running on stage to put it out. If the concert had been indoors, the potential for disaster would have been much greater.

Road Lifestyle

Much has been written about rock stars and their drug use, sexual activity, and spending of money. Because the technicians spend 16 to 20 hours a day with artists, some of these excesses rub off. The problems begin when the technicians and designers forget their purpose on the tour. It is not to be buddies with the stars or to see how many pickups they can make at the concert. Good technicians and sound engineers consider the production of the show the real reason for being there. Drugs and booze both are problems. A drunken technician is as likely to make a mistake and hurt someone as a drugged one. I have had more trouble with drunken than with drugged road personnel.

The actual workday is best illustrated with a typical schedule. Consider that this schedule is repeated five to six times a week for six to twelve weeks at a stand to really feel the strain and hardship with which people work.

Road Timetable

6:00 A.M.	Wake-up call
6:30 A.M.	Depart for airport
7:00 A.M.	Arrive airport; check bags and turn in rental car
7:30 A.M.	Flight departs
9:20 A.M.	Arrive next city
9:30 A.M.	Rent cars and collect baggage
10:00 A.M.	Arrive at hall (seldom time to check into hotel), begin setup
4:00 P.M.	Sound check (all lights, sound, and band equipment ready)
5:00 P.M.	Reset band equipment for opening act
5:30 P.M.	Opening act sound check
6:00 P.M.	Sound check complete
7:00 P.M.	Open house, crew meal
8:30 P.M.	Show starts
11:30 P.M.	Show ends
12:00 A.M.	Load-out begins
1:30 A.M.	Load-out complete, go to hotel

A person who goes out with a show like this must be able to handle himself or herself physically as well as mentally. The body can take the pace for only so long. You should prepare yourself as best you can, eat as regularly as possible, and organize your sleep and play time to benefit yourself the most. Sometimes it is play, because the body needs that, too, but most often it is bed . . . alone. Living out of a suitcase can be much more difficult than the physical pace of the tour. I know many road technicians who do not have a permanent address. Most humans need a place to call home, or someone waiting for them to return. A road technician often has neither. Think about it. According to the schedule I presented, you have less than four hours sleep a night. Think I'm kidding?

Even as I write these things, I know that most readers of this book will believe that the excitement of being part of this element of our youth culture and theatrical history outweighs all the hardships. Maybe that's what keeps us going. The newness of each day is at the top of my list. I do not believe I could be happy going to the same facility each day. The job certainly is not for anyone who wants security and a nine-to-five job. The day starts and ends in work-related activity. Sleep and attitude are important for surviving a tour. Very few minutes are spent that are not tied to the group or the people traveling with the show. All of you had better get along or tempers will flare.

Transportation

Methods of transportation are changing. In the early days of touring, it was "in" to fly everywhere. But the economy has caught up with us. Rockers now see the value in what many country and western artists have known for years. Customized buses, called motor coaches, outfitted for sleeping and riding in comfort are more practical than airplanes. The time taken in running for airplanes and the questionable safety factor of flight are now being replaced with the ease and security of the bus. After all, a rock star has never been killed riding a bus, even though there have been two highly publicized accidents, the most recent was Gloria Estefan's. But everyone lived, including the drivers. That can't be said about air travel.

Ninety percent of my tours since 1978 have used private coach or motor homes as the primary means of crew transportation. If the truck can make it with the equipment, so can the bus. We have returned to the old "bus and truck" touring companies of ten years ago. The difference is the comfort and class of the bus interiors. These custom coaches are hardly conventional buses. They are completely custom designed and fitted with sleeping sections as well as front and often rear lounges that have everything to keep the band and crew occupied on the trip. Most handle eight to twelve people comfortably for sleeping. That is why coaches are so popular. You maximize your sleep time, and the bus doubles as a lounge and even a place for a quick nap during the sound check.

My rule is that if a flight lasts less than 2 hours and 15 minutes, I'd rather have ground transportation. I don't have to keep loading and unloading bags, and my stuff is close by all day if I need to get something. Laundry? That's something for the day off when you are in a hotel. Some venues do have washing machines that you can use. But don't ask the house staff to do it for you—very uncool.

Figure 7–1 Custom motor coach, exterior.
(Photo by Florida Coach, Inc.)

Figure 7–2 Custom motor coach, interior.
(Photo by Florida Coach, Inc.)

Figure 7–1 shows a bus modified for a touring band or crew. Only the shell, engine, and drive train come from the manufacturer. The custom-coach builders do the rest either to their own design or often to specifications provided by the artist who will use the bus. Three commercial bus builders are used: Eagle, Prevost, and VanHool. These are not your family motor homes; they are top-of-the-line buses fitted with custom interiors. In Figure 7–2, the view looking toward the driver shows part of the lounge. Most are outfitted with microwaves, refrigerators, television, video cassette recorder, and stereo. Aft of the photo is the sleeping and bathroom area. The rear can be a second lounge or office.

Although some artists can afford a private jet plane, few groups are in this financial position today. More and more use scheduled airlines or ground transportation such as custom coaches.

An Established Field

Touring is now a well established theatrical field. In the first ten years it has developed into entertainment lighting's premier example of flash and spectacle. It has now heavily influenced television, film, and theatre. The most recent ten years have seen the lighting techniques adopted for architecture and retail sales. Touring has proved to have lasting entertainment and cultural value. The economy will always have its ups and downs, which affect what the ticket buyer can afford to spend on entertainment, but it has already been proved that concerts hold their own, even in slow economic times.

An artist who is now a superstar will continue to draw huge crowds, and, it is hoped, will continue to increase production values—and budgets. Artists in the production-show group have to spend even more production dollars to draw crowds. The 1996 Michael Jackson tour cost a reported four million dollars a week to put on the road. New bands are the ones who will be worst hit financially by increased production costs.

Whatever the state of the economy, production values, budget, and complexity of design continue to expand in the concert field. With this expansion will be a cross-over in the use of these techniques in other media. Technicians and designers who see the value in the advances made in concert lighting will be better equipped to deal with problem solving in other theatrical forms.

8

Road Safety

Anyone who has been on a stage realizes quickly how dangerous a place it can be if you do not watch your step. Scenery moving, pipes flying in and out, trapdoors opening, or risers that are not stable: all are accidents waiting to happen. So many incidents are reported that many states have tried to enact hard-hat area laws. Even venerable Broadway has its share of accidents and deaths each year. Stars are not immune—I remember when Ann-Margret fell from a platform at Caesar's Palace in Las Vegas while rehearsing. In that case, a quick-thinking stagehand broke her fall and possibly saved her career, if not her life. He was injured for his efforts, as are many stagehands each year.

It is difficult to find a stagehand who has not had a personal mishap or injury or does not have a friend who has had one. Usually the injuries are minor, but it is evidence of how often accidents occur. A sizable portion of these injuries happen during set changes on a darkened stage. When you have only seconds to make a scenery move and one person is off the mark that night or there is a substitute who has not done the work before, there is the potential for error and possible injury. Working with local crews who have not seen the show and are doing in one day what theatrical shows are allowed to rehearse over and over cannot help but be trouble. That more accidents do not occur is reason for kudos to the road crews and local stagehands.

The road offers enormously greater potential for accidents than does general theatrical production. When you consider the long hours and the travel, fatigue is probably the most important factor, followed by arrogance—the arrogance of a crew member who is tired or unhappy and believes everyone should be paying attention to him or her. Workers like this shove cases or bring down a truss without letting other workers know. That's when people are hurt. And the hurt might be inflicted by the rest of the road crew or house crew when they knock out the lights of the arrogant crew member!

The body cannot stay at peak performance week after week for months at a time. The pressure on the traveling road crew is tremendous. On average, the crew must load in the show, construct the rigging, conduct a sound check, work through a performance, strike the show, and conduct load-out in less than 12 hours and repeat that process five to six times a week for six to eight weeks at a stretch.

One of the main concerns of the now defunct Professional Entertainment Production Society (PEPS) when I helped found it in 1980, and subsequently served as its first president, was the safety of road crews.

Not only was our personal safety of concern, but also we wanted to promote the image of people who wanted to work as safely as possible. We felt that as a whole, our fellow road technicians had an outstanding safety record. But there were no statistics to support or refute our beliefs. Compiling such figures is not easy for a small, new organization, because even if the membership were polled, it would not be a large enough percentage of the total industry. The cost of a properly supervised survey was beyond our means. Nevertheless, our informal surveys seem to back my original belief.

Our concern for safety was so great that as a primary requirement for membership, a company had to have a $1 million public liability insurance policy. We wanted the hall managers, promoters, and producers to see our concern for not only our own safety but also for the audience's well-being.

A safe working area is critical. Our area is the stage. But what goes into making it safe? Most minor accidents happen because people simply do not think. We cut ourselves or bruise a leg and then say to ourselves, "What a dumb move," and that is exactly right. We really knew better than to do what caused the injury; so why do we let down our guard? A large percentage of incidents can be attributed to doing things too quickly and not paying attention to our surroundings. We are obsessed with how quickly we can set up or load out a touring show. That haste can be an important factor in an accident.

The constant, long hours of show after show in different cities without a break is not only physically tiring but also mentally boring. You establish a routine and do things mechanically without thinking. There is a positive side to that, but it also can be fatal. The positive side is that with so much to do and so little time in which to do it, things must flow and fit together without considerable effort. In most cases we do not even count items in a case; we "just know" it is all there. Instinct, I guess, but it also comes from repeating the process so often that it becomes an unconscious action. This is not meant to encourage beginners to disregard checklists and planned procedures; it is meant to point out that disregarding these tools can be dangerous.

Specific Areas for Safety

Where are the key areas to watch for potential accidents? The answer is, anywhere they are not expected. The following areas are worth discussing in detail.

Truck Loading

Workers brought in to load and unload trucks have no idea of the weight of an item, what is in a box, or how delicate the contents are; they are simply trying to fill or empty the truck. A forklift driver cannot be excused for dropping a case, but a loader who is trying to get a top-heavy case down a narrow ramp is always in danger of its tipping over. Make it a practice to have one member of the road crew outside the truck to assist the loaders with information about case contents, weight, and so on and to direct the movement of the cases into the hall for organized placement. Generally the truck driver is inside the trailer supervising the load. If the load has shifted in transit, an accident or at least severe damage to the equipment can occur.

Rigging

When overhead rigging is required for a show, most often a professional theatrical rigger is traveling with the show. The rigger may have a second, or ground person. The second sends up the cable, bridles, shackles, chain, and other gear needed by the rigger, or high person. The rigger is worth the added expense, especially during load-out. The correct packing of the cases can save hours on the next load-in. Simply eliminating the wasted time and energy of locating parts that were not packed in their proper places makes for a quicker, smoother, and safer operation.

If the show does not travel with a qualified rigger, it is wise to have one go over the plans before the tour starts and suggest a rigging plot, or, better yet, draw one out, giving insights into point placement, position, and weight configuration. This greatly helps the local rigger by providing an idea of what must be lifted. It promotes knowledgeable decisions based on load limitations at the specific facility.

After the rig is flown, have the crew place several safety cables. These are non–load-bearing cables attached between the portable truss and the physical building structure. They are there in case a chain or cable slips or breaks. A few years ago a truss did break as a cable was being released after a show. If the safety cable had not been in place, the accident could have happened while the show was in progress, causing injury to artists as well as audience members.

In recent years the U.S. Occupational Safety and Health Administration (OSHA) has stepped up its campaign to make mandatory the wearing of safety equipment during the rigging and focus process. There have been two recent cases of stagehands' falling. The first, in Memphis, occurred when a stagehand who was climbing a wire rope ladder up to a truss follow spot became exhausted and was unable to continue up or come down. He eventually let go and fell almost 40 feet to the concrete floor and died. In 1995, a stagehand on the Billy Joel–Elton John tour was climbing a wire rope ladder and missed a rung near the top. He was wearing a full body harness, and when he fell, the retractable lifeline stopped him from falling to the ground. He was able to regain his footing and complete the climb. The gear that saved the second man's life is referred to as *fall arrest* equipment.

In a broad sense, *fall arrest* or *fall protection* refers to all the effort involved in making sure workers are protected from accidental falls and that if a fall occurs, there is a system to save the worker before he or she hits the ground. All the rules are contained in the 1970 federal Occupational Health and Safety Act.

I have always respected riggers for their skill. I have a deep sense that they put their lives on the line each time they go high. I never thought there was much to do to help them if they did fall except scrape them up. Cold, but realistic at the time. Now, because of a push by both OSHA and, even more important, the riggers themselves, something is being done.

Frankly, there is another group who are not skilled riggers. In the past seven or eight years these workers, the truss follow spot operators, have been thrust into the need to climb high. These follow spot operators are not skilled climbers, and many do have a real fear of climbing a wire rope ladder or doing the focus, that is, working their way across a truss, bending over to focus a light, and moving on. It is hot, sweaty, exhausting work. This group deserves to be made safe. A number of concert rigging companies have spearheaded the effort with the use of fall arrest equipment, not only for the riggers but also for lighting crew members who climb to a truss. This gear is discussed later in this chapter.

Stage Support

When ground support for a truss is used, there is often little possibility of using safety cables, but you can still maximize the safety of the system. Check the stage surface carefully. When using a portable stage, check especially for weak spots or uneven sections. Next look under the stage. Are the sections secured together? Is the deck secured to the legging? You do not have to be a structural engineer—common sense tells you whether it looks unsafe. If it does seem unsafe, tell the promoter or facilities staff about it and make sure they change it. Even though stage construction is not a direct concern of the lighting technician, I always slide my foot over cracks and joints to check for leveling and open spaces that someone might trip over. Portable dance floor material is helpful in solving this problem quickly and at the same time improves the appearance of the stage floor. Even carpet pieces or throw rugs help.

Ground Support

The types of structures that are commonly used to support lighting are shown in chapter 13. In this chapter I discuss the safety involved in using these structures. Some structures have safety devices built in, such as the Genie Super-Lift. A braking device is designed to prevent the load forks from falling in the event the cable breaks. This lift is probably the best unit with regard to safety because a cable and winch design is used.

Hydraulic lifts do not have the cable problem, but they have problems related to leveling. Hydraulic lifts are so heavy that they can tip over if not properly stabilized, or if there is a weak point in the stage, they can break through the floor. In that case the lift does not fail, the stage does. Nevertheless, it is a safety problem related to the device and the stage. Use outriggers or stabilizer bars on all lifts to achieve the widest possible base.

Probably the two most common accidents that occur with lifts are pinched fingers (catching them between columns or joints as the device comes down faster than expected) and shin bruises when someone runs into the outrigger leg of a lift. No matter which lift is used, recheck leveling once the truss or load is raised.

Fixtures

Safety devices for fixtures are not common. Most PAR-64 fixtures have a spring-loaded clip to hold in the gel frame. I like to take a tip from television and film lighting, in which it is accepted practice to safety chain any barndoor or snoot to the yoke of the fixture. Usually, plumber's chain and an S hook are used. I prefer wire rope with a ring attached to a corner of the gel frame and a dog-clip on the other end. If color changers or other effects are added to the fixture, a similar device should be used.

When working with a triangle truss, I also safety all fixture yokes to the truss or pipe. If you are using lamp bars of four to six fixtures attached to a unistrut track, a "safety cable" should be added between the bar and the truss.

Another area of danger is lamp failure. The lamp manufacturers refer to this as *violent failure*, not an explosion. It can happen with an ellipsoidal or Fresnel lamp, but because of the lamp housing design, it would be rare for glass to fall out of these fixtures. However, the PAR-64 lamp has little or no real protection for this eventuality. The most extreme measure is to place a wire screen in the gel holder. Other than this, there is little that can be done. Hot glass showering down can cause serious burns and cuts.

The problem is intensified by the fact that quartz lamps are sealed under pressure. Therefore, cracked quartz glass acts like a punctured balloon—it explodes. The PAR-64 and the other lamps in this family have a glass lens sealed onto the face of the reflector-coated glass backing. If the cement has not completely sealed the gap, the heat produced by the lamp can expand the glass, allowing pressure to escape and causing further fracturing of the seal, which can lead to an explosion.

This is a layman's view and should not be considered a technical evaluation by an expert in lamp design, but it covers the popular views. The lamp manufacturers have taken great pains to ensure that the lamps are airtight before shipment. However, bouncing around in a truck can cause damage or cracks to occur. I have seen lamps come out of a truck neatly separated at the seal, and the lens lying against the gel frame. It is not practical to check every lamp every time they are moved because visual inspection does not usually reveal fractures. This is one area of safety concern that continually plays the odds.

Lamps in the PAR family have another problem in that they are focused by means of manual rotation of the porcelain connector cap at the back of the fixture. These caps are constructed of two pieces of porcelain held together with nuts and bolts. In transport they can come apart, exposing the metal contacts. Without looking inside, technicians reach in to rotate the lamp and can come in contact with these electrically hot leads. Always look before reaching inside or at least wear gloves as an insulator. It is wise to use gloves in any case, because the lamp housing is extremely hot.

Another part of your daily inspection of the truss should be for socket caps that are off the lamps or that have come apart. One method used to keep these caps from separating is to use a high-temperature glue in the hole that contains the hex nut. I have also seen wire wraps tied around the two parts. There can be a heat problem with this method and a fire hazard, so I do not recommend it. Some manufacturers have begun to install caps that go over the porcelain. It is a great idea and should be retrofitted to all PAR fixtures.

Focusing

Focusing is the most dangerous time of the setup day. When someone is high on a ladder or walking a truss, wrenches can slip out of hands or gel frames can fall while a color is being inserted in the holder, so use extreme caution on stage. Warn people to keep clear, that focusing is in progress. A must is to *stop all sound checks* and music being played over the PA system.

The falling wrench problem can be minimized if you attach a line to the handle and around your wrist. On tour, it is extremely difficult to keep people out from under the working area, because so much is going on about the stage at the same time. When something falls, the person hurt usually is the stagehand holding the ladder. This person should have been looking up, but that is not an excuse for an accident.

A constant problem is getting ladder movers (holders) to pay attention. If you are on the ladder, always make clear, before you climb up, how you plan to direct the movements. Only the person up high should call for the ladder to be moved, no one else. Try to have at least one person constantly looking up, both to hear you better when you call an order and to watch for falling objects. If no ladder is used, and a person is high on the truss, I always station a stagehand to watch for falling objects and to keep people away from the area.

Trusses

A daily visual inspection of welds is required. A fracture can occur in the best of units, and severe road conditions can do great structural damage. I believe that x-rays of trusses should be a yearly requirement. This would reveal any hairline fractures before stresses cause a serious structural failure. Second, but no less important, is to have one person responsible for rechecking all connectors—nuts and bolts, pins, and so on—that join truss sections together before the truss is raised in the air.

A high potential for truss failure occurs when the truss is being raised or lowered. Additional stress, as much as 350 percent of the static load, can be placed on any one section when the motors come out of synchronization or a corner of the truss is caught on a pipe or set unit. The motor may have no load for only a second, but when the truss comes clear it can fall with such a force as to break welds or the anchorage point of the motor.

Power Hookup

The potential for an accident with power hookups is tremendous. Because we are dealing with temporary hookups, it is not always possible to be sure the correct connection has been made. Another problem is that many situations necessitate that the road electrician give the pigtails to a house electrician to do the actual hookup. Take the time to clearly show the color code markings on your pigtails. Do not assume everyone knows green is ground (or earth). What kind of ground is available: equipment ground, grounding rod, or water pipe? Is the service single-phase or three-phase power? Check all of these things carefully. Then recheck everything at the source after the hookup is complete before energizing the lighting system. I strongly recommend voltmeters on each leg of the portable dimmer system you are taking on the road to double-check power before the system is energized. At least carry a good quality voltage or ohm meter.

Grounding is the primary cause of power problems. The two main problems are potential shock to someone working or touching the lamps, truss, or lifts and a buzz in the sound system caused by problems between lighting and sound grounds. The necessity for a good ground is essential, especially outdoors. Many road electricians take the added precaution of grounding the lifts by means of a ground stake at outdoor shows. It is an excellent practice.

Personal Fall Arrest Systems

Fall protection is one of the entertainment industry's hot buttons in the mid 1990s. In 1970 the federal government passed a series of laws administered by OSHA. The laws require that every employer protect every employee from injury in the normal course of work. The specific law regarding this is 1910.132.

Fall hazard is a technical term used to describe any situation in which a worker can lose balance, fall to a lower level, and be injured. OSHA defines fall hazard situations with the "six foot rule." If a worker is exposed to the possibility of falling six feet or more, fall protection must be provided and used. OSHA recognizes three basic methods of fall protection. The first is a guardrail system surrounding the walking or work surface. That is not practical on lighting trusses. The second is a safety net system installed below to catch a falling worker. Safety nets also are a problem in setup. Third, according to the OSHA rules, a personal fall arrest system can be provided to protect a worker in lieu of the foregoing methods. This is not simply a matter of putting on a rock climbing harness and attaching it to a rope tied around a steel beam in the building. OSHA says the system must meet the following conditions:

1. Be continuous
2. Be exclusive
3. Reduce the arrest forces communicated to the fallen worker to safe levels
4. Limit the free-fall distance before the arrest
5. Be composed of components of safe design
6. Be engineered as a total system
7. Incorporate rescue after the fall is arrested
8. Incorporate formal training in system use

What does all this mean? *Continuous* simply means that workers may not disconnect themselves from the system once they have more than six feet of potential fall. The system must allow the worker to move vertically and, when necessary, horizontally. In the old days, riggers would climb to the building steel or truss and attach a rope to their climbing harness. That is not allowable today. The system must be exclusive and not part of the anchoring for other rigging, such as a truss or sound system. The really new feature is that if a worker falls, the system must have an energy absorption system built in so that a worker who falls is not jerked to a stop at the end of the rope.

There are limits to the maximum distance a worker can fall before the system starts to work. That distance is 6 feet or not to fall onto a lower surface, whichever is less. It doesn't mean the worker falls only 6 feet; it means the worker can fall 6 feet before the absorption system starts to arrest the fall.

The components that are used in these new systems are very different from those a rock climber uses. In fact most of the rock climbing and rescue equipment formally used by riggers is not legal for fall protection. One obvious piece of gear is the seat harness. The fall protection model (Figure 8–1) is a full body harness that has an attachment point above the shoulders, so the person falling cannot become inverted and fall out of the rig, as has happened to climbers. That is why OSHA has designated that the system must be designed as a total system. The agency does not leave it up to riggers to put their own systems together.

Figure 8–1 Full body harness.
(Drawing by Steve Nelson.)

OSHA's concern is that it is very easy to mismatch components, which weakens the standards.

The final two points are very new. First is a rescue plan. When an accident has happened, how is the victim rescued? According to the law, the employer must have a written plan and personnel trained and ready quickly to implement that plan. Training before use of the equipment must include the specifics of the system components and assessment of the hazards to which the worker will be exposed during the production. Additional workers must be trained in rescue techniques for the eventuality that someone does fall.

Long time concert rigger Rocky Paulson, owner of Stage Rigging, Inc., in San Carlos, California, has been one of the top riggers for more than 25 years on tours with Pink Floyd, Neil Diamond, and Billy Joel, to name a few. The following is an excerpt from an article he and Steve Nelson wrote. It appeared in *Theatre Design & Technology*, the journal of the United States Institute for Theatre Technology (USITT), in the winter issue, 1996. The subject is so new that there are very few people qualified to write on this topic; I am not one of them. I felt that a much clearer understanding of the system would be given if a tour example were used. This was a tour of the group R.E.M. The authors have kindly given permission for it to be included here.

> The fall protection system that tours with the R.E.M. show consists of a vertical component for climbing the ladder and a horizontal component for traversing the truss.

The Common Elements

A full-body harness meeting OSHA and ANSI requirements for fall protection is an integral element of the system. As with all full-body harnesses, the only point of attachment to the fall protection system is the dorsal D-ring located high on the wearer's back [see Figure 8–1]. The Surety Model 809 harness used on this tour also has a chest level D-ring and two hip-level side D-rings intended for work positioning activities like rappelling. These harnesses are considered part of the total fall arrest system and cannot be replaced by harnesses owned by local stagehands or local venues. Attached into the dorsal D-ring of each harness is a four foot webbing lanyard with an integral rip-stitch type shock absorber (Surety model WL-202/RM). Specially for this fall protection system, Surety and Stage Rigging Inc. have incorporated a large D-ring between the webbing and the shock absorber of the lanyard for the retractable lifeline to hook into. The shock absorber end of the lanyard terminates in a locking snaphook that attaches to the harness dorsal D-ring. The opposite end of the lanyard terminates in a self-locking carabiner. The shock absorber element in the lanyard is designed to limit the Maximum Arresting Force (MAF) to under 900 lbs.

The rigging of this fall protection system requires just one modification to the standard way the trusses are rigged to the chain motors. Normal practice is to lead the two legs of the polyester roundsling supporting the truss to a $5/8$ inch anchor shackle and to hook that shackle into the chain motor hook. Because both the horizontal and vertical lifelines also need to attach in just below the motor hook, a $5/8$ inch pear ring is inserted between the truss sling shackle and the motor hook to allow attaching the additional carabiners used to anchor the lifelines at that point [Figure 8–2].

The Vertical Component

Just above the wire rope ladder, a retractable lifeline (Surety Surelock Retractable Lifeline BS-101/66) is anchored to the pear ring attached into the motor hook by means of an OSHA-approved self-locking carabiner. Retractable lifelines function much like an automobile seat belt—a spring-loaded

Figure 8–2 Horizontal lifeline rig.
(Drawing by Steve Nelson.)

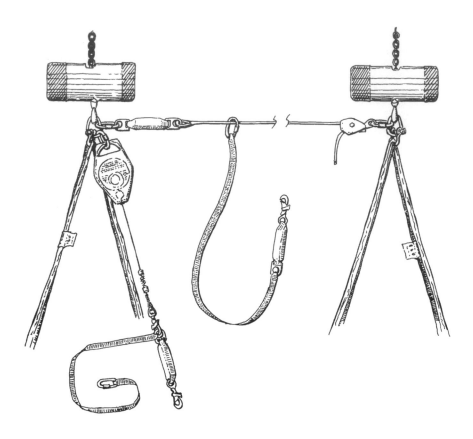

spool keeps just enough tension on the lifeline attached to the worker's harness that it will feed in and out easily under normal working conditions, but when the cable starts to feed out rapidly, as in a fall, centrifugal force acting on the turning drum activates a locking mechanism. Once the weight of the fallen worker is taken off the system, the retractable lifeline will once again feed in and out.

Using the System

After donning the harness, the stagehand uses a $^1/_4$ inch tag line to pull the retractable lifeline snaphook down. This snaphook is then attached to the connecting D-ring between the shock absorber and the webbing portion of the lanyard. The stagehand then proceeds to climb the wire rope ladder in the normal fashion with another stagehand steadying it at ground level (Figure 8–3). As the stagehand ascends, the lifeline retracts into the housing, keeping the line taut.

When a Fall Occurs

When a stagehand falls from the ladder, the centrifugal brake on the retractable lifeline engages, quickly stopping the falling worker. The worker is left in an upright position, suspended from the dorsal lifeline attachment point at the high center-back of the harness. Since the lifeline is located directly above the ladder, the suspended stagehand is left hanging near the ladder and can easily reach out, regain the ladder, and climb down to safety.

The Horizontal Component

The horizontal lifeline (Surety HL-1009-060 Surety Line Horizontal Lifeline) is an off-the-shelf unit intended for use in temporary situations. The horizontal lifeline assembly consists of a $^5/_8$ inch synthetic line with a rip-stitch type shock absorber on one end and a line tensioner on the other. The lifeline system is attached via approved self-locking carabiners between $^5/_8$ inch pear rings located just below the two chain motors. The shock absorber is placed in-line with the horizontal lifeline to perform two functions: The expanding

Figure 8–3 Retractable lifeline attached to truss as operator climbs wire rope ladder to spot light.
(Drawing by Steve Nelson.)

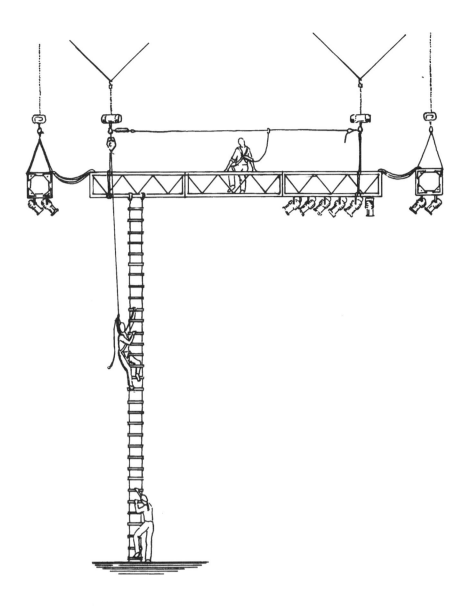

shock absorber absorbs some of the force generated by the falling worker; and as it tears open, it increases the length of the lifeline, thereby lowering the force the line must sustain by effectively increasing the length of the lifeline bridle angle. (Most riggers will remember from setting up bridles that the more shallow the bridle angle is, the greater the stress on the line and end anchorages imposed by a downward force, and vice versa.)

Using the System

Once the stagehand ascends the ladder and reaches a secure position on the truss, he or she clips the carabiner on the webbing end of the lanyard onto the horizontal lifeline. Only then is it safe to reach behind and unfasten the snaphook connection of the retractable lifeline. (Remember OSHA requires a fall protection system to be continuous.) Attached to the horizontal line, the rigger traverses the truss by either walking the lower web on one side of the truss or by spidering along on hands and knees across the top of the truss. Both of these methods of traversing keep the harness attachment below the horizontal lifeline, an important factor in keeping the worker's total fall distance to a minimum. Truss spot operators traverse the truss to their spot chairs, buckle their seat belts and then finally transfer their lanyard from the lifeline to the truss. This fall protection system is designed to accommodate only one person at a time.

When a Fall Occurs

No falls have ever occurred on the horizontal lifeline portion of this truss fall protection system, but tests with dummy weights have shown what can be expected. The stagehand free-falls until the slack comes out of the lanyard. The free-fall distance will vary depending on how much slack is in the lanyard, or more precisely, how close the dorsal D-ring on the full-body harness is to the horizontal lifeline—a standing worker will experience a longer free-fall than one who is sitting or lying on the truss. After the free-fall, which is only about three feet, the several components of the fall protection system begin to decelerate the falling stagehand and eventually bring him or her to a stop. As downward force is applied to the horizontal lifeline it deflects downward, or sags. A small portion of this deflection is due to elongation of the line and taking up any slack. The major portion of the deflection is in result of the inward movement of the attachment points at the chain motors and the ripping open of the in-line shock absorbers. All these actions absorb the force of the falling worker. As the system arrests the worker's fall, he or she will be jerked into a basically upright position and the force of the fall will be communicated primarily to the thighs and butt through the straps of the harness. The deceleration distance to full stop is about 10 to 12 feet after the lanyard takes up slack out of the lifeline and then there is an initial rebound of about 8 feet. After arrest, the stagehand will be left suspended in an upright position several feet below the truss, a position he or she will remain in until rescued. The plan for rescue in the event of a fall from the truss is to immediately lower the truss and remove the stagehand when the truss nears the deck. The elapsed time to rescue a fallen stagehand is about five minutes, the time it takes to lower the truss.

Limitations and Refinements

It should be noted that while this horizontal lifeline system, designed by Stage Rigging Inc. for use on suspended lighting trusses, is arguably the best available right now, it is still in development. Research into refinements and better solutions is on-going. Drop tests of dummy weights have raised some questions about exactly how the fall forces interact with the lighting truss. For instance, it has been noticed that the force created by a falling weight deflects inward the flexible vertical truss supports (the roundslings, motor chains and slings), which in turn jerks the truss ends upward and inward. This motion can be potentially dangerous on long trusses which have intermediate pickups: raising the end pickups will unload the middle pickups, possibly resulting in truss-span overloading.

Attempts to computer-model and calculate how a truss is stressed by the fall forces on a horizontal lifeline anchored to flexible truss suspension points have proved difficult because of the large number of variables involved. Stage Rigging, Inc. and truss manufacturer Tomcat USA are currently developing a rigid lifeline anchorage system that substantially reduces the variables. In November, 1995 at Lighting Dimensions International (LDI) in Miami a prototype tripod device was displayed [Figure 8–4]. By the end of 1996, following more testing and refinement, a truss lifeline system using these *rigid* tripod anchorages should be available. (From Rocky Paulson and Steve Nelson, "Fall Protection for Touring Lighting Truss," *Theatre Design & Technology* (Winter 1996): 20–23. Reprinted with permission of the authors.)

Although this excerpt only touches the surface of an area of safety that is of great concern to the concert market, the lighting designer needs to be aware of it because these systems must be built into the truss plan to meet OSHA standards. Heavy fines are now being imposed when riggers on theatrical events are found not to be wearing these devices.

Figure 8–4 Prototype of a structure designed to meet the horizontal lifeline requirement. (Photo by Stage Rigging, Inc.)

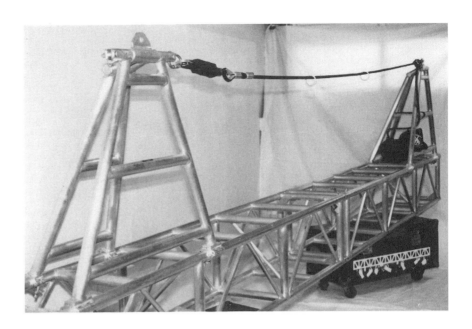

Smoke

Problems are associated with the chemicals used to make theatrical smoke (see chapter 10), used so that beams of light can better be seen. Actor's Equity Association commissioned a study to test the effects on dancers and actors. Although the 300-page report has not been officially released to the public, the results were not kind to the manufacturers of the smoke-producing devices. The report opposes the use of glycol fog on stage. Even before the report, considerable effort had been exerted by manufacturers of these devices to correct many of the problems. Chapter 10 discusses the materials and methods for making haze and smoke for theatrical purposes. It is wise to consider that some people have respiratory problems, and those persons should be warned about being in an environment too long with heavy concentrations of some forms of haze and smoke. Protective gear, such as masks, should be used when practical. We, as an industry, are always making the effort to make products better and safer. This is only one case that has received more publicity than other issues, such as fall protection. But each issue is equally important and must have continuous review to ensure that we are all working in as safe an environment as possible.

Murphy's Law

Murphy's law—If anything can go wrong, it will—is certainly true on the road. We place terrible strain on equipment and personnel. Fatigue can bring Murphy's law into action without warning. The main deterrent to accidents is to be aware at all times that they occur when least expected. So expect it or you may be a statistic. This is why I place so much importance on stress and fatigue on the road. You may have done the setup a thousand times and be able to do it in your sleep, but if you are asleep, you are an accident waiting for a place to happen. Insist that everyone on the crew be alert, because someone else's carelessness can be the reason you are hurt. I have at times told workers, "You might not care if you hurt yourself, but I want to be around to do this job for a long time."

Safety Problem Corrections and Solutions

There are four areas of concern in maintaining safety. First, during pre-production, check the certification for load capacity of the truss design, and check the safety record of the company or equipment to be used. Has the equipment been inspected recently? Even if you are "only the designer," you do have a moral as well as legal obligation to ensure that what is used on the production is safe. Do not try to put this responsibility on the head electrician. Everyone must be concerned with safety. As the designer, you must know that the design you have submitted can be safely executed by the equipment supplier.

Second, as the designer or crew chief, you have a continuing obligation once on the road to make sure the equipment is maintained and the crew is working in a safe manner. The third area relates to the safety of the work environment, specifically the stage on which the touring production is to be performed. Even if there is no lighting on the stage, as you walk around you should be conscious of wobbly sections or other signs of an unsafe stage. Report them to the stage manager.

Make sure equipment suppliers have proper insurance on equipment and the personnel working for them. Legally this is an area that is not clear. If you come into a facility and see or suspect an unsafe condition and report it, you cannot relinquish your responsibility if the house manager, promoter, or stage manager tells you it is okay or to mind your own business. If the safety problem is in your area of expertise, you can be held criminally negligent if an accident happens after you make others aware of the problem.

If you are going to be an independent designer, I suggest strongly that you obtain a public liability insurance policy. You owe it to your coworkers and to the public to protect them. I do not know of anyone ever being sued over this point, but legal counsel for PEPS advised its members of their ultimate obligation in this matter. You are responsible for the safety of others. Insurance companies pay large settlements on accidents that occur because people tripped on cables or had things fall on them during a show. Do not put yourself in the middle; avoid such a possibility by making your production as safe as possible.

9

Dealing with Problems

The human brain has selective memory. We tend to forget, or at least push into the far recesses of our minds, the disasters and unpleasant experiences we've all faced. You know the type: the important lamp that blows as the curtain goes up or the color that looked great in rehearsal but now seems washed out. These things happen to every lighting designer and are unavoidable. The important thing for a designer or technician to know is not how to place the blame or make an excuse but how to deal with the problem as quickly and effectively as possible.

Problem Solving, Stress Management, and Interpersonal Communication

The best designers are skilled in the art of problem solving. They communicate well and possess the ability to make on-the-spot decisions. They do not procrastinate. I've found that on a day-to-day basis, I choose to work with other designers who possess communication and decision-making abilities over more creative persons who cannot verbalize their thoughts and ideas. Concerts are a collaborative venture; when one member of a creative team is unable to deal effectively with the others, that person drains everyone's energies.

Let me tell you a story. When I was in graduate school I was assigned to stage manage a show. The lighting designer assigned to the show was highly regarded by his professors, who thought he had a bright future. On this particular production, the director was a visiting professional. He took a nontraditional approach to the play, forcing us to look at it in a new way. In the early meetings, we all heard his explanation, and in subsequent creative conferences, the design team contributed ideas. When it came time for the lighting designer to explain his thoughts, the director listened carefully. After hearing him out, the director commented on the approach, saying everything was fine except for one key scene, which he asked the designer to rethink. In the next meeting, the lighting designer reiterated the same concept. Again, the director said no, rethink it.

Technical rehearsals of the play began, and guess what? The look the director had rejected showed up on stage. Again, the director was patient—an uncharacteristic quality among his peers—but said, "Okay. I've seen it, and it still does not fit the imagery I wish this scene to create. Show me something different tomorrow."

As stage manager, I conducted a crew call for tech cleanup the next day before the dress rehearsal. The electrical crew was on time—but there was no lighting designer. We waited two hours, and still he did not appear. The board operator said, "What do we do? The director will hate it if I bring up the same preset again tonight." Figuring the designer had an emergency, we decided to cover for him and programmed a different look before the rehearsal began. At rehearsal time, the designer walked in. No emergency; he simply said, "I went to the beach to think."

We need not carry this story any further, except to say that this highly promising designer never made it past small community theatre. His talent was wasted, to be sure, but even more tragic was that his teachers did not educate him in the art and science of problem solving, stress management, and interpersonal communication.

Decision Making

As mentioned in chapter 6, part of my life was spent as an air traffic controller. How that happened was simple: I joined the Air Force, and they said, "You're an air traffic controller." Life often plays tricks on us; we may see no reason for certain events as they're happening, but they turn out to be pivotal influences later on. That was the case here, because air traffic control is essentially a game of juggling schedules and making commitments. The greatest lesson was: Do not be afraid to make decisions. Even the smallest hesitation in committing yourself, based on your training and experience, can be fatal to the people on the plane. Therefore, much time was spent teaching us to make decisions. The ability to make decisions is a learned skill. Working under great pressure is equally critical.

The failure of our educational system is the lack of instruction in the psychology of action or decision making. Theatre, film, and television are action-oriented professions. We all must work to a production timetable that, it is hoped, brings all the technical and acting elements together at the same time. My earlier story is a classic case of a creative mind unable to deal with the realities of group-created art.

The best designers seem to be those who work well under pressure. Sadly, many who have the creative and even the communicative skills necessary to be good lighting designers cannot deal with pressure. The best lighting designers know how to handle disasters, both physically and psychologically.

What do you do when you encounter a problem—for example, discovering you've used the wrong color? The solution is simple: admit your mistake and change the color. For most people, the problem is not changing the color, but admitting they could have made a better choice. It is no different when an actor cannot seem to find a special. Though it may be the actor's fault, I do not even think about arguing the point with the director. Change the special. And don't think the crew is standing behind you laughing; they'll only laugh if you are too foolish not to change it.

Design, Crew, and Equipment Failure

An important thing to realize is that we fail as often as we succeed. It's not all black and white either, because every success contains elements of failure, and vice versa. The types of failure lighting designers commonly experience can be put into three categories: design, crew, and equipment.

Design Failure

There is no such thing as a perfect design. According to that premise, all of our works fail in some way. Teachers, critics, audiences, producers, and directors all decide on their own terms whether a production succeeds, and their evaluations are important, especially in the professional world. But honest self-evaluation does you the most good. Learn to step back and go through your own checklist, asking if the show worked for you: as the director or artist defined the problem, as the physical limitations of the production required, and as you conceived it on paper.

Ask yourself what you learned from this design experience. What can you do differently next time? Each production requires you to rethink ideas or solutions that may have worked perfectly in other situations. To believe you succeed on the basis of your past glories will be the death of you as a creative person.

Crew and Equipment Failure

Regarding the crew, ask yourself if they failed, or if you failed because your training, your supervision, or your communication skills were inadequate. When crew members fail, look to yourself first and then do not look any farther. Did you give them all they needed to succeed? If they failed, it was probably because you did not communicate your needs adequately. You would be wise to study the many good books available about motivating coworkers. I particularly recommend *People Skills* by Robert Bolton, published by Prentice-Hall.

I work on a large number of television pilots. Because of the hectic pace of these usually underbudgeted projects, we often encounter problems that would be easy to blame on the crew if I chose to do so. It's not uncommon to be short an adapter or cable or to forget a lamp, especially when you're working on a limited budget. You can't bring the whole warehouse. Most likely, the problem is that I've put more effort into the complicated production and did not spend a great deal of time working out the nuts and bolts of this "simple" shoot.

Why waste time fixing blame? Do something! Maybe you can gang circuits or look for a place where a fixture can be moved and used to solve the problem. Maybe you did give the correct list to your gaffer or the rental shop, but that does not help you now. Before the next show, say a word to the person you believe forgot to check the equipment. The person will appreciate that you did not reprimand him or her in front of coworkers and will be more careful the next time.

No one is necessarily to blame for equipment failure, but you are responsible for finding a quick solution. While doing a series for the USA Cable Network, we shot more than 120 half-hour wraparounds. Those are the in-studio segments that lead into and out of a field report such as you see on "60 Minutes" or "20/20." These had been shot in groups of 20 with a month off between sessions. When we came back for a fourth session, I put the lighting in and couldn't achieve the same intensity on one part of the set dressings, even though we had the same studio, same dimmers, same fixtures, and same set. Why? We never figured it out. Under pressure to get tape rolling, my solution was to add a small fixture that was available and, to achieve the intensity, I put it at spot focus. About an hour into the taping, there was a violent failure (see chapter 8). Luckily, the Fresnel lens kept the hot glass fragments inside the instrument. We quickly changed the lamp and went on taping. An hour later, it happened again. We then exchanged fixtures, and the problem was eliminated.

When the producer asked, "What the hell is going on?" I could have blamed the lamp, the fixture, or the equipment rental house. What I said was, "I screwed up." Finding a scapegoat or going into a long explanation on focus and lamp failure would only have extended the problem and wasted everyone's time.

Dimmer Problems

Here is a common problem: dimmers that develop minds of their own. It doesn't happen often in permanent installations, but rental gear is subject to invisible damage. Portable control cables are run over by forklifts, and constant patching and bouncing around in trucks takes its toll on dimmers.

One of the live award shows I have done, "The Golden Globe Awards," had such a problem. The show was syndicated, and therefore did not have a large budget. I pride myself on being able to work with limited equipment, but this time it caught up with me. The stage was lit adequately, but I did not have a large number of "toys" to create different looks. I was depending on creating most of the livelier looks in one area where singers were to perform and otherwise keeping the lighting simple. In addition, because backstage space was limited, the fire marshall ordered us to put the dimmers outside the building.

About halfway into the live broadcast, one of the dimmer packs overheated and started flashing on and off. Naturally, it involved a critical lamp: the key light on the master of ceremonies' podium. The first time it went off I thought we had a blown lamp, so I quickly got a follow spot onto the speaker. Only a semidisaster, but I was saved—or was I? When we went back to the emcee, I put the follow spot on the podium. The lamp then came up. What was the problem? A short in the lamp? A bad twofer or cable? Frankly, the last thing I suspected was a dimmer problem, because the equipment was from a top rental company and had worked perfectly up to that point.

The next time we used the lamp, it came on as it should, but then started flashing on and off. Then I knew it was a dimmer problem. However, reaching the problem area took several minutes, and all the while the flashing continued on camera. Now that's a disaster. We shut the dimmer down and finished the show using a follow spot to cover the area.

This was not the time to remind the producer that he had cut the budget so tight that there was no money for backup fixtures, which normally would have been built into the design to cover such a failure. I, after all, had ordered the equipment. On live broadcasts, it is considered standard operating procedure to double hang areas such as the emcee's podium to guard against a critical key lamp's going out. I could have saved a couple lamps from other areas and used them to back up the emcee. I did not.

Computer Problems

My final example deals with computers. Now, I pride myself on being an early advocate of computer lighting control. I believe I was the first to use it on a concert tour with John Denver in 1974. But failures do happen.

My most recent failure came at a corporate show for a large auto manufacturer. We had rehearsed for a week, two shows were behind us, and we had one performance to go. After a quick run-through in the afternoon, we were ready for the audience.

I was sitting next to the console reading when my board operator returned 20 minutes before the curtain was to go up. As I looked up to greet him, I saw both of the video monitors go blank. My first thought was that we had lost power. We checked it, and the power was okay. I reset the switch, the screens came back on, and then we watched the computer go through its internal diagnostic program. The show program came up, and then went blank again. We went through the check and diagnostic program once more, and again the screens went blank—only this time smoke came out of the back of the console.

Now we knew there was a serious problem. While the operator opened the board, I ran for the telephone to find a backup console. Then I went looking for the producer to tell her we were dead in the water, so to speak. After the color came back to her face, she asked the obvious question: "What can we do now?" I calmly replied, "I'm not sure there is anything we can do."

By this time, the cover was off the console. We found burn marks near the power supply and a burnt wire lead. We replaced the wire and the computer was back on line—with no show program. The power failure had caused an electronic spike that destroyed the disk drive module. The backup console arrived, but it wasn't a match, so at this point, I had to make a decision. Should I go to the new console and reprogram the show from scratch, or stay with the one I had? I decided to use the original board. By reprogramming the soft patch and reassigning channels to the 24 submasters (and thankfully the board had that many submasters), I believed I could at least reproduce the basic show looks. To reenter all 137 cues would have taken too long, so while the board operator entered the dimmer-to-control channel patching information, I went to work laying out the submasters so we could run the show manually. The curtain went up 40 minutes late. That final show turned out to be better than the first two.

However, the problem never should have happened. I should have required a computer with dual power supplies, or a standby duplicate console. It's easy to say that in all the times I had used this particular board nothing had happened. I failed by falling into the *it never happened before syndrome*. There is always a first time.

Being Prepared

Early in my training as a designer, I learned a wonderful lesson from Dr. Sam Selden, author and for many years chairman of the theatre department at UCLA, who came to Southern Illinois University as a visiting professor. I was assigned to be his stage manager on a production of *Peter Pan*. Things had been going pretty well, and I was feeling cocky when he came up to me and asked what I intended to do if a particular hydraulic lift did not come up on cue. I hesitated, and he told me to come to him later with three solutions to the problem. It was a good point: we should constantly be considering *what ifs*.

Several of my colleagues brought up this point. A good production manager or lighting director always has Plan B *and* Plan C. So when a truck is missing, we move on to Plan B. When the house can't hang a truss where you want it, use Plan C. It's like being prepared with an excuse when you think someone is angry with you. Your mind races through all manner of possible excuses, doesn't it? Well, this is no different; you will be damned by someone no matter what you decide, so just do it.

I'm not saying we should or could build redundancy into every part of every system, because it isn't economically feasible. But we should always be prepared for the worst, and learn from our misfortunes. The greatest problem is being unprepared.

II

Equipment Designed to Travel

10

Technical Innovations

The explosion of technical innovations in the lighting field can be directly attributed to the demands and needs of the concert lighting industry. They have made their way into theatre, television, dance, live event production, film, nightclubs, restaurants, shopping malls, display windows, and architecture—virtually any medium in which theatrical lighting can be used. The areas that traditionally entailed a form of theatrical lighting were affected first. The packaging techniques were used for theatre and dance road companies. Then the design techniques started to bore a hole in the glass envelope called Broadway. Producers of musicals found that the audience wanted more flash, moving lights, and color. The audience had become accustomed to it by seeing concerts on television or going to live events. So Broadway was no longer leading, it was catching up.

Television and film found that there was a use for many of our ideas, such as with trussing. Several network television studios now have standard concert lighting trusses as the lighting grid. Moving lights have been used on everything from the leading game show "Wheel of Fortune" (my design) to televised concerts to national political conventions. Films like *Batman Returns* used a heavy dose of moving lights to achieve the magnificent effects for the Riddler's hideout. And the list is ever expanding. Look at the heavy use of concert design for the pavilions at the Atlanta Olympics or in theme parks and restaurants. Now whole facades of buildings, such as the Hard Rock Hotel and Casino and the Irvine Spectrum Dome, are washed with computer-controlled color changers. With the 1996 introduction of the High End, Inc., Eco-Dome, an all weather housing for moving lights, architects surely will become more interested in adding movement to their buildings.

Although there can arguably be a natural process of refinement and innovation in the products that manufacturers develop, there is no argument from them that to make some of these products they need to be assured of orders, and that is not something that normally happens in theatre. Theatre lighting has always built on outside innovations. The silicone-controlled rectifier (SCR) is a classic example. It was a development by the Navy during World War II. The lighting industry did not have the financial resources to develop such a device. Yet its adaptation for theatrical production was the key that allowed theatre designers to program much more sophisticated lighting cues and, by means of miniaturizing, allow more physical room to accommodate more dimmers. The growth of the postwar dimming business would not have existed without it.

The manufacturing portion of the theatrical business, by and large, has always been reactionary in nature. I was in the business early in my career, and I remember being told in no uncertain terms, "We sell what we have, we don't encourage the customer to ask for specials." Until the end of the 1980s, the advances involved standard items that had been modified or repackaged to meet the needs of our fledgling industry. Like legitimate theatre, concert lighting borrowed from any market or service that had something that could be adapted, modified, or used to its benefit.

But by the mid 1980s, things were changing. Manufacturers were going into business to meet the needs of concert and touring lighting. Products were appearing that were not adaptations or reworkings of old ideas. Exciting new products, cut from the whole cloth of a new vision, were becoming available to the designer.

Part II of this book gives an overview of the innovative concepts and products used in the concert lighting business. This section is by no means meant to represent all the ideas being supplied to the touring industry by groups as diverse as small touring companies and large multinational manufacturers.

Subsequent chapters are devoted to the main innovations: consoles, trusses, lifts and hoists, and computer-controlled moving lights. This chapter focuses on some of the other areas of development and products that have advanced the concert business. Also discussed are ancillary products and concepts that the designer needs to know about, use, or work with to realize a design.

Dimming

Dimming is an area in which packaging, not electronic innovation, was the real advance in the early years of touring. In the 1970s the established manufacturers were starting to market compact groups of six to twelve dimmers in a portable unit. What the manufacturers did not conceive of was mounting input connections as well as output strips directly to the dimmer packs so that there was much less to assemble each time the dimmers were set up. The first really portable dimmer racks designed specifically for touring came from British companies. These racks opened the way for many other advances that were not used simply for looks or to sell a new version; they were a practical solution to touring needs. The battle was on, and it only took a couple years for the United States to get in the game. Interestingly enough, it was not one of the old line names, but a relatively small company called L.M.I. that moved to the front. In later years L.M.I. was purchased by E.T.C., Inc., and the equipment is no longer manufactured under its original name.

Distribution systems with low-voltage control patching came next. This enabled the designer to assign one or more dimmers to a single channel on the console. Later, electronic or soft patch systems appeared in which a computer was used to assign control circuits by means of the console. Some British builders put a banana peg cord–type patch bay into dimmer racks. That system has never caught on with U.S. companies, who have instead gone directly to full electronic, digital interface systems.

The placing of several of these package dimmers in a single, castered road case meant that 24 to 72 1-kW dimmers could be connected and ready to operate in a fraction of the time it took to stack and wire each pack individually. Common were packages of 72 1-kW dimmers with 24 multipin output connectors for fast setup. The pin patch for the dimmer-to-control channel assignment panel was built into the rack. Shipping damage was considerably reduced with this arrangement. However, if you are not sure your dimmer units were made specifically for road use, you may want to take them apart to add lock washers and epoxy to keep the components from rattling to pieces in the truck.

U.S. electronic dimmers in the 1980s were being offered in a much wider range of capacities: 2 kW, 2.4 kW, 3.6 kW, 4 kW, 6 kW, and even 12 kW. But the British concentrated on 1-kW dimmers. That allowed each PAR-64 lamp (99 percent of all the fixtures on the road are still the 1,000-watt PAR-64 units) to be patched without twofers or multiple outlets. The low-voltage patch could take over and assign the dimmer and associated lamp to any control channel. The 1-kW dimmer also meant that more circuits could be housed in a single, movable rack with main circuit breakers and other elements fully enclosed in one unit.

One early road rack (Figure 10–1) built by Sundance Lighting Corporation used Skirpan 2.4-kW and 6-kW dimmer modules and a Rual slider patch system. The rear view (left) shows six Pyle-National multipin outputs. The slide patch assignment panel is on top. Designed with built-in breakers and hot bus, the slide patch made it easier to assign loads and eliminated patch cables. The three 60-amp connectors are the direct output for the three 6-kW dimmers. The minipin patch in the upper right assigned dimmers to control channels. The front view (right) shows the five of six-dimmer and one of three-dimmer modules that are the heart of the system. The right side contains the power section, in which digital meters are used to monitor all phases of both amperage and voltage. A 250-amp, three-phase main breaker and control cable connectors complete the panel.

The current push is for high-density dimming. The focus of research and development is miniaturization. There is also a tremendous interest in finding alternative devices to move beyond the SCR.

The concert field is currently dominated by manufacturers not known to the theatrical community ten years ago. Most started with consoles because the designers were in desperate need of innovations that would help them control the fixtures in new ways that would allow them to keep time with the music. The idea that you should be able to play the console like a piano was in a large number of heads. These consoles can be built in small quantities, almost built to order.

Dimmers proved to be more of a challenge. First, the technology didn't prove as difficult to advance as did the price. This is the quantity end of the game. High tech components are expensive, and only quantity

Figure 10–1 Skirpan/Sundance dimmer rack circa 1983 with 36 2.4-kW and three 6-kW dimmers with slide patch and six Pyle-National output multiconnectors. (Photo by Sundance Lighting Corp.)

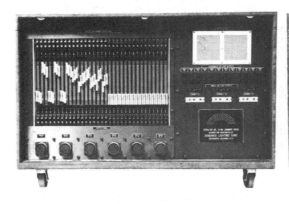

can bring the cost down. The tools concert designers needed were already widely known. Many small companies, like my own Sundance Lighting, had put together custom racks with a large company's dimmer module. They had survived the road on tours. The basic designs were proved in thousands of miles of trucking and rough handling, quick setup, and reliability. So why did it take so long for the front-line manufacturers to catch on? Does the answer lie in where they are now? One went into bankruptcy protection, and two have been sold to financial conglomerates for whom our industry is small potatoes.

It took the smaller, start-up companies to take the plunge. Now it is difficult to find a portable situation in television, film, or live events that does not take advantage of these road-style dimming packages.

What made them so different? First we must discuss the concept of the 1-kW dimmer verses the 2.4-kW dimmer. The British used a thyristor (optoisolated solid state relay). Designers in the United States used a device called a Triac to control dimmers up to 2.4 kW, but it was found to be unreliable. In the meantime, the British moved forward with the concept of dimmer per circuit much more quickly than the Americans. It comes down to inserting each lamp into a control circuit that can be operated alone or joined by means of a submaster to a group of similar-colored fixtures when needed. It also means that the cable sizes can be reduced to 14-gauge wire, decreasing the weight of the cables. Flexibility is the watchword.

The U.S. companies worked to catch up in the portable six and twelve dimmer, small package market. The difference was that they would place 48 2.4-kW dimmers in a rack that was of reasonable weight and size, and the British would place 72 1-kW dimmers in even less space. At some point we are splitting hairs, but size and weight when multiplied by four or six racks makes a difference in the truck pack. In both systems there has always been a limited need for a group of 6-kW dimmers to run cyclorama lights and audience wash luminaries, such as the eight-light PAR-36 or Mini-Brute units. On the whole, when dimming is needed on today's tour, it is likely represented by a dimmer per lamp style of packaging.

But these racks do not simply contain dimmers. The evolution to true road status meant that a number of things needed to become integrated into the same case. The first was that a power distribution system had to be built in. The idea of carrying a cumbersome, fused, "Square D"-style main breaker panel that had to be connected to each dimmer module was eliminated early on. Enter the use of Cam-Lok, a connector designed for #2/0 or #4/0 single-circuit power cable. For our purposes we can assume that one of these Cam-Lok #2/0 with appropriate cable is able to carry one leg of a 225-amp power service. Five of these (three hot legs, ground, and neutral) make up the connection to house power of three phase, five wire, as it is known in the United States. That is enough for 42 1.2-kW dimmers. Thus three-phase service of #4/0 handles 96 1.2-kW dimmers or 48 2.4-kW dimmers safely (always derate cable to 80% of full capacity).

The second feature added to these road racks was a digital multiplexed (DMX) capability. A Engineering Technical Committee of the United States Institute for Theatre Technology (USITT) devised what has become the industry standard of DMX protocol, called DMX 512. This digital control system also has contributed to the ability to link multiple road racks and also have the consoles control at one time any number of other devices, such as color changers and scrollers and moving lights made by any number of manufacturers.

The ability to patch any dimmer in any rack into any control channel was another part of what road crews wanted. The ability to lay out the console in the order preferred by the designer and also to link more than one dimmer to a control channel was highly desirable. At first there were banana-peg systems with small patch cords, so it looked like a 1940's telephone switchboard. But now, almost all manufacturers have added a small computer link with a keypad and two-line by 20-character backlit liquid crystal display (LCD) readout that not only can do this assignment of channels but also can actually record and play back a limited number of cues. This is great if the console fails. Some systems even allow you to change the dimmer curve as well as monitor the dimmer performance, so you have instant information about the status of each dimmer, such as whether it has a load on it.

Because almost all road racks use Socapex six circuit multipin connectors (Pyle-National and VEAM are also available), these devices can assign any one of the outputs to any dimmer in the rack. In the less suffocated models this can still be done with the older banana-peg system. Many also contain meters for visual monitoring of input voltage and hot for non-dim receptacles on the rack. All of these compact road racks require fans. Although noise is usually not a problem in a concert environment, most manufacturers are looking for additional sales in television and film, so they use whisper fans, which operate only when the rack reaches a preset temperature threshold.

All these features are designed by each manufacturer with a unique style, but they all have as a goal the ability to enable quick, reliable set-ups. Because there are so many, I will comment on only two units: the E.T.C. (Electronic Theatre Controls, Inc.) Sensor Rack and Avolites FD series. The first is from a U.S. manufacturer and the second comes from the United Kingdom. Both are excellent products and have large followings among road electricians.

The E.T.C. Sensor touring rack (Figure 10–2) comes, like most U.S. products, such as the Strand CD 90 system, with dimmer modules that are individual or dual, plug-in configuration models. All can be removed without tools. The British tend to go with a 19-inch rack version that has 12 dimmers in each module. The Sensor rack comes in two sizes: 49.75"H × 45"W × 30"D for a 48-position model and a smaller 24-position model that is 30 inches wide. With this as the shell you then have the option of having the rack built with 96 2.4-kW or 1.8-kW dual modules or 48 6-kW dimmers. Twelve-kilowatt (12 kW) dimmers are available but normally are not seen on concert tours. The output panels of these racks also can be configured to your needs. There are 36 Socapex six-circuit outputs on the large panel, which equals 138 individual outputs assignable to any dimmer. The panel shown in Figure 10–2 also has 72 20-amp female stage pin connectors as well as 2 additional 20-amp stage pin outputs for use as non-dim or hot and two duplex household outputs, one main breaker, and two sets of Cam-Lok input power feeder connectors.

The Avolite FD Series racks (Figure 10–3) look like their predecessors, but internally they are very advanced. As mentioned earlier, the approach is to build 12 dimmers into a 19-inch rack mount configuration, so they can virtually be stand-alone units. Each is mounted on a slide tray, so they can be removed without access to the back of the rack. They also have the feature of user adjustment of the control curve. This system does contain a fail-safe mechanism that maintains the last scene if control signal is lost with the console. Groups of racks are assigned channel numbers by means of a thumbwheel switch. They leave the dimmer to channel assignment up to the control console.

Figure 10–2 E.T.C. Sensor road rack with 96 2.4-kW dimmers.
(Photo by E.T.C., Inc.)

Figure 10–3   Avolite FD Series portable dimmer rack, front and back, with 72 1-kW dimmers. (Photo by Avolite, Ltd.)

This 72 10-amp dimmer module rack still uses the pin-patch system for output to dimmer assignment and contains a 96-channel DMX decoder. It does not have casters. These units are considerably lighter than the E.T.C. or Strand units. Setup and output panels are generally the same, with Socapex or other connectors as the user requires.

Although the Avolite unit does not have a built-in intelligent computer, it does allow lamp testing by means of a rotary dial on each group of 12 dimmers and indicator lights to show load. Avolite was one of the first British companies to have a marked impact on the U.S. concert market. The equipment is highly reliable.

All of these racks are also finding great favor in television studios and on film lots. The ability to move them to any location, to reprogram the configuration, and to set them up for different needs quickly, be it a hotel one night to a location film shoot the next, has made them desirable in the rental market as well. These are only two examples of what dimmers and their packaging have advanced because of the touring influence.

One manufacturer has taken a totally different approach. As is usual with products that are radical, even within concert lighting circles, the equipment has strong supporters and detractors. The IPS (Intelligent Power System) dimmer (Figure 10–4) is unique. Now owned by Rosco Entertainment Technology, the IPS-DS-1206 is a lightweight (32 pounds) and compact strip (5 feet long) that contains six 1,200-watt dimmers. The design of each dimmer incorporates a microprocessor and two isolated-gate bipolar transistors (IGBTs). The "intelligent" microprocessor adjusts voltage and current in response to changes detected in the load and electrical service, extending the life of the lamps. No filter chokes are used, so the units consume less energy than conventional SCR dimmers. They also can handle not only tungsten but also inductive and ballasted loads. Building these devices directly into a truss, supporters say, saves cable and floor space. Because the intelligent part of the system relays data to the console, information such as load status is available to the console operator. Changing fixtures is as easy as it is in a conventional theatrical pipe and raceway system, so it seems ideal for rental business, in which the fixture configurations must change from day to day.

Road Cases

One of the items that is not directly a lighting product but without which it would be impossible to tour is the road case. I say that in a loving way because when we first started touring, all that was available were wooden crates with steel casters or industrial clothes hampers. I have enough splinters in me from those crates to try out for a part as a puppet. The weight of the wooden crates and the steel casters were not the ticket when we were trying to pack the truck as tightly and efficiently as possible. Two methods have stayed around more than 20 years. One is actually modeled on a sound cabinet.

Someone saw sound cabinets being built out of tough but light cabinet-grade plywood that needed little internal reinforcement and said, "That would make a great cable box. To keep it nice and clean so we don't get splinters, why don't we glue some indoor-outdoor carpet onto it. To make it complete we'll buy good 2-inch neoprene casters. To keep the cases closed we'll add Session latches or Roto-locks" (practically invisible locks that need a hex-head wrench to open). Well, it was

Figure 10–4   IPS Intelligent Power System. "Distro" (distribution) strip with six 1.2-kW dimmers built in.
(Photo by Rosco Entertainment Technology.)

a good idea. The cases held the tremendous weight of #4/0 cable or multi-cables. They were also used for other heavy loads. That was overkill for storing individual lamps and protecting consoles, so a case made of PVC-coated plywood was used. The PVC (polyvinyl chloride) can be made in several colors for easy identification. These cases are great for lighter objects (Figure 10–5). Today these two types of cases remain essentially the same and are still the best anyone has come up with, so goodbye splinters!

Multi-cables

The use of portable, flexible multi-cables may not have been discovered in Rock and Roll touring, but they have certainly been refined to become a highly efficient and safe addition to the touring system. A multipin connector, such as made by Cinch-Jones, Socapex, Veam, and Pyle-National, is the only other item needed to make quick work of cabling.

The standard was a rubber jacketing for cable; other jacketing materials came later. A whole new market for cable manufacturers opened. The weight of rubber and the fact that it is not flexible when you have 22 to 30 #14-gauge stranded wires inside made concert lighting companies look for alternatives. The British again led the field because they had different electrical codes and voltages.

Although not approved by the National Electrical Code for portable use, the fact is that almost all early concert multi-cable has a jacketing of neoprene or PVC. A product called Cranetrol was first used in 1977 by my company after we saw it on a large construction crane. The cable had a neoprene jacket that could withstand severe heat or cold and yet not become brittle and crack as rubber does under similar circumstances. It is about half the weight of rubber, is more flexible, and can be purchased in colors. The advantages of multi-cable have given it supporters in installation as well. Multi-cable used in a nonpermanent installation is quick to install and flexible for many theatre situations. The bus-and-truck tours of dance and theatre can see the advantages of weight reduction and use of smaller, easily coiled cables. I have seen more and more semipermanent television studios taking advantage of these cables. If you have ever spent hours taping bundles of 12-gauge three wire cables together, you know why the "Hod" (a group of several cables taped together) will not be missed. ProCable by TMB Associates

Figure 10–5   PVC road cases.
(Photo by Excalibur Industries.)

has pressure-extruded black thermoplastic compound (proprietary) for its jacket. It meets the Underwiters Laboratories (UL) class 43 standard for portable cable. Each conductor is numbered so that it corresponds with Socapex conductor numbering. It is a #14 conductor cable that also comes in #12 and #10 wire gauge.

After several years the dust seems to have cleared, and the winner in the connector category appears to be Socapex. With a 14-pin connector as the standard, you have six fully independent circuits of hot and neutral plus two grounds for complete safety. Socapex also makes a 12-circuit connector used in television and corporate event production.

Lighting Fixtures Available in the 1970s

Because power availability was a serious problem in the initial days of concert lighting, a more efficient light source was needed. The Fresnel and the older plano-convex spot did not have the lumen output needed to project heavily saturated color onto the stage; the scoop and beam projector were also too inefficient to be of any use. They also did not go on the road well. They were heavy, rattled apart, and did not pack easily.

The PAR-64

In a medium in which bravado is a key element, the need for a light source that matched the punch of the music was needed. The answer was found in a relatively new lamp source being used on location shoots for film and television. The PAR-64 as we know it is a modification of the Cine-Queen fixture introduced in the early 1960s by Berkey-Colortran, Inc. (Figure 10–6). Chip Monck first used PAR-64 lamps in a concert, but the color did not hold up. It was the addition of a long snoot to hold color far enough out in front of the lamp so it would not burn that made it work for concerts so well. Altman Stage Lighting, at the urging of Bill McManus, made the first modified design, and it became the standard for concert lighting. The punch and reasonable control, even though the beam was football shaped instead of round, were what was needed to project strong, primary color onto the stage. The fact that it had its own series of built-in lenses was a bonus. The PAR-64 fixture made for an extremely simple housing design that could be trucked without falling apart.

In film the PAR-64 had been used as a punch light in banks of six or nine to replace the Brute arc-type lamp, which required 220-volt power and an operator to run it. (A punch light is a fixture with a highly concentrated beam that allows long throws.)

The PAR (parabolic aluminum reflector) lamp had the highest lumen-per-watt rating of any lamp then developed for 3,200 degrees Kelvin. This translated into a fixture that had no moving parts, no lens to break, and produced a great deal of light. Heaven had opened up for the concert designer. The PAR-64 meant a low initial purchase price and a long road life. The economics were clear: a PAR-64 housing cost about half that of a Fresnel and one third to one fourth that of the ellipsoidal reflector spotlight. This sealed-beam lamp offers a range of beam spreads from very narrow to narrow to medium to wide flood.

An aircraft landing light (ACL) can be fitted into a standard PAR-64 housing. It produces an intense, narrow beam of light. The limitation is that it is a 28-volt lamp. Although four can be ganged in series so that

Figure 10–6 Cine-Queen, in wide use in television and film and shown here with intensifier ring, was the original housing for the PAR-64 lamp.
(Photo by Colortran, Inc.)

120-volt dimmers can handle them, if one goes out, you lose the entire group. You also give up some individual control. And yes, they really are for aircraft. I remember an aircraft supply company calling me to ask how large a fleet of aircraft we had because our order had completely depleted their stock.

The cousin to the PAR lamp is called the Ray Light (Figure 10–7). The reflector fits in the standard PAR-64 housing but uses a DYS lamp, which is a small, minipin base lamp at 600 watts. It throws a concentrated beam, similar to that from an ACL, but operates on 120 volts. There is also a 30-volt version of the lamp at 250 watts. Reflectors also are made for the PAR-56 and PAR-36 lamps.

A new twist on the PAR lamp comes from E.T.C., Inc. They redesigned the housing and made the unit work like a Ray Light, but they added the ability to fix different lenses to the front. So far the unit has not seen wide acceptance in the touring field, but it is excellent for rental inventory because of its versatility.

Theatre at first ignored the PAR lamp because it was viewed as an uncontrollable source, but it has finally accepted this fixture, especially in musicals. PAR lamps are now at home in theatres and in concert halls. This is partly the result of audiences' perceptions of intensity and colors because they are influenced by the vivid and striking look of concert lighting and partly the results of designers' desire to explore all options.

Fresnels and Lekos

I leave it up to the standard theatre lighting textbooks to fully discuss the lighting characteristics and quality of light achieved with these workhorses of theatre. However, I would like to correct the misuse of a word I have often seen on light plots and in contract riders. The word is *Leko*, often misspelled liko or leco. The name is a contraction of the names of the two men credited with the introduction of the ellipsoidal reflector spotlight, Ed Levy and Edward Kook. It is the registered trademark of the old Century Lighting Company, now Strand, for their version of the fixture (circa 1932).

Figure 10–7   Ray Light. The reflector fits in the standard PAR-64 housing but uses a DYS lamp.
(Photo by Creative Stage Lighting Co., Inc.)

Figure 10–8   Source IV (ellipsoidal) light.
(Photo by E.T.C., Inc.)

E.T.C., Inc. recently brought to the market the first real redesign of the ellipsoidal reflector spot light since its invention some 35 years ago. The Source IV (Figure 10–8) fixture takes it and improves two important areas. First was a reduction in wattage while keeping a high or higher output (depending on lens and throw). Second, with the redesign of the gobo position, the patterns remain relatively cool and do not deform easily, prolonging their life. An improved lens system has made the field flatter and sharper. Although use of this style of fixture is not widespread in concerts, there are times when a sharp-edged light or a pattern is needed. Although it uses multiple lenses, with a little protection, it can withstand the rigors of the road.

The Fresnel lamp has not been totally abandoned, but it is rare to see any used. Other nonplayers in general are the scoop, the beam projector, and the border light.

Cyclight and Farcyc

Concerts have adopted one television fixture: the Cyclight is widely used for lighting backdrops. The design of the reflector and the light output, if not their size, have gained them favor. They take up a great deal of room and do take time to set up, but the advantages outweigh the shortcomings. Several versions are made. For floor mounting, a series of four to twelve lamps in three to four circuits, can be used. Overhead mounting favors the Farcyc, a square of four lamps first used at the BBC studios in London.

In the last few years a new source has been adopted for strip light units. The MR16 lamp has been designed into strip light housings and does find use in concert work. In a turnaround is fair play situation, it was Jules Fisher, famed Broadway designer, who first used the MR16 source in this configuration.

Follow Spots

Truss-mounted follow spots are a rather common device for providing concentrated light on a moving subject. Coupled with a mounting bracket and chair with a safety belt (Figure 10–9), a follow spot can be placed anywhere the designer chooses. The designer does not have to worry whether the building has positions where the lights are most needed.

The smaller HMI (metal halide lamp) units are popular. Newer versions are HTI lamps (metal halide short-arc lamp) in such models as Ultra-Arc's Mighty Arc II, which uses a 400-watt HTI lamp. Lycian's Starklite (Figure 10–10) uses a 1200-watt HMI source. These housings are short but give the throw necessary from on-stage truss positions. The HMI and HTI sources are from 5,000 to 6,000 degrees Kelvin; the lamps are most often used at 5,600 degrees Kelvin, so check the source and adjust your color medium to account for the bluer light.

Front-of-house follow spots continue to be a case of "what we have is what you get" from the venue. It is the unknown factor. Matching and balancing your needs with house-provided follow spots has always been trouble for concert designers. One night they are strong, too strong, and at the next venue they all are in the center when you wanted them on the sides. Or the intensity of two are about half that of number five. . . . It goes on and on. Bring your own? This option is impractical unless you have total control, such as in an outdoor sta-

Figure 10–9   Truss-mounted follow spot with operator.
(Photo by Gene Kirkland.)

dium tour. In arenas it is a problem simply to reach some of the positions to run intercom let alone change a follow spot.

There are several remote-controlled follow spot units on the market. These were designed to remove workers from the trusses, so certainly there is a safety advantage. The Pro-Spot by Morpheus is one such unit. However, you must control it from the ground much like a model airplane controller works. But another idea has hit the market—the Autopilot by Wybron, Inc. This is a system that locates the subject in three-dimensional space, translates the position to pan and tilt for any number of automated moving lights, and follows the performer around automatically. A small transponder is worn by the performer. Its signal is picked up by four ceiling-mounted or truss-mounted sensors that send the information to a computerized control box. The control box is then interfaced with the lighting console. As many as four performers can use this device on the same stage. No more follow spot operator on the truss, no more safety problem. It certainly has its uses.

Projectors

When it comes to projecting slides or intricately painted images, the old 35-mm projector is out. The old projectors do not have strong enough light output, and the slides tend to jam in the carousel when they are mounted on glass. In addition, the format is too small for hand-painted or intricately detailed projections. Enter the first really useful projector. Great American Market was formed to market a projector designed in Japan, the RDS (Ryudensha Co., Ltd.) (Figure 10–11). The projector has a varied array of front-end attachments that can mount 4 × 5 slides as well as moving effects of clouds, water, rain, and more. The lamp is a 2,000-watt tungsten. Although the projector puts out a large amount of heat, a series of heat-absorbing glass filters allows the effects to last without burning. A series of interchangeable lenses is available, and the size, 17"H × 14.5"W × 24" to 30"D (depending on focal length of lens), and weight, between 40 and 50 pounds, make it useful in concert application. I toured with these projectors for many John Denver shows and always found them to be reliable and give excellent images. Now there is a 2.5-kW HMI version 32"H × 24.8"W × 21"D (without effects) that

Figure 10–10   Lycian Starklite follow spot, used widely in truss-mounted applications.
(Photo by Lycian, Inc.)

Figure 10–11   RDS projector, 2-kW lamp
(Photo by The Great American Market.)

uses the same effects heads and lenses but compares favorably with 4-kW units that are much larger. As an example, the OL4 lens, at 25 feet, produces an image size of 24'7" × 29'9" with 42 footcandles; the OL8SA at 25 feet provides an image size of 8'9" × 11'9" at 154 footcandles. They can be flown on the lighting trusses.

The other contender is a European system called Ludwig PANI, represented in the United States by Production Arts, Inc. These are large and heavy units, as large as 4.9'H × 3.9'L × 2'D and weighing 105 pounds. The design and weight make it almost impossible to fly them on trusses. The sources are from a 2,500-watt quartz to 6-kW HMI lamp in the new BP6 Gold model (Figure 10–12). The image sizes can't be beat. The 60-cm lens at 200 meters (218.7 yards) produces an image of almost 40 feet. Their advantage is high-quality lens and lamp output. However, these projectors are designed to be operated by hand or by means of a motor-driven changer. They are built with European (in Vienna, Austria) precision. They are the Cadillac of projectors if you have the time for the care and feeding necessary . . . and have deep pockets.

Searchlights

Finding the strongest light source that can be put into a design seems to be the driving ambition of several concert designers. However, to the designers' credit, the effects and air light patterns they create, especially in the outdoor environment, are spectacular. There are several searchlight units available. Phoebus Manufacturing has a high-intensity xenon searchlight system. A variable speed, programmable revolver base also is available. It comes in sizes from 9 inches to 20 inches in diameter and from 1,000 to 7,000 watts. Sky-Tracker has been on the market for several years. First used as a replacement of the arc searchlights you saw in old war movies and Hollywood openings, these also use a xenon source of 2,000 to 7,000 watts. One of the unique things about Sky-Tracker is that it comes on a base with four heads that can be programmed to move in patterns. These can be seen for miles, like an old-fashioned searchlight in the night sky, and they do receive a great deal of use by auto dealerships, but like any tool available for the designer, they have their place. A single-head unit also is available.

Xenotech, Inc., has a series called Brightlight fixtures (Figure 10–13) that use 1,000 to 7,000 watt HMI lamps. The difference with this unit is that it fits onto the standard movie or television senior stand with a $1\frac{1}{8}$ inch pin. The ballast and control pack can be remote-controlled but it also can be mounted to a motorized base and controlled with a DMX 512 controller. Syncrolite Systems has a 100 SS7k Automated Skylight, which was specially designed for the 1996 Olympics. In Figure 10–14 the powerful beams can be seen shining from on top of the stadium during the Olympics.

Color Changers and Scrollers

The desire to make each lamp in a system serve as many functions as possible was felt right from the start. How could we make our rigs have more color washes and more specials? The physical facts were that we could place only so many lamps in or on a truss. How much dimming could we afford? Would the halls have enough power if we increased the system? With all these questions it is no wonder that at last count 14

Figure 10–12   BP6 Gold 6-kW projector.
(Photo by Ludwig PANI, Vienna, Austria.)

companies were making color scrollers and changers. None of these companies is a large theatrical manufacturer; they are small specialty companies.

A color scroller works by measuring movement of a cylinder. The motor moves the scroll according to how much DMX signal is received. The units all have thumbwheel counters that allow you to daisy-chain them together or retain individual control if you desire. These units can hold from 12 to 16 to as many as 32 frames of color. Most are built to fit the PAR-64 head, but in the past few years larger units to accommodate the eight-light PAR-36 units have been built. Some even fit 5-kW Fresnel units, cyclorama units and some of the searchlights mentioned earlier. One unit has appeared on the market to fit a standard $7\frac{1}{2}$-inch theatrical Leko frame and the smaller Source IV units. One problem has always been accurate return to a color. Wyborn, Inc., has the ColorRam II system (Figure 10–15). This system has sophisticated digital control and uses a self-contained diagnostic card to alert the operator to problems such as low voltage, incorrect gel-string position, head shutdown, or fan or motor problems.

A different approach is taken by Morpheus, Inc. The Pancommand ColorFader (Figure 10–16) is a dichroic color changer. The unit offers unlimited color choices, eliminating the need to assemble and change color strings for the scroller.

Smoke, Haze, and Fog

An important ingredient in concert lighting is some type of medium that enables the audience to see the beams of colored light. This is especially important when air light designs or moving lights are being used. The patterns created over and around the performers would not work if it were not for some means to accent the beams.

Enter theatrical smoke or, more correctly, what appears to be smoke. At least it is not smoke made from combustible materials. At first the only semisafe way to produce a controlled release of a smoky substance was borrowed from film. The Mole-Richardson fogger used an

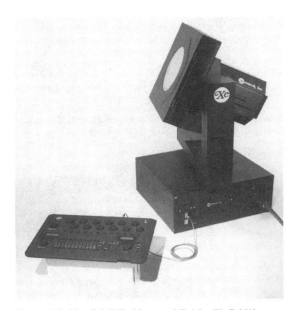

Figure 10–13 Brightlight searchlight with 7-kW lamp.
(Photo by Xenotech, Inc.)

Figure 10–14 Syncrolite system in action at 1996 Olympics.
(Photo by Syncrolite, Inc.)

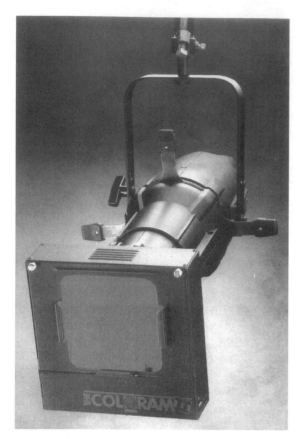

Figure 10–15 ColorRam II color changer.
(Photo by Wyborn, Inc.)

Figure 10–16 ColorFader system. It uses a dichroic system and never needs changing.
(Photo by Morpheus Lights, Inc.)

oil-based liquid that was heated until it vaporized into a cloud of smoke for the effects of night fog, simulated battle scenes, or fire effects.

This proved to be irritating to singers, and the search was on to find a more acceptable product. It didn't take long for researchers to develop products such as those introduced by Rosco Labs. Rosco was even given an Academy Award in the scientific and engineering category in 1984 "for the development of an improved nontoxic fluid for creating fog and smoke for motion picture production."

The current favorite on tour for keeping a haze in the air so that the beams of light are seen is the Diffusion DF-50 fogger made by Reel EFX, Inc. (Figure 10–17). This high-output hazer is approved by the California Occupational Safety and Health Administration (Cal-OSHA). It does not use heated glycol. One tablespoon of material fogs for 60 minutes. The fog is said not to set off ionization smoke alarms and has long hang time, a prime request for concerts.

Different needs demand different products. The dry fogger (Figure 10–18) made by Interesting Products, Inc. is exactly that, a fogger. Fog by definition is a cloud that touches the ground. It is not smoke, which rises when heated, so it gives a different effect. The dry fogger produces realistic low-lying fog effects. It is one of the new breed that does not use dry ice but a nitrogen and water vapor system. There are no chemicals or dry ice to buy, store, and break up for every performance. The nice thing about it is that the pressure is constant. Unlike dry ice, with which the vapor dissipates as the water becomes colder, the nitrogen stays at the same temperature and pressure.

Ultimately budgets and availability may necessitate the use of the tried and true dry ice machine. There are several still on the market. City Theatrical, Inc., of Bronx, New York, makes a good version. We used to build them out of surplus 50 gallon drums; the commercial systems are much better.

The Entertainment Services and Technology Association (ESTA, 875 Sixth Ave., Suite 2302, New York, NY 10001) has a standards program for effects. ESTA in 1996 produced a pamphlet called "Introduction to Modern Atmospheric Effects." In only 20 pages the pamphlet gives the reader an unbiased introduction to theatrical fog, the mediums of delivery, how they work, effective use, and some safety guidelines. To help in your understanding of these areas, I have reprinted the following definitions that appear in the pamphlet.

Cracker a fog machine that generates a haze by blowing pressurized air through a vat of fluid (typically mineral oil or a glycol/water mixture).

Dry ice frozen carbon dioxide (nominal temperature –80 degrees C), an effective cryogen.

Fog a mixture of liquid droplets in air that reduces visibility and reflects light.

Glycol an alcohol with a molecular structure having two hydroxyl groups. Common grain or wood alcohols have one, whereas glycerin has three hydroxyl groups.

Hang-time the length of time that a fog stays in the air without dissipating.

Haze an accumulation in the atmosphere of fine, widely dispersed, solid or liquid particles giving the air an opalescent appearance.

Mist fine droplets of moisture in the air, not as dense as fog, but often of larger size.

Nitrogen a colorless, odorless, non-flammable, gaseous element that constitutes about 80% of the volume of the atmosphere. When cooled to –198 degrees C, it becomes a liquid and an effective cryogen.

Smoke small, solid particles dispersed in air that reduce visibility and reflect light.

Vaporize to cause to change into a vapor (fog, mist, steam or visible exhalation).[1]

Because most of the products in question are of the glycol and mineral oil type, I reprint only the following two definitions from the pamphlet that explain how they work:

Pump-propelled glycol A fog fluid containing a mixture of one or more glycols and water is moved from a reservoir (either a bottle or an on-board tank) into a heat exchanger by a pump. The heat exchanger has been heated to the point at which the fluid vaporizes, usually less than 340 degrees C (644 degrees F). The fluid's own expansion into vapor forces the heated material out the front of the machine where, when it mixes with cooler air, it forms an opaque aerosol. The aerosol is composed of tiny droplets that reflect the light, which is what gives this type of fog its characteristic white coloring.[2]

Cracker [This] fog technology was developed in the 1960s as an improvement over previous fog-making techniques based on mineral oil. Previously, mineral oil haze had been generated by dropping the oil on a hot plate, which heated the oil to just below its flash point. The cracker method is considered to be a vast improvement, because it uses no heat at all.

For theatrical fogs, cracker does not describe a chemical process. These crackers work more like cracking a dinner plate; they enlarge the space between molecules.

The fluid used in crackers is usually high-grade mineral oil. The main advantages of mineral oil are its low vapor pressure and low rate of evaporation, which results in a fog with a long hang-time.[3]

Figure 10–17 DF-50 Fogger, nonglycol haze.
(Photo by Reel EFX, Inc.)

Figure 10–18 Dry fogger. Nitrogen is used to lay a low-lying cloud over a floor.
(Photo by Interesting Products, Inc.)

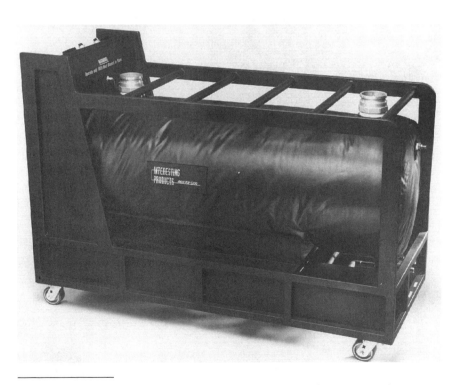

1. Entertainment Services and Technology Association, "Introduction to Modern Atmospheric Effects" (New York: ESTA, 1996), 19. Used by permission.

2. ESTA, 5.

3. ESTA, 12.

At about the beginning of the 1990s a hard look was taken at the increasing use of haze and smoke, particularly by the legitimate theatrical community. Actors and dancers had their misgivings about how the environment of the theatre was affecting their health. So Actors' Equity Association and the League of American Theatres and Producers, Inc., in separate requests asked for a study by OSHA. Their requests prompted the National Institute for Occupational Safety and Health (NIOSH) through its Health Hazard Evaluation Program to investigate. The revised report, Interim Report No. HETA 90-355, was issued November 1, 1992. The initial study was conducted in June and July of 1991: "Four Broadway productions which used theatrical smoke were selected and dress rehearsals were arranged to conduct personal breathing-zone (PBZ) and general area (GA) air sampling and to administer a questionnaire to the actors detailing the frequency and severity of irritant and respiratory symptoms (if any) when exposed to theatrical smoke."[4]

Many of the theatrical smokes currently in use in Broadway theatres, in television, concerts, and motion pictures are produced by means of heating of glycol fluids to produce visible smoke. Some use dry ice and nitrogen-based fog, and a few still use heated mineral oil–based smoke generators (oil crackers).

The NIOSH report continues,

Although theatrical smoke was visibly evident during all of the performances, results from all of the PBZ and GA air samples collected were very low when compared to applicable OSHA Permissible Exposure Threshold Limit Values (TLVs), or NIOSH Recommended Exposure Limits (RELs). For example, acrolein and acetaldehyde, suspected to be possible decomposition products from the heating of the glycol-based fog fluids, were not found on any of the PBZ or GA air samples collected during the survey. **None of the PBZ air samples** had detectable amounts of formaldehyde [bold in original].[5]

The report also analyzed the questionnaires given the actors. It was found that significantly more performers in shows that used smoke than performers in the nonsmoke control production, reported more mucous membrane irritative symptoms and indicated that they had a prevalence of cough, shortness of breath, wheezing, and chest tightness. However, the report concluded that "It is possible that the questionnaire was too sensitive in its design and caused an over-reporting of symptoms by the respondents."[6]

The report concluded in part that,

Although some of the constituents of theatrical smoke (primarily the glycols) have irritative and mucous membrane drying properties, the reason for the high symptom prevalence in the productions that use theatrical smoke is not clear, because the TWA [time-weighted average] concentrations of the glycols measured during the performances are quite low. It is possible, however, that the smoke concentrations can be sufficiently high during the short peri-

---

4. National Institute for Occupational Safety and Health, Hazard Evaluation and Technical Assistance Branch, Interim Report No. HETA 90-355 (Cincinnati, Ohio: National Institute for Occupational Safety and Health, 1992), 1.

5. NIOSH, 1.

6. NIOSH, 20–21.

ods of time that the smoke is generated to contribute to the symptoms reported by the actors.[7]

Although the excerpts must not be construed as a full analysis of the NIOSH report, there is concern enough always to check with the performers with whom you are working before production to see if there are any objections to use of smoke- and haze-producing units. Some artists have it in their concert riders that no glycol or mineral-oil products be used during their performance. So be forewarned.

Smoke is lighter than air. Therefore, air currents take the smoke wherever the wind or hot, rising air wishes to go—not necessarily where you would like to keep it: on stage. Placement of foggers can be a real science. Buildings often do not have the air conditioning or heating on until the audience is about to enter. Besides doors opening and closing, even the heat from the lighting influences where the smoke is carried. Bring along your own fans; one of the best is the Hurricane Blower from CITC in Prescott, Arizona (Figure 10–19). It is not quiet, but then if you are doing mostly concert work, who is quiet? These fans are used by fire departments and commercial services that need to dry flooring. CITC also markets a Director fan that is quiet and moves the smoke in a focused vortex action, allowing the smoke to be drawn up to 75 feet, and can be remote controlled. Last is the old standby, Mole-Richardson's 24-inch wind machine. It is noisy but rugged and powerful.

There is one other way to produce theatrical smoke—the use of some pyrotechnical devices. Use caution; most states require a licensed pyrotechnician to handle these effects.

Whatever you use, always be aware of smoke detectors and alarms, especially in hotel ballrooms. They can be set off by any of the smoke-producing agents. Second, even though all are said to be nontoxic, all carry warnings that irritation to eyes and lungs can occur among sensitive persons. Be sure to check with the artist before using these methods to generate smoke or haze. In many states and municipalities these are considered a pyrotechnic device, and you are required to obtain a permit.

Computer Drafting Programs

I realize that this is an area that strikes fear into the hearts of anyone over 30, but the facts are exceedingly clear. We cannot succeed in the business, or virtually any business, without some knowledge of computers and their ability to cleanly draw an accurate representation of our ideas. Some designers will support the pencil and paper method until the day they die. Their belief that hand drawings are faster and better cannot be shaken. I cannot fight it. Choose to believe what you will. But for the rest of us, computers are here. They help and they are now a necessity in the educational and well as the professional fields of lighting. My firm does not hire interns unless they have at least basic computer skills. We prefer those who have had some computer-aided design (CAD) classes. Because I am over 30, I have enlisted the help of one of my firm's associate designers, Jeremy Windle, to help sort through all the programs.

The first computer programs to assist the designer were tracking programs, such as Rosco's Lightwright®. This is a comprehensive software application that allows the designer to input information normally put

Figure 10–19 Hurricane Blower fan.
(Photo by CITC, Inc.)

---

7. NIOSH, 2.

on paper. The program lets you list each instrument, type and location, color frame size, color, dimmer, channel, gobo, iris, barndoor, and other elements. Lightwright then generates a complete lighting shop order: type of instrument, accessories, color order, and a cut size list. All this saves time. But these are basically bookkeeping programs.

Computer-Aided Design

Lighting designers eventually came to realize the potential of computer-aided design. There are two distinct views of CAD. Jeremy agrees that many who draft by hand can do the job quicker than some who use CAD. When CAD gains exponential value is in quick revisions and ability to run a series of originals on many different types of media in relatively little time. One of the advantages I like is that you can click on layers to see, for example, the set, then click it off for your final print. This keeps the drawing clear of elements that do not help the electrician put the equipment together.

CAD applications allow blocks to be quickly inserted and edited. In a rather simple example we'll define a block for a PAR-64 fixture as a series of lines that resemble a scale PAR can, such as the drafting templates you use in hand drawing. This block may be inserted and moved into the correct position. Information regarding focus, color, and channel is assigned to this block and appears within the instrument as in an ordinary light plot. Should you decide to move that PAR can six inches to the right, simply click the mouse, move it, and release the button, and your instrument is repositioned. No erasures, no mess. The numbers are far more readable than my penmanship! One limitation is that most CAD applications allow information from blocks to be exported to a spreadsheet, but information cannot be imported from a spreadsheet to a drawing.

Specialty Lighting Design Programs

Until recently, whether you were drafting or doing paperwork by hand or computer, it was necessary to list information regarding each fixture on both the drawing and the paperwork. When one was updated, the other had to be updated. With some of the current design software, Autolight Pro, Microlux 2000, JCN CadDriver, and Stardraw to name a few, it is possible for the information to be exchanged between the drawing file and the paperwork files. If an update is made in the drawings, it appears on the paperwork, and vice versa. This is becoming more important as new technology increases the number and type of fixtures it is possible to use. The other common feature is that you can draw the stage on one layer, draw the set on another, and then draw the light plot on one or more additional layers, so that all the information can be printed together or you can choose at any time to turn off a layer and print only the layers you desire.

One word of caution, most specialty lighting design computer programs do have proprietary or native software that might not allow interchange of information between the program you are using and what the equipment service company or theatre is using. Although all have interesting technical and educational assistance qualities, the cost is $1,000 or more.

One last word on the specialty lighting design computer programs. They offer many features, but when you are starting out learning about drafting by computer these features are almost overwhelming. Although these programs allow you to click on a fixture's beam and have it show you the intensity and coverage as you move the fixture around your drawing in two or even three dimensions, most professional designers don't have time for this. I have found myself playing with these features as if the program were a video game more than a design aid. I suggest that if you are not in a computer design class or have access to someone who can assist you, keep it simple to start.

Generic Computer-Aided Design

Generic CAD programs, such as CAD Lite (not referring to lighting), are available for less than $300. What that means is simple, no frills, no program to provide your lists of fixtures. You create everything you need for yourself. As a starting point for a new CAD applications user, this might be the best way to go. These programs do not have the paperwork interlace that the specialty programs do. But once you have mastered this simpler two-dimensional program, it allows you to step up to AutoCAD Release 12 or 13 (three-dimensional graphics) much more easily when the time comes. The CAD programs also allow you to open other CAD files that might be sent to you from a client. The specialty programs do not do this easily or at all. So buyer beware.

Most CAD applications allow you to save drawings in generic formats such as .DXF and .TIF files that can be converted easily into other drawing programs. All computer files can quickly be sent electronically from your computer to someone else's. It is now possible for a lighting designer to send a light plot by modem to the lighting supplier over the Internet in only a few minutes. This allows immediate response and quick changes. Again, I insert a note of caution. Of the equipment suppliers I interviewed for this book, one had CAD in place. Most said that because of the lack of compatibility of the programs, they send a file out to be downloaded and printed by a computer specialty company. I believe this is going to change soon.

How Wide Is the Use of Computer-Aided Design?

In the television field, I regularly receive CAD files of set designs that I can view on computer. I never need to have a hard copy. I can design and overlay my light plot to the file and send the entire integrated file back to the producer. When it comes to architectural work, there seems to be a wholesale shift to CAD, only a few small one- and two-person firms have not gone to CAD. We have found that it is so much trouble working with hand-drawn architectural plans that we do not normally accept jobs from these firms because of the added work we must do for the dollars the client is willing to spend. Economics pushes CAD. Every time a client changes his or her mind, new hand drawings can take weeks. With CAD a change order can take an hour, and you can print a clean set of prints with all the updates incorporated on each sheet.

What You See Is What You Get Programs

WYSIWYG: strange name, but completely clear once you understand where the acronym comes from. The FOUR TO ONE studio is working to meet the increasing need for pre-programming time in which the designer can play a tape and use the road lighting console to set up cues as represented by small lights on a model; however, this is limited to one location.

Pre-programming of light cues before the rehearsal is more the rule than the exception in today's economic environment. Rehearsal time with a full lighting rig and crew is difficult to obtain from the client. Part of the reason is availability of the venue, but the fact is the management is looking at the cost of the crew. Moving lights appear to save time, quantity, and trucking space. What they are is a beast that keeps saying, "Feed me, give me more programming! I can give you an even better show if you only feed me more!"

Once a lighting rig has been planned, it is possible to feed the monster in the comfort of your office or home. The computer, with the help of some programming gurus, has given us a virtual stage. Flying Pig Systems developed WYSIWYG software that interprets lighting console output and presents a graphic image of what would be happening on stage. Figure 10–20 shows a computer graphic made with WYSIWYG and a photograph from the show, "The '96 Juno Awards" television special. The software, including a custom computer card capable of reading DMX signals, is loaded into a computer. The program produces the plot by establishing a virtual environment based on a drawing of the stage that has been added to the computer drawing files. Stage walls, set pieces, risers, and anything else that might interfere with sight lines and that you want to see in relation to the lighting must be added.

Lights, both moving and conventional, are selected from the software library (all DMX controllable moving lights). Vari✳Lite series 200™ fixtures would not work here, but Vari✳Lite series 300™ fixtures would (see chapter 14). Place them where they would actually be in relation to the stage. This is a full three-dimensional simulation, so it is important that the instruments be assigned a height that corresponds to their actual show trim.

Figure 10–20   A. WYSIWYG computer screen showing graphic representation of look created with the light plot. B. Matching live production shot of "The '96 Juno Awards" television special.
(Photo by Steve Austin and courtesy of Flying Pig Systems and CAST Lighting.)

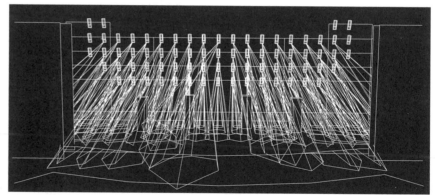

A

B

With the WYSIWYG software running on an independent computer, the lighting console with DMX output is plugged into the computer (consoles with proprietary software, such as E.T.C., do not work with this system). If both systems are configured correctly, it is possible to program an approximation of the show in a virtual environment without ever being on the stage or in a rehearsal hall. The price for all this is about $2,500 at today's price plus substantial computer memory to run it.

Jeff Ravitz used a WYSIWYG program to assist him on the 1995 Super Bowl Half-Time Show. He only got two evenings in the stadium, and one was a dress rehearsal on-camera. There was absolutely not enough time to program all the lights live, he told me. These programs also see wide use by designers doing large televised award shows. Even being able to pre-program looks for the musical numbers can mean the difference between a so-so show and a great one. The last one to get a budget is always lighting, and with the way clients are tightening their financial belts you can expect your request for an additional day of live rehearsal to fall on deaf ears.

Special lighting programs that show light beams, most in the color you select, can be a great help. It is possible to create screen snapshots of looks and after printing them, use them as a story board to guide you and the board operators through the programming. Some even let you write cues, such as LuxArt's MicroLux 2000 program, but they are limited in their ability to fully execute a show, as is a WYSIWYG program. But this is a hot area for competition, and I am sure more development is going on every day. Look for growth in this field over the next few years.

The Need for Better Equipment and the Solution

It would be easy for the lighting manufacturers to say that these advances would have happened eventually. But they cannot deny what Rock and Roll provided: ready cash and no-bid purchasing power. Theatres often take years in planning sessions developing specifications. Most touring lighting companies have one person, the owner, who makes all purchases, which often run as high as a quarter of a million dollars. Rock and Roll brought to the manufacturers a demand for prompt, efficient products and service. It has been a boon to all media because Rock and Roll stimulated the equipment manufacturers where it counted—in their cash flow.

In all the areas we have looked at in this chapter, one main need is present, the need for "roadability." The equipment must be able to withstand the constant bouncing around in trucks all night and be easily set up, used, struck, and packed back in the truck.

Once concert lighting techniques attained a proven track record it did not take long for other media that use theatrical lighting, and even some that have never considered its application, to jump on the bandwagon. The use of any and all of these products does have proved application in other environments.

Our continued livelihoods as designers and technicians require that we stay constantly on the alert for new ideas and techniques to better solve our design and production problems. Chapters 11, 12, 13, and 14 give a closer view of four of the areas I believe are the most important to the widest range of lighting in concerts as well as other fields over the coming decade—consoles, trusses, lifts and hoists, and moving lights.

11

Lighting Consoles

In the past ten years the proliferation of console designs has far surpassed work in every field except computer-controlled moving lights. The need for these new console designs is in large measure a response to what is required to control these same moving lights. Although it might be unfair to say that all the research and development came about purely because of Rock and Roll demands, there can be no denying that most manufacturers now look to our industry as the one with the purchasing power. When you have the purse strings, you have a manufacturer's attention.

Early Concert Consoles

At the time of the first edition, I said that concert designers were not moving to the new computer-based consoles as quickly as I thought they should. I argued that the repeatability they gave was a key to a designer's building a more complex set of cues than was possible with a manual board. At the time, I was talking about the wave of new consoles that had flash buttons and pin matrix arrays and multilevel chasers. As in any small industry, many designers were working quietly on things they used to meet their own needs. This group of tinkerers was really in tune with what was needed. My effort with Electrosonic, Ltd. of England to produce a console that, at the time, I thought was unique (Figure 11–1) was not all that was going on. Michael Tait was busy in England designing consoles. He relates:

> I was designing my own boards and then I ran across a company called Electrosonic. I met one of the engineers, Jetta Park, and at some point I bought a couple of their dimmers. That was in '73 or '74. I then got them to build me a console because I suddenly realized a couple of preset scenes was not what I needed. I needed to switch bunches of lights to keep up with YES. When you were doing all these other things there wasn't enough time to set a few channels and switch from A to B. With this pin program [Electrosonic had] I had this idea that I could have many more presets on full power. So they built the control board which was a 20-channel board with an A and B then ten extra presets on pin matrix. And I still have it; it is over 20 years old and we still use the damn thing.

Michael believes the pin matrix definitely was his idea, maybe not in the United States but in Europe. He realized he needed flash buttons that he could play like a piano. With those added and using a microswitch that Electrosonic built, Tait had the concert console he

Figure 11–1   Electrosonic console circa 1985.
(Photo by Sundance Lighting Corp.)

wanted. He could ". . . play it like a piano. More like an accordion. And flash as fast as my fingers could move; they would respond. No one could make their lights go that fast."

There were similar experiences in the United States. Bob See started building his own consoles. Bill McManus went to EDI (Electronics Diversified, Inc.) and had them modify their theatre console for Jethro Tull's Passion Play tour in late 1971. It was, in Bill's view, the first console with a pin matrix. "You could play it like a piano, and we preheated the lamps so that we got a very fast response and would be right on with the music," said Bill. All these experiences show that individually designers were searching for the most effective way to deal with this new style of lighting. We had visions of what we wanted to be able to do with the lights, but we lacked the technical research and development facilities to make the equipment. So we went to the established manufacturers and, using the power of cash, got them to build what we envisioned. Because many of the same ideas were surfacing at about the same time, it would seem logical that some of the manufacturers would take the ideas and expand on them. On the whole, they did not. Electrosonic in England did to some extent. They published a brochure and manufactured a small run of the console I designed, but their main market was audiovisual control, and they never penetrated the U.S. market. Electrosonic, Ltd. has since purchased another console company, Celco, which started in 1981 and is still active in the concert market.

Computers

In the United States small lighting companies were building early computers (Figure 11–2). I took on the road a computerized console built with components from a small California company called Siltron Corporation, which was headed by lighting legend George Van Buren. He had begun experimenting with computers earlier than anyone else I knew and was marketing a console he called the Sweet Sixteen. The idea was that every 16 channels of control had its own 128 memories. With three panels we had a 48-channel console with 128 storable cues. There was no disk storage for memory. Recording was done by means of manually setting each controller to the level desired and calling up a preset number and depressing the record button. That was it. After recording, you could use the single scene as a manual board. We designed a road case, added nickel-cadmium batteries to hold the memory and a mimic light panel (top right of console in photo). There were no flash buttons. This console was built in 1977 and I toured it with John Denver and then used it on a number of corporate and remote television shows.

I was going two ways. I wanted the hands-on multiscene preset board with flash buttons that Michael and Bill wanted, but I also had shows that I felt needed the accurate repeatability that cannot be achieved with a manual board. The computer also made for the smooth transitions and cross-fades in keeping with John Denver's style. When I would travel with Frank Zappa or the Eagles I would use the manual console Electrosonic had built for me. I matched my needs with clients' styles of music. Those experiences reinforced my belief that a true rock show can be run from a computer. I was able to purchase one of the first new Light Palette consoles from Century-Strand Lighting soon after they were introduced.

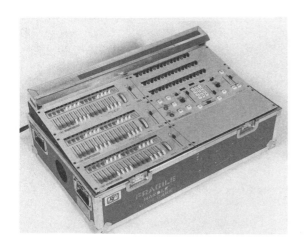

Figure 11–2   Siltron Sweet Sixteen computer console circa 1980s.
(Photo by Sundance Lighting Corp.)

The Light Palette console was delivered to my office and sat in a corner for a few days because there wasn't even an instruction manual for it. Dawn Chaing was writing it, but it wasn't finished. Every once in a while I'd take a break from office work and go over to the machine and push buttons to see what happened. That is how I learned how to run it. I never even hooked it up to dimmers before it was packed up and shipped to Germany for the start of a John Denver tour. I had See-Factor's London office build a black box to interface with their dimmers, which we were using for the European tour.

We had planned on having two days on site to work out the bugs. But the shipper messed up, and the console got there the day of the first show. I programmed it as fast as I could, making many mistakes that wiped out my cues, and I'd have to start all over. John did a two and one-half hour show with no opening act. I put "something" in the memory and held my head in my hands as the audience filed in. There was a preset on stage, and I was ready for my first cue. The house lights went down, and in the blackness of the velodrome I questioned myself. Should I push GO, or should I fade to black, clear, and enter the next cue number and manually fade up using the wheel? I did the latter, and nothing happened! The first several bars of John's opening song were sung in the dark. I reentered the cue number and hit GO. The fade-up occurred in the programmed fade time the way it was supposed to. My nervousness had forced me to question what I had done, and it bit me. After the show in the dressing room, John waited a long time before saying anything to me, and then said, "Did the new console screw up?" I said, "No, I did. The program was right and I questioned it." He never brought it up again.

Moving Light Consoles

Showco and Morpheus introduced their moving lights at about the same time, and we were all amazed. I thought they were going to be a special effect of which people would tire quickly. Michael Tait said he felt the same way when he first saw them, but we were both wrong. A full look at moving lights is found in chapter 14; here we discuss their consoles.

Showco, a successful concert lighting service company in Dallas, was to spin off what they rightly saw as a whole new business and later called it Vari-Lite, Inc. When I first saw the lights they were still under the Showco banner. The company had designed not only moving lights but also a special console to run them. And it used a proprietary computer language. Computer experts call these "native protocol" languages, because they are native to only a particular program. That way no one else could run their lights. The console looked like nothing we had seen before. It had dials and a computer screen and many buttons. It took a specially trained operator to run it. Showco wouldn't even let you look inside one of the lights in those days. Morpheus took a different road. They used a stock theatrical computer, Kliegl's Performance®, to control their moving lights. Of course, in those days, no computer was simple to use.

With the advent of a new type of console, designed only to run moving lights, we were faced with the fact that we, as designers, were not the only ones who were part of a band's creative team. Someone else was playing on our turf. To add insult to injury, they used their own secret language, computer talk. The console was asking us what we wanted to do with the X-Y axis. It was a whole new ball game.

There was a period when those two companies were the only ones in the game when it came to moving lights. Slowly others appeared. The drawback initially was that the lights came from disco equipment manufacturers and were built for installation, not the road. Although it is far from true that Showco and Morpheus had all the bugs out of their systems, these new pretender units were not road ready. But our interest is in the consoles. They certainly were different, and I believe they helped bring concert designers around to the fact that a computer can be used effectively to run a show.

Sophisticated Manual Consoles

At about this time (circa 1972) the theatre manufacturers were about to enter the computer age in a large way. They seemed convinced that there was no market for manual boards any more complex than a two-scene preset. They still did not see Rock and Roll as being a market. Not that the introduction of computers was wrong. Anything that gave the designer more flexibility was great. But the manufacturers saw their market as educational institutions. It is true that as far back as 1966 at UCLA we had a transitional console that was a computer-assisted, multipreset model. George Izenour had designed it and his students at Yale had built it. It used preset cards attached to two large rotating drums that spun to access the presets.

Computers were finding use in some Rock and Roll tours as stand-alone units. Early successes were the Kliegl Bros. Performer series and the Light Palette by Strand, especially with middle-of-the-road acts. In general, however, manual boards such as the Avolite QM-500 boards (Figure 11–3) had multilevel functions and features that allowed instant manual control of complex cues. All Avolite boards featured the now standard flash button array and pin matrix, but the larger units even had a computer to give 400 discrete memories on 20 faders. One unit came with an alphanumeric display available in several languages. The chase mode offered 20 memories in more than 1,500 steps. This was the start of the hybrid consoles. They incorporated the best of what was available from both worlds. Here again, it was the British and their thinking that gave us these sophisticated manual boards.

New or more powerful manual boards are still being brought to the market, and still it appears that the British are in the lead. Although Avolite still commands a large piece of the market, Celco of England, until recently, produced a line of similar boards. The Celco Gold (Figure 11–4) is a 90-channel, two-scene preset console that can control 512 dimmers. It has 30 cue faders and 15 pages of cue storage for a total of 450

Figure 11–3   Avolite QM-500.
(Photo by Avolite Production Company, Ltd.)

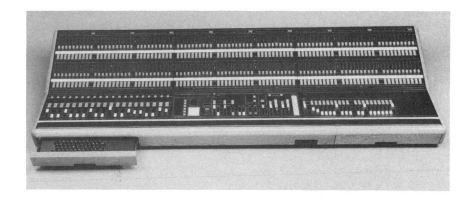

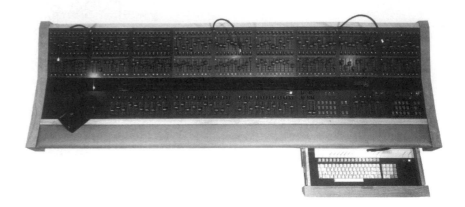

Figure 11–4 Celco Gold console.
(Photo by Celco, a division of Electrosonic, Ltd.)

cues. Its chase holds 24 sequence patterns in a total of 2,376 steps. It has flash buttons, a visual display, and cassette storage for the memory. Even though this console is no longer in the Celco catalogue, the company is taking about ten orders a year, especially from Japan, as reported by their representative.

The Avolite QM 500® has been around for many years. It is still the preferred console for many, many light board operators.

Hybrid Consoles

In the United States the race didn't seem to have anybody at the starting gate to join in. So there is a lag between the 1980s and early 1990s when U.S. as well as British manufacturers began introducing a whole new breed of consoles for the concert market. Part of the reason for this new style of console was the introduction of moving lights that did not have to be run by a factory technician. The Intellabeam® by High End Systems, Inc. was the first moving light built to be sold. And sell they did. Night clubs and discos wanted them. Tours wanted them, but the units had a rather un-user friendly rack-mounted console with a joystick. Not exactly what we wanted for the road. The new United States Institute for Theatre Technology (USITT) DMX 512 protocol made it possible to run these moving lights from almost any console. It was not easy and it took a great deal of channel space because one channel was needed for pan, one for tilt, one for color, one for the dozer, and so on. You had to multiply that by each unit you wanted to control.

As more and more manufacturers came on line with their own version of the moving light, it became obvious that there was a need for consoles to run them. Vari-Lite, Inc., still maintains its own line of consoles for its series 200 moving lights. However, the company does not sell the consoles; it only leases them. Morpheus Lights and High End Systems, Inc., maker of both the Intellabeam and the Cyberlight® as well as the new Studio Color® unit, do allow their lights to be purchased and run from any DMX compatible console. Vari-Lite, Inc., now has moving lights that can run on DMX 512. They can be rented and run with any compatible console without the company's technician. So there was a rush to design consoles to take advantage of all the things moving lights could do and make the programming process understandable.

There are a number of consoles designed to work with moving lights. These consoles differ from conventional theatre consoles in their ability to control a number of parameters, called *attributes*, simultaneously (some fixtures have as many as 20 attributes) and build cue sequences in an efficient, flexible manner. A parameter, or attribute, is any single function of a moving light, including pan, tilt, color, gobo (template), diffusion, or intensity. Instead of calling up one parameter and modifying it individually, a fixture or group of fixtures is chosen, and all parameters are edited at once. The designer no longer has to remember as many as 20 or more channels per fixture.

One early console came from a service company, See-Factor, Inc., in Long Island. As they tell it, when the first moving lights based on non-proprietary protocols first became widely available, it didn't take the company long to realize that programming them was a nightmare. At that time there was a console for each style of moving light, plus a console for the fixed lamps. To keep all the different consoles in rental stock was a problem. Enter the Light Coordinator® from See-Factor, Inc. (Figure 11–5). It can handle up to 500 moving lights or up to 500 fixed lighting channels simultaneously. It operates on any protocol, even different ones at the same time. The design is modular, so the console can be rearranged to suit the operator's needs. The cues can be accessed one of three ways: by means of the 20 submasters, as a one-key go sequencer, or stored as 20 separate chases with 250 steps each loaded into a slider. One of the nagging problems with moving lights is the number of attributes needed to run them. Most consoles require multiple wheels or handles for operation. The Light Coordinator handles the attributes as a unit, not as several channels. So programming is faster.

Celco, while building on its position in the manual board field, introduced the Navigator®, which would operate any DMX compatible moving light on 240 channels. It does not have a two-scene preset, instead relying on the wheels for programming the attributes of the moving lights. The operator accesses the channels, like those on a modern computer console, by entering a numerical channel number and then setting a level by entering a number as a percentage of the intensity. Show operation is by means of 12 submasters to access the cues or a time fader for the stacked cues. The more advanced Aviator® (Figure 11–6) handles 512 channels with a pre-programmed moving light

Figure 11–5   Light Coordinator console.
(Photo by See-Factor, Inc.)

Figure 11–6   Celco Aviator console.
(Photo by Celco, a division of Electrosonic, Ltd.)

library to save programming time. Attributes of most moving lights are already entered for quick access. The console has a 1,000-cue memory and 20 submasters for a sequenced playback mode.

Avolite with its most sophisticated console to date, the Diamond III® (Figure 11–7), keeps the familiar, tried and true design for which it has become famous. The company took a 60-channel, two-scene preset board with 20 submasters and added all the moving light control wheels and function pads. They advanced the two-scene preset idea by making all 120 faders available by means of function buttons to work as much more than a two-scene preset. With a cue capacity of 2,000 for 3,072 channels this is a powerful board. Avolite went one step further and designed a light-pen palette board to allow fluid programming of moving lights without use of the wheel (although the wheel is still there). The operator touches and drags the pen to indicate position and move the light or group of lights to the desired pattern. The operator selects a color from the rainbow color pad simply by touching the light pen to the desired color. The monitor shows a stage plan to make pre-programming easier.

As of this date, the console that has attracted the most attention for flexibility is the aptly named Whole Hog II® by Flying Pigs Systems, Ltd. (Figure 11–8). The concept is led by touch-screen window displays that can be arranged in any way and moved or sized to suit the operator. It has a complete library of fixtures, meaning that once told how many there are of each fixture type, the computer patches the parameters to the correct channels and names them. Along with the patch library comes a library of colors and gobos already programmed to match most manufacturers' standard fixtures. This library is constantly updated and easily obtainable from the Flying Pig Internet site (http://www.flyingpig.com). With the use of external monitors to show channel assignments and cue list, the console itself is compact. It also has a 2,000-channel capacity and is reported to have one of the most powerful microprocessors in the field. It operates on some of the ideas of the Vari✳Lite console, which is a dedicated or native protocol system and not available to the public.

Theatre Consoles

It would be unfair not to mention the many advances in what I would call consoles designed with more of a view to traditional theatre and

Figure 11–7   Avolite Diamond III console.
(Photo by Avolite Production Company, Ltd.)

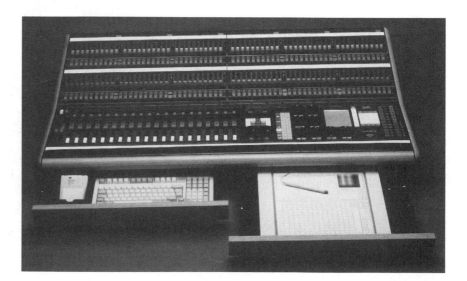

Figure 11–8   Whole Hog II console with expansion wing.
(Photo by Flying Pig Systems, Ltd.)

television—not that all of the aforementioned consoles have not been used and in some cases installed in large, nonconcert production environments. The field of computer lighting consoles has grown to the point that costs of the most sophisticated and feature-laden models are within reach of even educational institutions. Strand Lighting is still a leader in this area. The Light Palette series is still going strong with the latest version, the Light Palette 90® (Figure 11–9), which handles 4,000 channels and 600 cues. E.T.C., Inc., has risen to be one of the top manufacturers because of its innovative products. It also excels in consoles. The Expression IIX® (Figure 11–10) meets the theatre and television market of today. Both these consoles are flexible, allowing for multiple protocol access and programming and control of scrollers and/or moving lights. However, they both take the approach that moving light programming is not a priority function. You must still enter all the attributes. The consoles do not have pre-programmed groups for the available moving lights, as the hybrid consoles do. It is possible to control them, and if you have the time, to program, but what is becoming more and more popular is to link two consoles. This is not to take away

Figure 11–9   Light Palette 90 console.
(Photo by Strand Lighting, Inc.)

Figure 11–10 Expression IIX console.
(Photo by E.T.C., Inc.)

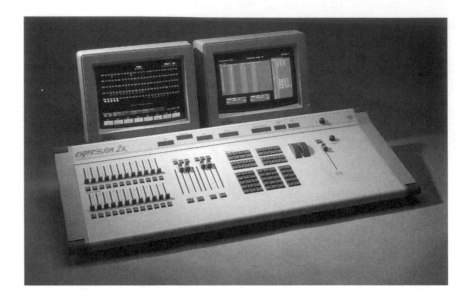

from these fine products. Many designers find that they can function excellently for concert production. There are many of both styles in use on the road.

In the first edition of this book I wrote:

> The shows are getting bigger and bigger and one console to run the PAR lamps and other dimmable lamps, and a second console to run the moving lights are needed. How long do you think it will take for someone to decide that what we need is a console that does both?

Strand recently introduced a concept that allows cues programmed on another console, such as a hybrid model, to be melded with cues programmed on its console. The show can be run from one console; the need is eliminated for two operators during production. This is a powerful advance. As theatrical musicals, corporate presentations, and Las Vegas shows and concerts have moved into the realm of more than 1,000 lamps, both fixed and moving, shows have needed as many as three and four operators. This advance should be a welcomed concept that makes production easier.

The Next Step in Console Design

I believe that the next step in console design will be a continuation of merging the consoles we now have to provide programming and show functions and address all a designer's tools, from fixed light to moving light to scrollers to show control of scenery and motors. An all-inclusive console that allows the designer to master all electronic functions into one console. The machine would have feedback loops that tell the operator whether a lamp is under load, check the circuits for overheating or potential shorts, indicate voltage at the lamp, and perform many more functions. We should have a uniform system of protocol or a device that allows a designer to pre-program a show in real time in three dimensions and then record a floppy disk and put it into any console and play it back. Right now almost every manufacturer has some sort of proprietary system that does not allow this to happen. Some of the walls are coming down, but it will take a while.

Actually, some of my dream has been realized in the WYSIWYG programs discussed in chapter 10. Because of the increased complexity of lighting, less time for rehearsal, and more demands on the designer to create more and more spectacular designs, we as designers need a full range of tools that allow us to program in advance what we need for a show. There is no longer the option of sitting with a director in a darkened theatre calling up one channel at a time and writing cues—in professional theatre let alone concerts.

12

Lighting Trusses

The use of found space for a theatrical production is not new. Barns, grassy fields, arenas, and all manner of multipurpose rooms have been used for stages. The elaborately equipped buildings designed for large symphonies and opera as well as those built specifically for drama in the early twentieth century are still in the minority. Because nearly all of the large theatres were built with stage houses of a similar size and design (except for thrusts), it was relatively easy to bring in a touring opera or theatrical production. Most of the buildings had permanent lighting pipes in neat rows to provide lamp support. But what about unequipped buildings?

The First Trusses

Early Rock and Roll concerts were deemed not of artistic merit by many city and college theatres and were generally relegated to the school's gymnasium. Where do you hang lights in a gym? Bring the structure to mount the lights with you. Create a performance area in the found space. Constructing portable units that could be trucked easily from show to show was the goal.

Portable units also needed time-saving features. To make money, recording artists traveled and performed in a different city almost every night. A play usually has a run of a week or two with possibly a day or two of rehearsal to adjust to the particular theatre. For concerts, speed was important. The solution to this new problem was hit-and-miss at first, but as more people took it seriously new design ideas emerged. Creative people took on the challenge, and a whole new design world was born: a structure, somewhat like a bridge member, that allowed the designer to place lamps overhead instead of on standing poles or trees.

The structures themselves have no historical precedent in theatrical design. The first truss for touring music was designed by Chip Monck and Peter Feller with Bernie Wise for the 1972 Rolling Stones tour. The lamps were not left in place when packed for traveling. The truss was ground supported. In 1973, a box truss with fixtures mounted for travel inside the truss was designed by Bill McManus with Peter Feller and Bernie Wise. It was the first (hung) truss grid and measured 50 × 28 feet flown with CM Lodestar hoists. It was designed for the Jethro Tull tour that year, The Passion Play. Other young Rock and Roll companies such as Showco, Tom Fields Associates (TFA), and See-Factor were right behind them in developing individualistic designs that with each new tour brought fresh ideas to the scene.

Triangle Truss

Triangle trusses fall into two groups: commercial towers and specialty trusses. Those built commercially as antenna towers are available in several widths and tubing sizes. Because these trusses are designed primarily for vertical stress, they usually cannot be used horizontally without some bowing or sagging. When the trusses are flown, however, the pickup points can be placed strategically so as to eliminate this problem (see Spans).

Commercially made versions specifically designed for lighting use copy this type of construction but are designed to withstand the horizontal stress and loads we place on them. Some of these specialty trusses are constructed of a heavy chrome-moly, but most are of a lightweight aluminum construction. Although the initial cost is low, repeated tightening of C clamps compresses the tubing, shortening the useful life of these trusses. Because more research and load testing have been done on these specialized trusses, such as the one shown in Figure 12–1, the safety factor has been increased. However, exercise extreme caution in the use of commercially made products that are not specifically designed for horizontal stress.

Two types of design are used in triangle trusses. The first is a solid triangle in 10-foot lengths. Widths range from 12 inches to 30 inches. The second design is constructed with a hinged joint at the top and a spreader bar attached on the horizontal side (see Figure 12–1). Removing the spreader bar allows the sides to close for compact storage. In both cases, fixtures must be attached once the truss is supported in position. For a one-time production, this may not be a problem, but the following disadvantages should be considered before using these trusses:

1. The fixtures can be focused safely from the ground only with use of a ladder.
2. Fixtures must be attached and plugged each time the truss is set up, a time and labor disadvantage.
3. Because fixtures must be attached to the triangle, the usual method is individual attachment by means of C clamps or hanger straps on

Figure 12–1 Triangle truss, folding.
(Photo by See-Factor, Inc.)

either end of a six-lamp bar. Adding 60 to 200 C clamps, at about two pounds each, is an undesirable weight gain.

A few modified triangle trusses do travel with fixtures inside the structure, but they are not the rule.

Square or Box Truss

Square or box trusses come in a variety of configurations. Some, even though constructed as rigid units, still necessitate hanger straps to mount the fixtures to the structures on site. Two such box trusses are shown in Figure 12–2. They can be used not only to mount lighting fixtures but also to rig drapery and sound systems. The center unit is a six-way corner block used to join trusses in several configurations.

Other box trusses are large enough for semipermanent internal mounting of the lamps to Uni-Strut bars or T connectors. The prerigged truss section shown in Figure 12–3 is 91 inches long and 20.5 inches square and holds two lamp bars of six PAR-64 fixtures in the transport position. Pins are released, and the bars extend below the frame for use.

Taking a cue from the folding triangle truss, Total Fabrication designed a folding box truss (Figure 12–4) for easy shipping.

Trusses can be built to accommodate single or double rows of fixtures. Figure 12–5 shows lamp bars in the lowered position. Casters allow easy movement around stage before rigging. The side view (Figure 12–6) shows the offset mounting used for a better focus angle. The lower left bar is removed after transport for unobstructed focus. In Figure 12–6 the casters are on the back of the truss so they do not hang below it.

Figure 12–2   Box trusses. Front, 12-inch square unit. Center, corner block. Rear, 20.5-inch square truss.
(Photo by James Thomas Engineering, Ltd.)

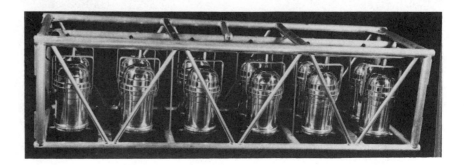

Figure 12–3   Double-hung box truss with fixtures loaded for transport.
(Photo James Thomas Engineering, Ltd.)

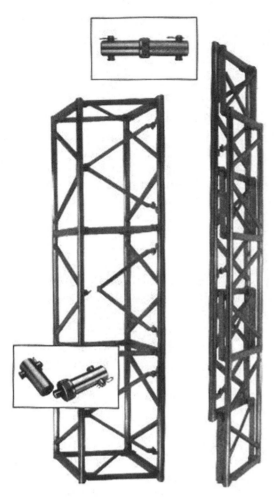

Figure 12–4   Folding box truss.
(Photo by Total Fabrications.)

Figure 12–5   Box truss, lamps extended.
(Photo by Pete's Lights.)

Truss Design

There are as many variations on the theme of truss design as there are companies designing and building them. Each company believes its design offers the solution to a particular problem, such as speed in setup, strength, lamp capacity, or method in which the sections are interconnected. For flexibility in design application, remember that whether you mount lamps internally or not, the four sides of the box and even the ends are available for mounting, so bottom corners can be used as well as top corners.

An advantage of truss use is the flexibility afforded by corner blocks and angle blocks to connect truss sections into shapes. The concert designer's truss layout is discussed toward the end of this chapter.

Because of the basic structure of a triangle, there is not much room for creativity in internal design. The box truss, however, has spawned some highly creative modifications of its basic form. One design by McManus Enterprises has a cable tray in the top so that cables need not be disconnected for packing in separate boxes (Figure 12–7). Another folds open to make two levels of fixtures; in the closed position, it provides its own protective case. In several designs, the lamps extend out from under the box truss when in position so that the structure does not interfere with the beam of light.

In location video lighting, the only problem in using trusses is that most are built to accommodate PAR-64 fixtures only, and a 2-kW Fresnel lamp might not fit inside. There are companies that provide trusses to hold some larger fixtures, but I know of no trusses that hold a standard-size 5-kW Fresnel lamp internally. When a 2-kW or 5-kW Fresnel lamp must be used, a large triangle or box truss on which the lamps are mounted externally is the easiest solution to a one-time location problem.

Moving lights have caused another problem: their size and electronics have made them not good for conventional premounted trusses. Both Morpheus (Figure 12–8) and Vari-Lite, Inc., have specially designed trusses for their fixtures. Recently the Obie Company introduced a generic moving light truss under its banner, CTS Trussing. This truss allows moving light fixtures to remain mounted during transport. The truss has a shock-mounted lamp bar. The truss units are bolted together while on their casters. The lamps are fully available to be

worked on or tested before the system is flown. The vertical truss cords provide a siderail to assist technicians working on the truss. Figure 12–9 shows how the system works.

Engineering and Construction

Most trusses are built of aluminum tube #6063-T5 in 1-inch and 2-inch outer diameter or HE 30 alloy, and with a fairly heavy inside wall thickness. Chrome-moly is being used less and less, although it is less expensive and easier to weld than aluminum. The added weight of chrome-moly, which is about twice as heavy as aluminum, is not desirable for touring. If the trusses are for semipermanent installation, chrome-moly should be considered for its cost alone. Its other advantage is that it can be welded whereas aluminum must be heliarced. A welder does not have to be as highly skilled to arc weld as to use a heliarc machine.

Although steel welding is less expensive in materials and equipment, and labor is more readily available, steel is seldom used in the United States, largely because of its weight and because of the controversy surrounding employment of amateur or semiqualified welders. This can cause a tremendous liability problem, which should be avoided. This is a highly experimental area, and the potential for a wrongful death or injury suit is substantial.

You can purchase trusses from one of the several companies in business strictly to sell trusses and not to design touring lighting. Make sure you are provided with engineering stress information, such as the form from Penn Fabrication, Inc., in Figure 12–10. Because it does not load the lamps on the trusses, the company cannot be held responsible if you misuse the truss.

The engineering of trusses is critical. This is the main reason one-time shows should not try to construct their own trusses but should lease them from an established concert company. If you are considering construction, I recommend you use only certified welders. Although

Figure 12–6   Double hung box truss, internal support, off-center lamp bars.
(Photo by Sundance Lighting Corp.)

Figure 12–7   Truss stack with cable trays.
(Photo by McManus Enterprises.)

Figure 12–8 Morpheus moving light truss.
(Photo by Morpheus Lights.)

actual construction time can be about five days for a 40-foot truss, it is essential to have a certified structural engineer design or check your idea. The added cost and time of this step are reason to lease if your project is short term or to consider purchasing if the project is long term. Be sure to ask the company for a certification of structural stress and load capacity. This can be done by specialized engineering firms and should cost less than one thousand dollars, depending on the procedures used and how far you carry the tests. Figure 12–11 shows the basic procedure to test trusses for load.

Spans

Because there is a large difference between the strongest and the weakest truss, a certificate of load capacity is important. Moreover, the clear spanning capability of the truss must be determined. Some trusses can be supported only up to a clear span of 40 feet. Not only the length but also the size of the tubing and design of the truss must be considered. Truss sections generally come in eight- and ten-foot lengths. The rental companies help you fit your design into the lengths they have in inventory. Even better, contact the company and obtain a breakdown on what is available before you begin a design.

Now that most trusses are flown, the full 40 feet of a standard portable stage is usable. (Ground support lifts reduce the usable width to 32 feet.) That is why 40 feet is considered the average truss length. Larger productions, however, are now calling for 50- and 60-foot lengths.

It is rare to see lengths more than 40 feet being ground supported. If your stage requires a truss more than 40 feet wide, it is time to consider a flown system. Why can a longer truss be flown when it cannot be ground supported? The solution is found in placement of the pickup points. Bridles (flexible nylon webbing or quarter-inch aircraft cable) are composed of two overhead load points of lesser load-bearing capacity joined to lift a heavier load. They help to distribute the weight evenly. It is common for a 40-foot truss to have two motor or winch pickup points approximately five to ten feet in from each end. These usually are bridled about four to six feet apart. The proper bridle configurations for a

A

B

Figure 12–9 CTS truss designed for moving lights. A. Truss turned on end with lights securely captured. B. Truss with sides folded up, feet extended, and security cage exposed. C. Truss with security cage disconnected and about to be removed.

(Photos by The Obie Company.)

C

given load must be determined by a qualified rigger. The example in Figure 12–12 shows some of the calculations needed to determine the stresses.

Flown trusses are safer than ground-supported trusses. Out of necessity, the ground-supported trusses are at the mercy of many factors, such as a stage with uncertain construction that can collapse under the weight. In several reported cases, lighting companies have refused to set up a ground-supported truss because they deemed the stage unsafe.

Integration of Electrical Connections

The electrical raceways and cables attached to a truss affect the structures. There are several methods of getting power to the fixtures; the simplest method is for fixtures to be wired on site. Other methods are use of standard Socapex six-circuit multi-cable and making a connection to the end of a six-lamp lamp bar, as in the Total Fabrications prerigged truss shown in Figure 12–13.

The standard electrical raceway takes this method a step further. It is either placed on the truss once on site or attached semipermanently to the truss. The inner connection of the fixtures can be easily accomplished if the lamps are to be mounted each time, or they can be patched and left for the run of the production if the raceway is an integrated part of the truss. The fixtures also can be permanently wired to a raceway. The last method, however, inhibits design changes and fixture replacement and is generally considered inefficient for any use other than a straight all PAR-64 production design.

Also available is the Intelligent Power System (IPS) shown in chapter 10. The system has dimmers as well as pin connectors fitted directly into the truss. Only a DMX signal and AC power for the six dimmers are required to be brought to the section of truss.

D

E

Figure 12–9 CTS truss designed for moving lights. D. Truss with legs ready to be retracted and system flown. E. Truss with four moving lights ready for show.
(Photos by The Obie Company.)

Figure 12–10 Sample structural stress test results, Penn Fabrication, Inc., Moorpark, CA.
(Reproduced by kind permission of Penn Fabrication, Inc., Moorpark, CA.)

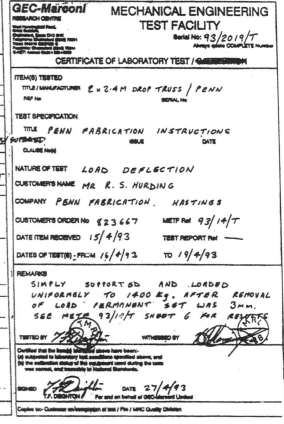

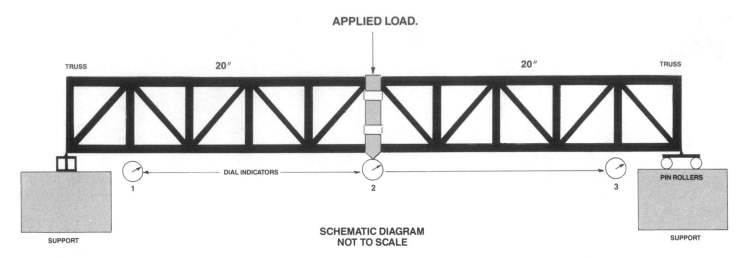

Figure 12–11 Sample truss load test.
(Provided by Rigstar Rigging Inc.)

Figure 12–12 Rigging bridle.
(Provided by Rigstar Rigging Inc.)

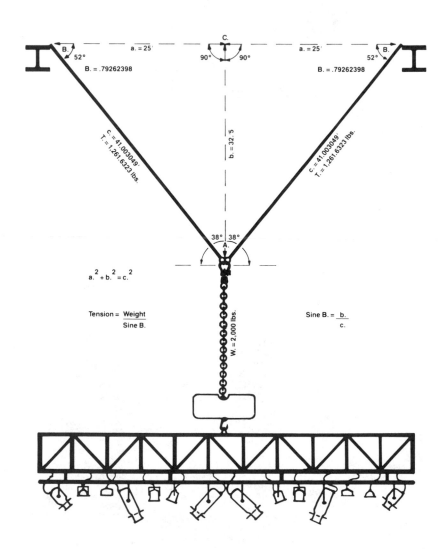

There are several choices to be made. Most limiting is what lighting equipment companies have in stock or what the show's budget allows for purchase.

Figure 12–13 Pre-rigged truss with six lamp bars.
(Photo by Total Fabrications, Inc.)

Figure 12–13 Pre-rigged truss with six lamp bars.
(Photo by Total Fabrications, Inc.)

Lighting Grid Design

A total lighting grid can be formed with one type of truss or with a combination of sizes and designs. It is not uncommon to see a single square truss in the front and on the sides and a double-row truss in the back for the more important back light.

Trusses are joined together in several ways. End blocks with bolts, aircraft fasteners with a ball-lock capture pin, cheeseboros as used on scaffolding, and other highly specialized connectors are designed especially for this use. Some trusses have been designed in such a way that a single-row truss attaches to another to create three or four rows of light. The way in which the designer lays out the configuration of trusses to accomplish the lighting needs is limited only by the load limitations of the lifts, winches, and motors used to place these structures in the air (Figures 12–14 through 12–18).

The simple tour design in Figure 12–14 consists of two 32-foot trusses supported by super lifts. The backdrop also is hung from the truss. Figure 12–15 shows a unique design that allows cable to be easily

Figure 12–14 Two stage-supported box trusses.
(Photo by Sundance Lighting Corp.)

Figure 12-15 Truss grid with catwalk.
(Photo by Showco, Inc.)

Figure 12-16 Overhead view of flown lighting trusses and drapery trusses.
(Photo by Sundance Lighting Corp.)

routed from truss to truss and gives a catwalk for focusing. The lighting trusses in Figure 12–16 were surrounded by a truss grid of drapery that was raised by means of motors. It created a three-sided house curtain to conceal the stage before the performance.

Figure 12–17 Mirror truss, Genesis show.
(Photo by Showco, Inc.)

Figure 12–17 shows a design of lighting trusses with motorized Mylar mirrors used by the rock group Genesis. Spots positioned upstage were aimed into the mirrors and the beam bounced back onto the performers. The angle of the mirrors was changed to allow the light to follow the performers around the stage. The early concert design for Kiss entailed a hexagonal configuration (Figure 12–18). The truss design was an important part of the total stage design.

The photographs for Figures 12–14 through 12–18 were taken before fall arrest equipment became available.

A designer should consider the capability of the roof structures of the halls before using a flown truss layout. Although the designer is not expected to be a qualified rigger, some understanding of the type of venues and what shows have played in the room previously is a good guide. Consulting a tour rigger before you are committed can spare you problems.

Advantages of Trusses

A truss that has been loaded with fixtures and cables and has been checked in the shop before going to the location saves on-site setup time. The efficiency of the structure means that less labor is used in the field. This does not mean the main reason to use a truss is to put people out of work. Trusses still require labor to prepare them in the shop. They do, however, reduce the producer's on-site costs and often also mean fewer people on the road, which saves hotel, travel, and per diem expenses. Use of trusses can mean savings of a day or more of on-site setup time, which translates into possible rental savings. More important, it may be the only way to enable the production to fit into the tight schedule of the facility.

Figure 12–18   Hexagonal truss grid.
(Photo by McManus Enterprises.)

Trusses provide a convenient, adaptable lighting system, but the safety element must be reemphasized. The problem of getting lamps to a fixed pipe 20 feet in the air produces a hazard. I have ducked out of the way of many falling items during such load-ins. The problem of working at this height rather than at ground level is obvious. Trusses have been in use since the 1970s and have proved themselves reliable and efficient in supporting lighting of all types as well as draperies, projection screens, and scenery. Their adaptability for use in film, television, and theatre rigging has brought them into common use. Use of trusses is a flexible and safe method of mounting lighting, drapery, scenery, and other materials under less than ideal conditions.

One other thing becomes attached to trusses—people. A popular design element is a follow spot placed on a flown truss to give creative angles not possible from house positions (see chapter 10) I have two notes of caution. First, never place someone on a ground-supported truss if movement has not been secured with a safety device of some type. Second, place someone on a flown truss only after the supplier and rigger have approved the trussing and its rigging for such use. If you climb the truss for any reason, wear your fall protection gear.

13

Lifts and Hoists

When trusses were first used as a solution to the problem of lamp support, they were, for the most part, ground supported. When they began to be tied to a building's structure, a process called *rigging*, several elements had to be considered.

First, many of the buildings did not have adequate structural supports to hold the added weight. Second, the cost of hiring riggers was prohibitive. As lighting systems and production complexity grew in later years, there was no choice but to use rigging. This meant that the tour had to be moved to larger indoor facilities such as basketball and hockey arenas. Or they had to be expanded outdoors to football and baseball stadiums, where the concert tour brought not only the lighting rig but also the roof.

The market for artists playing in smaller settings is still thriving. How can shows be expanded but avoid rigging? The logical solution is improved ground support. Devices used in the construction trades have been adapted for touring use. Units already were on the market to allow workers to change light bulbs and mount materials overhead in buildings.

What follows is a summary of some of the types of lifts both adapted for concert use and designed specifically for concert use. Not all manufacturers are represented, but every generic type of lift I found is presented. Special attention is paid to the ones that have received the most use through the years. These items represent savings of thousands of hours in labor. They make the difference in doing shows with the lighting available rather than limiting bookings to theatres with existing structures. These lifts are a key to bringing theatre, dance, opera, and other entertainment to portions of the population that do not have equipped theatres in their communities.

Nonhydraulic Lifts

Genie Tower

The Genie Tower lift is a commonly seen device originally designed to hold commercial lighting fixtures in position during installation. It was the first widely used lift for concert lighting. Fully extended, the unit has a maximum height of 24 feet. Compressed air is used to operate a series of aluminum columns. Maximum lifting capacity is 300 pounds up to 20 feet, 250 pounds up to 24 feet.

The advantages are quick setup and compactness in shipping. One disadvantage is that the lift can stop only in a fully extended position

Figure 13–1 Genie tower with light frame.
(Photo by Sundance Lighting Corp.)

unless restraining cables or chains are used. These cables also prohibit the columns from rotating freely. Another disadvantage is that improper leveling causes air to leak from the seals inserted between column sections. When this happens the tower loses pressure and the columns compress. Use of this unit for support of a truss is not recommended.

The most widely used application for the unit is to lift 12 to 18 fixtures, supported in a frame or on pipes placed in the holes in the head of the unit (Figure 13–1). Many crews also box the tower and lamps in a protective hard-sided case or open steel framework (shown in Figure 13–1) for transportation and quick setup.

I have not seen any of these devices on tour for many years, but I suspect that many regional rental companies still use them. Caution should be exercised, because the manufacturer did not design or approve these units for this use. I show them more for historical perspective than for recommendation as a modern device.

Genie Super Tower

The Genie Super Tower operates somewhat like a Vermette lift. Although it uses wire rope over a series of pulleys, it has a unique advantage. The safety braking system is approved by the Occupational Safety and Health Administration (OSHA). Another advantage is that the columns nest inside one another and are pulled out as you crank the forks (Figure 13–2). The telescoping sections allow the structure to be used at less than maximum extension.

There are two models of Genie Super Tower, 20-foot and 25-foot models, with a load capacity of 800 pounds for the ST-20 and 650 pounds for the ST-25. These units have three types of base configurations, all with excellent leveling jacks. It must be noted that Genie Industries was one of the first outside companies to take a real interest in concert touring needs. It was developed by company president Bud Bushnell and Bill McManus.

Air Deck

The Air Deck is a compressed air–operated lift that is an adaptation of the Genie Tower. Essentially, it takes three of the Genie air columns tied together with a basket on top to create a lift for a person (Figure 13–3). Normally not used in lifting trusses, the Air Deck is popular as a follow spot platform and as a focusing platform. It has operating heights of 24 and 36 feet. The unit weighs 351 pounds and has a traveling height of 7 feet, 5 inches. It is marketed by Upright Scaffolding, Inc.

Many of these units are purchased by facilities to clean windows and change light bulbs, so they are found quite easily. The air tank used is the same as that used by soda vendors, so often when we run low on air, we can borrow from the concession stand.

Hydraulic Lifts

Several oil-operated ram lifts are available. These also are borrowed from the construction industry. Although models can go high (45 feet), the weight and size usually prohibit using them for touring. Load capacities of 500 to 1,600 pounds are available. These lifts have the same disadvantages as Genie Tower lifts. If the load is not directly over the column, the seals are broken and the unit can slip. Although they are

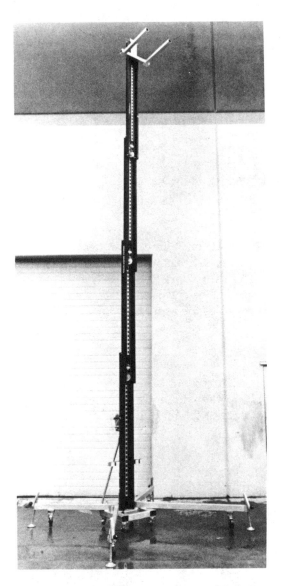

Figure 13–2 Genie Super Tower.
(Photo by Genie Industries.)

difficult to travel with, I have used these units on three occasions. It is a matter of finding the item that suits your needs, not of being restricted to what you see in theatre books.

Flying-Tiger

The Flying-Tiger lift is a sell-propelled, electrohydraulic elevating work platform that has a payload of 1,000 pounds and goes up to 27 feet in the air. It is of the scissor lift variety and weighs 1,200 pounds. The larger version is called a Flying-Carpet and extends to 36 feet with a larger working platform.

Tel-Hi-Scope

The Tel-Hi-Scope is only one of a large group of hydraulic, single-ram lifts that can be AC operated on external power or operated with batteries mounted on the unit. Models come in 24-foot and 45-foot versions and can carry loads up to 500 pounds. The 24-foot unit weighs 1,500 pounds and the 45-foot model weighs 3,900 pounds. The obvious first problem is weight. Other disadvantages are that these units cannot be disassembled and they have a minimum clearance height of 6 feet, 7 inches. Because of the oil reserve, they cannot be tipped on their sides. Double-ram units can go higher and carry up to 5,600 pounds, but the units can weigh up to 8,000 pounds.

Special Units for Lighting

Because of the unique problems of touring, several concert lighting companies have developed their own lifts. Although some companies are in the market to sell their lifts, most do not. Because of the nature of our work, it is good to see development of products to meet our specific needs. These products were developed on the basis of actual usage, so they are safe when used as recommended. If you need ground support, the first items you should check are products like the following ones. These units represent only a few of the ideas.

Show Tower

The Show Tower is a self-erecting ground support unit capable of lifting one ton to a height of 28 feet. It uses a CM Lodestar chain hoist for power. The base is constructed of carbon steel, and the mast is 6061 aluminum alloy. This design is not patented, and it has been widely copied in both the United States and Japan.

Thomas Tower

Although Thomas towers also use CM hoists to raise the trusses, the hoists ride up with the truss rather than being secured at the base as with the Show Tower. The lifting capacity of one ton is the same, but the Thomas lift is two feet taller than the Show Tower at 30 feet fully extended. The towers are erected after the truss is assembled (Figure 13–4) and are placed inside the box of trusses (Figure 13–5). Note that six towers in Figure 13–5 are lifting the total grid. The motors are not synchronous but travel at a close enough speed to keep the grid reasonably level. Control units allow a single motor or any combination of motors to work together.

The Thomas Tower is 12 inches square. The total system is designed to lift a box truss with a maximum span of 40 feet. An optional base with outriggers allows a tower to stand alone (Figure 13–6). Figure 13–6 shows the base detail with a CM Lodestar motor attached. The light frame holds 36 PAR-64 lamps.

Total Fabrications Ground Support Series

These products were designed specifically for raising full lighting grids. Two different load handling ranges are available. The 2,000 kilogram (two ton) version has a maximum height of 10 meters (32.8 feet). The 5,000 kilogram (five ton) version has a maximum height of 15 meters (49.2 feet). The structural calculations were done for Total Fabrications by a highly regarded engineering consultant and meet the British standards for their use category (Figure 13–7).

Crank Versions

Some towers use hand cranks. At one time Morpheus Lighting designed a flat ladder with a base and cables much like the Vermette except there are no lift forks. The Morpheus lift is easily climbed for focusing work. Stabil-lift is another hand-cranked lift; it uses a triangle tower but with much the same result as the Morpheus lift.

Rigging and Hoists

These are a few ways to accomplish rigging of trusses. Devices made for this purpose are limited. The other methods of rigging are ones developed by individual companies and have not gained wide acceptance.

Figure 13–3 Air Deck.
(Photo by Sundance Lighting Corp.)

Figure 13–4 Thomas Tower being erected.
(Photo by James Thomas Engineering, Ltd.)

Figure 13–5 Thomas Tower with lighting grid.
(Photo by James Thomas Engineering, Ltd.)

Figure 13–6 Thomas Tower as stand alone light tower.
(Photo by James Thomas Engineering, Ltd.)

Chain Hoists

On large systems, the circus approach to rigging is taken. By means of securing cables to the ceiling support beams of the building, a truss or grid can be lifted and suspended. The most widely used method involves a CM Lodestar motorized chain climber (Figure 13–8). For concert purposes, the motor is used in an inverted position. Special modifications must be made for this application, however, and they should only be done by a factory-authorized agent. CM Hoists, the manufacturer, is aware of the touring applications and works closely with road technicians and rental houses to ensure proper maintenance. A certification program is in effect through the manufacturer.

The load rating of the hoists in this series is from one fourth of a ton up to five tons. The main limitation is that the chain can fall out of the collector bag. There have been reports of slippage or brake release when the motor is disengaged. Many of these problems are due to poor operator handling and should not be interpreted in any way as the fault of an unsafe product. CM Hoists is a concerned and helpful company that has always worked closely with the touring market. The worker using the device has a great responsibility to make sure the device is checked frequently and used properly at all times.

How the hoists are attached to the trusses is up to the user. The placement and size of each hoist are determined by the rigger. Figure 13–9 is a photograph of a flown lighting system with at least eight chain motors visible. Note the bridles on the two upstage points. In Figure 13–10 the motor to the left is bridled to the lighting truss to distribute the lifting load to two points instead of one. The horse bucket catches the chain as the motor climbs up the suspended chain.

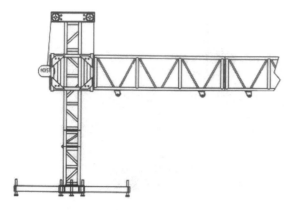

Figure 13–7   Total Fabrications tower.
(Drawing by Total Fabrications.)

Figure 13–8   Worker with CM Lodestar motor.
(Photo by CM Hoists, Inc.)

Other motors now are used for this purpose; Stagemaker by Verlinde of France sees quite a bit of use, as do Chain Master from Germany and Rigstar from the United States.

Motor Controls

At first the need to get the motor into the air was pretty simple. You plugged into power and pressed a rocker switch on what became known as the *pickle*. If you needed to raise two motors at once, you held one in each hand and had someone eyeball them as they went up to keep the truss relatively level.

When full grid lighting systems arrived, more coordinated control was needed. Panels were made that allowed the rigger to energize one or several motors on a single master switch. Other people spotted the movement so that everything stayed level. When it did not, the master switch was turned off, and individual motors were raised or lowered until everything was even again. Then the process started all over. The norm was that after the trusses were raised to the height the designer wanted, assuming the ceiling or high steel allowed for it, the control box or pickle was disconnected so that they were not accidentally moved.

When designers decided that besides having lights move why not have trusses move, more sophisticated devices were devised. At least a dozen companies make inexpensive motor control patch and low-voltage control devices. The skjonberg Control, Inc., CS-800 model (Figure 13–11) is designed for motion control of up to eight motors. Units may be linked to control up to 32 motors. There is a 25-foot remote switch control box with LED indicators for each hoist.

For more complex control, skjonberg Control has a hoist control system with a microprocessor base. Hoist-mounted sensors enable the user to execute complex hoist cues with precise repeatability and safety (Figure 13–12). This system is also used for in-show movement of trusses and other devices.

Safety First

The lift and hoist methods discussed herein are representative of what is now in use in the field. None of these items is foolproof. Accidents occur mostly because we are using these devices for purposes other than what they were designed for by the manufacturer. Safety should be the watchword for anyone using these methods. Consult the manufacturers. Most of them have become interested enough in the concert use of their products to offer suggestions for proper use. They want to protect you and themselves from lawsuits.

Use a skilled rigger whenever hoists are involved to protect the building as well as the audience and the production company. In the final analysis, the safety of the performers and the audience should be our prime concern. There are hoist schools that travel around the United States sponsored by CM Lodestar and other manufacturers. It is highly suggested that you attend one, even if you are not a rigger. It gives you a much better understanding of what you are asking for when you design your truss configuration.

Figure 13–9 Flown truss with at least eight motors.
(Photo by Sundance Lighting Corp.)

Figure 13–10 Chain motors with bridle.
(Photo by Sundance Lighting Corp.)

Safety is number one, so always call out loud and clear whenever a truss is being raised or lowered and keep the area under the trusses clear of people.

Figure 13–11   skjonberg CS-800 motor control for eight motors.
(Photo by skjonberg Control, Inc.)

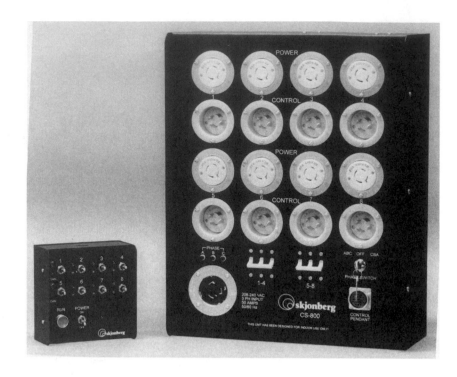

Figure 13–12   skjonberg Control microprocessor-based control system.
(Photo by skjonberg Control, Inc.)

14

Moving Lights

The most radical change in all of theatrical lighting in the past 30 years must be the advent of the modern, remote-controlled, computer-based (programmable), moving light. And the revolution is not over yet. The introduction of the Vari*Lite fixture in September of 1981 by Showco, Inc., in Dallas, stunned the concert community. They were surprised not only because of the innovative quality of the product but also because the manufacturer was not looking to sell a product. It only leases the system.

How could the giants of the lighting world miss this idea? Remote control of fixtures actually has been around for a long time. In my trips throughout the world, specifically what I saw in Japan's NKH television studios and the BBC studio in London in the early 1970s, as well as in Germany, I became aware of the early use of motorized lights. What made this such an historic introduction? One explanation is that the established lighting community saw it as a Rock and Roll effect only and did not visualize its potential for use in theatre and television. This is not the first time the mainstream has been slower than Rock and Roll to pick up a concept. (The list is long, including PAR-64 lamps, trusses, multi-cable, and portable packaging of dimmers.) Again tour lighting ingenuity had taken an existing technology and improved it tenfold.

The History of Moving Lights

While trying to put this new development into perspective I contacted some people who I hoped could fill in some of the historical background. One of those conversations led me to Mr. Louis Erhart, a Yale graduate who had assisted the legendary Stanley McCandles from 1932 to 1934. Erhart joined Century Lighting in 1937. In 1941 he helped establish the West Coast factory operations, retiring as vice president in 1972. I called him to find the historical facts on these foreign installations only to be told that American ingenuity had not been lacking. Erhart produced a copy of a data sheet on a fixture Century marketed as the Featherlight. It was the outcome of a joint venture with Paramount Studios to develop a commercially salable remote-controlled fixture.

The story of that fixture started at the end of 1949, when production began on Cecil B. DeMille's cinematic spectacular *The Greatest Show on Earth*, which was released in 1952. A unit was desired that could be mounted high in the big top without an operator. A Mr. Hissorich is credited by Erhart as the developer for Paramount. The joint venture ultimately produced a fully automated television studio in New York in the mid 1950s (NBC Studio H). Unfortunately, some people thought that it meant the potential loss of jobs, so they reportedly did everything possible to sabotage the concept. It is too bad they did not realize that automation increases productivity, thereby increasing usable production time and the need for even more crew. This has been proved in studios in Japan and London. Sadly, the Century/Paramount project was dropped soon after the studio opened. The designers cited technical shortcomings in motor design, which could have been resolved if they had been willing to stick with the concept. Several of these units still exist and were in working order at Los Angeles Stage Lighting until that company closed in the 1980s.

A British firm also has come forward with information about an early product. Dennis Eynon founded Malham Photographic Equipment, Ltd., in the early 1950s. He met William Cremer in Paris in the early 1960s. Together they collaborated on many projects, including the Top Rank Bristol Suite, circa 1963. They installed Cremer's Mixlights (Figure 14–1) to project patterns onto the balcony walls and with 45-degree mirrors to project patterns onto the dance floor, according to James Eynon, Dennis' son and currently codirector of a company called Malham Lighting Design, Ltd., in London. To quote a letter written by James Eynon on August 7, 1995:

> The Mixlight was a development of a 1000w spotlight which contained 2 colour changing systems. One was a conventional colour wheel with gel colours in an aluminum segmented wheel. The other was a four blade paddle wheel with perforated gel panels, which rotated axially in a plane at 90 degrees to the conventional color wheel.
>
> These projectors could also take gobo's (made from perforated metal) or glass patterns made from standard patterned glass. These projectors were not remote controlled, but changed continuously and used mains 240w ac synchronous motors supplied by Crouzet of France. The projectors had been formerly used at an exhibition "Formes et Lumieres" in Liege (commissioned by Phillips).

William Cremer was somewhat eccentric it seems. In a few years he left the company in the hands of his secretary, bought a yacht, sailed the Caribbean, and wrote novels. He returned to Paris and ran a restaurant until committing suicide in 1980. Dennis Eynon now lives in Ireland.

The letter goes on to recount that after a falling out with the Rank Organization, Cremer concentrated on television studio designs for his remote-controlled devices. He developed a 1,000 watt spotlight that had motorized pan and tilt and could be focused remotely. After, the Rank Organization, persuading Cremer to sell them components, continued supplying Top Rank, Bristol Suite, and at least two other ballrooms.

The units in Croydon, England, had six functions: pan, tilt, focus, iris, blackout shutter, and color wheel. It is thought that the iris mechanism was supplied by Strand Electric. The motors were from Crouzel of France, and as far as can be determined were 240 volts AC. Control was by means of hard wiring through spiral cables to an operator panel, which had momentary switches.

In more recent history Showco, a successful concert lighting and sound equipment supplier in Dallas, started working to develop a color changer for a PAR-64 fixture. Finally in 1980 a team headed by Jim Bornhorst, then an audio engineer and console designer who worked for Showco; Brooks Taylor, software designer; Tom Walsh, digital hard-

Figure 14-1 Photo circa 1960 of William Cremer, holding the control of his Mixlight, and Mr. Dennis Eynon.
(Photo courtesy of Malham Lighting Design, London, England.)

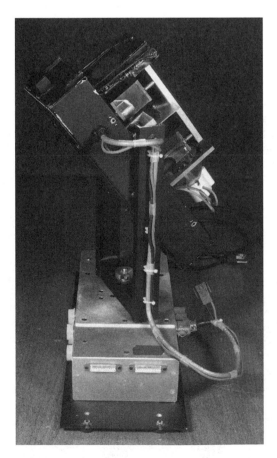

Figure 14-2 Bench test of original Vari✳Lite (VL Zero).
(Photo by Showco, Inc.)

ware designer; and John Covington, analogue system designer, drew upon a couple of emerging technologies: dichroic coated glass and metal halide lamps.

Rusty Brutsché was president of Showco, Inc., and guided the project from start to finish. He was considering dropping the add-on color changer idea for a completely new fixture. In the fall of 1980, Brutsché and his partner, Jack Maxson, along with Bornhorst and other Showco employees were having lunch at a local barbecue restaurant. In a discussion of the feasibility of building a new dichroic filter-based fixture, Maxson remarked, "Two more motors and the light moves. . . ." An all-out building effort ensued and by December of 1980, a prototype and a controller existed. Brutsché decided that the group Genesis would be a likely candidate to preview the system, now know as VL Zero (Figure 14-2).

Brutsché and Bornhorst flew to London to present the idea to the band members. In a hayloft of a 500-year-old barn in the English countryside, they executed two simple cues. A band member exclaimed, "I expected the color, but by Jove, I didn't know it was going to do more." With that an active personal and business relationship began between the two groups.

On September 25, 1981, in a bullring in Barcelona, Spain, Genesis opened their Abacab tour with 40 Vari✳Lite prototype luminaires. The audience gave an immediate reaction the first time the lamps came on and moved into the crowd. Each time it happened crowd reaction grew. "I remember thinking that we had seen our little system work its magic with the music and knowing that things somehow had changed," said Bornhorst on the occasion of the 15-year anniversary of that night in Spain.

According to Tom Littrell, also with Showco in those early days,

Vari-Lite, Inc., engineers began the entire project which was to become the Vari✳Lite by thinking in terms of a wholly unified system of automated luminaires and control. The GE Marc 350 bulb, designed initially for slide projectors, had made its appearance in the entertainment world in truss-mounted follow spots and came to the attention of Jim Bornhorst and his team in the late 1970s. They also began to investigate dichroic glass as a permanent color medium not susceptible to heat. The Vari-Lite, Inc., engineers created a practical fading color changer built around the properties of dichroic glass and packaged it, along with the new arc source, into a realistically sized stage lighting instrument.

Photographs of the bench model (Figure 14–3) have only recently been revealed to the public. I thank Rusty and Tom for sharing this wonderful piece of history with all of us. For many years, Vari-Lite, Inc., was very quiet about how everything worked because they feared patent infringement. Their fears came true, and for the past few years they have had to defend their patents in court. There have been lawsuits between them and both of the other large manufacturers.

As a personal note: It is a sad part of any business, but it is correct for anyone to defend what they believe in. I have worked for years with all companies involved and believe that they entered into their designs honestly believing they had created something unique. But, just as you have heard in other parts of this book, it is easy for people working secluded in various parts of the world to believe they were the first. I hope that the outcome of all the lawsuits is that we move forward with everyone having their rights protected equally.

Current Development

None of this historical look at early development of some form of motorized, remote-controlled lights should be taken in any way as lessening the efforts of the highly inventive work done in the late 1970s and present. I am in awe of the later inventors' creativity and desire to advance our media.

The sudden rash of moving lights, motorized yokes, programmable fixtures, and computer-controlled fixtures, all names for the same general product, started with two nontraditional manufacturers: Showco, Inc., a touring lighting and sound company in Dallas, followed a year later by Morpheus Lights, Inc., a San Jose, California, touring lighting company. The development of each product took a similar path but had interesting variations on the theme. Some two dozen other companies are now in the field with more offering new entries every month. Some are close copies, but to their credit, many have added features that have enriched this

Figure 14–3   VL Zero.
(Photo by Showco, Inc.)

innovation. So the Rock and Roll moving light has obviously outlasted expectations that it was only a gimmick or short-lived effect light.

If there was a stigma on these lights as being Rock and Roll lights, that prejudice seems to have been overcome. Television, especially, took to them. Vari-Lite, Inc. even received the Award for Outstanding Achievement in Engineering from the Academy of Television Arts and Sciences at the 1991 Emmy Awards for the development of the Vari✳Lite Series 200™ automated lighting system. It again was honored in 1994 for the development of the silent, compact VL5™ Wash Luminaire.

Corporate theatre is a large user of moving lights, and Broadway has started to make them indispensable, starting with *Starlight Express*, *Will Rogers Follies*, *The Who's Tommy*, and *Miss Saigon*, to name just a few. Films such as *Streets of Fire* and *Batman* have also used them.

Rock and Roll has proved that each fixture, with its ability to be repositioned, change color, add patterns automatically, and even sometimes change focus, is a very valuable tool. Even the least expensive units can give you a ballyhoo effect for your money. The range of functions is as wide as the companies the lights come from. Whereas it was a very small group that had the money and ability to use these lights in the 1980s, in the 1990s and beyond the market is open on every level. Moving lights are as likely to be seen in a display window as at a Broadway show, in a corporate show as in an opera. The uses and variety of the tools available under the generic name *moving light* have not seen their zenith. I could never hope with this book to cover the entire field. The fixtures shown are among the leaders for a number of reasons that are explained, but that does not mean that other units do not have value.

Cost and Availability

Pancommand Systems was a sales company formed by Morpheus Lights, Inc., to handle their moving lights and their own console, the Commander. The company stopped using the Kliegl Performance console in 1992. Although the company was closed by Morpheus around 1995 because of financial reorganization, the present company, Morpheus Lighting, is coming back strong with a new range of products. It has used its unique take on the moving light and color changer to develop fixtures that designers have requested. Vari-Lite, Inc., continues to handle all its own marketing and does not sell the fixtures or the technology. They do provide leases and long-term rentals as well as touring systems. They have, at today's count, 19 offices to make the equipment locally available.

Another company, High End, Inc., has concentrated on a sales effort for its products. The company works with local lighting companies to make rental systems available around the world. Martin also has an extensive sales effort for its Roboscan series of moving lights. The introduction of the Coemar NAT 2500, a very powerful moving light, by The Obie Company in Los Angeles, exclusive distributor in the United States, put that company in the game as a major player. Light & Sound Design, Inc., in Newberry Park, California, has its Icon family of luminaires and consoles that are only leasable. This company has offices in several large cities in the United States and abroad.

It should be clear by now that although some companies want to keep a very hands-on approach with their clients, even Vari-Lite, Inc. has relaxed its hold, no longer requiring that one of their employees run the system. The company offers a school at its facility in Dallas to teach operators the system, but it still does not sell the product. More companies sell their moving lights than do not. Your needs and budget are the determining factor on which units you use.

As a purchased item, the cost of moving lights is unquestionably the highest of any lighting product we use. The lease cost has been reduced substantially. With concert lighting equipment supply companies making purchases of some of the higher-end units, the prices have become competitive. Recent figures supplied by Bill McManus suggest that, as an example, he can rent ten Intellabeam units and an operator for $2,500 a week. Vari-Lite's price for a minimum order of 12 lights depends on the units, length of rental, and other factors, so no pricing is available. So many new products are currently being introduced that it is difficult to say what the next step will be. Certainly we have not seen the end of the expansion in this area.

Vari-Lite, Inc.

A separate company was set up to handle the manufacturing and marketing of Showco's new product. The Vari✱Lite® is described as "a self-contained computer-controlled lighting fixture." The unit consists of an upper box assembly that houses the lamp power supply, pan mechanism, and other electronics. The lamp housing, or head, contains the lamp, color mechanism, mechanical dimming system, and tilt control. The upper box is also where all the mounting hardware attaches. All of the fixtures are controlled by a multiplexed digital signal distribution system. This means that a single three-wire microphone cable from the computer provides the control data for all fixtures.

The original Vari✱Lite used a GE (General Electric) Marc 350-T16 lamp that could produce 140 foot-candles at 40 feet with a color temperature of 5,600 degrees Kelvin. It took two seconds to rotate the unit 180 degrees, and the position was accurate to within one degree on either axis. It had a mechanical douser that went from full on to full off in less than one-half second. The beam spread was varied by means of choosing any of eight available aperture openings.

Probably the most important feature was the color system. The unit produced 60 colors by means of dichroic filter wheels rather than standard color media. It could change color in one tenth of a second. Besides the 60 preselected colors, it is possible to dial in a mix of your own colors at the computer console.

The original fixtures were controlled by means of a custom computer console with proprietary protocol processing. The processors and cue memories were in the lights themselves, and a high speed bidirectional datalink allowed them to achieve a sophistication level that a central processing system can't give in large rigs, according to Rusty Brutsché. Because of this, Vari-Lite products cannot be run from any other console, except those designed by Vari-Lite. The original console could store 250 cues for 96 fixtures. There was no tape or disk-drive storage; the unit used an integrated-circuit storage. Cues were written for each lamp or for groups of lamps and could be retrieved at will or in sequence. The board operator also could manually control any feature of any fixture during a cue.

Keeping the company vision of providing a fully functioning automated lighting system, for the next string of introductions, the talk turned to "intelligent" lights. The Vari✱Lite 2™ (VL2) was a high-performance unit that could produce 1,000 foot-candles at 20 feet with an HTI lamp.

Tilt was increased to 270 degrees with panning ability of 360 degrees. The unit weighed 58 pounds, and at 8 $\frac{1}{2}$ inches by 17 $\frac{1}{2}$ inches it was quite compact. The full unit, with control head and lamp, is 25 $\frac{3}{4}$ inches high. The unit was given a precision iris and could be remotely focused to a hard or soft edge. It had an aspheric lens system. Reflecting advances in dichroic technology, the unit had 120 colors that could be accessed in 0.12 seconds. Another unique feature was something called Vacu✱Dep™, which allowed the user to design custom patterns (very expensive). The unit held nine standard or custom patterns on top of an internal pattern-gobo system.

I wrote *was* because Vari-Lite, Inc. introduced the 200 series with an updated console, called The Artisan®, to handle increased abilities. The 200 series included the VL2 spot luminaire, which was soon eclipsed by the VL2B™ (featuring the Dichro✱Wheel for instant access to more than 120 colors and a 400-watt arc source) and VL2C™ (a 600-watt metal halide arc source, enhanced focusing and defocusing of gobo patterns), and the VL4™ wash luminaire (featuring the Dichro-Tune™ color tuning system and a high-speed douser). The 200 series was the second generation of advances from this highly inventive company. But the company still wanted to control the systems and did not allow other consoles to operate the fixtures. Most of the VL2Bs are gone, but some of the VL2Cs are available.

The Vari✱Lite 3™ (VL3) was soon replaced by the VL4™ wash luminaire in 1989. Described as a "wash luminaire" by the manufacturer, it uses a new 475-watt, 53-volt tungsten lamp at 3,200 degrees Kelvin that was custom designed for the unit. A beam spread ranging from an aircraft landing light (ACL) type beam to the field of a medium PAR-64 lamp is possible with the unit. The color system for the VL3 uses a Dichro-Tune color-tuning system. It has a fully tunable system that allows the designer to gradually dial through the spectrum to achieve the precise color desired. "Some designers just get hung up on one they like and won't let go," said Suzan Tesh, of Vari-Lite's Los Angeles office.

The third generation of Vari✱Lite is now with us. There are many changes, but the change that pleased other manufacturers of consoles was that the 300 Series of luminaires can be controlled with any DMX console. The main physical change was that the lamp power supply was moved to a remote location and the upper housing eliminated, making the unit smaller. The electronics that were in the upper enclosure are now in the yoke. Vari-Lite also finally let others into their game. You can still only rent or lease the fixtures, but you no longer

Figure 14–4 The Artisan® Plus Console from Vari-Lite, Inc.
(Photo by Lewis Lee © 1997 Vari-Lite, Inc. All rights reserved.)

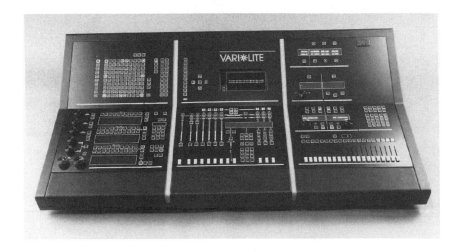

Figure 14–5 **VL5™ wash luminaire from Vari-Lite, Inc.**
(Photo by Lewis Lee © 1997 Vari-Lite, Inc. All rights
reserved.)

Figure 14–6 **VL6™ spot luminaire from Vari-Lite, Inc.**
(Photo by Lewis Lee © 1997 Vari-Lite, Inc. All rights
reserved.)

need the company technician to run the console, and you can pick from
any console capable of moving light control.

Vari-Lite, Inc. did add a new version of its own console. The Artisan®
Plus (Figure 14–4) console and the mini-Artisan® 2 console are what run
the family of fixtures today. The Artisan® Plus provides manual and
programmed control of up to 1,000 channels and 2,000 control cues per
channel. This console comes equipped with a Power Macintosh 6100/
60AV including a 230 MB Magneto optical disk drive. The miniconsole
also can produce 2,000 cues for the 1,000 Vari✳Lite fixtures or conventional lighting instruments and is linked to an outboard Macintosh.

Noise from cooling fans is not a problem in Rock and Roll, but it is in
other markets. Fan noise was the issue that was holding back acceptance of the fixtures in musicals and opera. The newest of the family
that address this problem are the VL5™ wash luminaire (Figure 14–5)
and the VL6™ spot luminaire (Figure 14–6).

The VL5 wash fixture uses either a 1,000 or 1,200 watt tungsten halogen lamp coupled with a cold-mirror reflector that removes heat from
the light beam, eliminates internal fans and associated noise, and
reduces heat on stage. The prototype of this fixture was unveiled at
Lighting Dimensions International (LDI) Trade Conference in 1991.
They were answering the cries from designers who wanted a warmer
light, low maintenance, better cross-fading color palette, and DMX on
board to widen control access. They also wanted to get the price down
so they could use larger and larger quantities on productions. Because
the VL5 is an incandescent lamp, it needs an added dimmer.

The VL6 spot fixture is low profile, lightweight, and virtually silent,
because it has two wheels for interchangeable color and gobo selection.
It used the Philips MSR 400-watt short arc lamp in a cold mirror reflector to provide superior brightness in an affordable package.

Is this the end of the VL series? Not according to anyone at Vari-Lite.
The company has a 60-member-strong research and development force
in Dallas that works to push the technology forward. Just before I completed this manuscript, Vari-Lite announced the VL5A™ wash luminaire. The advance is a new 700-watt, 5,600 degree Kelvin arc lamp
combined with a fluid-filled plastic membrane diffusion mechanism to
provide powerful automated beam angle variation. There is also a
VL5B™ for those who want a pastel color palette. These lights are
housed in the same VL5 frame and can hang on 18-inch centers.

Morpheus Lights

When Morpheus Lights entered the moving lights market soon after
Showco, the company initially introduced two fixtures, a spot type and
a wash type luminaire. These lights were an immediate hit with
designers because they were two of the main beam styles with which
the designers were used to working. Morpheus also has moved on to
second-generation innovations.

The PanaSpot® is a unit much like the Vari✳Lite fixture. It has a single housing for all control functions and motors. The General Electric
Marc 350-T16 is the lamp of choice. A mechanical douser is used to dim
the light, but the unit does have a fully functioning iris instead of the
template idea Showco used. There is a slot for a mini-ellipse-sized pattern. The beam size is altered by a magnifying iris. The beam varies
from 2 degrees to 25 degrees. Color was provided with a boomerang
setup of seven user-selected colors.

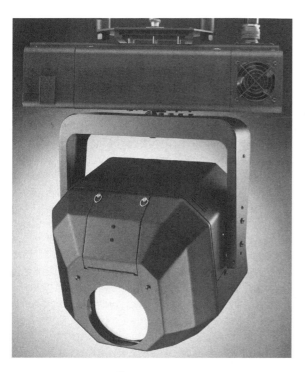

Figure 14–7 PCSpot® from Morpheus Lights, Inc. (Used with permission.)

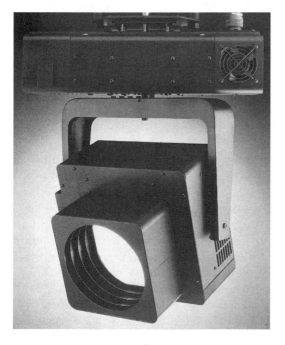

Figure 14–8 FaderBeam® from Morpheus Lights, Inc. (Used with permission.)

The other fixture from Morpheus is the PanaBeam®. Although similar to the PanaSpot in size and somewhat lighter, the light source is a standard PAR-64 lamp. Any beam width can be used, including an ACL lamp. No dimmer is built in, so provision needs to be made within the regular dimming system for intensity control. This unit uses a scrolling color changer with six colors and clear.

Morpheus took a different road by not designing a custom console. Rather they chose to use a stock Kliegl Bros. Performer 2 computer console, assigning each unit a position by means of the soft patch. This console allowed 125 lamps to be controlled and 225 cues to be stored. The thinking was that because the console was mass manufactured by a mainstream lighting company it would control the moving lights and any standard theatrical lights at the same time. Repair and replacement were easily provided by the Kliegl dealers around the world, so service was simplified. Morpheus also uses a native protocol to run its systems.

The new family from Morpheus contains many advances. The PCSpot® (Figure 14–7) has a new lamp source, a 600-watt HTI. An important factor is that the complete unit weighs 50 pounds. Centering is reduced to 20 inches. The tilt coverage is increased to 270 degrees and 360 degree continuous pan. Proven zoom optics provide a 5 to 35 degree beam spread.

The PCSpot is the first unit other than the Vari✳Lite to use a dichroic color system. However, it adds a ten-frame scrolling system to provide color correction, diffusion filters, or special colors the designer may require. Nine pattern holders are built in, and four are capable of rotating with programmable speed and direction, which makes for some very nice added movement in the light besides pan and tilt. Patterns are combined with the zoom lens to control the actual pattern size. Remote focus of beam from hard to soft is still possible.

The other fixture is the PC-Beam®. The lamp was a 1,000-watt FEL, and the unit has an internal dimmer. A parabolic reflector produces variable beam spread from ACL-type to wide floor PAR fields. Color is provided by means of an 11-frame scrolling changer. Weight is a lean 20 pounds per unit, which includes dimmer, fixture head, and electronics. This unit also is preprogrammed with looks built in; 100 are stored. These looks can be used as programmed or modified for user needs.

Morpheus exchanged the PC-Beam for the FaderBeam® (Figure 14–8) in 1992. It is similar, but has some advances. The same FEL lamp and internal dimmer are there, but the color system has been replaced with a patented fading color system that can bump or fade to and from any color in the spectrum. The weight increases to 35 pounds with the addition of the color changer, but the unit can be operated without this accessory.

With this generation of lights a new custom computer console was developed in 1993. Called the LDS MP-100, it is slightly smaller than the Vari✳Lite Artisan® console and uses a detachable monitor for graphic display of cues and function of the fixtures. Because each fixture has its own on-board computer, which in this case is an Intel 8088 processor with 64K RAM, the console does not need to contain all the functional information. This is another example of the "intelligent" lights that are the future in theatrical lighting.

Morpheus has packaged these lamps into a system that comes complete with trussing. A fold-up truss (see Figure 12–8) contains 12 Morpheus units or any combination of conventional theatrical fixtures in each section. If all moving lights are used, setup and focus time are reduced dramatically.

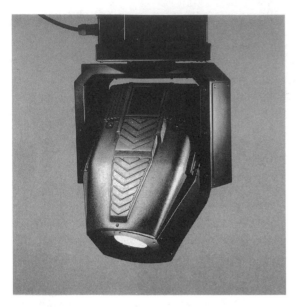

Figure 14–9 Icon® luminaire from Light & Sound Design, Inc.
(Used with permission.)

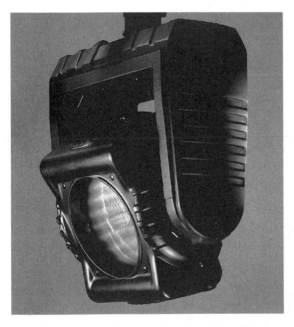

Figure 14–10 Icon® washlight from Light & Sound Design, Inc.
(Used with permission.)

Icon Systems

Light & Sound Design, Inc. (LSD), in California and England, had been working on developing its own moving light. Like Showco and Morpheus, LSD was first a supplier to concerts and found that the large lighting manufacturers were not responding to the needs of the concert designers and technicians. The prototype was later replaced with what they call the Icon® luminaire (Figure 14–9). It uses a 600 watt HTI source at 5,600 degrees Kelvin and a 45-degree dichroic cold mirror for superior light output. It has a synchronized variable speed shutter and can provide a strobe effect. The Icon includes a dichroic color system, seven indexable rotating gobos, and seven interchangeable fixed gobos or effects with the capability for customizing. A 2:1 zoom lens and iris system provide beam angles from a hard-edged pin spot to a soft-edged super wide floor. The Icon has 360-degree pan and 270-degree tile motion.

The Icon® washlight (Figure 14–10) weighs less than 25 pounds and can hang on a 16-inch center. It uses a 575-watt HPL incandescent lamp at 3,250 degrees Kelvin. The optical system was developed in conjunction with Entertec, developer of the Source IV profile spotlight. A unique feature is that it has an automated lens-rotating facility to allow remote control over the fixture's two lensing options. Option 1 involves interchangeable conventional PAR-type lenses with the ability to position or continually rotate the oval beam shape characteristic of the wider lens. Option 2 entails a unique variable beam spread system that gives the user remote control over the beam size, from very narrow to wide floor. It also has LSD's proprietary graduated color media system.

The Icon console (Figure 14–11) is a 1,000-channel unit. It is called a *soft configuration* with liquid crystal display switches that provide total flexibility with maximum ease of operation. It also supports control input and output of DMX 512, MIDI, and Ethernet.

Mirrored Lights

Whereas Vari-Lite, Inc., Morpheus Lights, and Icon Systems took the design direction of mounting the lamp in a yoke that provides movement, another group of designs moves only a mirror, leaving the lamp housing with the rest of the electronics and power supply in one large, often heavy, unit. Often called *wiggle mirrors* by the designers, and I am sure to the annoyance of the manufacturers, they do not have the ability to pan as much as the yoke type. When you design them into a system, take care to leave room for the housing and to make sure the housing is oriented so that the mirror reaches the positions desired. The advantages are that all fixtures in this style of which I am aware are controllable by means of DMX, and all are for sale. They also can be rented or leased from equipment suppliers.

High End Systems

Based in Austin, Texas, High End has been in business since 1986. It was not a concert lighting supplier before beginning business to design moving lights. The company started with a directed program to design and manufacture a microprocessor-based lighting system. It has grown very rapidly to be a major player. The first big success was with the

Figure 14-11 Icon® console from Light & Sound Design, Inc.
(Used with permission.)

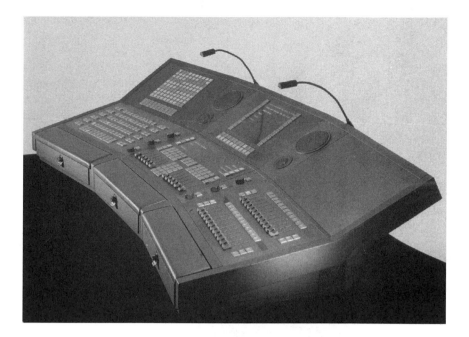

Colour Pro in 1987 and 1988. The Intellabeam® (Figure 14-12) was introduced in 1989 and quickly became the moving light for clubs, tours, and television shows that could not afford or did not want a fully automated rig. It is the first wiggle mirror light discussed in this book but not the first one introduced. Bill McManus introduced a floor-mounted unit several years earlier.

The design takes the position that the head remains static and a mirror redirects the light to where it is needed. The mirror can scan rapidly to 170 degrees of pan and 110 degrees of tilt. That is far less than the other fixtures discussed. Depending on user needs, however, it is quite acceptable in many productions. The current model is the Intellabeam 700 HX. It uses a 700 watt, 5,600 degree Kelvin metal discharge source (MDS). It has 11 dichroic colors plus white, 12 dual colors, and 11 gobos plus one open. There are 10, 12.5, and 17 degree lenses available. The unit weighs 66 pounds, so is much heavier than the other products mentioned. It is also larger: 36.5"H × 13"W × 8"D. But it runs on a DMX 512 protocol, making it capable of control from almost any lighting console, an important advantage.

The Cyberlight® (Figure 14-13) was introduced in 1993–1994. It is based on the Intellabeam but has a stronger light source and more features. The 1,200-watt lamp is housed in a larger package, 90.5 pounds and 42.25"L × 12.37"H. But the larger number of features necessitate the size. First, the unit has a cyan-yellow-magenta (C/Y/M) dichroic color mixing system in addition to an eight-position color wheel with seven saturated dichroic colors (user can change if desired) plus clear. The unit also has a C/Y/M color mixing system for selection and number of colors and subtle hues; a CTO color corrector (converts from 5,600 degrees Kelvin to 3,200 degrees Kelvin for balance to television); upward, downward, and centered color correction for modifying selected colors; four variable speed rotating gobos plus a gobo wheel with two fixed and five replaceable gobos; a remote zoom from 13 degrees to 22 degrees or 16 degrees to 26 degrees with the wide-angle lens; and 180-degree pan and 90-degree tilt with the motorized mirror assembly.

Figure 14–12   Intellabeam® 700 HX by High End, Inc.
(Used with permission.)

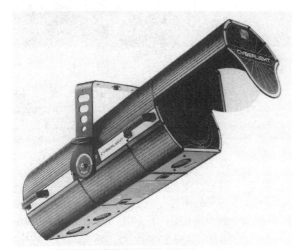

Figure 14–13   Cyberlight® by High End, Inc.
(Used with permission.)

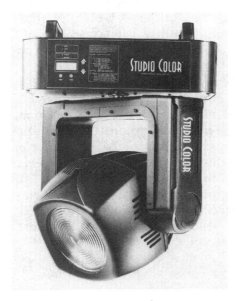

Figure 14–14   Studio Color® fixture by High End, Inc.
(Used with permission.)

In 1995, High End changed concept and introduced a yoke-type design, the Studio Color® wash luminaire (Figure 14–14). This unit made a pronounced impression on designers. First, they could rent or buy it. Second, it was DMX 512 controllable from any console. Third, the light output from the MSR 575 discharge lamp was very good; the company says it is twice the output of a 1,000-watt halogen lamp. The Studio Color luminaire can be fitted with a color corrector when 3,200 degree Kelvin use in needed. For color selection it is similar to the Cyberlight, using the C/Y/M system and six-position color wheel for selected colors. One of the outstanding features is its exclusive variable beam profiling. The standard beam angle selection of 8 to 22 degrees may be user shaped through the use of secondary effects lens systems. This exclusive system delivers virtually unlimited radial beam profiling in both the horizontal and vertical planes. It also features a frost effect, which when selected provides progressive beam diffusion enhancement. What that means is the beams match smoothly across a plane of several fixtures with the beams side by side. This is a highly desirable feature in television, theatre, or film. At a weight of 47 pounds and centering of 24 inches, the fixture is usable in portable situations and touring.

Coemar NAT Light

Based on the wiggle mirror idea, this is another innovation in the moving light field. Introduced at the 1996 LDI convention, by Italian manufacturer, Coemar, it is the highest wattage light source available thus far. A 2,500-watt HTI source drives this monster (there also is a 1200-watt version in a somewhat smaller housing). The NAT tm® (total movement) light (Figure 14–15) has, without doubt, the strongest output available to date. In another exclusive feature, it can pan and tilt a full 360 degrees (thus "total movement" in the name), another first. It weighs a hefty 130 pounds for both the power supply (separate) and the main unit. It has a 16-unit positioning system and ten interchangeable gobos that can rotate in both directions and at variable speeds. It uses the C/M/Y color-mixing method of producing color and adds a nine-place color wheel for mix effects. The iris, strobing, and blackout facilities are on high-speed motors. The NAT series of lights can come with no mirror, the more conventional mirror design similar to Cyberlights, and the total movement adaptor. It also comes in a 1,200-watt version. It is exclusively distributed in the United States by The Obie Company.

The Future of Moving Lights

There can be no question that the versatility of moving lights has application not only in concerts but also in all forms of theatrical lighting. The costs are dropping. Recently I was quoted a price similar to that of a standard 300-lamp system for 120 moving lights. There is no comparing the design flexibility that is possible over conventional lighting. The state-of-the-art quality and cutting edge of these developments do not seem to be finished. When we can focus, color, and even dim a source of such brightness and high color temperature remotely, the time has come to integrate our thinking. There have been two attempts to make a moving light that has the basic features of a leko, that is, remote positioned shutters. One is by Martin Systems. Even more radical designs are being tested as you read this. The uses of these new marvelous

Figure 14–15   NAT tm® 2500 light by Coemar.
(Photo by The Obie Company.)

lighting tools are endless. Designers have finally acquired the physical means to design almost anything they can dream up. What does the future hold? I am sure that before this book goes to print there will be an even more exciting development in this highly charged field.

Plate A John Denver during in-the-round performance. (Photo by James Moody.)

Plate B John Denver in performance with stained glass and aspen tree gobos. (Photo by James Moody, courtesy of Sundance Lighting Corp.)

Plate C John Denver performance in proscenium setting with film of *Calypso* in background; still reads well against hot concert lights.
(Photo by James Moody, courtesy of Sundance Lighting Corp.)

Plate D Reba McEntire '96 tour, close-up.
(Photo by Lewis Lee, courtesy of Vari-Lite, Inc.)

Plate E Reba McEntire '96 tour, wide shot.
(Photo by Lewis Lee, courtesy of Vari-Lite, Inc.)

Plate F   Styx 1995 Return to the Paradise Theatre tour (with roll down drop). (Photo by Jeremy Windle, courtesy of M/R/H Lighting Design, Inc.)

Plate G   Styx 1995 Return to the Paradise Theatre Tour. (Photo by Jeremy Windle, courtesy of M/R/H Lighting Design, Inc.)

Plate H   U2 ZOO TV tour. (Photo courtesy of Willie Williams.)

III

Practical Examples of Techniques

Parts I and II of this book covered the basic concepts of concert lighting. How you progress beyond the basics will be based on how you respond to circumstances and opportunities you find for yourself. No book can make you a designer. A book can only explain current tools, procedures, and criteria. What makes a design is that inner voice that takes your accumulated knowledge and arranges it into something uniquely yours.

This section includes examples of the lengths other designers and I have gone to achieve our designs. The projects described have many elements that also can be used for theatre productions. The techniques used to mount and move the show from city to city are cut from the whole cloth of touring.

Our choices of fixtures and how we used them may seem a great departure from what I have described as a typical concert. Don't let that throw you; all creativity is a departure from the norm. No matter what mix of tools you use, the object is to achieve a unique result.

With each project, we also talk about the staging. The concert lighting designer is often responsible, to a full or lesser degree, for all of the design elements. What follows are examples of the integration of concert techniques, also applicable to theatre-in-the-round staging of a play or musical, that can be used in any place other than a specifically designated theatre space. What is described for the proscenium staging of concerts is also applicable in its use of color, position, and cuing.

Following these are two examples of what to do when there is no roof. We also receive insight into how a designer revisits a project 15 years later and what a designer does when faced with the problem of an artist's wanting Bigger, Bigger! Last I discuss what happens when you go overseas to Europe, Asia, and South America.

15

Designing to
Fit the Space

In-the-Round Performances

I was fortunate to design for an artist who welcomed change and
encouraged it in his productions. This chapter gives the example of two
types of staging. Both were unique for their time, 1974 through 1978. I
don't believe, within that musical style, they have been eclipsed yet.
These examples and the examples in chapters 16 and 21 on lighting a
facility without a roof are my designs and show some of the unusual
situations regarding location of a show that I have faced over the years.

I received a call saying we were wanted to do an in-the-round concert setup for John Denver. He was performing at a political benefit,
and the committee had already sold the arena for that style seating. The
easy way would have been to drawn on my theatre training. That
would have entailed lighting the concert as if it were a play in the
round, segmenting off the stage into pie wedges with a warm and cool
color in each and a number of specials to add focus and color. I couldn't
leave it at that.

The general opinion around John's management office was, "Let's
do this as best we can and get back to reality." But I was intrigued by
the challenge. It presented a perfect opportunity to do some cross-over
experimenting. I saw a fantastic opportunity to depart from the harsh,
primary color, concert look and present John not as a performer standing on stage with production behind him, but as a storyteller singing
with his friends and fans. To create a feeling of intimacy in such a large
space was my goal. Part of what I felt I needed to accomplish this goal
was to also have control of the stage design because I didn't think any
scenic designer would understand what I was trying to do. I felt the
scenic artists would be too interested in making their own statement.
Besides, in those times it was highly unusual to hire a scenic artist.

Stage Design

The first problem to be overcome in the stage design was the stage
itself. Dan Fiala of Concerts West, John's national promoter in those
days, went so far as to set up a stage and some audience chairs in a
shopping center parking lot to see how high the stage should be for
optimum viewing. These same promoters were also handling the
Sinatra shows—done in the round but with the band seated at audience
level on one side of the raised portion of the stage—and had experienced obstruction problems before. On the basis of Dan's investigation
and ours, it was agreed that a low stage (two feet) was best. We found

that if John were placed in the center with the players around him, as the height of the stage increased, the obstructed view for the audience increased logarithmically.

The first leg of the tour had stages provided by each hall; these varied from two to four feet in height. The hall management fought us on stage height almost everywhere we went, believing that crowd control would be a problem. People jumping on the stage can interrupt the show. We were fairly confident that John did not have the usual rock concert audience. Spectators did not try to tear his clothes off, and it was generally a family night, from parents with babes in arms to grandparents. In all the shows we did in this manner (some 200), only three people got onto the stage. This was partly because of the audience makeup and partly because of a good security and usher system. It was a system that used a very low-key approach designed to spot potential problems before they happened. Our feeling was that if you trust the audience to respect an artist enough to remain in their seats, most of them will do just that. Most problems occur when the artist calls for the audience to disobey security rules.

As to the physical setup, John stood on an 18-inch high by 6-foot round turntable in the center of the stage. The band on the first tour was relatively easy to work with; there were four musicians with minimal gear. Each musician was placed at a corner, putting their backs to the main aisles, and therefore did not block people close to the stage, breaking the stage into pie wedges. An usher was seated, facing outward toward the audience, at each corner of the stage. We intentionally planned the seating layout with the venues to leave aisles directly in front of these points.

The next year, 1978, the problems were compounded when John brought in nine musicians, including three singers, and a baby grand piano. I spent several days constructing a model stage and photographing it from the audience point of view at each corner.

When I originally set up the stage with four musicians I used my own representation of a Hopi ceremonial sand-painting design for the floor. I was interested in this art form, and it fit right in, complete with an eagle feather pattern and the symbols of life from the Hopi tribe.

With the expansion of the players, I knew the design would be lost, so I changed to a carpet to cover the stage. The carpet hid three items: the plywood stage flooring, the holes for the microphone cords, and the sound monitors, so they could be connected beneath the stage, keeping the floor clear of cables. The carpet was a three-tone, golden brown, high-low cut. It held up very well through some 120 shows, even with all the holes cut into it. Redwood around the turntable and planters added to the earth-tone design, as did a dozen Boston ferns, which covered the backs of amplifiers. We rented the plants at first, then decided to purchase them because local florists were charging too much for a one-day rental. The plants lasted three to five days while being transported, and the cost of purchase turned out to be half the rental cost. I made a lot of people happy because I would take the plants that were starting to wilt and distribute them among the facility staff and the stagehands. Why didn't we use artificial plants? They would last the whole tour. John wouldn't hear of it (Figure 15–1).

Lighting Design In-the-Round

There is no creative challenge in producing designs that are safe and that you are sure work. We should not discard our knowledge, but we cannot be slaves to it either. When you are sure of your basic skills as a

Figure 15–1   John Denver at Madison Square Garden, in-the-round sound check.
(Photo by James Moody.)

designer, then you are able to challenge yourself to find new ways to accomplish a task. The John Denver project allowed me to do just that: take basic knowledge of theatre-in-the-round and combine it with my knowledge of concert colors and positions to achieve a totally new look for a concert.

No Follow Spots!

To make the show intimate, I believed that follow spots had to be eliminated. I felt strongly that I could light the stage in a theatrical manner without them. Because of the distance of the follow spots from the stage, the beams' ambient light would illuminate much of the audience. The angle, which varied radically from arena to arena, was the primary problem. In some venues, the follow spots are no higher than 20 to 30 feet above the stage. This means that the first five to ten rows of people are blinded when looking directly at the artist. When other artists work in the round, they are constantly moving, and this problem is diminished somewhat. With an artist standing in one spot for two and a half hours, it would be unbearable to try to look into those beams for that long a period. The problem also extended to the fixed lighting. To achieve an intimate look, no single source of light can be overpowering compared with the rest of the light. A follow spot is five times brighter than fixed illumination, and I believed that would be too much for the soft look I wanted (Plate A).

No matter how I reasoned, some management people insisted that follow spots be used. The answer turned out to be simple, however. Before the first show I told John to tell me if he felt the audience was being annoyed by the follow spotlight. It only took one song, after which he said over the sound system, "Jim, you were right, kill the spots," at which the audience applauded.

Technical Specifications

I feel obligated to have an idea that the design I have created is technically sound and can be set up within a timetable that is reasonable. To that end, I, as a designer, must know the available equipment that can accomplish the task. If there is no available item that can do it, then I must design it myself or find someone who has the expertise to do it. This project led to the development of several new technical items. It also challenged me to find equipment that could fit into my plan and make the production workable. The following describes how this work was done.

Mounting and Rigging

The problem of minimizing setup time was a constant concern when I was working out how the show could be hung. I wanted to have as few rigging points as possible, and because of the great cooperative effort between light and sound, the answer was already there. Stanal Sound's Ernie Zillinger had designed flying platforms for his company's sound system that formed a grid for the speaker cabinets on which to hang the cabinets. This allowed the technicians to focus horns and cabinets at angles not possible with other rigs used at the time. These grids were flown with $5/8$-inch aircraft cable with the motors mounted on top of the grid (Figure 15–2). The advantage in this rigging was portability and speed. The four sides required only two cables each instead of the common four-point system used with chain hoists. These $5/8$-inch stranded steel cables were rated to safely support 5,000 pounds each.

The cable drum used was dual-sided so that both cables on the grid went through a pulley block to a single motorized drum mounted in the center of the grid. This ensured that the grid would go up preleveled. The total load per side was certified at 3,000 pounds for both lights and sound. The cables, bridles, and other equipment required to hang the system were easily portable. A second set was taken along so that the rigger could fly to the next arena the day before the show to do a pre-rig. When the usual chain-type hoists are used, their bulk and weight rule this out, unless they are trucked.

Lighting Support

The width of the sound grid was sufficient to allow a small 18-inch triangular truss with lighting fixtures to be suspended from the onstage side without interfering with the sound system. Balance was maintained by moving the speakers forward. The lights were electrically isolated from the PA (even though this was a highly specialized concert sound system, it was still referred to with the old term *PA*, not as public-address system) by means of wrapping tire inner tubes around the grid between the cables attached to the lighting truss. Each of the four grids had individually controlled motors so that the grids could be flown to the height required for the best sound, even if that was at dif-

Figure 15–2   Stanal flying system.
(Photo by James Moody, rig by Stanal Sound, Inc.)

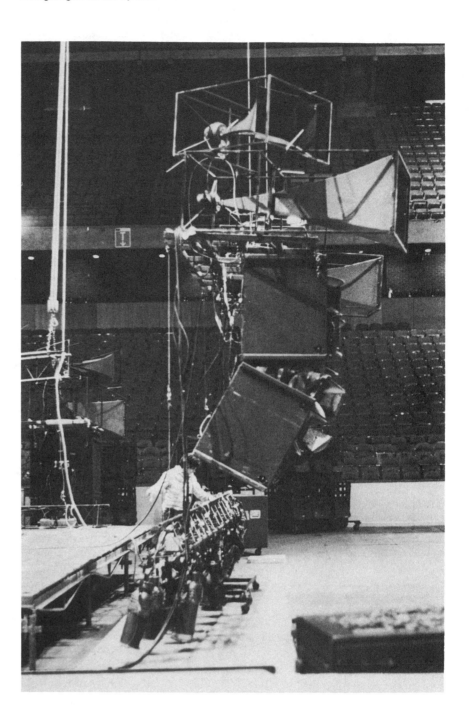

ferent levels in arenas that had high seats on the sides and low seats on the ends. A center grid was flown separately, either attached to the scoreboard in a basketball arena or with block and tackle.

The sound system must be positioned at a height that equally splits the seating, according to Ernie Zillinger, the show's audio engineer and mixer. This theory differs from that of other flying sound systems designers, who usually keep low (16 to 20 feet from the floor and a bottom speaker) no matter what the height of the building's seating. I am not an audio engineer, but I know our sound worked very well for John's style of music.

We had to be able to extend or reduce the cables on the light trusses to maintain a constant position no matter how high or low the building's seating. Lighting trim was best at 24 to 26 feet from the floor for this show. That allowed for the two-foot-high stage. That made John's face light higher than a 45 degree angle, but more important, it kept the spill light on the stage and out of the audience.

Enclosed square trusses that travel with fixtures prehung and cabled, of which I am very fond, were not used in this case because of the extra weight, size, and light beam obstruction. Because the fixtures were not mounted in a box truss or attached to bars in groups, the yoke of each fixture was secured to the grid with safety cables to ensure that no fixture could fall on the audience or a performer. All color frames had safety wire cables attached to them. We tried to have people not sit directly under the grids. Management wanted a six-foot walkway around the stage for traffic control and safety. But some halls pushed seats to within two feet of the stage.

Lighting Console

I had used computer consoles on the show since 1977. I started with a Siltron System 120 console and later moved to the Strand-Century Light Palette when it was introduced. I believe we got one of the very first ones produced. Because concerts do not get the weeks of rehearsals that theatre productions do, to get each cue down perfectly, you must build the design as the songs are staged. The computer allowed me to start with the basic look and then build during the song and record what I saw. Because of the length of the show and the computer technology of the day, it actually took two $5 \frac{1}{2}$-inch floppy disks to hold all the cues that could be used in the show. John performed a stock opening set and closing group of songs, but the larger middle of the show would change from city to city. John was sensitive to how an audience was reacting and would tailor the show to them. That meant that I could be called on to light any one of about 50 songs.

To make it easy to gain access to any song, I developed a plan that had each song starting at a multiple of ten, that is, song one started at cue 01, song two started at 10, and song three at 20, and so on. Because the Light Palette had the ability to add .1 to .9 between each cue, I always had plenty of room for each song's cues using this system.

I also programmed a series of basic opening looks into the additive submasters, so if unable to access a cue series quickly enough, I could bring up a submaster to cover until I could find the right cue sequence. It turned out that I did not have to resort to this backup very often. Even when an artist does not let you know which song will be next, you get a sixth sense for what will happen. In this case, sometimes the guitar John picked up or how the band changed instruments would reveal the song to me.

I had both consoles fitted with dual power supplies and battery backup so that instant changeover could be made if a power source were damaged in traveling or if a console lost power during the show. Those features are now standard on most consoles.

Focus

Because triangular grids cannot be climbed on for focusing as most square trusses can, we carried two 24-foot Air Decks (see chapter 13). They were also used for tying up the cables once they had been hoisted up. Many halls did not have catwalks to allow the tails to be pulled up and snubbed off, so the rigger came up with the idea of tying the tails off and using duffel bags to hold the loose rope. The rigger then clipped the bags to the block to keep the look cleaner and make sure that the rope would not uncoil and come tumbling down during the show.

In focusing, the two Air Decks were used simultaneously on the arena floor next to the stage edge. The two technicians doing the focusing were pulled around the perimeter of the stage in opposite directions as they worked. The center grid was focused in a similar manner, but with one Air Deck on the stage before the band equipment was in place.

Dimmer Racks

A 60-channel 3.6-kW Berkey-Colortran custom rack was constructed in the Sundance Lighting shop for the first tour (Figure 10–1). Only the dimmers and their connector hardware were from the manufacturer. The case and all wiring for output panels, meters, and so on were designed by Sundance specifically for road use. After consulting with the manufacturer's engineers, we were able to load the 3.6-kW dimmers with 4 kW on a regular basis without any strain on the devices. The main breaker was a 600-amp motor-operated, three-phase unit with constant digital metering on all phases. The rack was very large, had very good casters, and was quite manageable.

Later we built smaller racks containing 30 2-kW and three 6-kW Skirpan Lighting dimmers (see chapter 10). Again, we designed and built the case as well as all the interconnecting wiring, pin matrix patch, main and sub-breaker panels, and output panels (slide patch).

Multi-cables

Because I wanted an unobstructed view of the stage from all sides, I needed to avoid what I had heard about and seen at shows where the lighting cables hang down at the four corners like the posts of a four-poster bed. So all the cabling from the lighting trusses to the dimmer was 350 feet of Cranetrol multiline cable. (Sound also ran their cables away from the stage.) It took ten cables, two per grid plus two in the center, which contained nine 120-volt circuits that terminated in Pyle-National's

Figure 15–3   Sixty-channel 3.6-kW custom Dimmer Rack built by Sundance Lighting with 350-foot multi-cable reels.
(Photo by Sundance Lighting Corp.)

Star-Line series connectors for quick, secure attachment. The cable reels made it easy to store and move such long lengths (see Figure 15–3). We could fly the cables to the corner of the arena floor and not make the stage seem like a canopy bed with four cable posts around it. The reels did not have to be fully unwound. The excess remained on the reel. A set of short feeder cables made the final connection between the reel and the dimmer rack.

Fixture and Color Chart

Because John stood on a center platform on a 20-foot-square stage, I started with a fairly standard formula for in-the-round theatre lighting. I wanted to have very tight control of the light and contain it within the confines of the stage. To do this, almost all 123 fixtures were ellipsoidals—a mixture of 6 × 9, 6 × 12, and 6 × 16, with only a few PAR-64 mediums as down light. Most of the 6 × 16s were the Colortran 20-degree models, which at the time gave the best lumen output. Certainly this fixture complement was unusual for touring. But the desire to control spill light was uppermost in my mind. As you can see in Plate A, the lighting emphasized the use of people on stage as scenic elements, an essential ingredient in concert lighting even if there is scenery. Eight 1,000-watt Colortran 20-degree fixtures for face (key) light may seem like overkill, but I wanted two lamps on each corner (each on separate circuits) so that in the event of a burnout there would not be a dark side. Each truss therefore had two circuits (one warm and one cool color) of two lamps (one lamp at each end of every truss) to provide the key lighting.

In the center of the truss were 6 × 16 ellipsoidals that provided the full color wash (red, blue, blue-green, yellow, lavender, and white). Each color was broken into two circuits (north-south as one and east-west as the second), and the shade of color changed from one circuit to another; that is, a red #821 was on two sides and an orange #819 on the opposite two sides. This gave a nice modeling to the body even if I used only the red full-body channel from all four sides. Added to this were four PAR-64 medium fixtures overhead as down light pools in red, blue, amber, and blue-green to round out John's lighting.

The band was illuminated with five color washes of eight PAR-64 fixtures equipped with medium flood lamps, two from each side. Again, the colors were divided and shaded from side to side, as was done on John's washes. This procedure was repeated for the four color washes on the center truss. In addition, each band member had two key light specials (warm and cool) with a single Colortran 20-degree instrument. The light plot (see Figure 15–4) shows rigging, circuit chart, and sectional view all on one sheet.

Scheduling

John believed in a tight schedule. On the Spring 1978 tour, we played 57 shows in 61 days in 54 cities. That's a heavy schedule for any artist, especially when he did close to a 2 1/2 hour show each night and frequently did a second show at midnight. (See Plates A and B.)

End-Stage Productions

We often alternated between the in-the-round show and an end-stage or proscenium show because of the facility availability. *End-stage* denotes a portable stage placed in the same manner as a proscenium, a traditional theatre stage, or in the case of an arena or coliseum where seats circle the stage area, placed so that most of the audience views the show from the front. As the designer you want to be sure to find out if seats are to be sold behind the stage (usually with tickets stamped "Restricted Viewing"). You cannot use a backdrop if those seats are to be sold. You might want to negotiate to keep the backdrop and convince the promoter beforehand not to sell those tickets.

In some cases of end-stage configuration a full orchestra was added and I had to be prepared for them whenever they were used. However, as was true with the in-the-round shows, the foremost factor to John was the audience's unobstructed view. There was no scenery for the in-the-round design, but when I deal with an end-stage or proscenium show in which there is no hard proscenium, the design concept grows. Most of the audience is much farther away from the stage than for an in-the-round show.

In any concert design I want to create an environment for the artist that can make a statement about the music. If the group is Metallica, U2, R.E.M., or Kiss, you give them flash and nonstop color changes, like the pace of the music. If the performer is Barbra Streisand, you drench her in beautiful colors to make the stage reflect her bigger-than-life image.

So, for "country boy" John Denver, I not only saw a man who had a very definite public image but also heard in the lyrics of his music a very definite statement about family life and our use and abuse of planet Earth. The public's concept of John is that of a lover of nature and the wilderness. The Rocky Mountains and the sea became an important part of the visual image he wanted to convey to the audience. My desire was to do a design that placed him in a scenic as well as lighting environment that matched his lyrics. The peace and beauty of lyrics such as

> You fill up my senses
> Like a night in a forest
> Like a storm in the desert
> Like a sleepy blue ocean[1]

had to be imparted to the audience visually.

Stage Design

Before I could design the lighting I had to visualize the setting. Once I had an image I liked, there was no longer a need for a scenic artist to redraw what I saw. So I also became the set designer. This is not unusual in concert touring. Unless the artist has the need for a very elaborate set, it is usually left to the lighting designer to at least specify the size and color of risers, backdrop, and carpet. This is 180 degrees from the usual Broadway method that has the scenic artists doubling in lighting so that they can ensure that the end product will have the color and shading they had envisioned in their scenic design.

This set for John Denver had as its focal point four 8-foot by 4-foot leaded, stained-glass windows, each depicting a season of the year and framed in redwood. We found a stained-glass company to do the actual graphic design and build the leaded-glass windows. I added a scenic

---

1. From "Annie's Song," lyrics by John Denver. Copyright 1974 Cherry Lane Music Co.

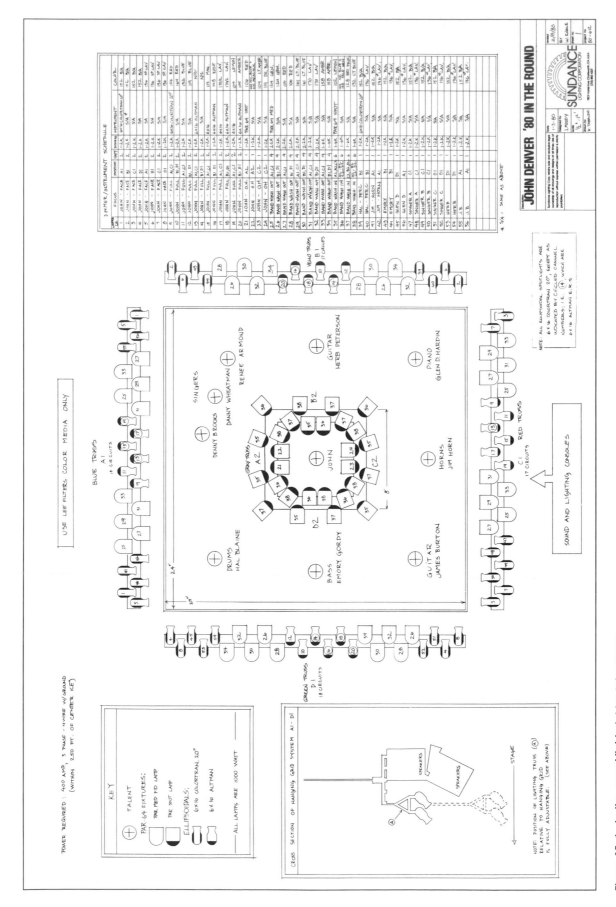

Figure 15–4 In-the-round light plot for John Denver. (Design by James Moody.)

element of redwood trim and support structure around them once they were finished. A rolling cart, well padded and with a protective cover, was specifically designed to minimize damage. To the great credit of this case and exceptionally fine leaded-glass work, the windows traveled all over the world without a serious mishap.

The stained-glass windows were free standing to make it easy to adjust their position to match the physical restrictions imposed by the various stage sizes. If an orchestra was used, the windows were placed to the side so the full orchestra could be seen. Both floor stand supports and hanging hardware were carried to cover any situation we encountered.

The risers for the drummer and other musicians were also faced with redwood and carpeted on top. Planters with live green plants rounded out the set, which was all placed on a tri-colored (browns to red) carpet. Carpeting had worked so well for the in-the-round tour in tying the set together that I kept the element. Even the sound-monitor system was carpeted to make it less conspicuous. John, however, stood on an authentic Navajo rug, another subtle statement tied to the in-the-round tour motif.

Rather than using the windows as the surface for changing images, I completed the stage design with a full cyclorama (a curved curtain background). It served as a surface for film, slides projected with a scene machine, patterns, and color washes. The combined effect of the stained-glass window and cyclorama gave the audience the feeling that they were viewing the show from inside John's living room. Occasionally a stage allowed for additional scenic elements such as a ceiling piece. These elements were the mind's eye to the lyrics, suggested in images and light.

Lighting Design

Now that the set was complete, I had my surfaces to light, whether cyclorama or performer. In concert lighting our most important and one of the most useful canvases is the performing group. The first thing I plan in a design are cyclorama colors and the back light for the star and band. After I am satisfied that I have the colors and circuit control I need, I work forward. The reason the cyclorama and the back light are viewed at the same time is that there must be a contrast between the colors so the back light does not get lost in the cyclorama.

It may seem odd at first that I start lighting from the rear of the stage. Theatre-trained designers usually start from the front of the house and work toward the rear of the stage. But I got involved in film production and learned that most directors of photography and gaffers (lighting electricians) proceed from back to front when lighting film. I find the technique similar to laying on the broad strokes for an oil painting. In film the canvas begins with the set (the walls of a room, for example), followed by general illumination that creates the mood of the scene. Only after that are the front light sources put in. If you pay attention to the layering, the portion of your audience sitting 100 feet away will see the difference.

It must also be realized that in concert lighting the key light—the follow spot—is known, so less attention needs to be paid to it. It is the most common factor. I say this with reservation, but I have expanded on my feelings throughout this book.

My choices of colors are largely in the primary and secondary range. I am not prone to mixing gels in a single light source. When I apprenticed with Jules Fisher, the innovative Broadway designer of such shows as *Hair, Jesus Christ Superstar, Lenny, Dancin'*, and many more, one part of his design criteria especially impressed me and has had a great impact on my designing. He believed that with primary and secondary colors he could achieve almost any color during the cue-to-cue rehearsal. When you finally sit in the theatre with a director who wants the set a little warmer or wants a magenta feeling, if you have picked colors that do not mix well, you are forced to re-gel and delay the rehearsal. Jules, on the other hand, had his palette in the air ready to mix instantly to his or the director's pleasure. With time being money on Broadway, this technique helps to make him cost effective to the producer. This is a simplification of his principle, but when I went into concert lighting I found this concept served me well. With minimal rehearsal time, I would use my blue or red back wash or combine them to create magenta or lavender, depending on how I varied the level between the circuits. This saved me lamps and dimmers, both of which were at a premium in the early days of touring.

After the back light, I looked to the band side light, then John's side light. Next, pools and specials for band members and other effects were added. Just as with the in-the-round design, the contrast between colors on different levels or sections of the stage is important in creating depth of field. Next the patterns for the cyclorama, floor, and set were determined. Last, as in film lighting, the key light colors were chosen.

In this design I had decided to eliminate all follow spots because John does not move around the stage. I chose to use 6 × 16 ellipsoidals placed on a truss out in front of the stage in a fixed key light position. My system provided for warm and cool cross-key face light plus a no-color circuit positioned straight on. Two lamps per circuit were used to increase intensity and as a safety measure against lamp burn-out during the performance. After these straight-on key lights were focused at a waist-to-head shuttering, I put in several front-crossing full-body circuits of pastel colors.

I was shown films that had been produced especially for the show as backgrounds for several songs. One was shot on the ocean research ship *Calypso* (Plate C), another in the Rocky Mountains, and yet another in black and white depicting a farmer in a field with a horse-drawn plow. My personal favorite was a beautiful film of soaring bald eagles. I had to be a part of the decision about the order in which the songs were sung because the films, slides, and other effects had to be arranged throughout the set for maximum impact.

Because the films were done well in advance I knew which songs needed other visuals. So I started finding existing slides, or in some cases, I had them shot specifically for the tour. The slides were processed and mounted for use in a scene machine (see Figure 10–11). The 4 × 5 inch slides were great for realistic images such as the snow-capped peaks of the Rockies or the ship on which John wrote the song "Calypso." Besides holding film slides, the scene machine is excellent for hand-painted images. I also used another machine to create moving clouds on this tour.

Last I added metal gobo patterns for several songs that needed a more abstract image. John sang frequently about trees and forests. I used some stock patterns but modified designs of the realistic stars and a reverse pattern of a stock leaf pattern done by the Great American Market. I have never understood why most people use a leaf pattern that makes the leaves the shadow area and the sky between the leaves the light transmission part of the pattern. Most tree patterns are done the same way. My design centered on first washing the cyclorama with the base color, that is, the blue sky, then laying over the white stars, the green leaves, or the green and brown trees. This follows the painter's broad stroke and finishing detail method. Andrea Tawil of the Great American Market and I created new designs of aspen trees and hanging leaves with branches, as well as an eagle.

The overall effect was to create an environment that reflected the music and gave a large enough image (cyclorama with film or slide or pattern) to be seen by the person in the last row. The audience needs a picture to view even if it cannot see the expression on the singer's face from 150 feet away (let alone be absolutely sure who it is standing on the stage).

This design is not a light show. This artist's music is unique, filled with beauty, not pulse-pounding power. In either case I am still guided by the principle that good lighting is judged by where you do not put the light more than by where you do. It is true that there are few situations in concert lighting that adhere to this philosophy. I firmly believe in it and fight to keep the quantity of fixtures down. I do not look for ways to increase the size of the system. See Figures 15-5 and 15-6 for the light and circuit plots for the end-stage performances in the John Denver tour.

Giving all your looks away in the first song by flashing through every preset you have is not design. I take a strong stand against the flashing light school of nondesign. There is a difference between creating movement and excitement and simply flashing lights to the beat of the music.

Before anyone says that my theories work only for John Denver or other middle-of-the-road music acts, take a close look at the excellent recent designs for David Bowie and Whitney Houston (Allen Branton), Michael Jackson and Madonna (Peter Morse), John Mellencamp and Bruce Springsteen (Jeff Ravitz), Peter Gabriel (Jonathan Smeeton), Alice Cooper (Joe Gannon and Ed Geil), Genesis (Alan Owen), Bob Dylan with Tom Petty & The Heartbreakers (Stephen Bickford), Neil Diamond (Marilyn Lowey), or Jackson Browne (Marc Brickman), to name a few. The Rolling Stones 1982 tour, also designed by Allen Branton, showed great thoughtfulness of design.

Critical Acclaim

The results of these designs were displayed for more than 2.5 million people to see, now a small number for a tour. From 1976 through 1978 some 350 shows across the United States were viewed and praised by audience and press alike. *Performance* magazine said of the Chicago Stadium show, "... the staging was a masterpiece of large concert production" (May 20, 1976). Philip Elwood of the San Francisco *Examiner* saw what I had tried to create when he wrote, "During the entire performance ... the lighting was perfect, spotting soloists on schedule and making the small stage seem like a cozy general store where all the gang gathers round for a song fest" (May 12, 1978).

In 1980, *Performance* magazine awarded me its first Readers' Poll Concert Lighting Designer of the Year Award for the outstanding design of this tour. The United States Institute for Theatre Technology (USITT) presented a Juried Scenography Exposition in 1982, and this design was one of only five designs exhibited, and the only nontheatre design. It was the first time a concert design had been so honored.

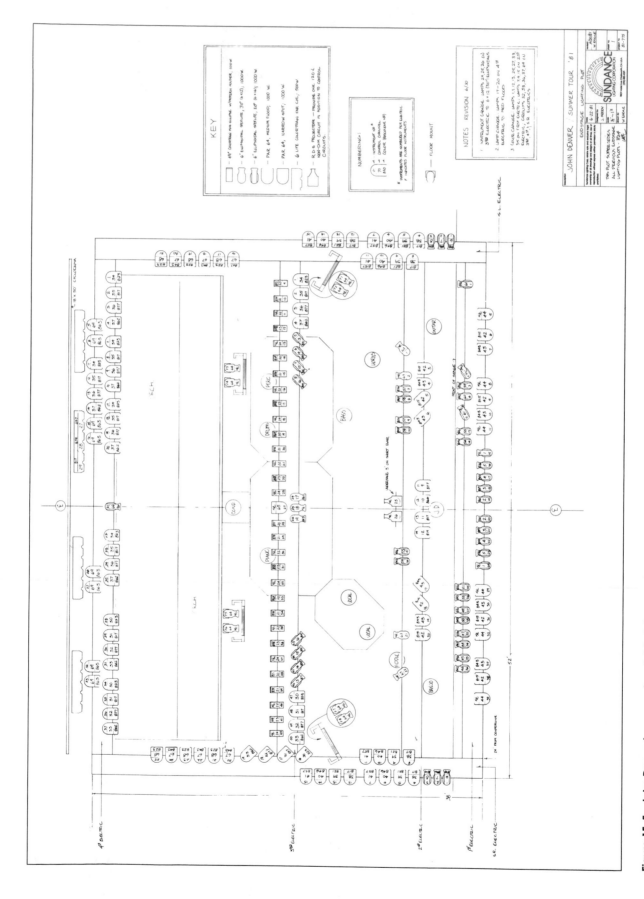

Figure 15–5   John Denver's proscenium light plot.
(Design by James Moody.)

CIRCUIT / INSTRUMENT SCHEDULE

DIMMER NO/	LOAD	CONTROL CHANNEL	INSTRUMENTS TYPE	AMT	NUMBERS	LOCATION	DESCRIPTION	FOCUS	COLOR DESCRIPTION	NO/	NOTES
	2K	1	6X16ERS	2	12, 23	1ST ELECTRIC	KEY	JOHN	N/C	–	
	2K	2			16, 18				LT. BLUE	861	
	2K	3			15, 20				STRAW	809	
	2K	4			14, 21				SP. LAV.	842	
	2K	5			17, 19				FL. PINK	826	
	2K	6	6X16ERS	2	1/1	S.R./S.L. ELECTRIC	SIDELITE		MAGENTA	838	
	2K	7			2/2				DK. LAV	846	
	2K	8			3/3				MED. GREEN	874	
	1K	9	PAR M.F.	1	11	2ND ELECTRIC	DOWN POOL		BLUE/GREEN	877	
	1K	10			13				URBAN BLUE	866	
	1K	11			16				DK. AMBER	817	
	1K	12			18				LT. RED	819	
	2K	13	6X16ERS	2	5, 47	3RD ELECTRIC	CROSS. BACKLITE		LT. GREEN	871	
	2K	14			6, 48				LT. MAGENTA	837	
	2K	15			7, 45				RED	821	
	2K	16			8, 46				STRAW	809	
	1K	17	6X12ERS	1	25	3RD ELECTRIC	BACKLITE		LT. BLUE	861	
	1K	18	6X9ERS		27				N/C	-	
	1K	19	6X12ERS		28				MED. LAV.	843	
	3K	20	6X9ERS	6	10, 16, 17, 23, 35, 41	3RD ELECTRIC	PATTERNS	CYC	ASST. GREENS	871/869	PALM TREES
	3K	21			12, 18, 19, 30, 37, 42				MED. GREEN	874	ASPEN TREES
	3K	22			11, 20, 24, 34, 36, 40				N/C		REALISTIC STARS
	3K	23			13, 15, 21, 29, 33, 38				LT. GREEN BLUE	858	TREE TOPS
	3K	24			14, 22, 31, 32, 39, 43				N/C		CLOUDS
	1K	25	RDS. PROJ.	1	14	2ND ELECTRIC	5 - 4x5 SLIDES		N/C		W/EDM DISC MACH. AND TP-5 TURRET PLATE – USE OL-4 LENS
	1K	26		1	15		5 - 4x5 SLIDES		N/C		
	4K	27	CYC. STRIP	4	–	U.S. FLOOR	CYC. LITE		MED. BLUE	857	
	4K	28			–				MED. GREEN	874	
	4K	29			–				DK. AMBER	817	
	4K	30	PAR N.S	4	50/31, 35, 39	3RD/4TH ELECTRIC	BACK WASH	VOCALS	DK. RED	823	
	4K	31			49/30, 34, 38				DK. AMBER	817/2	DOUBLE COLOR.
	4K	32			52/33, 37, 41				BLUE-GREEN	877	
	4K	33			51/32, 36, 40				BLUE	862	MAY USE No 857 IF COLOR NOT AVAIL.
	6K	34	PAR NS/MF	6	2/4, 8, 12, 18, 25	3RD/4TH ELECTRIC	BACKWASH	BAND	DK. RED	823	
	6K	35			1/3, 7, 11, 17, 24				DK. AMBER	817/2	DOUBLE COLOR.

DIMMER NO/	LOAD	CONTROL CHANNEL	INSTRUMENTS TYPE	AMT	NUMBERS	LOCATION	DESCRIPTION	FOCUS	COLOR DESCRIPTION	NO/	NOTES
	6K	36	PAR NS/MF	6	4/6, 10, 14, 20, 27	3RD/4TH ELECTRIC	BACKWASH	BAND	BLUE-GREEN	877	
	6K	37			3/5, 9, 13, 19, 26				BLUE	862	MAY USE No 857 IF COLOR NOT AVAIL.
	6K	38	PAR NS/MF	6	4, 5, 12/4, 5, 12	S.L./S.R. ELECTRIC	SIDEWASH	BAND/VOCALS	DK AMBER/2	817	DBL. COLOR
	6K	39			6, 7, 13/6, 7, 13				RED	821	
	6K	40			8, 9, 14/8, 9, 14				DK. LAV	846	
	6K	41			10, 11, 15/10, 11, 15				MED/BLUE	857	
	8K	42	PAR M.F.	8	2, 6, 31, 32/1, 8, 21, 27	1ST/2ND ELECTRIC	FRONT WASH		MED. AMBER	815	
	8K	43			3, 8, 29, 33/2, 9, 20, 28				MED. LAV	843	
	6K	44	PAR M.F.	6	10, 11, 13, 22, 24, 27	1ST ELECTRIC	DNSTAGE WASH.	S.R. EXIT & RETURN	N/C		
	1K	45	6X16ERS	1	28	1ST ELECTRIC	SPECIAL	BANJO	FL. PINK	826	
	1K	46		1	30				SP. LAV.	842	
	1K	47		1	25			FIDDLE	FL. PINK	826	
	1K	48		1	26				SP. LAV	842	
	1K	49		1	24	2ND ELECTRIC		VOCAL	FL. PINK	826	
	1K	50		1	25				SP. LAV	842	
	1K	51		1	22			VOCAL	FL. PINK	826	
	1K	52		1	23				SP. LAV	842	
	1K	53		1	17			PIANO	FL. PINK	826	
	1K	54		1	19				SP. LAV	842	
	1K	55		1	10			BASS	FL. PINK	826	
	1K	56		1	12				SP. LAV	842	
	2K	57		2	4, 6			DRUMS	FL. PINK	826	
	2K	58		2	5, 7				SP. LAV	842	
	1K	59		1	4	1ST ELECTRIC		HORNS	FL. PINK	826	
	1K	60		1	5				SP. LAV	842	
	2K	61		2	1, 9			GUITAR	FL. PINK	826	
	1K	62		1	7				SP. LAV	842	
	3K	63	6x9ERS 750 W	4	1, 2, 21, 22	2ND ELECTRIC	FRONT WASH	STAINED GLASS WINDOWS	N/C		
	6K	64	6x9ERS 750 W	8	F1 – F8	MOUNT ON FLOOR	BACK WASH		N/C		
	1K	65	PAR SPOT	1	26	3RD ELECTRIC	COND. FRONT LITE	CONDUCTOR	N/C		
	1K	66	6X16 ERS.	1		4TH ELECTRIC	COND. BACK LITE		LT. BLUE	861	
	6K	67	PAR NS/MF	6		SL/S.R. ELECTRIC	ORCH. SIDE LITE	ORCHESTRA	LAV	842	
	6K	68		6					RED	823	
	8K	69	PAR MF	8	1, 2, 15, 16, 22, 23, 28, 29	4TH ELECTRIC	ORC. BACK LITE		DK. BLUE	863	

Figure 15–6 John Denver's proscenium circuit plot.
(Design by James Moody.)

16

Rigging with No Ceiling

Even after the touring design has been done, there is no guarantee that everything will just drop into place to suit your plans. For an unusual rigging application we look to the John Denver show that closed the old open-air Universal Amphitheatre, Los Angeles, in the fall of 1980. The next year the facility was enclosed, eliminating the problem I had to deal with one last time.

Problems

This was the last summer that the Universal Amphitheatre would be an open-air facility. Plans had already been drawn for a beautiful, new, fully enclosed facility. This show was to be the final performance under the stars. John's doing this final show was fitting because he had opened the facility in 1973. I had been there as the in-house lighting director at that time. The problems I had fitting our production on the stage were as follows:

1. We were outdoors with no covering over the stage.
2. The stage was just deep enough to hold the set and orchestra, but the front of the stage had been cut with a very large radius, which would not allow us to keep the normal musician placement.
3. There was no apparent way to build structures that would support the trusses without obstructing the extremely wide audience seating plan.

Because of John's having opened this facility, both staffs were nostalgic and wanted to go out in style. Therefore, I had to try to mount the full production, including slides and patterns, with the full orchestra added.

Sky Hook

The solution to the main problem of truss support came, as many good ideas do, as a joke. "Let's get a sky hook!" And that is exactly what we did (Figure 16–1). I contracted a construction crane company that had experience working on movies and sports events. Often a camera will be put in a basket attached to a crane for a spectacularly high shot. I merely wanted them to suspend our lighting trusses instead.

The mathematics were fairly simple. The weight of the truss was 2,800 pounds, the lighting cables were 1,500 pounds, and fixtures came

Figure 16–1 Crane behind stage at Universal Amphitheatre.
(Photo by James Moody.)

in at 3,000 pounds, for a total of 7,300 pounds. This was not a problem for a crane with the required reach. Luckily there was an access road directly behind the backstage wall, and we were able to get the crane into this area to the rear of stage left.

The last factor to consider was possible slippage during the week's time the truss would be in the air. A hydraulic crane with a 160-foot mast was used because it had accurate gauges that read out angle and boom-arm extension. I insisted on a guarantee in writing that it would move no more than one inch in the full week.

Set and Schedule Modifications

All preparation was accomplished in one 12-hour day, including staging and band setup. Winds at night in the open amphitheatre were a concern, so I did not want to use a cloth cyclorama or projection screen. Rather I had 4 × 24 foot hardwall flats built, covered with muslin, and painted white. To frame the stage picture, I added black soft goods from the top of the 50-foot rear wall, approximately 50-feet wide, but I did not put any drapery legs in as they would only blow around in the wind. The movement of the black drapery was not a problem because the hardwall white cyclorama was in front (Figure 16–2).

I wish at this point it could be said that everything went off without a hitch. The fact is that after the truss was attached to the crane cable and the fixtures were put on, I realized that the lighting design was not completely symmetrical. Also, all the lighting cables were led to one point of exit off the trusses, stage left. With the imbalance of the fixture layout, that put a great deal of weight on that corner, which made the truss lean. The only solution was to add a guy-line to the back wall for balance once the truss was in place. We added two more guy-lines off

Figure 16–2 Front view of stage.
(Photo by James Moody.)

stage left and stage right to keep the truss from turning like a top while suspended from the single center hanging point.

The actual performances started the next day after sound checks. The longer than normal setup was scheduled to allow for the anticipated problems that could result from the unusual production technique we were attempting with the crane. A break was planned between the expected completion of the setup and darkness. I wanted to be sure the setup would be complete before we lost the light of day. Then we could focus the lighting in the darkness. Because the system was almost half ellipsoidals and projections, shuttering and focus were more critical than with PAR-64 fixtures. I have focused PARs in bright sunlight many times, but this was a very special show so we were allowed this luxury.

Rehearsal and the Shows

Day two started at one o'clock with a full orchestra rehearsal for the opening act: God himself, George Burns. Another fitting touch, as John had made his film debut with Mr. Burns in *Oh God*. Then came a rehearsal for John with the orchestra, and we were off and running, almost. Actually, so much publicity was generated by these being the final performances in the facility and the appearance of John and Mr. Burns together that the press consumed more than an hour taking pictures and conducting interviews.

Opening night went very well, and we were ready to settle back for a nice run while everyone had a chance to go home to their own beds for a few days before hitting the road again. However, when we returned the next day, the crane operator assured us that the crane arm had not moved, but the crane body had! Apparently, the amphitheatre had been built on the site of the trash dump for the movie studio, and the concrete slabs that were placed over this landfill had cracked at the front left leveling pad of the truck. The crane operator leveled the truck quite easily with the hydraulic leveling devices in the truck, but we were concerned that the ground would continue to give way. After consulting with the Universal Amphitheatre staff, we decided that if the weight was distributed over a broader area, the ground would hold. Large 4-foot long, 2 × 2 foot wooden beams were placed under the leveling pads. That accomplished the weight distribution needed and kept the crane from sinking further.

The effect for the audience was unique. Many patrons had attended concerts in the facility for years, and such a large concert lighting rig had never been used since the stage had been reshaped a few years prior. The photograph looking across the front of the stage (Figure 16–3) shows how far the truss had to extend past the lip of the stage. If floor supports had been used, many seats would have been obstructed.

Although cranes have been used for outdoor festivals to hold up roofs, I believe this was a unique application of the sky hook. It shows how a tricky problem can be solved when you are not afraid to try something out of the ordinary. When faced with a seemingly unanswerable question, look for an unexpected answer. Nothing is gained by saying, "It can't be done."

In chapter 21, I explore another time that a roof was not available. In that case I suggested that the production still could be done if we used a concert technique.

Figure 16–3   Side view of stage.
(Photo by James Moody.)

17

A Look Inside Design:
Designers Talk about
Their Designs

When I first thought about writing a book on concert lighting I had it in mind to do a second book compiling a pictorial with interviews of all the early concert lighting designers and their work. I knew that if it wasn't done, the history of our profession would be quickly lost. True, the technology has advanced so far past those early efforts that they seem like a kindergartner's first use of finger paints as opposed to a modern computer program. But that is not truly the point. In virtually every area of human study we have learned and grown in our knowledge and thus improved the future by looking at and studying the past.

I insisted that at least a small part of that book idea be added to the second edition. Although I knew I personally did not have the time to go out and interview all the great designers of the 1960s, 1970s, and 1980s, I felt strongly that the history should be preserved. If that meant my only adding a few interviews, then so be it.

So be it for a number of reasons. First and foremost I must take the blame for not having full time to devote to it. My own design schedule proved to be simply too busy. Second, the designers' own schedules made it very difficult to catch up with them. Our work keeps us on the move. From city to city and country to country and even continent to continent it was a struggle to get three designers to slow down long enough to do an interview. One was in my own backyard, my partner, Jeff Ravitz, and his turned out to be the last interview, done moments before my manuscript deadline!

Why am I telling this story? Because I want you to know that I do not feel the job is complete. Just as I felt from the first day my book was published that someone was bound to come along and do a bigger, better, more insightful book on the subject of concert lighting, I felt someone would do a book on the designers working in this new media. But it did not happen; why? Please do not let our history be lost.

With that said, I feel the three designers that follow represent three very different styles, in both the music their shows represent and their personal approach to design. One is a theatrically trained person but was not a lighting design specialist in school. One was a professional singer with some acting training before turning to road management and ultimately lighting design. Another is an unschooled Englishman who has created a whole new vocabulary and mix of design talents to create his lighting. I myself have an advanced college degree in theatrical lighting. Although my designs do not appear in this chapter, you should compare the styles and then read the next chapter to see how our backgrounds and education played a part in what we have become.

The first two interviews are telephone interviews I conducted with two of the designers. Willie Williams was already at work in Dublin on U2's 1997 tour. I sent him a set of questions, and what is printed concerning the ZOO TV Tour comes directly from his written response. I have tried to make very few editorial changes.

What I hope you get from these interviews is an insight into how the *process* of design works. Not what symbols get drawn on a piece of paper, but how you get to the paper and what you do with it once the paper is made a reality. Each designer's light plot is included, and color photographs of the tours are presented.

The 1996 Reba McEntire Tour by Peter Morse

Q Who actually hired you?

A Narvel Blackstock, Reba's manager, husband, and show producer. Obie lighting had recommended me. They had done the tour in 1994, and Narvel saw some of my shows on tape and realized he had seen Madonna's Blonde Ambition tour I had designed and he liked it, so I was hired. He had a lighting director, Gayle Hase, who had been with them for about eight years. He told me he needed a new dimension, Gayle is great but I want to bring in someone who is really a designer, not someone who is just a lighting director. Can you work with Gayle? he asked. Well, I already knew Gayle and said, more importantly, can he work with me?

Q How many designs had you done for Reba in the past?

A Just one. She does a new show every year, working about ten months a year. It was a very nice proscenium show and they were really happy with it. Now I'm working on my third for her.

Q Was there a budget?

A No. Narvel goes with the preliminary. If he likes the concept, he will go with the flow. The bids were rather high, but he fought for the bid, he wrangled that with the production manager, Brian Leedham. I stay out of that part of the process.

What is really funny, every production manager, every manager that comes to me saying the bids are too high you've got to cut, I say wait a minute, go back to the vendor first and make sure you've got their very best price. That is what Narvel does. So he was happy with the design and just went with it.

Q What was the type of venue proposed for the tour?

A Strictly arenas. But we make plans for A and B sizes.

Q How many dates?

A One hundred and fifty in ten months. We are talking 20 trucks on one-nighters.

Q Who was involved in the initial creative meeting?

A The interesting thing was that the year before, on opening night of the 1995 tour [the first Peter designed for her] Narvel turned to me and said, "How do we go bigger next year, how could we possibly go bigger?" I said by going smaller. By doing it in the round, bring her closer to the crowd, get rid of some of the gags. Show them

Reba! So late that year when he called me and sent a fax of his design for 1996, it was not just in-the-round but it was three stages at opposite ends of the arena. I told him that was not exactly what I had in mind. He asked me what I would do regardless of budget. I drew up a plan and faxed it to him at the same time he faxed his to me and they were almost identical! It was basically three stages drawn together by ramps.

To me intimate was getting the people closer to Reba, not necessarily physically, as much as spiritually, musically. For me it just meant less gags. Narvel loves the gags. He interpreted it as meaning getting her closer to the people *with* the gags. Basically he connected the stages with a means of transporting her to various areas. As an example, she was put on a dolly and carted from one end of the arena to the other and all of a sudden she would reappear at the other end of the stage, magically to those people. Of course they forgot there was a raised ramp between the stages, but it was still a lot of fun. He really thought it out carefully.

Q So he, Narvel, is the set designer too?

A No, we talked Michael Tait out of retirement to do this one. Michael first of all brought the technology of in-the-round. And there is a big technology to it. What it really revolves around is sight lines. He's done a lot of shows in-the-round starting back with YES. He's got an ideal stage height that works and that is 44 inches. Nothing else works. So we had to come up with lots of alterations to the stage in certain areas where she could stand up and make costume changes and everything else.

Q Was that the only addition to the creative team?

A No, we brought in John McGraw [Plan View, Inc.]. Because of the time element and the fact that there was one gag that was very difficult. It was built into the top surface of the ramp at the north end of the arena. It was an articulated arm that went up some 60 feet, higher than the lighting trusses, and swung out over the crowd with Reba standing on it. It was an engineering marvel. Everyone agreed it was like a Rolls Royce of design. It had to fit perfectly flush with the stage so the dancers could use the surface. It was an historical occasion, working from coast to coast to bring this thing together. [McGraw] worked very closely with Michael on this.

Later, there was a choreographer, Jerry Evans, because she had ten dancers.

Q Who did the set construction and who was the lighting contractor?

A Tait Towers in Pennsylvania did most, except for the one unit John McGraw built on the West Coast. The Obie Company was the lighting contractor, but I am not sure if the Vari✳Lite package was direct or not. [Note: The Obie Company did contract all lighting services.]

Q Give me the chronological order of events.

A Narvel called me in and we met with Michael Tait around early December 1995. Within two weeks Michael had set drawings and two weeks later I had a preliminary design done. What is unique about Narvel is that he always goes with the preliminary. He loves just going with the flow as long as it is in reason. Of course, this was not, but it didn't matter. He loved the graphic of the design so much that he just trusted the rest of it and went with it.

I told him I needed three weeks of programming without band, sound . . . anyone . . . nobody hammering and sawing . . . total silence. So we set up a mock stage in Pensacola, Florida, with the full lighting rig. After that we had three weeks of rehearsal with Reba and the band and dancers. Again, the uniqueness of this is that they ceded to my vaguest wishes. The drawback was that it was prior to rehearsal, so I only had a vague idea of some of the stage plans.

Q When did reality set in, or did it?

A Narvel loved it from an artistic and maybe even an egotistical point of view, the pure size of it. But Brian Leedham, the production manager, called me and said OK, now we've got to move it. Now we've got to get realistic. So I spent a week refining it about 20 percent and that was basically with conferences with the producer and the production manager who had to do the day to day running of the show. It turned out to be a four hour out and a six A.M. load-in with a three P.M. sound check. Pretty amazing for 20 trucks on one-nights. The thing is that I remember Dolly Parton telling the story about how she didn't know she grew up poor because no one around her knew what it's like to be rich. Well, these people get up in the morning, have their pancakes and bacon, and say let's do it. I know that is a very loose comparison, but these guys don't know what it is not to make a show. All I know is that it works, I can't explain it.

Q Have you ever had that much time to program another show?

A No, a week, ten days. The irony with Michael Jackson last year was that it was as big or bigger, and they gave us ten days total with all the other people who needed to come in and do work, and it was awful. But I told them [Narvel] from the beginning. In fact the first year I told them I needed it, there was no question about it. Total darkness, daylight hours, waking hours, so the brain tissues are at their best. This is the most unique because they take the time to create. They are really concerned about the time, I don't know, it was just very comfortable.

Q So what happened when you got to rehearsal?

A The first day of rehearsal with the band in place and all of us sitting beside the stage with note pads in hand, having programmed the basic show already, Narvel comes out and says, "Well, let's see, how are we going to do this opening?" Then he turned to me and said, "What did you have in mind here?" So I said, OK, what I'd like to do is this and this. Well basically we had enough in the can so to speak so that whatever he threw at us it was easier to edit than start from scratch. We were much closer than if we had waited for him to show us what he wanted, so the show just evolved.

Q You haven't said much about Reba being involved in the creative process. Don't you want or need her input?

A Her creativity is certainly the obvious part, the music. We are building a show around her. As far as the input into the staging of the show, from my experience, the biggest input is in the rare time when she won't do it! She'll try anything. I don't know how much input she has, at least it is not visible to me. At the kitchen table or in the dressing room alone with Narvel possibly, but it is not obvious out front. But when something is done to upset her you know about it in a very quiet way.

Q   Got a story?

A   Well, because of the time element there was one gag that was thrown in late in the game. That was the one John McGraw designed and built that we spoke about earlier. Well, as I said the arm extended out about 60 feet that could swing out over the crowd. It had a two foot square platform with a pole and waist strap. But they had installed a full railing for rehearsal to help make her feel comfortable during rehearsals. But with the idea that they would get rid of it and it would look like her feet were glued to this tiny platform suspended in space.

  Well, she was willing to try it, she's a real trouper. And a week into rehearsal Narvel decided to take the handrail off but forgot to go and warn her. And the only way I can explain her to you is by telling this story. So the number comes, music starts, she jumps out there and all of a sudden the lights come up and the arm is up and she is terrified. But she is not saying a word but you read in her face a mixture of terror and absolute anger. She sings the song, the arm comes down, she pretends to do her bows and exits. You can see she is upset.

  Narvel comes out to give notes and says, "Where's Reba?" And nobody can find her. So he says, "We'll do notes later." But that's as much as *we* heard from her. She went through it. She did what he wanted her to do, and they had words later, but she will never make a scene with us. She's the sweetest person, I can't explain it. That's the country attitude. None of the others [artists] are like that.

Q   Do you use an assistant? How many people help you?

A   No. I do the design work myself and the drawing. I don't use an assistant at all. Gayle has become my assistant on these tours. I'll do all the design work and all the interface work. He doesn't want to get involved. He steps aside and lets me get it all ready. Then during the programming process he sits there with me and takes notes of everything I call out to the programmers. Any cue I call up, he tells me exactly what is happening in the articulated range and the conventional range . . . what color we are in, etc. A complete notation of everything that's happening in each cue. So if there is any disagreement as to what I asked for and what is delivered, he can read it out. Which is kind of interesting. He writes a veritable book every time we do this. And of course we go through spot cues and he calls the show. It's a very cooperative arrangement.

Q   What about method of drawing, CAD, Mac, pencil?

A   For a long time MacDraft. Pretty basic. Michael Tait was all over me because he's on AutoCAD and he would send me these wonderful drawings to which I would fax him a MacDraft layout, which never came close to matching what he was doing. So I started Mini-CAD this year.

Q   In production mode, who calls the show and how many board operators did you use?

A   Most shows what I will do is bring in someone, or I will work with the band's lighting director. I'll tell any artist who says they have a lighting director, will [I] work with him? Yes, I'll tell you if I can't, but I certainly will give it a shot. And there have been a couple of cases where it has been difficult, but in most cases that's fine. I'm not there to take someone's job, I'm there to help them, maybe teach them and expand their horizons a bit. The real question is can he work with me? I am invading their territory.

For this artist, as I've said, Gayle Hase calls the show on the road. For the first couple of weeks he'll call follow spots and boards. After that the board operators are on their own and he calls only follow spots. There were only two board operators on this tour; one Vari✳Lite operator and one Animator board operator. The thing is that there were actually four full-size Animator boards slaved or daisy-chained together so one person could operate in show mode. The reason for this was that we could have fit everything on two or three, but I broke it down because I wanted several people from the crew to sit and do various elements of the focus during the day. That way one person wasn't laden with the whole thing. Plus, if there was a breakdown on any element of the lighting, the boards could pick it up and continue the show.

Q   Crew size?

A   I don't remember. Obie would have that. [The Obie Company gave the following:

Crew Chief: Kevin Tyler
Programmers: David Arch, Michael Keller
Operator/Technician: nine
Vari✳Lite Crew: three]

Q   What were some of the nightmares, problems, things that didn't go as planned?

A   People not delivering. . . . That happened here, too. Although Michael Tait really came through, there were pieces arriving right up to the last minute. We started planning with Michael in December and said we wanted a show by the end of February. That's ridiculous. So given that, we knew things were going to be late. So we worked around that.

During rehearsal I would look up and during the programming process I found several lamps that were not useful where they were located. And either they were dropped or moved. In most cases I eliminated lamps that I was not using. And in effect this eased the weight situation and the load and everything else. I found ways to cut some lamps and move some cables that actually saved a truss here and there. And that happened through rehearsals. Not in programming, oddly enough, it came more in the rehearsal.

Actually, by the first show we were locked. It's funny, there were changes during the rehearsal, but we loaded in and out of three different venues during the rehearsal period, so we could try A systems and B systems and to get the load-in time, truck packs, etc., down. *So* by the first show everything was running smoothly. Narvel does this on purpose. During these parts of the process we make our cuts, refine it. I have to say that opening night we were happy. I stayed out a week or two taking notes and refining the programming, but the design was there.

Q   So there were no big problems, nothing didn't work as you expected?

A   Everything you could absolutely hope for. I can die happy. I have lived every dream. But at the same time you can't write a book about it because there was nothing dramatic. The drama comes when there is poor planning.

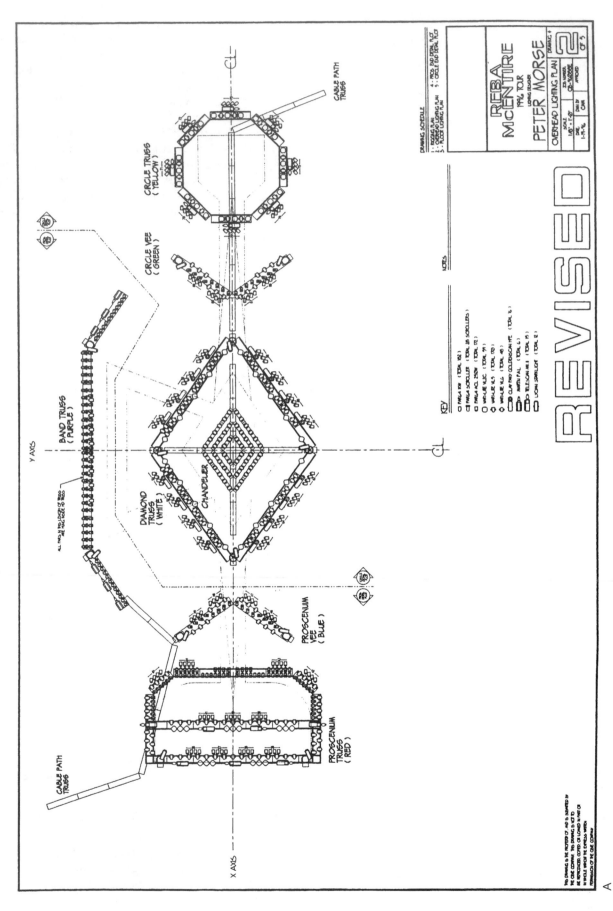

A

Figure 17–1 A, B. Reba McEntire's 1996 Tour light plots by Peter Morse.
(Courtesy of The Obie Company.)

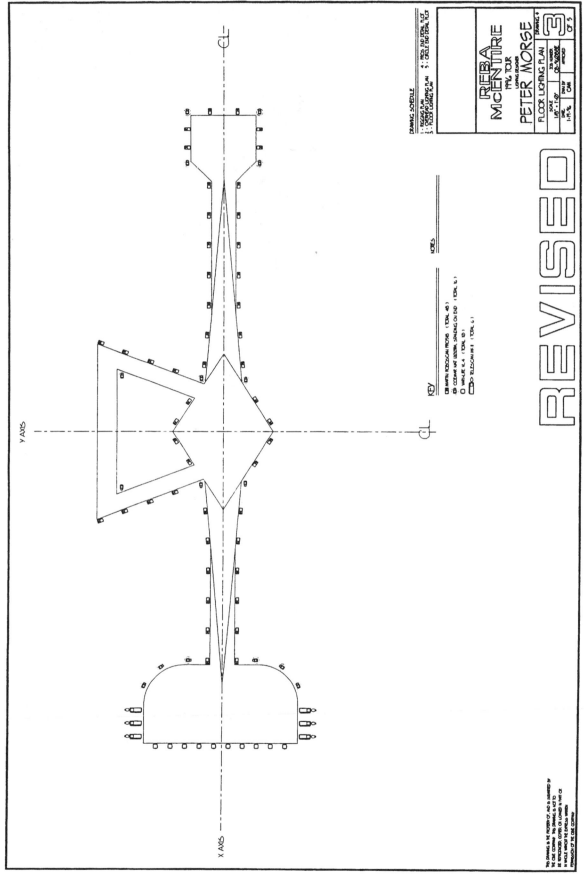

Figure 17–1   C. Lighting rig flown.
(Photo courtesy of The Obie Company.)

C

Figure 17–2   Reba McEntire lighting equipment list.
(Courtesy of The Obie Company.)

Reba McEntire Tour 1996
February 14, 1996
EXHIBIT "B" -Revision II

Quantity	Description
MOVING LIGHTS	
21	Telescan Mark II
16	Coemar NAT
16	Goldenscan HPE
48	Roboscan 518
6	Martin PAL
CONVENTIONAL LIGHTS	
178	Par 64
43	ACL Bar
12	1200w Starklite
EFFECTS	
6	DF 50 Fogger
6	Reel EFX Fan
26	Par ColorRam
CONTROL DESK	
3	Animator
1	Avo Sapphire
DIMMING	
6	ETC 48 x 2.4k Sensor Rack
6	ETC Data Splitter
INTERCOM	
1	24 Headset Intercom System
TRUSS and HARDWARE	
436'	CTS Truss
20	CTS Corners
180'	HD Truss
4	HD Corners
270'	Triangle Truss
120'	12" Box Minibeam
5	Underhung Chair
7	Rotating Spot Chairs
3	CM 2 Ton Motor
50	CM 1 Ton Motor
12	CM ½ Ton Motor
52	Rig Sets
1	Skjonberg 30 way Controller with Computer
10	Skjonberg 8 way Controller
SAFETY SYSTEM	
21	Horizontal Lifeline
12	Vertical Lifeline
14	Full Body Harness
CABLE & POWER DISTRIBUTION	
	Necessary Cable and Power Distribution
VARI*LITE EQUIPMENT	
59	VL2C
48	VL6
14	VL4
170	VL5
1	Artisan Console Package

The 1996 Styx Return to the Paradise Theatre Tour by Jeff Ravitz

Q Well, this is a little different. The tour we are going to talk about is not "new." You did essentially the same music and production design a long time ago, right?

A Styx and I go back a long way. After I got out of Northwestern University I started working as a freelance lighting designer and occasionally as a technician for Upstaging, Inc., in Chicago. I was working with Bill Quateman, who had a national hit, off and on. In between I'd fill in with whatever work was around, including touring with Kiss as a technician. Styx did some dates as their opening act. And I also ran into them around gigs in the Chicago area, also their hometown, opening for Rush and other bands. But the band had a spotty record. Some national exposure, but really hadn't broken out until a couple of years after their first release and subsequent hit "Lady." I actually turned down going to work for them several times. I was content with what I was doing at the time. But I did finally take the job they offered to me, but I have a story. . . .

I had actually lit a show for them a few years before and never met the band that night. I had gotten a call to do a one-nighter in Michigan City, Indiana. Just a half a truck, trees, autotransformers, Lekos, etc., and one helper. The night before the show, my helper's dad found out we were doing an out of town gig and called to tell me he was not letting me drive because his kid was only sixteen! So I was out a helper. I loaded the truck, drove to a high school in Michigan City, unloaded without help, set up, fought the janitor about hooking up power into the electrical panel (he thought the outlets on the front of the stage were enough), had no follow spots, and on top of that the band seemed to also be having a bad night. After I packed up, their road manager, Jim Vose, asked me how much I was getting paid, and I said, $35.00 and $8.00 per diem (I jacked the price up $10.00 because I didn't have any help). He thought I was making far too much and grumbled as he peeled off the bills. I never even met the band!

Q After that I'm surprised you wanted to.

A Well, I just kept bumping into them around the Chicago area over the next six months. I had met them by now in a casual setting and felt that it would be the right move, so I quit all my other involvements. Things change and they made me a very nice offer that allowed me a lot of creative freedom, so I took it.

We continued to open for Rush and Kiss and others while squeezing in a few headliner dates. We traveled in rent-a-cars, but I never had to drive because I was always in the back seat with a pad on my lap doing a light plot for the next date. We'd stop at rest stops so I could go to a pay phone and advance the date.

Q When did Styx get their real big break?

A In 1977 a Gallup poll named them American's number one rock band. They were riding very high on the success of the *Grand Illusion* album, and we were doing very large shows by that day's standards. Pink Floyd and maybe David Bowie were the only other bands doing concept albums and tours. In 1979–1980 we were touring the world.

Q What was the spark for the *Paradise Theatre* album and tour?

A Dennis DeYoung, the singer and piano player, was having dinner in a suburban Italian restaurant near his home in Chicago and noticed an oil painting on the wall. It was a strikingly beautiful picture of a rundown theatre with the name Paradise Theatre on the marquee. He was so taken that he bought the painting from the owner and took it home thinking there might be an idea for a song in that painting.

They usually worked on a tour idea a year in advance. We'd talk about an idea and then he and I would bring in the rest of the band. Everyone would come up with ideas that were a great contribution to the shows.

The part I came up with is the concept of starting the show with a blank stage except for the traditional theatre ghost light and an old janitor sweeping the stage. We had a backdrop that was painted as the rear brick wall of a stage with ladders and props painted on it. As he sweeps he reminisces about the old days, and slowly the scrim backdrop would illuminate the band behind it and the show would begin. Dennis had written the theme for "Rockin' the Paradise," which opened the show. Then the rest of the album, which somehow they had found ways of working in the word *paradise*. It would be played as a total beginning, middle, and end theme.

I experimented with front-back painted scrims that look one way when lit from the front, and when lit right from behind, you see a whole different painting. We used this technique in the show.

Q Did you have a scenic artist involved in the design?

A No, Dennis and I would talk and I'd sketch out the idea and then I took that to a scenic studio where they did the graphic and painted the drop. I also designed the risers and any backdrops the band used in those days. But that wasn't unusual for a lighting designer back then to have these additional duties.

Q In the case of Paradise Theatre all this happened before an album was even written or recorded, correct?

A Yes, again very unusual. But Dennis wrote several Rock and Roll songs that stood on their own but made them fit in. All in all the tour lasted over a year and played extensively in the U.S., but also did Europe and Asia. I called and ran every show.

Q But Styx dropped from sight rather quickly as I remember. What happened?

A Based on the success of the *Paradise Theatre* album and tour, we mounted an even more ambitious tour called Kilroy Was Here. That tour took its toll on the band and after it they decided to take a break even though a live album had been recorded and released that did well also. With nothing happening with Styx, Tommy Shaw, lead guitarist and singer, eventually formed another band with Ted Nugent, and some believed that divided the band members forever. The rest of the band did do a comeback tour in 1991, but not very successfully. That was all very sad because they had been an extremely theatrically minded band, and it was great creating these stage shows for them.

Q Then how or when did you get a call that they were re-forming?

A I was doing a project in Boston when a friend called the hotel and said turn on the Regis and Kathie Lee show. There were Dennis,

Tommy, and JY playing an acoustic set together. They told them that they had gotten together to play and it sounded good, so they decided to try touring again.

JY called me two weeks later in October of 1995. He said Bill Stern would be the production manager. That was great because he had been my favorite electronics technician on the road with the band and had since moved up to production management in the years between tours. He was the ideal person, I thought, because he was already part of the family.

I flew to Chicago and we went to the warehouse where the band had stored all their things, but found many missing including the old upright player piano we had used; the Paradise Theatre drop was also gone. But the Grand Illusion drop was there, a little mildewed. That actually turned out to be good because we soon realized that the size of stages had changed in the intervening 15 years. That drop was only 16 feet high and 36 feet wide. In those days a 40-foot truss was the standard and you trimmed the trusses at around 20 feet.

Now we use 50 to 60 feet length trusses and trim at 25 feet plus, so it looked like a postage stamp! Fortunately I am a stickler for documentation, even then, so I had a full set of the drawings and records. I was able to find the same guys that had painted the original drop still working in the area, but under a different shop name, American Scene. They were thrilled to do it again. But we wanted more, so we hired David George of G&G Productions to design and build some new drapery and additional items. I wanted a very grand set of drapery to hide the trusses and festoon the stage. But they also really framed the Paradise drops well. We did find the old marquee sign and with a little paint and rewiring it was used again (Figure 17–3; Plates F and G).

Q Fast forward, what do you do to make a 15-year-old concept fit 1995?

A Well, there were a couple of things at work here. One is the incredible leap in technology over the years since that tour began. There wasn't a Vari✳Lite. But by the start of the Kilroy Was Here tour, we were one of the first five bands to have them.

Such an advancement in technology demands an acknowledgment of that in the new look of the show. And the lighting was dated by the style of cuing and so forth. So the second thing in play was really my own personal development as a lighting designer in all those years. I feel that I have advanced so much in my way of lighting a stage, my way of lighting performers, my cuing style, and my own musical sense have evolved over the years. All of that growth had to be focused on my favorite and most dearly beloved group. The group that had given me so many fabulous opportunities to do everything that I loved to do back in those days (Figures 17–4 and 17–5).

Q So it was you and Dennis at a kitchen table again?

A Not really. It was not so much Dennis and I concocting ideas on our own because, in a sense, it was an established concept. What we really needed to do was bring it into the nineties and see what was missing. Here we had an opportunity to revisit something 15 years later when we were older and wiser. So the entire band jumped in. We started by doing a number of two hour conference calls

A

Figure 17–3 A. Paradise Theatre marquee, circa 1980 with Jeff Ravitz on left.
(Photo courtesy of Jeff Ravitz.)
B. Paradise marquee refurbished, 1995, with Jeff Ravitz.
(Photo by Jeremy Windel.)

B

between L.A. and Chicago with all the usual suspects—production people, band people, etc.—to flesh out the new ideas. I had already begun to get prices from all the various sources that I needed to get

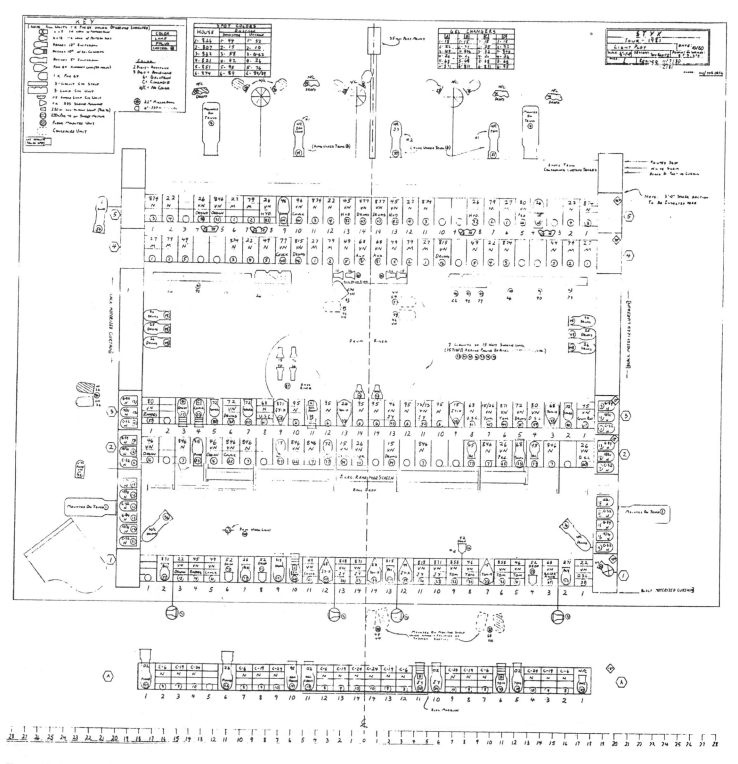

Figure 17–4 Styx's 1980 Paradise Theatre light plot.
(Courtesy of Jeff Ravitz.)

costs. We followed those calls up with a full scale production meeting in Chicago, around Dennis's kitchen table. I started by showing sketches and moving little matchsticks around the table to see what the actual progression would be.

"Paradise Theatre" Tour '80 Lighting Equipment List	
PAR-64	160
ACL	24
10 degree Berkey	20
5 degree Berkey	8
6x16 Leko	18
Single Cyc Units	8
Berkey 3 circuit cyc units	3
Altman Satellite	
Truss Mounted-	
follow spot	4
Lighting Consoles	
Computer console,	
96 ch.	1
Manual, 3 scene	1
Dimming	
12 kW dimmers	12
6 kW dimmers	18
2.4 kW dimemrs	remaining
Truss	351 ft. total

Figure 17–5 Equipment list for 1980 Styx tour.
(Courtesy of Moody/Ravitz Design Partners, Inc.)

Q When was that?

A February of 1996. At this point we had basically been in a go mode for about a month and it was me that suggested that we all needed to be in the same room at least once to move things also. So we went through the show storyboard style from beginning to end. We decided that the janitor would return at the end of the show and watch Dennis fade back behind the scrim and then sweep the stage as the lights faded.

Q How long before you had a light plot and how many revisions did you make?

A At that point it was about four weeks. There was only one minor budget go-around. The biggest thing was me trying to reconcile the trussing. The old configuration was very much like a grid. Because we had so many drapery, curtain, roll-drop, and scenic elements we ended up using a fairly large rectangular truss grid with cross-stage truss members. It served our purposes even though the innards continued to change from tour to tour. The basic shape of the truss rarely changed because it was so conducive to all the scenic elements. I always felt that rectangular truss configuration was best for lighting anyway because it gave me tons of positions over the stage. At virtually any point I could rig a light if I wanted to even after the plot was set. The original show also incorporated a front truss 15 feet out over the crowd. It gave some fabulous front light elements. I always try to minimize the use of follow spots because they are a kind of imposed element on a clean lighting setup. All of a sudden you've got this big light coming from who knows where from night to night and an unknown angle or intensity on a day-to-day basis.

I wanted to catch a guy at his mic with a sharp Leko cut to his head and shoulders. Then I'd put a PAR-64 with a color changer head to toe. That way I could change the color in the soft edge of the light and have a clean head shot I could completely control.

That works well in arenas, but we were doing sheds and only a few arenas, so there weren't the hanging points available. Instead I cantilevered a truss from the basic grid as far out front as I thought safe. I toyed with the shape to try and get a more pleasing variation. I also went quite a bit wider and that gave me the opportunity to do some really good off-stage torm sidelight.

Q But this time you went with an automated light package.

A Yes, Morpheus. I was really ahead of the game on this one because everyone was so nervous. The light plot was finished in March, and in April I actually went up to Morpheus's office in Santa Clara, California, and did some of the preprogramming sessions in their shop. The three days equaled about 36 hours of programming time and basically in the process my programmer, Mike Hall, and I were able to develop a color palette and come up with a series of basic focus or designs [in Morpheus's terminology they call each patch and set of basic focuses a *design*]. So we developed a series of designs. I had actually done most of them in advance of my arrival because I had worked with Morpheus fixtures before and knew what was needed. So we could go right to fleshing out the skeleton of what the cuing would be. After 36 hours we had barely begun but it was a great start. Programming time . . . there never is enough and it is so hard to get clients to realize what it takes (Figures 17–6 and 17–7).

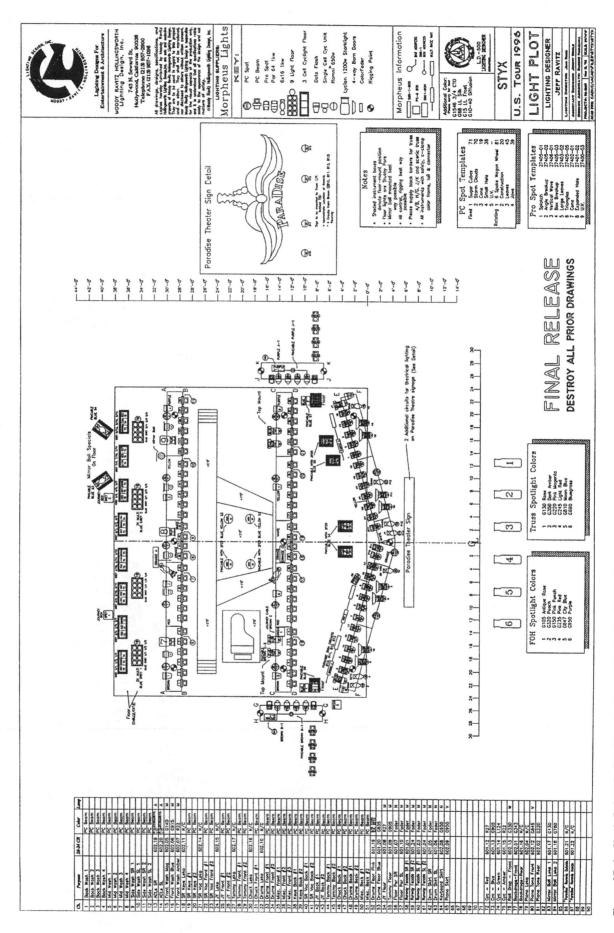

Figure 17-6 Styx's Return To The Paradise tour light plot by Jeff Ravitz.
(Courtesy of Moody/Ravitz Design Partners, Inc.)

"Return To The Paradise Theatre" Tour '95 Lighting Equipment List	
PAR-64	28
ACL	8
6x16 Leko	6
Romni	4
Moving Lights:	
Morpheus-FaderBeam	64
PC Spot	12
ProSpot	4
High End Systems Cyberlight	4
8-Lite Fay Units	3
Truss Mounted follow spots	
Lyscian	4
Lighting Consoles	
Computer console, Morpheus	1
Manual, 3 scene	1
Avolite QM 500	1
Dimming	as required
Trussing	578 ft 6" total
Truss	351 ft. total

Figure 17–7 Styx's 1996 lighting equipment list.
(Courtesy of Moody/Ravitz Design Partners, Inc.)

Q When and where did rehearsal start?

A On Mother's Day, May 12th of 1996. We rehearsed for six days in Gary, Indiana. Basically rechoreographing the show and getting the bulk of the cues down. We then shut down for three days and moved it to the first show venue in Cedar Rapids, Iowa, set up there for another day and a half of rehearsal and opened the tour.

Q What was your road crew complement?

A Four people on the road. A touring lighting director, John Rossi, and three crew members to set up and run the boards with John able to pick up the slack a little bit on the day-to-day setup. John ran the Avolite QM 500 for the conventional lights and Libby Gray ran the LDS-MP500, Morpheus moving light console. Brad Brown and Tim "Squid" Fincannon rounded out the team. Rossi called the follow spots too.

Q After the first show how long did you stay out?

A I was there another five days. At that point we were still really making the transition from my running the show. Things happened so fast that before we left Gary, Indiana, we had an invited audience dress rehearsal. I ran that show and called the follow spots because John was not fully trained and up to speed. At the first show I called follow spots and John ran the QM 500. We switched off until John was completely comfortable. You know, I feel the show was under-rehearsed by five to ten days.

Q In this case the show wasn't exactly brand new, but did things happen on opening night that had to be changed? Did it not play as well as it did 15 years ago?

A There were a number of little elements of the show. There was a very nice moment in the middle, an acoustic set, that the band came down in front of the roll-down drop and sat on stools to play guitar, bass, and congas. That part needed to be finessed quite a bit. The Rock and Roll numbers were fairly in line. And really the beginning and end of the show were major production moments that needed to be rehearsed and altered after opening. The timing was off, the exact sequence of events changed two or three times before we finally decided what it was we wanted it to do.

Q Again, I must say you have a unique opportunity to revisit something you did years before but with different, more sophisticated equipment. Was something lost, was it better simpler?

A I'll tell you: Absolutely. There were some cues that I did with just fixed lights that are just impossible to re-create any other way. I had a really bizarre complement of lights in the old days; beam projectors, 5-degree Lekos, etc. Just a lot of strange things because I liked the mixture of beam sizes. And it wasn't so much because I had come from theatre. As I was developing my ideas, I'd say I wanted a sharp light cutting through this soft wash or I want a gobo here or a hard cut on this guy at the neck . . . things that are harder to do with the moving lights unless you incorporate many different types of automated fixtures. And I spent a lot less time programming in the old days! Ha, ha.

Q How do you do your designs . . . the process and equipment you use?

A I use a Mac with the Mini-CAD program. I sometimes do the full light plot myself; it is just easier than trying to explain things to someone else. However, what I usually do is use the 3-D feature of the Mini-CAD program to put in all the risers of the set, etc., and then the trusses. That way I can see what form and shape the stage takes. Then I lay in the basic instrumentation. I can turn that over to a full AutoCAD specialist in our office who would then turn it into a final light plot. I would give all the color and focus information and he would put it into the drawing. We have our own large printers for that system and we can produce full size blueprints and reproducibles right in the office.

Q In rehearsal you used an assistant. Tell how you work with him or her?

A I am very meticulous in my documentation. I'm insistent on excellent documentation and I was even so when I did it all myself. Because of the number of choices you can make in any given situation now, you are deciding on actual focus, what color, where does the light move to, does it have a gobo, what is the beam size, etc. It's no more a simple judgment of off or on!

I need the ability to retrace my steps. Not only for security in the case the system crashes, but there are a lot of decisions to be made and a lot of consoles still do not have the ability to print out a hard copy of text information. Now I do extensive song breakdowns of all the music. And extensive tracking of all the cues as well as keeping all the drawings updated on AutoCAD.

I've gotten into the habit, and the luxury, of an assistant out on the road. When I'm putting a tour together, and it is much more of a necessity now because of all the documentation you must have for these shows. I realize that there are a lot of people who do not document their shows and it hasn't come back to haunt them . . . yet! But I just have this feeling that if I want to re-create a show two years later when someone decided to remount the tour in Asia, I have saved myself and ultimately the client, a lot of time, i.e., money. The ability to pull the information out and get things up and running quickly is money in the bank because you don't have to rehearse.

So when managers grouse at the idea of paying an assistant out there because they think it is just someone to get coffee for me they ultimately come to realize, as does everyone on the tour, that my assistant has expertise they can use too.

Q So, sitting back now, how was revisiting the Paradise Theatre and working with an old client feel now?

A Totally satisfying. Other than the frustration of my lifestyle no longer allowing me to go out on the road, if there were any group that I would hate to miss even one performance of, it is Styx. It's bittersweet having to turn it over to someone else, but a totally satisfying experience. I think the audience loved the show and the members of Styx were never in better voice or form. Sadly the original drummer, John Panozzo, was too sick to go on the tour and tragically passed away midtour. That put a damper on the experience, but artistically it was a great success for the band.

And we are now getting ready to revisit the Grand Illusion show, but not so much of a re-creation as the first outing, a lot of new concepts.

The U2 ZOO TV Tour by Willie Williams

Prologue

It is interesting to note that a rock show is the only kind of staged live performance that does not have a director. Add to this the fact that the cast (i.e., the band) is in charge (not to mention funding the event) and you have a curious power structure, one that would give most theatre directors nightmares.

By default, this is the role I tend to adopt when I am involved in a production, and in the rock business this is not uncommon. On large-scale rock shows the lighting designer quite often will take responsibility for the entire visual content of the show, particularly once the show is on the road.

Having worked with U2 since 1983, my role as show designer and director is official, which is helpful in that it allows me to concentrate on the big picture and gives me the freedom to delegate more responsibility to a lighting director and video director.

For ZOO TV my lighting director was Bruce Ramus, with whom I have had a long creative relationship. The video director the first year was Carol Dodds and for the second year Monica Caston. Given the extreme nature of the ZOO TV show, in parts highly synchronized, in other parts highly free-form, I was very fortunate to work with people who were able to grasp the concepts, develop them, and have the instinct necessary to make the best decisions when there was no time to say "stand by, and go. . . ."

ZOO TV

U2's ZOO TV tour was very much a child of its time. By the end of the 1980s the whole notion of the stadium big rock show was clearly in need of reinvention. Rock audiences were coming to expect a higher level of visual content than had previously been seen on traditional "festival" type outdoor events. Given the level of visual sophistication in many rock videos, it seemed quite ironic to me that in a live situation the visual accompaniment to most bands' performance would still be the very Victorian concept of a light show.

At the time, U2 as a band had reached a pivotal point in their career and were in the process of reinventing themselves entirely. Given these two factors, I saw an opportunity to take the vastly underused potential of live video and make it the central focus of U2's show.

Concept Meetings

Concept and design meetings commenced a little over a year prior to the start of the tour. U2 were in the final stages of making *Achtung Baby*, their first album of the nineties. This was a complete departure from the 1980's version of U2, and as a result the band members were full of ideas about where they wanted to go next. Bono, the singer, was already toying with the phrase "zoo TV," being a play on the free-form style of American "zoo radio" phone-in shows.

With all things to do with U2, ideas tend to form though much discussion and (usually highly entertaining) think tanks. In a moment of clarity after many sessions of brainstorming ideas regarding new and exciting uses for live video, Bono hit upon the notion of going the whole hog and actually taking a TV station on the road. From here the rest of the idea would grow, over the course of the 12 months' pre-production and the two years of what would become the ZOO TV tour.

Tour Venues

The tour was to begin as an indoor arena tour, to run for six months before going outdoors into stadiums for a further 18 months. Essentially this meant designing two entirely separate shows, but the plus side was that we were able to start small (with merely ten trucks of gear) and get a feel for how the show might develop before expanding to the absurdly vast proportions of the stadium show.

Staging

I designed a simple indoor stage to house four 8-foot square walls of video cubes and 32 36-inch video monitors. An additional 16 × 20 foot video projection screen, in portrait aspect ratio, was deployed via a roll drop, in the enter of the front truss. In the original scheme of things this projection screen had been intended to be video cubes too, but proved too costly. This was to be the first of many such compromises. Despite its lavish appearance, budget was to be an ever present concern throughout the life of the ZOO TV tour, simply because on this scale the opportunities for overspending in all areas are inconceivably vast.

From the stage a camera track ran out into the audience, on the end of which was a small second performance area, called the *b-stage*. This was something which U2 had wanted to do in previous tours but had always been thwarted by regulations, fire marshals, and so forth. This time the band were not taking no for an answer, and after much negotiation with buildings their wish was granted (Figures 17–8 and 17–9). [Ironically the b-stage format has since become something of an industry standard.]

Lighting

Lighting ZOO TV clearly called for a unique approach. I have always favored a very homemade approach to lighting, over an off-the-shelf one. This has usually resulted in the need to find or make individual lighting instruments, which in the past this has included recycling trash cans, buckets, furniture, and so forth to create fixtures. Hence the ZOO TV Trabant!

The Record and the Trabant

U2 recorded *Achtung Baby* in Berlin in the period when Germany was reuniting and the Berlin Wall was being pulled down. The Trabant (or "Trabbi") was the "people's car" of Communist Eastern Europe. They were mass-produced vehicles, highly unreliable, and horrifyingly pollutant with the engine power of the average American lawnmower. They were also, though, very small and rather cute, and as such they became a symbol of the liberation of the East—the ultimate underdog. The members of U2 took quite a shine to these vehicles, photographing each other in them and acquiring several of them as runabouts. (You could pick one up for about the same price as a five minute cab ride in the West.)

In the Trabbi I saw the perfect lighting instrument for ZOO TV. By removing the entire contents of the vehicle, I could imagine being left with a shell about the same size as an old-fashioned carbon-arc Fresnel, so the rest was obvious. The Trabbis could provide a suitably surreal and symbolic scenic element whilst also functioning to light the stage. Seemed like a winner to me.

Selling the idea to the band I could see might be tricky if it wasn't presented well. Consequently I went to the engineering department of

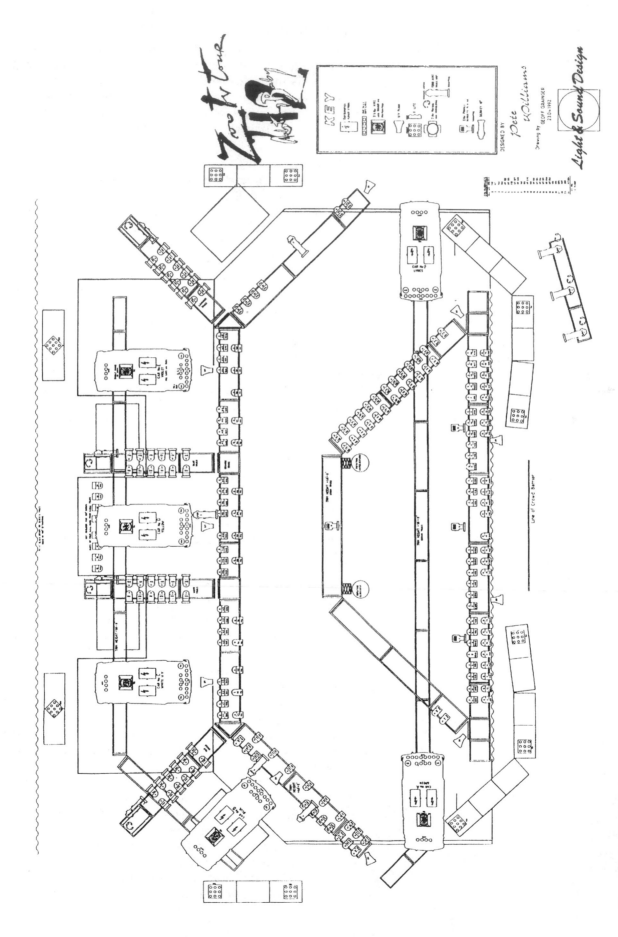

Figure 17–8   U2's ZOO TV tour lighting design by Willie Williams.
(Courtesy of Light & Sound Design, Inc.)

Figure 17–9 U2's ZOO TV tour lighting equipment list.

(Courtesy of Light & Sound Design, Inc.)

LIGHTING EQUIPMENT SPECIFICATIONS
U2 Outdoor Zoo TV Tour
Light & Sound Design

Structure
16	8ft. A-Type Truss
2	Mega Pods

Rigging
4	1 Ton Hoists
4	½ Ton Hoists

Fixtures
7	2.5HMI
3	2K Xenons
57	9-Lights
38	4 way Par 36 Molestrips
80	2 way MR 16 units
2	8' MR16Ministrips
2	MR16 Minicools
20	Car Headlights
284	Par 64 Lanterns

Control
4	Triple Remotes
2	Mains Systems
1	30 way Intercom System
2	Power distros
	cable as required
	Dimming as required

Color Changers
145	Color Mags
10	Mini-MoleMags with Radial Dousers
2	MegaMags
4	ColorMag Consoles
	cables and PSU's as required

Spotlights
15	HMI Starklights

Strobes
30	Mirror Strobes
22	Terra Strobes
38	Data Flashes
1	Data Flash Controller
4	Optikinetics 8 way Controllers

Smoke
4	F100 Smokers
4	Kraxoil Machines
4	Wind Machines

Specials
2	Pantographs
2	Mirror Balls
1500	Feet of Christmas Lights
4	Control systems for Architectural Lighting
4	Cable systems for Architectural Lighting
4	Power systems for Architectural Lighting

Light & Sound Design in Birmingham, England, and asked if they would help me create a prototype. Once they had finished rolling around on the floor laughing, they threw themselves into the project with unparalleled enthusiasm. The engine, seats, and front windshield of the car were removed, and all the other windows were replaced with sheet aluminum. A PAR-64 Ray Light reflector just so happened to fit nicely in the headlight bracket, and a metal bar which had previously held up the back seat proved to be the ideal place to mount a large Fresnel fixture. Trabants are constructed from a kind of low-grade fiberglass made from a mixture of plastic and cardboard, so HMI fixtures proved to be more successful than incandescent in terms of heat damage.

Brackets were welded to the wheel hubs of the car, to which chain hoists could be attached. This meant that using a motor manager, they could be tilted, pivoted on its own axles, thus avoiding costly engineering. Finally, a psychedelic paint job was added and we were ready to rock. I shot plenty of video footage of the Trabbi-light's maiden voyage and returned to Dublin to make the presentation to U2.

Once they had finished rolling around on the floor laughing, the band gave me a major thumbs-up and we went into production. LSD's warehouse came to resemble a Warsaw parking lot, and the rig began to take shape. There were seven Trabants in the indoor lighting design: six above the stage and one out in the house, which served both as a pre-show DJ booth and as a mirror ball, being able to revolve and entirely covered in glass mirrors.

Video Footage

The months prior to the tour also saw the making of a great deal of video material which would run during the show and indeed would be the principal visual element of the show. As usual the band members were highly involved in the process, from concepts and storyboards through to approval of the finished footage.

Almost every element of ZOO TV would continue to evolve over the course of the tour, but none so much as the video footage. New video elements were being made right up until the final weeks of the tour, as the show changed and new songs were added. Over the course of the tour the band, incredibly, managed to write, record, and release an entire new album, *Zooropa* (the album named after the tour, incidentally, not vice versa), so were keen to introduce new material and new visuals to go with it.

The first consignment of video footage was made by myself, Brian Eno, and Mark Pellington, the man largely responsible for creating MTV's hyperactive television style. Over the course of the tour new footage was made by almost a dozen video makers, including Kevin Godley and Rhode Island's Emergency Broadcast Network. Subsequently my role became one of curating the video content rather than making it, directing its deployment and use in conjunction with the lighting and music (Plate H).

Initial Response to the Tour

The tour was greeted with wild enthusiasm from press and public alike. It was quite the triumph for U2 as a band, many of their detractors having previously written them off as having passed their creative peak. This was clearly far from the case, as ideas continued to flow from them. Literally every single day there were new ideas, new additions, new toys to play with. It was a most exhilarating period.

Realism to a Fault?

Despite the fact that it would have been easier to fake a lot of the show effects, it was important to me that all of the show elements were real. The satellite TV pictures on the screens should be real. When Bono changed the channels with a remote control, I wanted him to actually have control. The phone calls should be genuine and to unsuspecting people, the Trabbis should be actual cars from the streets of Germany. Unbelievably all of this was achieved.

Looking back on it, I think my obsession with authenticity got a little out of hand (at one point we were genuinely corresponding by E-mail with a Russian cosmonaut in space), but it led to some quite extraordinary moments. In conjunction with MTV, U2 ran some competitions where the winner would get the show broadcast live to their TV and their TV only. A camera crew would be dispatched to the winner's house, and a two-way satellite link would be established. During the show pictures from the winner's living room would appear on the show screens as the band's performance was relayed back. Between songs Bono would talk to the living room full of people and they would talk back. This feat was achieved several times, most notably with a live link to the MTV Awards, where Dana Carvey played drums in Los Angeles accompanying U2 who were simultaneously playing in Detroit.

The Outdoor Version Takes Shape

As the tour got up onto its feet, we were already well into planning how this indoor show might be transferred to the big outdoors. Given that we were on tour, it was clear we would require outside help to effect this process, so set designers Mark Fisher and Jonathan Park were brought into the picture. Their work with Pink Floyd and the Rolling Stones had showed them to be leading innovators of large-scale productions. They came to see the indoor ZOO TV show and set about making proposals for how it could be repackaged and expanded.

Fisher Park's proposal included a row of ten 90-foot high pylons to support the required technical equipment, sound system, eight video screens ranging in size from huge to enormous and the Trabbis reborn, moving through free space on cranes and manlifts.

Lighting the Outdoor Version

Lighting this structure was clearly going to be a much larger task than lighting the indoor show. There was no stage roof at all, and much of the lighting was going to be for the structure, so I opted to use mostly outdoor architectural units which would survive the inevitable weather conditions. To create distinct moods on this scale, I chose instruments of various color temperatures, sodium fixtures, metal halides, incandescent quartz, floodlights, DWE 9-lighters, and so forth.

The lack of roof presented me with a dearth of places to hang lighting—the nearest available solid object suitable for lighting equipment deployment was 60 feet away from the singer and behind him. I experimented with a series of trusses which would overhang the stage, cantilevered from the rear, but these were rejected once the band saw them. It's true they would have been useful, but they broke up the clean lines of the stage structure, so were jettisoned almost immediately. Consequently, the band's key lighting would be just from Gladiator follow spots in the house, with another couple of dozen HMI spotlights strategically placed in the structure behind them.

The lighting would be used principally to change the shape and mood of this structure, whilst the video footage provided the bulk of the visual display. Obviously the two had to be complementary in terms of mood, color, etc. Most of the time the video would take the lead, but equally some of the abstract video footage I made was created specifically to enhance the mood of the lighting (Figures 17–10 and 17–11).

Outdoor Show Budget

Creating the stadium show brought with it a whole host of new budget nightmares. There were many bloody battles, some of which I won, some of which I lost, but without exception the show and the band's performance proved strong enough to continually make what was available into something quite extraordinary. The second year of the tour was largely in Europe, where the summer nights of the more northerly regions remain in daylight far later than the USA. For the American tour, the larger video screens had been projection screens, which would not

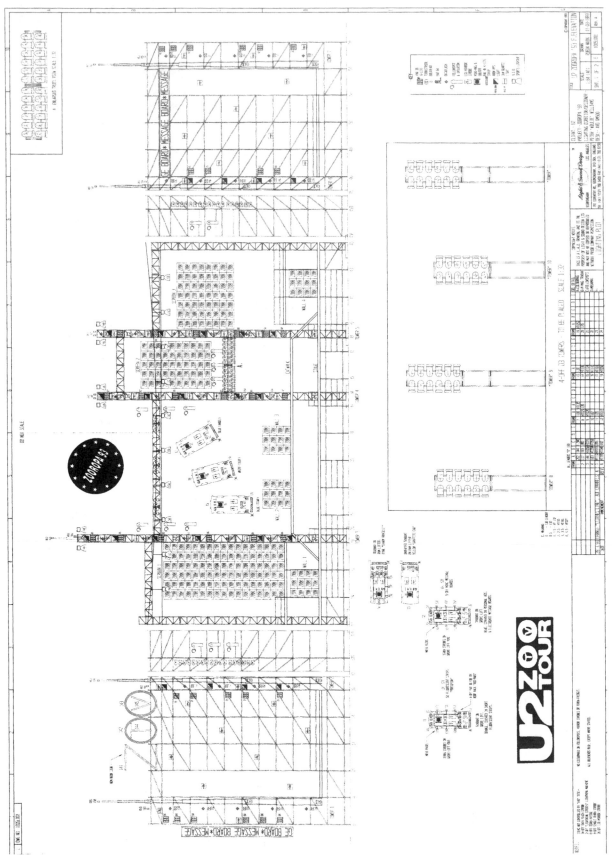

Figure 17–10 Zooropa '93 lighting design by Willie Williams.
(Courtesy Light & Sound Design, Inc.)

Figure 17–11   Zooropa '93 equipment list.

(Courtesy Light & Sound Design, Inc.)

ZOOROPA '93
Light & Sound Design Ltd. (UK Head Office)

2x Active Lightning Strik	3	TERRA Strobe	
72 way Avolite Rack C/ F.D.	4	TERRA MAG Classic	
48 way Avolite Rack C/W F.D.	1	Mirro Strobe	
36 way Avolite Rack C/W	2	8 way STROBE Controller	
20 amp 12 way Dimmer Modules	31	P64.110v 1000w.VNs1.	
10 amp 12 way Dimmer Modules	2	P64.110v 1000w.Ns2.	
Litton Patch Elbow	26	P64.110v 1000w.Ms5.	
Litton Socapex Rack Link	10	P36.28v.250w.ACL	
4 way Remote - Socapex	1	PAR36.110v 650w. DWE	
Triple Remote - Socapex	2	0 - 5M Multicore Cable	
Triple Remote Litton-Soca	2	5 - 10M Multicore Cable	
400 amp Power Distro	1	15 - 20M Multicore Cable	
200 amp Power Distro	1	25m Multicore Cable	
70mm 5 wire Mains - 20 meters	8	30m Multicore Cable	
70mm 5 wire Rack Links	5	35m Multicore Cable	
8' D3 Truss Sections	11	40m Multicore Cable	
4' D3 Truss Sections	4	45m Multicore Cable	
12' D3 Ladder Beam	2	50m Multicore Cable	
20' Ladder Beams	7	60m and over Multicore Cable	
LODSTAR Hoist ½ tn.	8	32amp.Legrand - 32amp. Legrand	
LODSTAR Chain Hoist 1tn.	18	LEGRAND - 6 X 15 amp. Sockets	
LODSTAR MTR. CNTRL. Module	2	Misc. Scaffold Pipe	
16 amp MOTOR Cable - Assorted	20	Swivel Clamp	
32 amo LEGRAND Y Splitter	6	Half Clamp	
3.25TN. Bow Shackle 5/8	135	1TN. LODSTAR MORE CASE	
2.00TN Bow Shackle 1/2"	50	Motor Control Case	
1MTR.2000KG.Spanset	30	1/2TN. LODSTAR MORE CASE	
4MTR.2000KG.Spanset	62	2x6 Lamp Bar Case	
6MTR.2000KG.Spanset	60	6 way Leko Case	
2MTR.2000KG.Spanset	12	6 way 8 light Molefay Case	
1' Steel Wire Rope - 1 Tonne	10	Colourmag Unit Case	
5' Steel Wire Rope - 1 Tonne	20	MoleMag Unit Case	
10' Steel Wire Rope 1 TN.	24	Intercom Case	
20' Steel Wire Rope - 1 Tonne	4	Hydrovane Compressor Case	
30' Steel Wire Rope 1TN	2	KRAXIOLK Smoke Machine Case	
30' Wire Rope Ladder	4	MUT Case	
5 Tonne Load Strap - 2"	12	Double MUT Case	
1 Tonne Load Strap - 1"	3	General Case	
PAR 64 Lantern-Black	216	LYCN HMI 1200 Spot Case	
PAR 64 Lantern - Short Nose	12	Hyper Towerr Leg & Jib Case	
Dolly - 8 x 6 Lamp Bars	2	Zvoboda Case	
18 Lamp Medga Pods	4	ColourMag PSU Rack Case	
BAR-6	37	Toolbox Flightcase	
9 Light MOLEFAY UNIT	22	3 way Mirrorstrobe Case	
4 Lite MOLEFAY (4x1)	10	West Mid Fan Case	
COLOURMAG Colourchanger	120	TERRA Fridge Flightcase	
MiniMOLEMAG Colourchanger	7	MR16 Birdy Black	
MEGAMAG Colourchanger	2	MR16 Transformer	
COLOURMAG PSU	33	400AMP. BAC.Cabe 7.5MTR.	
C'MAG PSU Rack & Mains C/W	1	16amp.EXT.Cable 10MTR.	
Mini-Mole 5K. Extender	1		
MiniMoleMag ROTARY DOWSER	4		
3K. XENON GLADIATOR SPOTLIGHT	6		
3K.GLADIATOR B;'LST.STAND CASE	6		
LYCIAN HMI 1200 Spotlight	14		
On-top Spot Seats	5		
Beyer Headset-Double	34		
1 Channel Belt Packs	26		
2 Channel Belt Packs	10		
Clear Com Main Station	1		
Cable Drum 100m. - Intercom	6		
KRAX Oil Smoke Machine	3		
Hydrovane Compressor.	3		
West Mid Fan Square	6		

have had sufficient punch in dusk conditions. Consequently these were replaced with an entire system of video cubes (300 in all) and became the largest touring video facility ever created. There were sacrifices as a result. Some of the physical staging elements were reduced or discarded, the Trabbis on cranes and manlifts, for example. These were hard choices, but the new video system was so vastly superior it allowed us to use it in far more subtle and interesting ways than before. So again the show grew, changed, developed, and improved on a daily basis.

Moving on to Asia and Australia

The final leg of the tour was Asia. From Sydney, Australia, the show was broadcast live to the world and captured on videotape for what became the home cassette. By this time the show has become highly polished with a greater degree of band interaction than we could have anticipated upon starting out. The Edge, U2's guitar player, was himself triggering video samples from a pedal board, a virtual Lou Reed would appear on the video screens and sing a duet with Bono. (Bono's voice was live, Lou was on laser disc.) Audience members were appearing on the screen nightly from our video confessional. Bono was using a Handi-cam video camera himself, and many of the video sequences were running to time in split-second accuracy.

However, my personal favorite moment from that video shoot was none of the above. In Sydney, God smiled on us, and gave us unique atmospheric conditions for the night of the show. There was not a breath of wind, and over the course of the night the stadium filled with a gentle haze of smoke, the like of which you'd be impressed with indoors, never mind in a stadium. The quietest, most poignant moment of the show was a song called "Running to Standstill," performed by Bono way out in the crowd on the b-stage. No video, no tricks, just one tiny figure in a vast stadium lit only by the front-of-house follow spots. This particular night, however, due to the stillness and the haze, the follow spot beams were bold and visible from Bono right the way up to the beam's source 300 feet away. The slightest wind and it would have looked like nothing at all, but that night it was a sublime moment of lighting and performance. Utterly simple, utterly beautiful, utterly huge, and captured on film. In my book, those are the moments that make it all worthwhile (Plate I).

Summary

The reflections of these great designers on one project out of very long careers should be reread and reread. Because what they have told you can't be found in a class, can't be fully learned by working in the business, can't be read in any other book. The essence of design is in the soul. These people have found their soul and transmitted out of their bodies and into designs that work far beyond illumination. I thank them for opening up and giving us a piece of that soul.

18

Concert Designers:
Art versus Business

In chapter 17 you had a chance to hear from three very talented designers. Although it may seem backward, I have waited to tell you about their backgrounds because I wanted you to consider the design and the solutions reached by the designer as a stand-alone discussion. Given what you have already read, now you can learn more about the individuals behind those designs.

What I have done is expand the biographic information on each designer. When it comes to what and how a person designs, I feel you see a lot of their personal history and background in their work. To follow the format of the first edition, I include myself in this look at the background and education of the designers.

In the first edition I put ten questions to four designers. One of those is a repeat interviewee, Jeff Ravitz. It should be of interest to see if his answers have changed over the past eight years, so go back and look at chapter 22 in the first edition. I have used only two new designers, Willie Williams and Peter Morse. While I would have loved to have interviewed even more, the lack of availability of some very sought-after designers made it impossible. I spent months and months trying to get more stories to no avail. I hope that someday there will be a book that brings a large group of these talented designers onto the printed page. It would be a shame for our industry to realize too late that we had lost their thoughts forever.

Peter Morse

Born and raised in the Chicago area (Glencoe, Illinois), Peter Morse attended New Trier High School and the University of Illinois, Urbana-Champaign (major in premedical studies). A singer, Morse recorded his first album at sixteen. He traveled and performed extensively on the folk circuit through the 1960s, took a break, and studied music and drama at New York University for three years. Morse went back on the road as a member of the New Christie Minstrels while continuing to write and record through the 1970s. He released several singles and albums during those years, but says not to hold your breath trying to find one. He turned to road managing for Mac Davis for several years. He started lighting Mac's shows, and there the interest began.

When Morse started road managing Mac Davis, it was Davis, Morse, two suitcases, and a guitar. Transportation was a rental car. One day

Mac phoned Morse and said he was adding a band and wanted to add lights. Did Peter know a lighting person? Peter asked how much more would Davis pay for that service. Whereupon he says he told Mac of his never before mentioned (even to himself) lighting prowess. Mac said "Great."

Morse immediately called his music teacher back at high school and requested a one-day cram course from the theatre department. He wanted the job, not so much out of a desire to learn about lighting, but to better his weekly salary!

Morse started with a few odd Lekos, or whatever was lying around each venue. Slowly, he learned the characteristics of each fixture and the hardware behind them. He progressed to designing the small touring systems that Mac started to carry on tour. Eventually he was designing and directing Mac Davis's Las Vegas show.

Peter has lived at Lake Tahoe, Nevada, for a number of years because he loves the summers and the opportunity to use is 1940 Garwood speedboat on the lake. He collects antique cars, something he has done for many years, and now he collects boats.

Morse is a prolific designer. In recent times he has designed for Michael Jackson, Madonna, Janet Jackson, Reba McEntire, Bette Midler, Barbra Streisand, Dolly Parton, Paula Abdul, Tina Turner, and Melissa Etheridge, among others. He received the 1991 Lighting Dimensions International Designer of the Year Award. He also has won two Cable ACE Awards and has had an Emmy nomination for his televised work.

Jeffrey Ravitz

Jeff Ravitz grew up with an intense interest in the performing arts and the entertainment business in general. This was spawned by his exposure to television in the 1950s. Ravitz says, "I was mesmerized and decided, as early as age four or five, to be a part of it." His introduction to Broadway was next and he was really hooked. Before kindergarten he was taking singing, tap, and acting lessons. Music came easily to him, and he was told he had a good ear. So it came as no surprise to his family that he went after whatever opportunities his small town in the New York metropolitan area had to offer. In high school, Ravitz was active in dramatics, but as an actor. "Lighting—what's lighting?" he asked. Then the Beatles hit and Ravitz was off to Rock and Roll land, even playing keyboards in a small but locally celebrated band.

Off to college, Northwestern University, in Evanston, Illinois, to pursue a theatre degree. In those days the popular advice to kids interested in theatre was to get an English degree and teach as a fall-back measure. That was Ravitz's plan until the voice of wisdom told him not to dilute his efforts but to go after his dreams with full energy. Northwestern was a well-regarded school for its drama program and had spawned several celebrities of the time, including Charleton Heston.

Ravitz decided to hang up Rock and Roll for a while and study acting. But his roommate loved lighting and shared his enthusiasm until Ravitz caught the bug too. A few inspiring professors, some real equipment, and some talented grad students showed him what it was all about. Then art history, classical music, musical comedy, Jimi, Jim, Janis, and Vietnam all began to combine to give Ravitz a point of view for the first time. By the time he graduated he was rarin' to go.

But careers in the theatre flow and ebb. Ravitz found himself doing more lighting than acting—mostly on the recommendations of his acting buddies. He found himself thinking more about the old band days. In early 1973 Ravitz saw an ad in the paper looking for a lighting designer for a national touring recording artist. He was hired not on the basis of the quality of his experience, but because he had *any* experience—even one experience would do! "Who cared?" he asked, "I was in."

> If I stood out from the crowd at all it was because I had a way of approaching the music from a theatrical vantage point. It was all just another monologue being presented to an audience that needed the designer's interpretation to put the message across. And the frustrated musician in me kept the rhythmic pace. Not note for note, like some of the shows I was seeing, but waiting, choosing the right beat or counter melody to base a cue on. This got me work.

Nowadays, Jeff would like to move away from concerts, even though he is still a highly sought-after designer. He received the *Performance* magazine Readers Poll Award for Best Concert Lighting Design in 1986. He also received an Emmy nomination for a Cher taping in Las Vegas. Ravitz still designs for former clients: Bruce Springsteen, John Mellencamp, Ringo Starr, Steely Dan, Styx, and Boston. He has added many new projects, including Natalie Merchant. But he is moving away from concert designing because, as he states,

> I do not really enjoy concert lighting any more because of the process. It's too little too late for me in every instance. Tight budgets are one thing, but the intense pressure to create a good-looking two-hour original show in the course of three or four all-nighters is just not satisfying anymore. More often than not, I come away from opening nights wondering how it all got done and vowing to swear off once and for all.

Part of Ravitz's feeling comes from a desire to make his family and marriage a priority in his life. "It's something I seem to be able to do, and it is the *only* thing I do that truly makes a difference." He does have other interests, skiing and scuba diving, but vows to get a hobby someday!

Willie Williams

Willie Williams grew up in Yorkshire, England. He advanced through high school but has no formal college training. He began designing lighting in 1977 with local pub bands. He worked his way up from there.

In the late 1980s Williams became interested in video and multimedia, which he has been incorporating into most of his shows since then. The past 20 years of designing shows has moved him from lighting designer to, often by default, assuming the roles of director and choreographer. "A Rock and Roll show is the only kind of staged performance that does not have a director. Nowadays when I begin a new project, this is instinctively the role which I take on."

Willie's approach is far from the norm in this field, which makes him difficult to label. People within the industry tend to view him either as, "a leading visionary or merely as an eccentric outsider. To be honest, the latter is probably nearer the truth," he told me.

Although a fixture in the music business for years, Williams attained notoriety with his creation of the 1992 U2 ZOO TV tour. It was a breakthrough production in many more ways than lighting. It received coverage in magazines as widely diverse as *Scientific American*, *Auto Week*, and *Vogue*, besides the lighting and music industry magazines.

Williams has designed for David Bowie and R.E.M., for whom he also used multimedia techniques. Williams was honored with the Lighting Dimensions International Award in 1992 as Lighting Designer of the Year and received the *Performance* magazine award for Concert Lighting Designer of the Year in both 1987 and 1992. As of this writing Williams is launching U2's latest outing. Reports are that it is another full leap forward.

Other interests are photography, writing (he has kept a diary for many years), collecting vintage photographs, and stand-up comedy. Williams is fascinated with kinetic sculptures and surrealism.

James Moody

Born in Joliet, Illinois, in 1942, I was reared by my grandparents most of my life. My mother frequently married and divorced, so I had no stable home life with her. My step-grandfather was my first hero. A railroad worker and union official, he treated all workers—Polish, black, Italian, German, Irish, Greek, and Jewish—the same. I have a profound respect for all these cultures because my grandfather believed in the basic goodness of working class people. He taught me that hard work is its own reward. He never favored one religion over another but took me into many homes, varied religious services, and introduced me to many folk entertainments. My grandfather was German by birth and my grandmother was Irish and English. My father was Irish, but I never met him.

My grandmother was a self-taught artist and loved to take me to museums and music performances, including Broadway shows that toured in Chicago. I attended music and acting classes given by the local Catholic Sisters of Mercy.

After traveling throughout grade school, I insisted that I wanted to live permanently with my grandparents so I could stay at one high school. At Joliet Township High School I was involved in the music department, but I acted in the drama department musicals. I took lessons on drums, steel guitar, accordion, and guitar, but was not particularly good at any of them. Private voice lessons were required to be part of the school's highly-awarded Madrigals group, and I won many ribbons at state competitions both with that group, the full chorus, and as a soloist.

I started college in 1960 at Bradley University in Peoria, Illinois, as an advertising major with an art minor. I left at Christmas and joined the Air Force. I was frustrated even though I was pledged at a fraternity and was elected president of the freshman class. I was there because my grandparents wanted me to be successful. I didn't want to look at another book as long as I lived when I left college.

Right from the start the Air Force opened my eyes to the fact that education and advancement were essential to having the nicer things in life. For some unknown reason I was assigned to Air Traffic Control School. That would be a fateful move, because the first day in class the instructor told us, "If you fail to do the job correctly people will *die* and you'll spend the rest of your life in Leavenworth [the military prison]." A hell of an incentive to an 18-year-old to study and succeed! Out of the experience a seemingly unrelated skill developed. The job of a controller requires an ability to deal with stressful situations on a moment-to-moment basis. Keeping your cool during an aircraft emergency is critical to the pilot's survival. Organizing your facts and resources goes hand in hand with the job. We were taught techniques to be able to listen to several conversations at once while writing down information on flight-following strips that track the plane's movements.

After tours at several lower-forty-eight and Alaskan bases, I was ordered to a small Asian country called Vietnam. While the experience wasn't as bad for me as for those who followed in later years, there is no question the experience had an emotional, if not physical, impact. It was many years before I would even admit to having served there, shunning the Veterans organizations that tried to help us deal with what we saw.

I was accepted to Southern Illinois University in Carbondale, Illinois, and started back to college as an English major with a theatre minor. I saw my future as a high school English teacher who helped out with the school plays. Marrying my hometown girlfriend meant that the GI Bill would not cover all our expenses, so I worked in the library. During military service I had managed to take correspondence college courses and attend local colleges near the bases to complete enough work to re-enter as a junior. I found I liked the people in the theatre department and spent most of my time there. Always needing money, I was interested in a job that was announced to assist a visiting professor. I had no interest in the person, only the extra money. It turned out that the professor was Samuel Selden, recently retired head of the theatre arts department at UCLA.

Sam took a liking to me, and I soon realized a real love of theatre under his encouragement. One day Sam said, "You'd do very well in theatre." I responded that I was an English major and had no aspirations to a theatre career. But I thought back to my grandfather, who always had said that we need to walk our road, but don't be blind to the interesting things that may lead down a new path. So I asked Sam how I could proceed. I was older and married and couldn't afford to start all over on another degree. Sam said he could get me into UCLA's theatre master's degree program without my completing a theatre degree or the requisite portfolio review. I thought again and then asked, "But what would I do? I'm not even a decent actor. I have art training but don't see myself as a scenic designer. What?" Sam looked up at me, pointed a finger, said, "Lighting," and turned back to his papers without another word.

In 1967 I entered the two-year master's program and graduated in 1969 with a specialty in theatrical lighting. Sam's faith in me sat on my shoulder guiding and encouraging throughout that difficult time. I couldn't have done well otherwise, because I did not have the background other students in the program brought to the game.

Upon graduating I felt my education was not complete and took a job at a small lighting company called Berkey-Colortran, Inc., in Burbank, California, to be the assistant to the newly appointed president, Joseph Tawil. A Carnegie University theatre graduate himself and former Kliegl Bros. salesman, Joe was the third person to heavily influence me. I spent five years working with Joe during a period of great growth for the company. But all along I was doing community theatre lighting at night and on weekends. A classmate of Joe's was Broadway designer Jules Fisher. When I told Joe that I needed to try to make it as a designer, he got me an interview with Jules, which led to my becoming Jules' assistant on the *Jesus Christ Superstar* production at Universal Studios. After that I did the premier production at the newly completed Shubert Theatre in Century City, California. Called *Mary C. Brown and the Hollywood Sign*, it was a bomb, but by then Jules had shown me what a truly talented designer is all about.

I wanted to stay in Los Angeles for my young family's sake, so I returned to doing small regional theatre until I received a call asking if I would light a concert. "Sure!" Only having seen Chip Monck's Harry Belafonte concert at college and a few minimal staging performances by Peter, Paul, and Mary and a few other folk artists in clubs, I didn't have a clue as to what was required, but I needed the money, so I jumped right in.

The promoter stiffed us for our money, but the sound company told me about a couple of young promoters who were about to launch a series of shows at the Hollywood Palladium and needed a light guy. That led to my lighting virtually every artist, U.S. and British, of the day because at 5,000 capacity the Palladium was bigger than any club in the area. It was a jump into the ocean by a fresh water guppy. I didn't know anything but concert lighting. Then again, not many other people knew anything about lights either (see chapter 1 for similar comments by Bill McManus and Bob See). I faked my way past a lot of artists. It was a great, quick two-year education.

The promoters moved on to larger shows at the Hollywood Bowl. I went along to call the lights for any opening act. In walked the headliner's road manager, Richard Fernandez, and asked if the promoter knew a lighting guy; he pointed across the stage to me, and I left the next day on my first road tour, with Rod Stewart. Chip Monck had designed the tour, and it had the lighting truss Chip had designed for the Rolling Stones the year before. Bob See was the electrician, and he taught me all about a road system. We worked together on several other tours after that, including the first U.S. appearance of David Bowie, the famous Spiders from Mars tour.

Later I would design and travel on tours for Frank Zappa, Dolly Parton, Blondie, Donny and Marie Osmond, Billy Preston, Seals and Croft, Captain & Tennille, Andy Gibb, Ronnie Milsap, Bay City Rollers, War, Stevie Wonder, Merle Haggard, Sergio Mendes & Brazil '77, Barry White, Captain Beefheart, Kenny Rogers, John Denver, Linda Ronstadt, the Eagles, Jackson Browne, America, and more than 30 other artists. It was with the Eagles and Linda Ronstadt that I really felt most comfortable. Then came John Denver, and I found a canvas with which I truly felt at one and was given total creative altitude. Denver's encouragement and willingness to spend what was necessary to give the people a great show, when he could have sat on a stool on a blank stage, was my opportunity to go completely theatrical, not flash, flash Rock and Roll.

I have received more than my share of awards in several fields of lighting: theatre, film, corporate theatre, and television. The most dear to me is the *Performance* magazine award because it was the first time an award was presented to a lighting designer. The 1980 Lighting Designer of the Year plaque hangs on my wall as a reminder of what so many people worked so hard to create—a new industry. I was just a small part of it, but to quote Jack Nicholson's character in the film *Easy Rider*, "What a ride, what a ride."

My other interests are collecting Southwest American Indian kachina dolls and sandpaintings and first edition books on the American Indian (I have 450). I enjoy sailing my 42-foot Hunter and hold a Coast Guard Ocean Master's License in the 50-ton division. I also have a Private Pilot License for single-engine planes. I serve as a captain in the Coast Guard Auxiliary on air and sea search and rescue missions and as a boating safety instructor and boat crewmen trainer. Theatre is still a part of my life. I design five to six shows a year in Los Angeles and in Telluride, Colorado, where I have my second home.

The Questions

I put the same ten questions to each designer. I wanted to learn how they felt about their relationship with concert lighting. They all approached the job with professionalism and concern for the clients or artists they served. I have not paraphrased their answers, rather this time I have let them speak their minds fully because I feel it is such a magnificent insight into minds that have created such magic on stage. I do add my own small thoughts at the end of the chapter.

Q What is the most important consideration when you first approach a design situation?

A **Peter Morse:** The most important consideration when first approaching a design is that of the type of music and type of performer that I am designing for. Eventually the reality factors, such as lighting budget, touring budget (number of trucks and crew), and venue size come seriously into play. However, the very first consideration I have is for the artist and his or her music and style of performance. If you think about it, the lighting designer's job is to assist the artist in projecting his passion and emotions visually to the audience. The key: support and illuminate the performance, don't *be* the show. There are exceptions to this rule, of course—primarily with the newer musical trends. In these cases, it is really fun to let go and design for tricks—the old *"ooohs* and *aaahs!"*

Jeff Ravitz: My 1985 answer still holds up pretty well: content and style. What is it that I am to design for? Is it instrumental music, narrative story-telling lyrics, or stylized poetry? Do the performers move, dance, or do they let the music do these things? Are they avant garde or conservative, literal or figurative in what they deliver? These things are going to give some shape to my thoughts.

Willie Williams: When approaching a design situation, the first consideration is to identify the key creative players. These people fall loosely into two camps: the people with the ideas and the people with the power. In an ideal situation these will be the same people or person, but usually there's a modicum of diplomacy required in order to keep all players happy without compromising the show to an unacceptable degree.

Q What one area of the finished design will you not compromise?

A **Peter Morse:** The one area in the finished design that I try not to compromise is that of *position*. Relative position of the lighting to the performer or the performance area is imperative. There are alternatives to any fixture or color, depending on budget, space, and live versus video/film formats. But the angle of the focus is very important to me.

Jeff Ravitz: Over the years, I've learned a great deal about survival, stress, and picking my battles wisely. Compromise now seems as natural as breathing. You want blue? Bingo . . . it's blue. Does it really matter that much? Would they ever understand your reasons for wanting it magenta? Not bloody likely. Getting it finished by opening night, that's what counts in the long run, as rehearsal periods grow shorter and expectations longer. Who's gonna care that you got bogged down doing the greatest cue the world has ever seen and it put you behind six hours, so the last half of the show is just recycled cues from the first half because you never got that far.

What do I really have control over that allows me to retain the standards of quality that have put me in a position of self-imagined strength? My level of preparation, for one thing:

- I will not be put in a position of not knowing the music backwards and forwards, because that will result in a clearly mismatched performance on my part. So I will insist, or beg and plead, for set lists, and live show arrangements of music long before most bands will want to commit. Sometimes, it is this pressure I put on the performers that gets them to conceptualize their show before it is too late to do anything special.
- I also do not have to compromise my preproduction relationship with the lighting vendor. However foreshortened the prep period may be, I endeavor to give them what they need to get the job out the door in good shape.
- I would not work for a band that wanted only bump and flash type cuing. I feel it is the cues that you do not do that makes the ones you do mean something. And fades are like a fine wine swallowed slowly.
- I do not like being told not to light the band but only the lead singer. Every person on stage is a great surface to bounce light off of to create a total composition—even if they are not lit prominently.
- I am disappointed when a performer who is better lit with fixed instruments insists on a follow spot to satisfy their ego. Most follow spots hardly enhance the careful sculpting accomplished with interestingly positioned lights in contrasting or harmonious colors. (But it makes those clueless chaps so happy, how can you deny them?)
- I hate turning on the house lights "on command" from the stage. (But, in certain circumstances, it has supercharged the audience in a way I would not have believed.)
- I used to refuse to overlight the stage to accommodate the video crew. (Now, I am committed to helping them find a way to accomplish the same results with a better look.)

The fact is, for many compromises to which I have yielded, I have learned something new and possibly valuable.

Willie Williams: Compromise is an inevitable part of teamwork. Rock and Roll shows are especially curious, because the "cast" are funding the performance, so are ultimately in control. Fortunately, many musicians find that visuals are not their strongest suit, so are happy to delegate that responsibility to their designers. More often than not it's quite an easy working relationship. I rarely find myself "compromised" in a negative sense. The only area I won't compromise is having fun. That and the design fee, of course.

Q   What is the most important factor in a successful design?

A   **Peter Morse:** In my opinion, the most important factor in a successful design is its effectiveness in complementing the artist, the music, the set. Most importantly, I feel strongly that the actual drawing is only a fraction of the overall design. The most important part is the programming and cuing. Without imaginative and thoughtful programming, and without attentive cuing, the most practical and beautiful light design is wasted. We have all experienced creative lighting that was accomplished with very small, traditional packages. In contrast we have all witnessed rather dull, unrewarding lighting when the director had all the latest technology at his fingertips, with no sense of creativity when programming or operating the system. It relies so much on the way the fixtures are "mixed" and melded into the performance.

Jeff Ravitz: A design that carries the viewer through the performance with a sense of progression, not repetition. Orchestration.

Willie Williams: For me, the most successful elements in design are simplicity, originality, and humanity. Of course, simplicity is the most difficult to achieve.

Q How heavily does budget figure into your lighting design?

A **Peter Morse:** Budget figures heavily into my design. Over the last several years I have been involved with several large productions. Believe it or not, budget has been a bigger factor in these cases than in the smaller shows. It seems easier to stay within the boundaries of reality with the small shows. In either case, once I have some idea of where the budget is, I am able to lay something out that hopefully is within those boundaries. Most larger shows have only a vague idea of what their initial lighting budget is. So my first draft is usually (and purposefully) a "dream list" of everything I would love to have on the show in question. Once the initial estimates are in (and the accountant picks himself up off the floor), I am better able to judge how the finished design will evolve. I always have an alternate plan in my head as I draw the initial plot. This way I am better able to "let go" of certain aspects of the lighting in order to come in on budget. In the smaller shows I try to "nail it" budget-wise on the first draft. That way I can refine the design without worrying about the cost, but thinking more about the actual application. Sometimes the quoted budget has *nothing* to do with reality. That is when it becomes extremely difficult to design the proper lighting. At this stage, politics begin to overshadow the craft. That is my greatest regret in the evolution of the large production show.

Jeff Ravitz: Significantly, but not how you might think. I have seen an unlimited budget be a designer's undoing. Knowing what to do with any budget, large or small, is a valuable skill. I have seen some very creative solutions achieved on budgets that I perceive to be "too low." The problem is, there can be little orchestration, because there is nowhere to go (see my answer to question 3).

Willie Williams: Budget is, of course, the ever present scourge of show design. If there were any justice in the world, designers would be shielded from such rude and brutal realities and left to be fabulously creative and irresponsible with other people's money. Really, the only gripe I have with budgeting is when the client's mandate is "We don't know what we want, but we need to know how much it'll cost." This, sadly, tends to be the norm.

Q What tells you a design has succeeded besides your own satisfaction?

A **Peter Morse:** In most cases I feel that a design *fails* if all I hear about the show is comments about the lighting. In most cases lighting is there as a support element—not the star attraction. The less said about the lighting, the more comfortable I am. Certainly it is important if the performer or performance is complimented by the design, wherein everything seems to fit like a fine puzzle.

Jeff Ravitz: If the design is effective, it carries the show to heights that it might not have achieved without good design. The message of the show is delivered with more impact. The audience reaction will indicate that the right nerve has been touched. And all of this might be accomplished with a design that is "transparent" to the viewer.

Willie Williams: Success, in design terms, is hard to measure. Really your own satisfaction is the only true yardstick, though a happy client is obviously the key to a quiet life. An ecstatic audience brings instant gratification. A good review in the paper is a bonus, but at the end of the day you know whether it worked or not. I'm pretty hard to please when it comes to my own designs.

Q Whom do you prefer to deal with: artist, road manager, or personal manager?

A **Peter Morse:** They all matter. However, I prefer for the primary input or communication to come from the artist. It is the artist I am there to serve; it is his or her creativity I am there to interpret and illuminate; it is their performance I am there to help magnify. The road manager and personal manager have their own criteria, which, while serving the artist's best interest, usually is secondary in priority for the lighting design. True, the artist may want more than he or she can afford. Then the personal manager's involvement becomes tantamount. However, in the creative realm, the artist's involvement is first and foremost.

Jeff Ravitz: I want to establish my artistic relationship with the person who knows the most about the show's intentions and concepts and the one who cares what the final result will be. It helps if this is also a person in a position to help the process along political and financial paths.

Willie Williams: Many years ago a good and wise friend advised me to "never deal with the feet, always deal with the head." You can't always get the access to the artist that you'd like, but be sure that "the head" has the only opinion that really counts.

Q Will you adapt a design to changing venues or start all over?

A **Peter Morse:** Wherever and whenever possible, the design should adapt to the various venues—even by going so far as including a B version of the show. I have yet to totally redesign a show for a specific venue. Fortunately most designs are malleable, as are the set and the performer.

Jeff Ravitz: When a design has been created to match a show's content as perfectly as possible, it would be like fixing something that is not broken to not use that design for different venues. Even if the show is changing daily from theatres to arenas to in-the-round, the basic elements of cuing and focus want to remain similar in order to evoke the same response.

Willie Williams: In context of a rock tour, especially doing one-nighters, a change in venue type has to be dealt with on the fly. Consequently, flexibility and adaptive initiative are vital. I would usually use a change of venue type to experiment with a rig, rather than unrealistically try to make the original show work in an inappropriate space.

Q How important is formal theatrical education?

A **Peter Morse:** I am not the right one to ask this question. My formal theatrical education came about on the road—first as a performer for 15 years, then as a lighting designer/director who literally learned as I went! My education was on stage, by trial and error. I was fortunate in that in those days there wasn't much competition in the concert field, so I was able to stumble along and learn at my own pace. However, in today's atmosphere, the competition is intense, and the need for proper knowledge is tantamount to properly and creatively designing and directing a show. The technology has advanced to the point where one *must* have a formal theatrical education just to understand the nuts and bolts of the designer's tools.

Jeff Ravitz: What is learned in a formal theatrical education can also be learned informally. It just takes a great deal more time and energy. It takes a highly motivated individual to do this. This person usually has an abundance of talent as well and will soak up the lessons that self education can teach. That being said, I do believe that the training that should accompany any formal education is valuable to receive, however acquired. This should include an understanding of the evolution of the dramatic process and why some things work on stage and other things do not. Development of an eye that sees the world in a way that appreciates subtleties of shape, composition and color, and, of course, light. Mastery of the skills necessary to communicate design intent, such as drawing, drafting, writing, and speaking. An appreciation of fine art and music and what those things have bequeathed to contemporary art forms. Knowledge of the scientific explanations of the phenomena of light and electricity.

Willie Williams: Theatrical education? I seem to have got away without having one. I suppose it could have been a useful thing to go through, as I still feel like I have enormous gaps in my knowledge of traditional theatre craft. Rules, conventions, and training can only be seen as tools, though. If you start treating them as rules I think it would seriously hamper your creativity. Man Ray said, "Inspiration, not information, is the force behind all creative acts," which I'd go along with. Mind you, I'd be bound to say that really. . . .

Q Should a person go on the road as a technician before becoming a designer?

A **Peter Morse:** In line with my response on question 8, I would say yes. First of all, no matter how much technical knowledge one gains in school, the practical applications are the most important background for understanding today's technology and the performance styles the technology is meant to support. Politically speaking, I think being a technician is the most direct route to a successful career as a designer. I'm afraid it's the old "coming up through the ranks" approach. A full knowledge and background in the technical field will give the designer a much better grasp of his tools and his creative environment.

Jeff Ravitz: Yes. If your designs will be for the touring industry, it is vital to gain the experience of traveling with a show. Only then can you see, firsthand, what works and what doesn't in a show that loads in and out on a regular basis. More importantly, future designers who work as technicians learn many valuable skills that enhance their insight as designers to create lighting designs that work on the hardware level. Being the person who sets up and maintains equipment on a daily basis develops a sense of what is efficient, fast, and safe. A designer who has come up through the ranks also has a healthier respect for the crew that makes the day to day operation of the lighting system a reality. Furthermore, as a technician, a person is in a position to learn techniques they might otherwise not be exposed to. This enhances creativity by giving the designer the knowledge of the limits to which the equipment can be pushed.

Willie Williams: If designing is really what you want to do, then it would be better to be the designer of a small show than a technician on a large one.

Q What do you, as a designer, feel is the most important personal quality needed to be a successful concert designer?

A **Peter Morse:** I was about to joke and say, "one should not be color blind," but Beethoven was deaf. So, I don't think that idea would matter! Seriously, I think the most important personal quality is to be observant and sensitive—observant of all motion and direction of action and sensitive to the lyrics and music. All of the performer's message and passion is contained in the lyric, and the physicalness of the performance. All of this must meld in order to project the "poetry," and the lighting is a necessary component to completing the total image. The lighting may be anything from minimal to overabundant. This is only determined by being sensitive to *all* the performer is attempting to transmit; and by being observant of the action that takes place on the stage as a result of the music and lyrics. Be sensitive to the artist and the performance. The designer is there to illuminate an event—not create one.

Jeff Ravitz: The possession of an open mind is a critical prerequisite to working in the concert field and design field in general. This makes a person receptive to new ideas, unusual music, unconventional people, and unique experiences. This helps make an individual tolerant of change, without which no creative breakthroughs can occur.

Willie Williams: A designer needs to have the obvious qualities of imagination, vision, understanding of how shows work, sympathy with the performers, and so forth. The single most important quality? Confidence, probably. There's an unattributed quote: "If you're not panicking, you obviously don't understand the current situation." When you've got a hundred people at rehearsal in a state of frenzy, I think a certain amount of detachment can be a helpful thing.

My View

Each of these men entered concert designing by a different path and achieved a place as a top designer. My choice of these men in no way is meant to imply that women do not do exceedingly well as concert designers. There are very well known women in touring, including Marilyn Lowey in Aspen, Colorado, and Candice Brightman in San Francisco.

When you first approach a design project, your most important consideration can be as varied as your own background. Just as color or space may be important, so can acceptance by the artist, band, and road crew of the fact that you are in command. I use command in the sense of having thoroughly prepared yourself to undertake the project. Do not let the crew get the impression that you cannot deal with problems or are not flexible and willing to work with them.

To compromise a design can be as simple as making the cyclorama green instead of blue-green because the artist likes green. We all compromise, daily, so why not in lighting designs? This is a medium in which factors concerning sound, musicians, space, time, and money all come together. There are bound to be compromises with all of the variables in the game. Simply face them and do not feel that any problem or obstacle cannot be overcome. Sometimes you have to stand your ground, but in the end, it is the artist's show and whatever is done must satisfy him, her, them, just as in theatre or film, in which the director has the ultimate control. The truly final word is your paycheck: do well and you get one, do badly and they are few and far between.

A very important factor in a successful design is simply you: your own instinct and understanding of the problems. Your feeling for the needs and limitations of the artist is what makes each design unique. We work within a very tight time frame. Given enough time and money, the places to put lights, a stage, and crew, anything can be accomplished.

To me, budget is the thing. Sure, I like it when a client does not appear to care how much it costs, but I care. I know I will not be back if the client does not make money. I prefer to deal with a client knowing that I have a ballpark figure with which to work up front. I may exceed it, but at least I had a guideline. Maybe I am more comfortable in this area because I owned equipment for a number of years and perhaps have a better sense of what things are going to cost.

A design is a success for me when the house stagehands tell me it was good. They see show after show, and for them to take the trouble to come and find me after the show and compliment me means a great deal. Besides this, I also agree with the maxim Chip Monck quoted concerning successful designs, so I hope people will not go out "humming the lights."

Naturally, the artist can lay down guidelines, but some do not. I have worked with clients and not met the artist until dress rehearsal. Then I take the advice of a good road manager who has been with the artist for a year or more, because he or she sees the show the artist never sees. The road manager handles the manager's complaints about money and the artist's gripes. He or she is on the firing line. The show must be good but still make money or the road manager is out of a job. This person is the balance point between the artistic and monetary sides of the show. However, I do take the artistic comments of a road manager with a grain of salt, because I have been misled before.

If I find out that a show I designed for arenas is going into Las Vegas, I want to start over. I may still use the ideas that worked in the original design, but it gives me a chance to take a fresh look at the concept.

I like young designers who come to me with a college degree under their belts, but professional experience outweighs education. Most schools do not offer advanced studies in this medium. After school, put in time on the road. An old Air Force technical school sergeant once told me, "Okay, you know the book, but you learn the really important stuff like who goes for coffee when you get out in the field."

There is another aspect of working on the road as a technician. In several instances, I have had excellent theatre students work for me who simply could not adjust to living out of a suitcase. Doing a show for two weeks in one town is quite different from 40 days of one-nighters.

Always working against the clock to get the show up on time or get to the next town on time is physically and emotionally draining. Some people like to be free, with no base; others need a home. Ties break easily in touring.

The ability not to be afraid of making a decision is the most important quality a concert designer can have. This comes from being confident in yourself. Decisions are asked of us every day of our lives, but seldom with more urgency than at three o'clock in the afternoon in Des Moines with eight channels of dimming blown up. Sure, the show will go on anyway, but you have to make the best of it. So do something, anything, but take a stand and follow through.

19

Touring in Europe, South America, and Asia

When U.S. artists decide to go on tour outside the United States, one of three approaches can be taken to their technical needs. What was most common in the 1970s was that the lighting designer was told by the artist's management that all arrangements had been made through the local promoter and that a local supplier would provide equipment as available. You were expected to "make it work, and besides, this is not the United States!" But that is no longer the rule. In a second approach, you may be asked to submit a lighting plot, but from there on you are told that you must accept what they give you because of the costs. That hasn't changed in 30 years! The bean counters rule now more than ever. And since most have no concept of *production*, they try to hold the cost of lighting as close as possible to U.S. tour costs. Touring overseas or in South America adds a tremendous amount of cost to the budget, such as fees for translators, higher hotel costs, higher travel costs, and higher per diem costs. Some of that will be paid by the local promoter, but there is no question that the bottom line is raised for tours overseas.

In the third scenario, you can actually get just about anything you request. This is not the exception to the rule anymore. Not only are bands demanding their shows be equal to a U.S. show, but also the suppliers in other countries, eager for U.S. business, have stocked the U.S. and British equipment the designers want. A few British and U.S. companies have opened branch offices outside their home countries. The cost, however, is higher. They have import costs, a larger spare parts inventory, higher taxes to pay, and fewer actual days the equipment is working, so they need to make more per rental day to keep their doors open.

Many British firms do have manufacturing facilities or supply depots in other countries. That is most often in the United States. Head Water Industries, under the name Penn Manufacturing, a truss builder, builds its product in the most overseas countries: Japan, Mexico, Germany, Spain, France, Australia, United Kingdom, and Canada. High End Systems, Inc., has a German operation, rather different from the others in that area of the business. Vari-Lite, Inc., because it does not sell its product, has taken to adding its own subsidiaries in some 13 countries, and there are eight series 300 dealers overseas. Vari-Lite, Inc. is by far the best-networked company in our industry. It takes an aggressive position to make its product available under controlled conditions that ensure product availability almost anywhere and with the proper maintenance.

There is one other avenue. Some companies have made warehousing deals with local suppliers. Morpheus has done this as a way of keeping some of its systems in Europe. Morpheus still owns and controls the equipment rather than having a "dealer" arrangement. Do not worry much that your favorite light or console is not available. Worry more that the management will cough up the extra money to make your design happen.

Touring Europe

If you are touring in Europe, you will find virtually everything that you need and are familiar with in the United States. Added to all the United States–built equipment that has been exported to Europe are the English and European fixtures, especially excellent dimming and consoles. To my way of thinking, Europe is a candy store for designers.

Besides the English companies, several of the U.S. tour lighting and sound companies have branches in England. Bandit Lighting, See Factor, Inc., and Light & Sound Design have fully stocked operations in England and on the Continent at the time of this writing. Check with them or any other U.S. company early in your preparation for your overseas assignment. It might be smart to work through them to arrange your European needs, even for the accountants, because payments can be arranged here, and often other cross-over deals can be cut that will save money.

These companies combine European and U.S. technology to create their systems. This includes having the solutions to the various power services you will encounter. Therefore it is relatively easy to tour in England and Europe as far as the equipment is concerned. Just about any piece of equipment is available. However, quantities are still limited, and early commitments are usually necessary if you want to be assured of getting everything you want.

Effects of the European Common Market

The biggest change for tours in Europe is the noticeable dropping of barriers. First is the use of passports. After initial customs clearance in the first country in which you land after leaving the United States, the chance of having your passport stamped again is almost nonexistent. People pass from member country to country in the European Economic Community (EEC), more commonly referred to as the Common Market, very freely now. Soon even a common currency will be accepted in most member countries.

For equipment, there has been little change. You must make sure that the paperwork you prepared before you departed is accurate and complete. And I mean complete! A customs agent having a bad day could go through every piece of equipment you have just to find some small item not listed that could hold up the clearance for a day or more. Don't take the chance.

As the designer you probably will not be directly concerned with this issue. But make sure if you are taking any U.S. equipment for which you are personally responsible, that the serial number, estimated cost, proof of country of manufacture, and other information is given to the person preparing the *carnet*. This is the document prepared before you depart your home country that lists all the items leaving the country that you expect to bring back. The U.S. Customs Service will inspect and stamp those papers before the equipment leaves as verification that it originated in the United States, so that when you return you will not be charged import taxes. While traveling in other countries the carnet is used to keep a paper trail of its movement and to certify that you plan on removing the equipment that you have brought into that country and do not intend to sell it. The form is checked at departure to ensure that all the items that entered the country leave the country, eliminating any sales taxes or special tariffs or restrictions of selling a product.

Either the tour manager has been through all this enough to make sure the paperwork is correct or the band's management has hired a specialty firm that is in business to handle this type of freight-forwarding paperwork. Equipment suppliers may try to handle their own equipment, but this is very rare now. This issue is very near to my heart, because I have been delayed in receiving equipment on site too often to believe that "someone" is taking care of everything! That "someone" better be known to you and the tour manager. You need to know how to contact that person 24 hours a day. I can guarantee you will need him or her sometime during the trip.

Cultural Differences

Customs as they apply to the way Europeans take their breaks and meals, the hours they work, and even crew availability can vary widely throughout the continent. That is not to imply that they are not as good as, if not better than, U.S. crews. It is just that you must keep in mind that they were raised with different working standards and ethics and it can take some getting used to on your first overseas tour.

Language also comes into play. You can carry one of the handy translation books that cover theatre or film terms, such as *Theatre Words*, available in the United States through the United States Institute for Theatre Technology (USITT), but that will not be the total solution to the problem. Many promoters do hire English-speaking crews on the Continent; in some cases they are U.S. servicemen or their dependents stationed in the area. I find the best solution is to make sure the head electrician you get from your British equipment supplier is able to converse in French and German. That is not too much to ask, because many Britishers do speak some of both languages.

Working through an interpreter is difficult, because most are not familiar with the theatrical terms we need to have communicated. I also find that the interpreter ends up spending more time with the management personnel than with the crew. I have gotten pretty good at the few words and numbers you need to communicate, and I usually find that enough people speak some English so that you can get your point across. Patrick Stansfield, now Neil Diamond's road manager, years ago worked for the Rolling Stones when they were virtually unknown in the United States. They toured small places throughout Europe. Patrick is American and continually became frustrated with people when he thought they knew he was American and still tried to speak to him in their native language. He had a feeling they spoke English but were just trying to put him down. So he learned a phrase something like, "No, no, let's not speak in Italian [or German, etc.] today, why don't we speak in English?" with a perfect accent. He contends he was never challenged. They always switched to English and never knew he didn't speak their language. This is a story, but it is true that most educated Europeans do speak some English out of the necessity of doing international business. The Japanese are the same, but there is one difference, which I will discuss later.

I did do a show in Berlin in which it turned out only one crew member spoke a little English. We were playing the then new International

Congress Centrum. The plan was to use only the house lighting crew and equipment for this corporate show. Because we had a two-day load-in scheduled, I agreed to try to work with the crew. We had a translator, but I knew she would be busy with other people most of the time (and I was right). I was told that the crew all spoke some English. The fact was that the facility's technical director was an American, but he could not be around all the time to lend a hand, because he had a very large facility to run with several other theatres and convention spaces. So, I was left to my own devices.

With a great deal of gesturing and the few words I knew, we got the show mounted. The real problem was in calling the follow spots. What I contrived was to write out all the cues and spend plenty of time with my one English-speaking crew member going over each cue until I thought he understood. Then I would point to the cue that was next up, and he would read the cue in German to the follow spot operators and I would give the *Go* or *Black out* (*Hauptregler*) or *Fade-out* (*Ausblender*) in my best German.

The crew tried very hard and did an admirable job. Of course we had two days of rehearsal besides the load-in time, so I could take this chance. On one-nighters, I would not recommend trying this at all.

Another situation, also in Germany, came about in trying to persuade the local officials that it was safe to rig a lighting truss from a catwalk in their beautiful and very old municipal theatre. Every official we talked to passed the buck up higher. Finally we had to call in the town's Burgermeister (mayor). The German promoter was acting as translator and go-between, and they were all talking so fast that I could not understand what was going on except that it did not look like I was going to get my truss hung. I finally got them to stop long enough for me to motion that we should all go up on the catwalk so I could show them what we needed to do. Once on the catwalk I asked the promoter to tell them that all of us were standing at the very point where we wished to attach the truss. And we collectively weighed more than the lighting truss! In that case a picture was worth a thousand words. We hung the truss and did the show as planned.

Responsibilities

In most European countries, especially Germany, the technical director is personally responsible for the safety of the theatre. He can be legally held liable, fined, or jailed if there is an accident. Of very great concern to the authorities throughout Europe is the rigging. Many of the buildings are very old and highly suspect as to their actual load-bearing ability. Do not be shocked when a rigging plan representing all the rigging and bridle points and their respective weight loading is demanded in advance of the show. In point of fact, the Greater London Council (the GLC, as it is commonly referred to by Londoners) will request such a plan and they will need to approve it several days in advance or there will be no show. Figures 19–1 and 19–2 are examples of rigging plots.

This is a practice I wish were more prevalent in the United States. I believe I have worked with the finest riggers in the world, and safety is always a top concern. Even they would be the first to admit that many buildings have not had a safety test inspection in many years and that structural load limits can change from day to day owing to weather such as heavy rain or snow buildup. Any touring designer or rigger who does not worry about each building he or she enters is a fool. And that high level of concern is what keeps our industry safe.

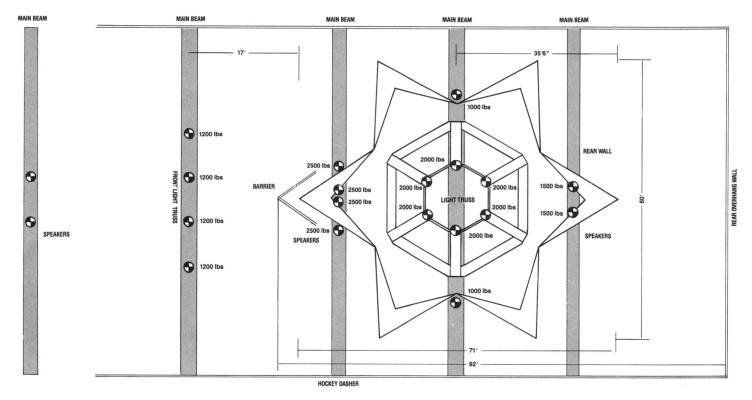

Figure 19–1 Rolling Stones tour, 1975, stage rigging plan.
(Plan by Brannam Enterprises.)

George Gilsbach, a well-known rigger, says that he is actually encouraged when facilities want to see his rigging plan. That they are knowledgeable about the potential risks is actually reassuring. Gilsbach went on to say that more and more buildings are asking for plans. The Palace of Fine Arts in San Francisco, a recent stop for George and me, requested plans for their structural engineers to do a stress analysis of what we planned for in that wonderful old building.

Power Supply

Power problems are not serious if you are using one of the British concert equipment suppliers. They are prepared for the different power set-ups in each of the countries and have adapters to do the job. However, if you insist on bringing your own lighting console from the United States, either make sure it has a switchable power supply (most do, some do it automatically) or request a transformer into which to plug it, or you will be out of luck. Many of the Rock and Roll lighting consoles do have a built-in switch, especially those made in Europe, so they will work on 110 and 220 volts. Any band gear with motors or fans will need 50-cycle adapters, which are expensive, so it is better to rent that equipment (such as electric organs, computer-based keyboards) in England.

Touring Latin America

The market for artists touring in Mexico, Central, and South America, Brazil in particular, is tremendous—not only English-speaking artists but also Latin artists draw huge crowds. They are as keen on large touring systems as we are. Demand has brought many U.S. and English

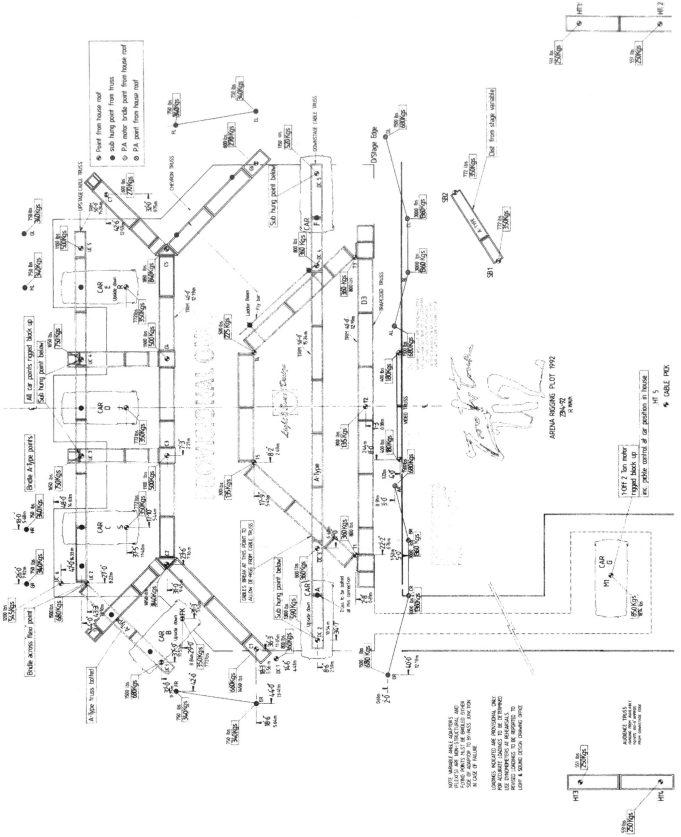

Figure 19–2 Rigging plot, ZOO TV tour.
(Plan by Light & Sound Design, Inc.)

companies to Latin America, to sell, start join-venture companies, or establish their own entity, as Vari-Lite, Inc., did.

Although equipment availability is nowhere near what it is in the United States or Europe, the desire of Latin artists is to put on spectacular shows that are just made for moving lights. They created enough demand for many manufacturers to want to get into the market. Vari-Lite, Inc. started making its lights available in Mexico long before it did in Japan. The glitzy, almost Las Vegas type production has always been a trademark for Latin shows, so it is no wonder they pushed for the United States–style Rock and Roll lighting earlier than any other country outside the United States. I built custom touring systems for legendary Mexican crooner José José back in the early 1980s at a time when he was number one in Latin America.

Power

Power is without a doubt the trickiest part of touring south of the United States border. Power changes not only from country to country but also from city to city. The U.S. Government Printing Office in Colorado publishes a useful pamphlet on power requirements outside the United States. But the problem is not limited to voltage. The cycle problem also is changeable from place to place. That is definitely the tougher problem when it comes to any motor device, so plan very carefully if motors or flown lighting systems are a part of your design. One last note: power is such a problem in even the largest cities that you can meter the input service and see a 20 or 30 volt change at the time the factories shut down. During rehearsal the voltage might be close to 100 volts and by show time the voltage could have gone as high as 135 volts. The overvoltage is potentially damaging to electronics. At 100 volts or lower, however, computers tend to shut down.

As in Europe, having a head electrician and a lighting supplier familiar and experienced in the countries in which you are touring is most important. Go over the potential problems as they see them and discuss what their plan would be if one of these problems were to arise. How do they plan on handling it? Planning for problems and emergencies is just as important as preproduction show planning.

Culture

Although Europeans often expect white, Anglo people to understand and speak some of their language because of cultural ties, the Latin world, which is much larger, is not so prone to discrimination on this point. Although I am not an expert on linguistics and the percentage of populations that speak second languages, I have found in my travels that fewer Latins speak English than do Europeans. It also seems, however, that most of my acquaintances know more Spanish words than German or Italian words, so I guess we are a little more at ease with our Latin neighbors when it comes to communicating. Portuguese, spoken in Brazil, although having more similarities to Latin than Germanic languages, is a little more difficult to learn. In my experience, it is such a pretty, sexy language, that Brazilian road crews do not seem to mind teaching it. The people are easy going and want to be helpful. I found them always to be eager workers. Many crew members know the main English words for the stage terms; that helps.

Mexico and Central and South America have been portrayed as "mañana land," where people are slow and uncaring about a timetable. That is an unfair stereotype. Warmer climates bring with them a style of dealing with the conditions. I have never experienced a show's being late because of a lazy or unproductive crew in Latin America. True, I have worked with crews that can be called less skilled, but that was in the early days of touring, when few professional stagehands anywhere were familiar with equipment and techniques. It is generally true, however, that skilled stagehands are not readily available in the quantity we would like. With good supervision, the job can be accomplished in any country.

Touring Asia

Asia was late to enter the concert market as packagers of tour systems. Led by the Japanese, Asia has become a big market for U.S. and European artists as well as a thriving local music scene. Because of extreme cultural and language differences, which are a seemingly insurmountable wall to the Occidental, I concentrate on this market because it presents the biggest difficulties.

The astute Japanese business mind quickly recognized a market for touring lighting in the 1980s. It was not long before a group of companies appeared in Tokyo, eager and willing to serve foreign lighting designers' needs. With expansion of touring into other areas such as Malaysia, Thailand, Singapore, and Hong Kong, the market has rapidly expanded.

The Lighting Industry in Japan

The cultural differences separating the United States and Japan would take volumes to explain, even superficially. This is acknowledged even by Ken Lammers, who was born in Japan of American parents, and has spent all but three years of his life there and worked his way up to become a manager in one of the largest Japanese lighting companies. After seeing and working with several U.S. and British production companies, Lammers started his own company to supply bilingual backstage coordinators. He would be the first to say that he will never be completely "Japanese."

Inadequately stated, the Japanese view theatre as an art refined to its most simple common denominator. Light is there to make it possible to see and is not a dramatic part of traditional Japanese theatre. Therefore the light should be bright, even, and clean so the audience can see the subtle lifting of an eyebrow, or the twitch of a finger during a scene from a Kabuki or Noh play. Form and economy of movement are the keys in these ancient dramatic arts. Until recently, schools did not teach western theatrical lighting techniques, and the theatres were not equipped for western lighting designs. But here too, the western influence has made Broadway shows extremely popular, and that has begun a change in the Japanese view of theatre.

Theatres and Concert Production In Japan

All the large theatres, some 2,000, were built after World War II. Most are government owned, whether by city, school, prefectural, or federal authorities. These theatres were built for community use, and each was designed as an all-purpose facility equipped to handle all the performing arts. Most theatre systems were standardized for time efficiency. Because the theatre has to serve the entire community equally, no one person or group can book the hall for a long period. This means that most shows must start to set up on the morning of the show. Other than in a few privately owned theatres, it is difficult to have more than three or four hours to set up and focus before rehearsal. This is why zoom-type ellipsoidal, plano-convex (box) spot, and Fresnel lamps were used and are still in use today.

The use of color media and more complex control entered Japan in two ways: western-style theatre and American modern dance. Taking their cue from the likes of Martha Graham and others, the modern dance of Japan is very experimental and innovative, and this sparked new uses for lighting.

In the early 1960s there were no equipment rental houses except those that catered to the movie industry. When television came out of the studio and began shooting in the theatres, a few lighting rental companies started to appear. This was when the six-channel, 6-kW dimmer packs were first introduced to the market.

When Rock and Roll concerts came to Japan, it was a surprise to the Japanese that people wanted to take a full lighting system into a theatre that already had one. For a long time artists had to use the house system unless they brought the whole thing with them from overseas. Finally the Budokan in Tokyo opened its doors to concerts, and the shows produced there were to become the most important influence on touring in Japan. Trusses started to be used, although they were constructed of steel. Most rental houses were using the United States–made 120-volt lamps because these fixtures were economical. The lumen output and color temperature were bad because they were being used at 100 volts. In the late 1970s, one of the lighting rental companies, Kyoritsu, made the first 100-volt PAR-64 lamp. Even with this new lamp, most shows did not carry their own dimmer or console. This was because most of the halls did not, and sometimes still do not, let you into their main power. This means that even if the hall has enough power for the show, you are forced to rent a generator. Most of the promoters have accepted the need for a generator as part of the production cost, so most tours from overseas now can have their own control consoles and dimming. A few large pop-music Asian artists tour with portable systems. The 1980s saw great change in concert production.

Lighting Companies

In Tokyo alone there are now about 110 lighting companies plus some theatrical groups that have lighting departments registered with the Lighting Engineers Association of Japan. But most of these companies only have crews and not rental equipment. Of the companies that do have rental equipment, only seven do concert touring for western performers. These are Kawamoto Stage Lighting, Ltd., Kyoritsu, Ltd., Lighting Big-1, Inc., Lighting Version, Ltd., Sangensyoku, Ltd., Sogo Butai, Inc., and Tokyo Lighting, Inc.

Two or three rental houses cater to the remaining companies, which do not own their own equipment. There are no full-service companies that provide sound, trucking, rigging, staging, and lighting, although Kyoritsu, Ltd., comes closest with the addition of their subsidiary companies that provide sound, stage carpentry, and video services.

Lighting companies normally do not take care of rigging of trusses, drapery, or risers. This means that more than one company is needed to supply a tour.

Power

Japan is the only country in the world that uses 100-volt AC power. It is also useful to know that northern Japan is on 50 Hz (Hertz) while southern Japan is on 60 Hz. Grounds are required for installations up to the main breaker box, but the individual outlets do not have to be grounded. If you bring equipment that needs to be grounded, make sure you do it yourself and do not depend on the house having a ground. Check before you connect anything.

Part of the reason for not simply putting a company disconnect in the theatre has to do with the electrical laws of Japan. Any temporary hookup that is more than 100 kW (about 300 amps) needs to have a qualified electrical supervisor on hand. It is easy to see that this would become expensive just for the six or seven shows a month that would need the service. This also applies to generators, but as long as there is an operator from the generator company on hand, they seem to allow it.

Generators

Because of stringent noise pollution laws, generators must be extremely well sound insulated (blimped). The most common size is around 120 kVA (kilovolt-amperes). The largest available are around 300 kVA. Taps can be changed on all sizes, so the voltage between the hot legs is either 440 or 220 volts, and then varied as much as plus or minus 50 volts. In this way all needed voltages can be obtained. The cycles also can be varied between 50 Hz and 60 Hz.

Equipment Availability

Although many western manufacturers do sell equipment in Japan (E.T.C. recently opened a sales and service office there), a few manufacturers build right in the country. One is Penn Industries, makers of trussing and outdoor portable roof products. Vari-Lite, Inc. has a presence in several Asian countries. So a reasonable amount of western-style lighting equipment is available. But the prices are high for rental. The main block to realizing your full design is the deal the local promoter makes with your artist's booking agent. That usually restricts the local promoter's financial obligation for touring equipment to a fixed figure. The artist must pay anything over that fixed number. And pay dearly. Costs for rentals are 200 percent of U.S. prices. Your ability to mount the same show in Asia as in the United States may not be limited by equipment availability but by financial restriction.

Can and do people bring U.S. lighting systems? Yes. But shipping costs are high, often equalling local rental costs. There is the option of bringing an Australian lighting company you may have used on earlier stops in that country. That has worked for several acts.

As for the locally built Japanese equipment, in 1984 a 500-watt very narrow lamp was produced. This light is so efficient that it is brighter than the 120-volt 1,000-watt lamp when used on the 100-volt systems. There also is a family of very narrow, narrow, and medium floods; a 1,000-watt, 100-volt PAR lamp; and 100-volt models of several popular theatrical Leko lamps.

Follow spots are not a problem. Most of the theatres are equipped with 2-kW xenon units. There are usually four in a theatre. For performances in other types of venues, the rental companies can supply your needs. It is interesting to note that most Japanese operators disdain color changers, and they place colors manually. Ken Lammers said that he gets quite a reaction when he tells foreign designers that their show was done this way. The smooth and accurate operation the technicians achieve, even on fast rock shows, make it undetectable to most people.

Aluminum trusses are available but quantities are limited. Hoists are Japanese-made because of voltage differences from the United States and Europe.

There are no federal laws on laser use, but some local restrictions do apply. Lasers are available, and the promoter can put you in contact with a specialist.

All trucks are 11-ton, straight bed frames, 36 feet long. Few tractor-trailer rigs are available in Japan, and no air-ride boxes are available. Luckily, all Japanese roads, even in the countryside, are excellently maintained.

Crew and House Staffs

There is no union of stagehands in Japan, although some of the privately owned theatres have in-house labor unions. The government-owned halls have a two-person lighting staff to act as supervisors only. Between shows they maintain the facility in top form. The crew needed to load in and work your show is contracted from the outside. This is usually done by the promoter, and the theatre has no say in which firm is hired.

If the show is going to travel outside Tokyo the key people travel with the show and local crews are picked up at each stop. This is arranged by the lighting companies through regional offices or agreements they have with local companies.

Crews get no set breaks or minimum guaranteed hours. They are paid a flat rate for the day with a bonus if the work goes through the night. The full crew stay through the load-out, even if that is the next day. Most Japanese have the attitude, "Let's get the work over with and then rest." Most crews want to work until the focus is finished before taking a break, even if that means no lunch. Japanese promoters are not in the habit of feeding crews. If they do, make sure special meals are ordered for the American and European crew members. Typical Japanese workers' meals are not palatable to most outsiders, even if they believe they have eaten true Japanese food in other countries. The diet is very different and takes some getting used to before you can eat whatever is available.

Payments and the Promoter

The promoter normally contracts for the lighting, sound, trucking, rigging, and staging for a tour. In the United States, Latin America, and Europe the artist's manager does this. No Japanese promoter enjoys exclusivity in any facility. The lighting and sound companies have ties with different promoters, and there is no bidding, as is encountered in the United States. In the past it was difficult to persuade a promoter to take a lighting system on tour. Now almost all tours travel with a full system.

Just as in the United States, production costs are mounting in Japan largely owing to bigger and bigger designs. As mentioned earlier, it is the rule rather than the exception that a promoter writes into the contract that the artist is limited to a fixed cost for production. If the artist wants more, they reimburse the promoter back for the additional cost. Lighting plans may be reduced during production meetings between a Japanese promoter and the equipment company, so be prepared to persuade the artist or his or manager to pay up or be willing to cut back on the design. The cost of a crew is about one-third more than the cost in the United States.

Theatres and Other Halls

Most theatres in Japan have fewer than 3,000 seats, but they have very wide stages by U.S. standards. A 100-foot wide proscenium is not uncommon, but the working depth is very shallow. This is owing to traditional Kabuki needs. The larger halls are usually gyms, which hold 5,000 to 7,000 seats. There are about four halls in all of Japan that hold 10,000. Artists such as Madonna and Michael Jackson have used stadiums because of the greater demand for tickets.

As mentioned earlier, most halls are government run. Thus there is often no discernible logic to the rules they impose, even discounting the cultural differences. A bureaucrat is a bureaucrat the world over.

Booking a hall must be done well in advance, usually one year. This means that many times a promoter will book a hall even if there is no artist scheduled at the time. The halls, being government owned, have to give equal opportunity to all who apply for dates, thus it is impossible to get more than a couple of days back to back. If an artist wants one or ticket sales demand longer runs, the promoters often get together and shift schedules when possible, but it is not a given that an agreement can be made, so do not count on an extended run.

Each hall has a different starting time. But the common rule is a 7:00 or 7:30 P.M. show. Halls want the show to end by 9:00 P.M. This is not only because of the work schedule of the hall staff but also and most of all for the audience. Most concertgoers come to the theatre directly from work or school. Public transportation is used by most people, who then face an hour to an hour and a half ride home, so they need to be on their way by 10 P.M. It is common to see people leave a show before the last song to catch their train, not because the show was bad.

One other reason for the early stopping time is noise. The legal penalties are very harsh on a promoter for violating the noise pollution laws. Because homes are built on all available land, the loading doors probably face directly into someone's bedroom. Noise after 11 P.M. is not tolerated, and the theatre will receive complaints immediately if this law is disregarded.

Rigging

Arranging the lighting system on straight pipes makes life easier for everyone involved. Theatres do not like to see trusses hanging from their grid, even if they are lighter than the equipment they replaced. If you have to bring a truss, be prepared to ground support it. Fire curtain laws are strict, so no box truss configuration can be hung unless it is behind the curtain line. Most halls do not allow hanging points in front of the proscenium. The only answer is to move the artist back away from the audience, which does not make the performer happy. Gymnasium-type halls are gradually allowing rigging, but each has different weight restrictions, and most seem to be ridiculously low compared with U.S. limits.

The Budokan, one of the best known and biggest venues in Japan, has gone through a few stages regarding rigging. The hall was built for the 1964 Olympics and has a concrete false ceiling. One foreign group did rig, and there was some damage, so rigging was banned for about six years. After long consultation with the architects who designed the building, rigging points are now installed. Each point has a dynamometer in it that gives an instant readout. If the point goes over the weight restriction, a warning bell rings and work stops until it can be fixed. Each point has a different weight limitation depending on how the other points are being used. Only designated bridles and Japanese-made cable hoists are allowed. A computer controls all the points, and there are ten patterns that it will allow. You must design the grid to fit one of these plans. The total weight allowed is 7.2 tons, but because of the weight distribution restrictions, only about 5 tons can be over the stage area. If you ground support, there is no restriction.

Pyrotechnics

Pyrotechnical regulations are up to each hall, city, or prefectural fire marshal. Permission can take up to a month and advance notice may be required in writing. On the day of the show an inspector has power of disapproval, even if you comply with the written order that was issued.

Business Ethics

The way business is conducted in Japan will be a puzzle to you. We have all heard about the Japanese being interested in saving face above all other considerations. The formality of business entertainment also is strange to westerners. In Japan, 4 percent of a firm's gross revenues are tax deductible for business entertainment.

It is more than being friendly to ask a client out for dinner and drinks; it is part of the normal business day. I have often seen a businessman, briefcase still in hand, leave a bar at 9 P.M., bid goodbye to a group of similarly briefcased men, and head for the subway train to go home for the first time that day. It is an expected ritual for corporate executives, and it is a great offense to decline such an invitation.

Another facet is the pecking order within the firm. If your boss (usually translated as *superior*) is to have dinner with an important client, you may be asked to attend. And if you supervise a department, your assistant also attends. This is a show of status and position, not a need for the advice of employees.

This brings up another rule of business in Japan. Often a question is asked directly of a technician, and a clear answer is not given. The Japanese system requires that when a superior is present, the question must be answered by the higher ranking person. Westerners usually view this as subservient behavior, but you should realize that it all fits into the Japanese sense of order and respect for elders and those of higher position in business.

Respect for Other Cultures

Touring in Japan, Brazil, Russia or any foreign country is exciting and challenging. Before you condemn methods or work habits you encounter overseas, look to the social and economic structure of the individual society. We in the United States have cultural links largely in Europe. No matter what country you travel in, remember that the people there are on their home ground. Respect their beliefs and ways of conducting business.

That goes for another group. Any military organization—of the United States or any other country—with which you might come in contact has a very special set of rules to live by. Although most of us would not like the strict rules, these organizations are set in tradition, just like the traditions of any other large group. The following example happened with I was to shoot a television program aboard the U.S. aircraft carrier *Dwight D. Eisenhower*.

The crew and officers had been most kind and cooperative and tried to meet our every demand. Although our presence was a huge disruption of normal routine, they even bent a few rules such as allowing us to work after normal lights out and letting us bring fast food aboard (a no-no for seamen). Very late one afternoon we were having a meeting with several officers and chiefs on the hangar deck. At sundown a boatswain's whistle sounded over the loudspeakers, and all crew stopped work or walking and turned and faced aft (rear of the ship). I did do service in the Air Force and now I am active in the Coast Guard Auxiliary assisting with search and rescue, so I am familiar with the general rules of service. I too stood but did not salute as the others were doing because I was not in uniform. In a couple of minutes another whistle sounded and everyone returned to their activity. I assumed everyone understood what had happened and because none of the officers offered an explanation, we went back to our meeting.

We were going over the schedule and I noticed we were scheduled to be shooting, with an audience made up of mostly military personnel, during the hour of sunset. I brought this to the director's attention and said I think we need to schedule this differently. He asked why, and the senior officer at the meeting simply said, "Because that represents what and who we are, we pay our respects." What he was referring to was *retreat*. The time each day that the flag is lowered on board a ship or military reservation. That is just another example of being aware of your surroundings as an outsider in a different environment from your own.

Take time to prepare for your overseas tour, not only technically but also emotionally and culturally.

IV

Cross-Media Use of Techniques

20

Industry-Wide Benefit from New Developments

The previous chapters give you an update of the newest lighting specialty and unique ideas developed to meet today's and tomorrow's designers' needs. In the chapter that follows, I present one case study of how these techniques can be used to solve a production situation for a television location. Then I discuss the visual definitions used in film and video and how to be prepared to adapt your concert for videotaping.

In this chapter I look at how concert lighting techniques and equipment can be applied to theatre, corporate presentations, sales displays, and architecture. First let us review some of the important elements in concert lighting and how they can be useful in other media.

Lighting Structures

The development of portable lighting structures is certainly concert lighting's most unique achievement. This was an area virtually unknown by theatre, film, or television. These highly portable structures have become the basis for development of new television studio lighting support systems at several new network facilities. The labor coefficient cannot be ignored. The research and hundreds of thousands of hours of in-use applications in concerts must be taken advantage of by facility planners in the future.

The true advantage is not classic design or engineering skill. It comes in the form of a practical structural concept that has been time tested. Size or weight-bearing factors change with application, but the utilitarian construction of the devices must be recognized as a great innovation. A young group of people faced a problem with which they had no expertise and devised a solution. We have not seen the end of development in design and additional study is needed if full benefit is to be gained from what concert people have started.

Theatre Use

The use of trusses to house fixtures in trouping situations has moved to Broadway. Side-lighting structures in which the lamps, whether PAR-64s or ellipsoidals, can be mounted, circuited, and stored all in one convenient case, are seeing wide acceptance. The truss is highly usable in this manner for dance troupes who want a convenient, quick setup system that is easy to operate.

235

Other trusses can provide a multiple-use structure to handle scenery support, drapery track, or even the skeleton of a portable proscenium arch. When historic Royce Hall at UCLA badly needed a second front-of-house lighting position but could not construct a permanent position in the ceiling, three holes for chain motors were cut and a truss was added. This was a practical solution to the problem. Two motorized winches raise the truss or lower it to the floor when it is not in use. This system retains the architectural and acoustical integrity of the hall for functions that do not require heavy front illumination.

Television and Film Use

The value of trusses in television and film have even more possibilities than in theatre. Portable truss sections outfitted with 2-kW or 5-kW Fresnel fixtures that can be stored then rolled into position for quick rigging on a sound stage or in a studio are a good example. On television locations, trusses pre-rigged with PAR-64 or Fresnel lamps can provide audience lighting quickly and efficiently. The increased safety factor over a single pipe is a great advantage.

Corporate Presentations and Displays

The truss has made it possible to advance the auto industry's design of eye-catching displays at auto shows. The moving light has added attention-getting appeal. Even department stores have used some of the smaller moving lights to attract attention to in-store, point-of-sale displays. The corporate presentation business would not be competitive without the use of splashy shows to introduce new products and get representatives and clients excited. The use of concert lighting techniques has become the head cheerleader for product introduction. Some shows encompass the entire floor of an arena. These shows cannot be done on time and with reasonable staffing requirements without these advances. The International Alliance of Theatrical Stage Employees (IA) is worried that these techniques have cut jobs and worker hours in this segment of the business. As with any advance, there comes change. The union is reassessing the needs of the marketplace and is meeting the future with well-trained, technically aware workers who can keep pace with this demanding business.

An example of how corporate America is using concert lighting was obvious at the 1996 Atlanta Olympics. Even white-shirt-and-tie IBM hired Rock and Roll designers, led by Candice Brightman of Grateful Dead fame, to light their pavilion. The need to appeal to Generation X, the MTV generation, has placed these corporate giants in the position of matching their sales image to what the mass media are doing. That responsibility is placed squarely on the music industry as the leader of American taste. Concerts and the artists who bring you the Mega-tours led the way.

PAR-64: Fixture for Any Media

The size and weight of a PAR-64 fixture are a great advantage when fixtures must be quickly put into position on scaffolds or noncounterweighted pipes. The low maintenance factor is also appealing to television stations, as is the comparatively low purchase price. Television has already made great use of the PAR-64. Audience lighting has virtually been given over to the PAR fixture. Other uses, such as musical numbers on shows from prime time to late night talk shows, now simulate the concert look with heavy color from PAR-64 fixtures. Television also gains greatly from the flexibility of the PAR-64 as a broad fill light on locations such as outdoor pageants, sports, and parades.

Those who work in theatre realize they have had open-faced sources as a mainstay going back to the 1940s. Fixtures such as the scoop and beam projector have been in use for a long time. Because the PAR-64 is a self-contained lamp, reflector, and lens, theatre has questioned its controllability. But with four separate fixed-beam spreads and several wattage sizes available to project from a broad field to a very narrow beam, the objection of poor control seems to lose force, and the introduction of the E.T.C. PAR that has a round beam is even more useful. Legitimate theatre has traditionally been slow to accept change. So it is not surprising that the PAR-64 fixture is only now beginning to be accepted. Theatre eventually will see the great opportunity it has to take advantage of this new idea developed elsewhere and make good use of it.

The use of the PAR-64 fixture has restrictions, as does use of an ellipsoidal or scoop fixture. When used for punch lighting when no shuttering or dooring is desired, however, it proves a valuable tool. The fixture is available with accessories such as a snoot to help block and restrict some of the ambient (spill) light. Barndoors are also available for shaping of the light, but either one of these accessories is only minimally effective.

The greatest use of the PAR-64 fixture is for back light, for which reshaping of the beam is not critical. Next in order of importance, it has great use for special effects such as beams of light or intense color. When the PAR-64 lamp is used for side light, the potential spill on set walls can be avoided if you are careful in positioning the units.

Dance companies can be the greatest benefactor of this new light source. Because dancers often use minimal sets and rely on light to convey mood and form, the PAR-64 is an ideal source for them. Dance generally desires more color than legitimate theatre and thus can gain the benefit of the high light output of the PAR to compensate for reduction in lumen output caused by saturated color use.

Architectural application of the PAR family is already widely seen. The sealed-beam nature of the lamp makes it an ideal candidate for outdoor environments. A housing that protects the connections and a weatherproof housing for wet environments have been marketed. These have found wide use in theme parks and other nontraditional applications.

Moving Lights

The remote-controlled, computer-operated fixture is currently the bright star in theatrical lighting. Its impact is already being extensively felt, not only in concert lighting but also in television, theatre, and film. With the introduction of a weather-sealed, outdoor housing there will undoubtedly be a rush to use these fixtures as attention getters at malls and as exterior sources for illumination on buildings. Vari-Lite, Inc. has premiered an architectural fixture called the Irideon® wash luminaire and is planning a full family of fixtures designed specifically for display and architectural use.

The moving mirror style of moving light can be used in limited outdoor applications with the introduction of semi-enclosures in the form of soft covers. This is not a fully enclosed, all-weather type of housing, but it does afford some protection. The recent introduction of all-weather enclosures by High End Systems, Inc., called the *Eco-Dome*, will be a big boost for all moving lights and color scrollers for applications around water or in general outdoor applications. The basic housings designed for moving lights have proved adaptable as newer, more powerful, lamp types have been developed (600 and 700 watt metal halide arc source and recently 1,200 and 2,500 watt HTI sources), making these lights even more appealing to other media.

When I wrote in the first edition that we were seeing only the tip of the iceberg I could not have imagined that in eight short years we would already be into a third generation. The second generation opened even more avenues of design possibilities. Those advances are already in place and have proved that the units have increased reliability and lower cost. With the wave of the second generation came a whole new group of manufacturers. That stimulated development and competition. The third generation has brought faster, more accurate movement, more effects and even shutters. Certainly we will see even greater use of these flexible fixtures throughout the full spectrum of the lighting industry in years to come.

The initial high cost of renting these units did not help their growth in theatre. However, as with any new product, the costs have dropped. One way was to manufacture units that had fewer features. Theatre was a bit overwhelmed, I believe, so it was good marketing strategy not only to reduce the price but also to make the fixtures not so foreign to theatre practitioners. Mass production has helped to saturate the market and make sales departments look for new markets. The clones with fewer features may be just what dance and theatre need. One clone even emulates an ellipsoidal fixture with remote-controlled shutters. The speed and large number of colors desired in concert lighting may not be necessary for most theatre work, so the marketing angle makes sense. In display and architectural uses, the more advanced features, at least at this point, are not needed. All this goes to making the moving light the most sought after of the developments in concert lighting.

Multi-cables

When it comes to cables and the search for lightweight, flexible, cost-effective materials, concert lighting again did the field testing. Although most installations are restricted by electrical code to certain cable types, concert designers experimented, not always by the code I concede. What has evolved may well rewrite the code. Currently, new jacketing materials are being discussed for code consideration in the theatrical field. Again, the field studies were done, in effect, by the concert technicians. I am not condoning or encouraging the violation of electrical codes; I am just stating what has happened to bring these materials out in the open for study and inspection.

The use of multicircuit cables for nonraceway theatres or portable facilities has many possibilities. They need not be restricted to portable truss situations only. The traditional taping together of single runs of cable to the end of a pipe, called a *hod*, is not as efficient as multi-cable on two counts: first, size, and second, weight. From a storage standpoint, a hod takes up more room and is heavier and harder to handle. It adds unnecessary pounds to an electrical pipe that is often too heavy anyway. A hod also does not coil well and is unruly to handle on the pipe.

Dimmers and Consoles

As for dimmers and consoles, it is true that it was the established manufacturers with their larger financial resources that first brought out the computer lighting consoles. It was the imagination of concert designers, however, that figured out how to make them be more than a storage facility for basic file information. The push from concert lighting that made dimmers smaller and more reliable is also quite apparent. Packaging techniques for the road have been incorporated into almost every one of the newer models by all the manufacturers. If they can stand up to constant pounding on the road, the dimmers can surely handle normal installation situations in a relatively maintenance-free manner.

One idea in dimming has not been greatly used by the large U.S. manufacturers; that is the 1-kW dimmer. Most of the progress in this area has been left up to small companies and designers. If a dimmer per circuit plan is of value to you, these companies warrant more investigation. Again, because their bread and butter has been made on the road, the reliability factors of these dimmers are in general very high; therefore maintenance should be at a minimum with these units.

While the large manufacturers were busy developing computers, concert technicians were looking for manual boards with more versatile functions. The old ten-scene preset board with its huge wing was not practical on the road. When a small lighting company developed the pin and pushbutton matrix and introduced it in 1973, theatre people were surprised it came from Electronics Diversified. This was only one of the small companies that had its eyes on what the young concert industry was doing. This board was a practical alternative to the computer both in size and cost and had validity in television as well as theatre and dance. Here again, small companies did the research, and the benefits were seen in competitive prices to the consumer.

The British companies that worked to integrate the old manual boards with features that would make the concert designer happy also led to the integration of computers in consoles, but in a nontraditional way. The hybrid consoles that have appeared on the scene to control the expanding number of DMX 512 controllable moving light fixtures are the latest development that can be attributed to the concert lighting industry.

Summary

The important developments of concert lighting have been portable lighting structures or trusses, the PAR-64 lighting fixture, moving lights, multi-cables, dimmers, and consoles. Now that these features of concert lighting have been accepted in the main stream of theatrical lighting and have been introduced to a whole new world of applications, it is appropriate that we continue to look toward the future and drop all barriers based on labels of *concert lighting* or *theatre* techniques and use the wonderful tools that are available to meet our design needs.

What's next? Many of the people to whom I posed this question say that lighting is moving toward an integration of video. One recently talked about development of a pixel screen in the gate of a light to project any pattern or picture that can be provided by a computer program. Another use of video is as the illumination source. These and many more developments are only months or years away. We can no longer speak in decades to see change. Our technology is moving so rapidly that I dare say that before this book is published we will have seen another pivotal advance in the industry—something that only a few people have dreamed about.

Education

Although this book is an attempt to educate and I have taught a class and lectured on concert lighting at several schools, it is time to call for a structured training format. Although that may not mean a whole department at a university, so many areas have originated or been redefined by the concert field that there should be some way to bring education to people who want to explore this field as a career. The rigging seminars sponsored by CM Hoists is wonderful. The many special sessions at both the Lighting Dimensions International (LDI) and United States Institute for Theatre Technology (USITT) annual conventions are very helpful, but they do not fully meet the demand.

There are many forms training can take. Two methods are the in-house training that most of the concert lighting suppliers give employees and the school Vari-Lite, Inc. runs in Dallas to train technicians in the use of its products. I like the concept of extension programs of film schools, such as those of New York University, the University of Southern California, or UCLA. It is time for the formation of accredited programs that can offer classroom study and practical, hands-on work with the equipment that would lead to a formal certificate of competency, quite possibly a trade school system.

There are advantages to potential employers. New employees would not start in the shop learning techniques as on-job-training on company time. They would come to the job with tested skills. The companies could also send employees to this type of school and be much more cost efficient. It could serve as a postgraduate educational opportunity for theatre undergraduates looking to work in the industry. The uses are not limited.

The courses would range from Road Management and Tour Accounting to computer-aided design (CAD) courses to certification as a Moving Light Technician, Audio Technician, or Rigger with several layers of instruction. The advantage to the industry would be that manufacturers would have more trained workers who know how to operate the products, increasing the market for these products. Suppliers would have better educated and trained new employees and thus be more cost efficient. The advantage to a designer would be more knowledge about how systems and products are used.

The establishment of such a school is a long way away, but I feel very strongly that if our industry is to continue to grow and stay innovative, a solid base, rooted in formal education, must be established.

21

Concert Techniques in Television Production

By 1987 the bulk of my lighting design work was in television. I qualified for the Hollywood Producer's Roster in 1980 (a classic catch-22 wherein you can't get on the roster unless you work for a producer who is a signature to the roster, but it is against the rules to hire someone who is not on the roster) and received my union card in the International Photographer's Guild in 1980 (International Alliance of Theatrical Stage Employees [IA] local 659 changed in 1996 to local 600). I was a fully qualified director of photography (DP) and could work on the film lots in Hollywood. They do not use the term *lighting director*.

I was designing "Entertainment Tonight" and "Hard Copy" for Paramount Studios full time and doing a series of game shows designed for the Latin market on the side. They were produced by legendary game show producer Dan Enright. He was teaching me a lot about what is needed for that special genre of television. You had to have a lot of respect for him even though he was made notorious for being one of the producers of "The $64,000 Question" back in the early television days. Dan was highly regarded and was especially well liked in the television community. He had given many people their breaks in the business, both on camera and off. One day he received a call from the associate producer of "Wheel of Fortune" asking for a recommendation on someone who was an established television lighting designer who also had experience in handling location lighting in large theatres and arenas.

"Wheel" was and still is the number one syndicated television show in the world. It is seen nightly in the United States alone by more people than voted in the last presidential election. Apparently for Americans, seeing what Vanna is wearing and playing the game at home are more important than who runs our government. But for me, the opportunity was very interesting for two reasons.

First, mounting an established show like this in "found space" offers the challenge of doing a design with concert lighting and rigging techniques. Second, it is the number one show and has already been renewed through the 2002 season!

At that time the show was shot at CBS Television Center in Los Angeles. The distributors of the show, King World, had devised a plan to get stations to renew the show through the year 1999. They said, "We'll bring the show to your town!" Unfortunately, or fortunately for me, no one asked the technical staff or designers what that would mean physically, let alone financially. "Wheel" is not your typical game show.

Besides the game pieces, the wheel, and the puzzle board, there is a 20 × 80 foot area with large prizes in elaborate settings that are upstage of the game pieces and changed every five shows (one taping day). I started calling it "That Little Game Show" when we had meetings with potential venue managers because they just did not realize the magnitude of the production. It needs a minimum 60 × 90 foot clear area for the staging and cameras and more space for an audience of 2,500 to 5,000.

I met with the associate producer, Wally Weltman, and the director, Dick Carson (as it would happen, I had worked with him on a pilot several years earlier) and was hired. The plan was for them to continue to do the studio shows at CBS with the staff lighting designers, and I would do the road shows three times a year. I was still with "Entertainment Tonight" year round but I thought I could take the time off.

Some 16 locations have been used since that first location at the Arie Crown Theatre in Chicago. We have done the show in wonderful theatres like the Wang Center in Boston and the Fox Theatre in Atlanta and twice at the Palace of Fine Arts in San Francisco. Convention facilities in Seattle, Philadelphia, Miami, and San Diego, and outdoor amphitheatres in Dallas and Phoenix also have been sites. We did several sessions in the studios at Disney World in Orlando, Florida. The truly unique location was aboard the U.S.S. *Dwight D. Eisenhower* aircraft carrier. I used concert trusses and other techniques learned in concert lighting in all of these places. But the one where I really pulled out all the stops was on the Big Island of Hawaii.

Game Show Lighting

I need to take a moment to discuss the basics of game show lighting. The key is to make the contestants look happy and excited. Harsh key lighting with shadows does not convey that to the home viewer. The lighting cannot be distracting or cause glare for the contestants. The contestants cannot have lights in their eyes or obstructions to their field of vision. I have often told friends who say they could be a good player that answering the questions from your easy chair is a very different from standing behind the wheel and looking about 40 feet over to the puzzle board while hundreds of people stand around and cameras are moving. I took my first cue from the fine job the CBS lighting staff was doing and made sure that I continued to light the game cleanly. The game areas are not lit with broad fill-wash lighting. I have refined the studio lighting since I became the full-time designer. The show was moved from CBS, where it was a part-time studio tenant, in the fall of 1995 to Sony Pictures Studio, where we have a dedicated stage. Every source is tightly focused and shuttered to meet a specific need for scripted camera shots.

Although not unique in the game show genre, "Wheel" has the added element of prizes on stage. The difference is that we do three very large prize sets, each filling a 20 × 25 foot area. That is 1,500 square feet that must have new scenery, props, and a re-light every shoot day. From cars to boats to full ski packages with snow, you name it. As a side note, all the plants are real. Orchids and other tropical flowers are flown in when we have the need, as is real grass sod. But the snow is *not* real! I have a meeting with the art director, carpenter, and prop departments one week before the shoot day, so I can plan the re-light. It must go quickly and efficiently each day before the afternoon taping. These new lights must balance with the game illumination, so the video controller is not forced to constantly adjust the irises on the cameras. In addition, the prizes are often behind Pat Sajak, the host, during the game and must balance with his lighting. Each of the six cameras has specific game shot lists that must be illuminated from the proper angle.

Hawaii Calls

We were on a plane flying back from Minnesota, where the producer, production designer, director, and I had gone to survey a possible site. At one point the producer came to us and showed a brochure of a hotel in Hawaii and said that if we didn't like the site we had just visited we could go here. It is pretty obvious which one we all voted for, and we were off to survey a site on the Big Island of Hawaii. The site was to be the Hilton Waikola Village, but initially it was assumed we would shoot in the hotel's convention center ballroom. It was soon apparent to Dick Styles, the production designer, and me that we could not fit the staging and audience into the space. So the producer asked if there was anywhere else we could shoot. Hotel management said there was nothing bigger inside but there was a beautiful space that "Live with Regis and Kathie Lee" had used. It, too, was not large enough. It was the old problem of people just not understanding that we mean it when we ask for a 60×90 foot minimum stage space.

We started walking the lovely property but did not find anything until it was suggested that there was a point of land that an ESPN exercise show had used for a taping. Arriving there we knew we had our spot. That section of the property faced back across a small bay to the other part of the hotel complex, which was fronted by a palm tree–lined walkway. The sun would set off to our right just past a point of land that would be perfect for a backdrop of setting sun. The white coral shoreline that surrounded the small bay was a perfect tropical image. The crashing blue-green surf against the black lava rock sent up spray that when lit at night would be beautiful. There were hotel rooms right next to the site (they became our rooms and production offices), and there was access for large trucks between the hotel and golf course. But there were problems.

All our previous locations, even the aircraft carrier's hangar deck, had provided a roof for support of lighting and scenic drapery. Here, we were completely in the open. The producer turned to me with a "Well?" look, and I replied that I could make it work.

Portable Roof

I asked if there were any portable concert-type roofs on any of the islands. The Eagles were scheduled for a stop in Honolulu a few weeks before our tentative shooting days, and I hoped they would be bringing a roof. A quick call to the promoter scuttled that idea. The only way to do it was to ship in a roof from California. A huge expense. No problem, I was told. The production designer and director wanted as little an obstruction to the vista as possible. My first thought was to do it with two cranes much like I had done at the old Universal Amphitheatre (see chapter 16). Scaffolding-type roof support systems were quickly placed on the bottom of the list.

As soon as I returned to Los Angeles, I called John Brown of Brown/United Productions. I had worked with him for years and knew him to be good at problem solving and to be reliable. In addition, Jeff Ravitz had just used one of Brown/United's roofs for Farm Aid VIII and spoke highly of one roof that needed only four posts to hold up an 80 × 100 foot roof with a 60 × 80 foot footprint. I did contact two other companies to ask about availability as well as size and type of roof structures, but they could not meet our needs or availability.

I was still thinking about the cranes so there would be no obstructions. A call came from Hawaii saying that there were no hydraulic cranes as large as we needed on the island that were not in use. Besides, they had checked and couldn't get them down a bottleneck on one of the access roads.

Jeff's suggestion sounded better and better. But first, was the roof available? John Brown confirmed the roof was available for that period, even the time it would take to barge it over and back. The entire roof structure, cover, and posts would fit in the space of only two 40-foot flatbed trailers. It is widely referred to as the *Elton John roof* because he was the first to use it, but it had been used for other big outdoor shows (Figure 21–1).

The next step was to return to Hawaii and with the art director, René Hass-Johnson, lay out the grounds to see if everything would fit: bleachers for the audience, stage, support gear, generators, portable toilets, video trucks. As we marked off the space and talked the hotel into tearing out a berm of low-lying plants (we didn't want to, and as it turned out did not have to, cut down or move any palm trees). As one of the checks I wanted to see how deep the soil was before we hit bedrock. I was reminded that the Big Island is the result of a volcano's lava flow and that the area we were standing on was the result of an eruption as recent as 100 years ago. Quite recent by geological time. The problem with lava is that it is not always solid. It creates air pockets and voids as it rolls and pushes its way to the sea. Would the footings for

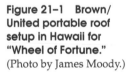

Figure 21–1 Brown/ United portable roof setup in Hawaii for "Wheel of Fortune." (Photo by James Moody.)

the posts be strong enough to hold up the roof? A call to Brown/United had a specialist on a plane to survey and evaluate the site.

The report was that foundation supports 8 feet deep by 4 feet square might have had to be poured to hold the bolts if voids were found in the lava at the points we needed to place the structure. Our plan turned out to be feasible according to Bruce Magnusun from the Brown/United office. The hotel said OK, the producer said OK, now let's put on a show!

Scenic Elements

The next step was to wait for the production designer, Dick Styles, to lay out the elements around the game wheel and puzzle board to see if they could fit within the 60 × 80 foot supports. Dick did a wonderful job, including designs for waterfalls with tropical flowers for masking (Figure 21–2), two miniature volcanoes that had smoke, water, and special lighting effects behind the stage (Figure 21–3), a floor covering design with the islands of Hawaii, and special contestant backings. He also agreed with me that we should light the palm trees behind the stage as well as the small bay and 800 feet of palm trees across the bay.

Lighting Concept

This is a nighttime show, but I proposed we shoot the first show each of the three taping days at sunset (golden hour) and then continue into the night. The sun would set behind the stage, upstage left. It was the perfect "money shot" to have Pat and Vanna walk onto the set with all the palm trees and the sunset behind them. The sun would set before Pat

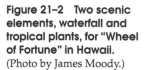

Figure 21–2 Two scenic elements, waterfall and tropical plants, for "Wheel of Fortune" in Hawaii. (Photo by James Moody.)

Figure 21–3   Scenic elements, volcanoes with smoke and fire, for "Wheel of Fortune" in Hawaii. (Photo by James Moody.)

started the actual game, so no distracting natural light would interfere with the stage lighting.

The first thing I needed to determine was at what f-stop we could see all the elements. I went back to the location and with the assistance of a local crew, ran several light tests. One test was to determine how best to illuminate the water in the bay, in terms of possible sources and direction. I found that a string of PAR-64s with medium lamps placed just above the high water line on the far side of the bay and pointed back at the stage would give the streaks of light we associate with lights reflecting across the water and moonlight. A $^1/_4$ Booster Blue was added for the effect. Next we lit the palm trees from the front and then from both sides in white light and colors.

The test shots were taken back to Los Angeles and discussed with the production designer. It was agreed that the palm trees illuminated with color looked like a bad Elvis movie. It was also agreed that light from the side gave a more defined outline to the trunks and fronds of the palm trees. Another test was conducted on the 800 feet of palm trees across the bay. How many lights would it take and at what intensity? Then everything was re-shot with a man standing at Pat's position. Various light levels were recorded on the film to see what, if any, of the water and palm trees could be seen as the intensity of the talent key lights were raised and lowered.

I used a 35-mm camera to shoot stills of all these elements onto Kodak 5279 negative color film. The range of f-stops at which I exposed the film was determined with the assistance of Ross Elliott, the show's video controller. Before the trip, we had shot a roll of the same film at the studio to match the film's speed and ASA with that of the latest charged coupled device (CCD) cameras we would be using on the location. This test can be used as an equivalent of the video camera exposure levels. Once Ross had set the speed and ASA, I could use a 1-degree spot meter to read the illumination from across the bay and photograph the setups for review back in Los Angeles. The film would confirm that I was seeing all the elements in balance and in the values we desired. This is a technique similar to the one a film DP uses when scouting locations. Viewing the stills helps determine the ambient light present and areas that need fill during filming. A series of Kodak negative color films is available in Hollywood for use in a conventional 35-mm reflex camera. They are popular for this type of test, because it is the same film stock often used for motion pictures and thus has the contract latitude and color rendering properties most DPs use.

I determined that I would be able to focus on the talent and still see the palm trees, water, and far line of palm trees with a maximum of 65 fc (footcandles) of key light. This meant that I had to reduce all my normal light levels, but the CCD cameras could handle this decrease. The question was what would happen to depth of field. The ability of lenses to produce a sharp focus on a subject near the camera as well as in the distance has much to do with brightness, or the illumination ratio between the foreground object and the background object. In general (within the latitude of the specific film you have), it can be assumed that as the light level drops, closer and closer objects behind the primary subject appear out of focus. Although I did not want everything to be in focus, we did need to retain the ability of the audience to differentiate the distant objects. That meant that the distant line of palm trees needed to be illuminated at 250 fc. The footcandle level on the water appeared to make no difference; angle to the lens did. The near palm trees required 110 fc.

The final test had to do with the color temperature change as the sun set. I had to determine what color temperature shift I could handle as the sun was setting as well as for about half an hour of afterglow. I chose to light everything at 3,200 degrees Kelvin and let the setting sun appear even warmer than it would to the eye. The bluish cast to the sky gave that Kodachrome look of a postcard to the event. This was achieved by means of working with the video controller to set up the cameras for 3,200 degrees Kelvin and not daylight (5,600 degrees Kelvin). Therefore he did not have to make major adjustments to the cameras as the last of the sun's warm glow faded to night.

The slick, clean look I want to achieve for the show when it is in the studio changes when we hit the road. One of the things the producer now believes makes a good location is how well it "says" where we are (Plate J). Otherwise we could shoot on our stage in Los Angeles; who would know? This is certainly a debatable point when it comes to convention centers that have no style of their own. But the old theatres we have shot in do have character that identifies them and places you in a specific location. Disney World and the U.S.S. *Eisenhower* certainly fit that bill. So the surroundings really make for an outstanding location. What the production designer adds to the location is icing on the cake (Plate K).

It can be argued that many years ago when television shows went on the road, they more or less expected that because they were out of the studio, they would not get the level of technical support they enjoyed at the studio. Things would not be as slick, clean, up to their high standards, so to speak. Edges would be rough. Now it is often said that an edge is a necessary element. To me, the edge can be the element needed to convey to the viewer that the program *is* shot on location. With full use of the technology available, there is no excuse for not being able to create any lighting position or use any type of equipment you want.

Lighting Equipment Supplier

Because virtually every concert lighting equipment supplier I spoke to this last year said that more than 50 percent of their business is now outside concert touring, finding all the lighting equipment you need for a location shoot is pretty easy. The only problem I have encountered is that most of the concert equipment companies do not keep a large enough supply of the studio-type 2-kW Fresnel fixtures. With subrental that problem is minor. The main items—truss, portable dimmer, multi-cable, and any type of lighting console—are plentiful.

After all that, however, I must admit "Wheel" has only used one lighting supplier for our location shoots the past four years. Given that most of the equipment might be considered equal, VANCO, out of Orlando, Florida, is our primary lighting supplier. We have found that having an ongoing working relationship with one company saves us a tremendous amount of pre-production hassle, shop assembly time, and load-in days. The same head road gaffer and head electrician come on each shoot and already know the framework in which we operate. There is a decided decrease in lost detail and missed communication. It helps make things work smoothly. Angus Sinex as gaffer and Mike Reason as head electrician work out of VANCO and have done more than eight of our locations as of this writing. Although the show also brings my studio gaffer, Jimmy Holt, along to assist me, the local crew is run by Angus. I do try to involve local suppliers, and VANCO has often subcontracted moving lights and generators locally. On the Hawaii location, all the trussing and 100 PAR-64 fixtures for palm tree lighting were subcontracted from Hawaii Stage Lighting to save space in shipping.

We have actually saved an entire load-in day or more because of the past experience Angus has in doing the show and the planning he is able to do before the equipment leaves Orlando.

In Hawaii, it took two days to put in the roof, two days to build a custom stage under it (the ground was not level), one day to place the set in position, one day to decorate the set and bring in audience chairs and bleachers, and one night to focus all the lighting. Of course, all the trussing and lighting were raised when the roof went up. While the stage was being built, the dimming and control elements were put in place and checked so that we would be ready for the focus. An evening of camera rehearsal was held, shortened by a brief rain shower.

Technical Support

To shoot this show, the production used seven CCD cameras: three pedestal, two 12-foot long arm "Jimmy Jib" mounted units, one handheld, and one on a 24-foot overhead track. The show brought most of the studio camera operators, video controller, audio engineers, and technical director, so there was only a small learning curve to add to the unique elements of the setting that everyone had to learn. The technicians already knew the game.

The production required more than 800,000 watts to light the stage, audience, palm trees, water, and prefabricated waterfalls and volcanoes. We used every portable film generator (seven 150-kVA generators for lighting, one 100-kVA for staging, one 60-kVA for audio and video) available on the Big Island.

The light plot (Figure 21–4) shows more than 465 lighting fixtures and 300 feet of 12-circuit multi-cable. All the trussing was subcontracted

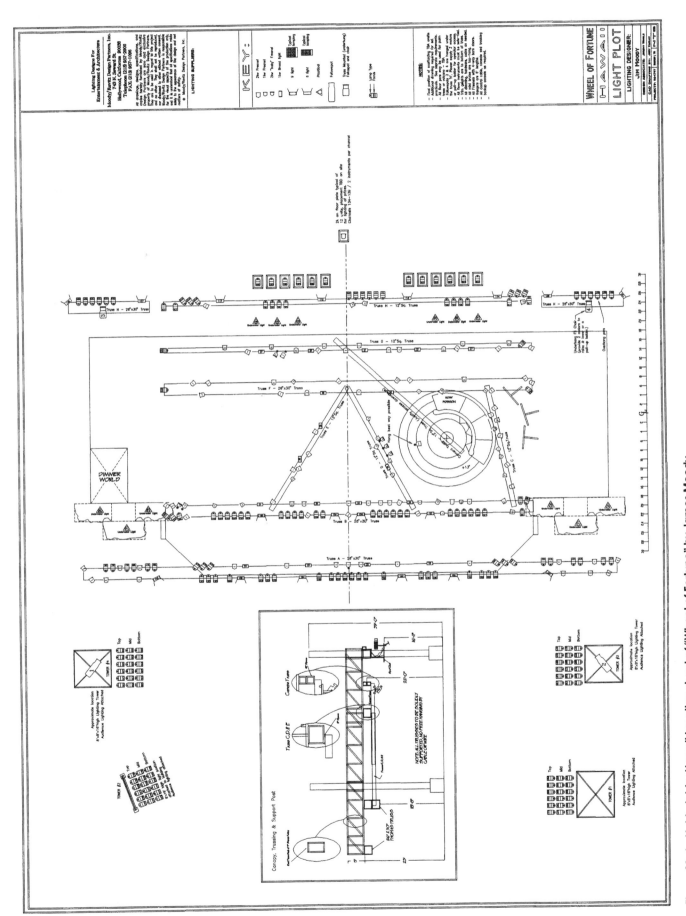

Figure 21–4   Light plot for Hawaii location shoot of "Wheel of Fortune" by James Moody.

locally as were an additional 100 PAR-64 fixtures used to light the palm trees across the bay.

It took 65 local IA stagehands and our staff of more than 80 people from Los Angeles and Orlando to mount this production. The eight days of load-in and rehearsal, three shoot days (Plate K), and then two days to tear down and completely clean the area made for a total 13 days on site, not including site preparation.

Why Go to All This Trouble?

The costs to use such a location were enormous, but the return was even greater. The ratings numbers jumped, and the Big Island recorded a tourist boost attributed directly to the airing of the shows. Officials from the tourist office have already requested that we shoot there again. The design and technical staff love the challenge and for the most part enjoy traveling to the locations. Lighting is the one element of such a production that has gone through the most advancement over the past ten years. What makes this sophisticated location shoot possible is directly attributable to concert techniques now available to the television market.

22

Music Performance on Tape and Film

Live rock concerts used to be just that—live! If you missed them, your next opportunity to see the band came the next time it toured. Rock concerts are being taped and, less often, filmed to be aired on cable, pay-for-view, or network television. Individual songs are used as promo spots or music videos, such as those seen on MTV and VH-1. Many series type shows feature rock and country music video venues: NBC's "Friday Night Videos," "Top of the Pops," which is shot on video in London and Los Angeles, syndicated shows such as "MV3" and "Live from the Palace," as well as full-length performances such as Diana Ross in Central Park, the final Who concert, or Bette Midler's 1996 pay-for-view event from Las Vegas. These shows alone add up to nearly 30 hours of programming per week. That does not include the full-time music cable channels around the world. Those channels account for 60 to 70 percent of the music videos aired. And after the success of a European version, Latin and Asian versions have been launched.

Another link between video and concerts is the display of live pictures on huge screens while the concert is in progress. Large-screen video projection or JumboTron™ systems are an integrated part of many live concerts. Virtually all recent summer outdoor stadium tours used these means of allowing fans 200 to 400 feet away from the stage to see the star "up close." Figure 22–1 shows such a close-up.

Several companies specialize in this type of video production. Nocturne Production in San Francisco, VPS in Hollywood, and World Stage in Los Angeles are long-time providers of video systems for the road. They work along with the tour lighting director to achieve an acceptable balance between what the designer wants to create for the live audience and what the camera needs to reproduce that image. The lesson is simple: to be a successful concert lighting director and qualify for today's big tours, you had better know something about video and its lighting requirements.

Film versus Video

Because of the increasing transfer of live performances to other media, debate rages between video and film makers over which medium most faithfully recreates the atmosphere of the live performance and over the technical and aesthetic merits of each medium. Film usually dominates for promo clips (commonly referred to as *music videos*). Video is used

Figure 22–1   Live concert video magnification. (Photo by Randy Bachman for Nocturne Productions.)

more often for full-length performances, although some of the classic rock performances like the Band's *The Last Waltz* and Tina Turner's *Private Dancer* were recorded on film. One recent Rolling Stones tour was both videotaped and filmed by famed director Robert Altman for release as the full-length film *Let's Spend the Night Together*.

Although I join a growing number of cinematographers who believe a production should be recorded in the medium in which it will ultimately be viewed—silver screen or tube—there are technical considerations that often influence decisions from a practical perspective. Ease of editing, ability to capture the ambience of the performance, and necessity for readjustment of the concert lighting are some of the considerations in choosing between film and video.

Film

The logistical problems of filming live concerts often determine the choice of medium. Five to nine cameras usually are set up to cover the action. Film cameras must be reloaded frequently, because 16-mm and many smaller 35-mm cameras can only take 400-foot loads, which translates to a maximum of 10 minutes of 24 frames per second (fps). Even the most popular motion picture camera, the Mitchell BNC, can accommodate magazines only up to 1,200 feet, and that is while the camera is mounted on a tripod. For handheld work, the magazine length drops to 400 feet. There are cameras that can take 4,000-foot magazines, but they are not generally used in this type of photography. A concert does not stop for film reloads; therefore each camera is down for several minutes during critical performance time. There are no retakes in live performances, so any missed action is lost forever, or you must go to the expense of shooting a second performance, almost doubling the budget.

A helpful addition to filming a concert ironically comes from video. The video assist system allows a small black and white video camera to pick up the image in the viewfinder of the film camera. Although the clarity or resolution is not broadcast quality, it does send back to the director an image that he or she can use to see framing and action, making decisions for cameramen to change shots that are not working or to stay with some action. Shots on which the director counted on getting may turn out to be out of focus when the film is developed, even overexposed. So it does not solve all of film's problems of recording this type of event. Some directors have insisted they need nine or ten cameras to record a concert. Even if they can cut a very good deal on the crew and cameras, the costs skyrocket in editing.

Video

Video offers greater flexibility. A video director is in direct communication with the camera operators and sees what the camera is recording. Duplication of shots can be avoided. The director sees the big picture, being able to view all the cameras at once (Figure 22–2).

Depending on the budget and capability of the mobile video truck, the program (linecut) is double-recorded on two 1-inch tapes with a $^3/_4$-inch copy containing time codes for off-line editing. The program is the real-time mixing of multiple video camera shots or taped feeds onto one master tape or onto a live line transmission. *Off-line* refers to the time the director can view the tapes without the heavy cost of an editor and the expensive equipment in an editing suite, another cost savings. One or two 1-inch isolated (*iso*) tapes are recorded for cutting in the post-production editing session. Depending on the union situation, either the technical director, who also switches the linecut, or the assistant director is responsible for switching cameras onto the iso feeds. Iso feeds are switched as straight cuts. No dissolves or fades are done on the iso tapes. This is possible on the linecut, however, as are split screens and other electronic effects, which again saves time in editing.

Figure 22–2 Road video system setup.
(Photo by Bexel Corp., Burbank, California.)

Iso feeds are used for three reasons. First, they cover other action in case the on-line camera has technical problems or the cameraperson loses focus. Second, they allow the director to concentrate on the main action, although the director can ask for a particular shot to be isolated. Having that extra tape avoids having the director make quick judgments on unplanned shots. Third, the iso feeds can be used to lay in audience shots or other cutaways for the final edit. They can cover a composition error that is not seen until editing or can be used as the second image in split-screen or other effects on the final cut.

Each director has his or her own way of switching isos. Some keep the wide camera on iso throughout the performance and switch only close-ups to the program feed. Others have the assistant director (AD) keep an eye out and switch cameras into iso that are not the same as the on-line (program) camera.

The Debatable "Look"

Picture quality can be a debatable point when deciding on film or video. The film look is highly regarded as the equivalent to our concept of fantasy. Video is often talked about as too slick and real-life, too 5 o'clock news, for entertainment. You have to decide which image is right for your artistic goals.

There was an attempt at melding the two media. Two companies, a film camera manufacturer and a video camera manufacturer, independently introduced digital video cameras that were thought to produce a film-like look. Panavision, a leader in 35-mm motion picture cameras, marketed a video camera that used the widely accepted Panavision film lens system and operation characteristics. Its operating parameters also offered a low-light-level feature that allowed lighting to remain in the range of film production, a nominal 50 fc, instead of the 125 fc necessary for the average studio video camera to produce an f/2.8 iris setting.

Ikegami, a highly regarded video camera manufacturer, offered its EC 35 model with essentially the same film-like characteristics. However, the company stayed with the camera-operator characteristics of the video camera, that is, no need for a focus puller as with the 35-mm film cameras. Many people in video believed that the EC 35 had the best electronics then available. Its image-enhancement circuitry had a low noise device, resulting in a signal-to-noise ratio greater than 57 dB rms (root mean square) and a new low capacitance diode-gun tube capable of producing an extremely sharp picture edge to edge with improved resolution and detail.

But for any number of reasons, neither system caught on, and they have been abandoned.

A cross-media trend is developing in which performances are shot on film then transferred to videotape for editing and viewing. There is a film format that has an aspect ratio of 1.33:1 for both 16 mm and Academy 35 mm, the same that is used for television. Wide-angle Cinemascope-type lenses should not be used, however, because too much of the image is lost when viewed on the home television receiver. It is difficult for a cameraperson to keep in mind the Television Academy safe area when shooting. That is why you see boom microphone on television series shot on film more often than in series shot on tape. Here again, the director and technical director can see exactly what they will get while it is happening. With film there is only a black and white low-contrast image not found until screening the next day, when it is too late to re-shoot.

The Television Academy technical specifications state that as little as 35 percent of the image on standard 35-mm film will actually be received in the home via television. The safe area for video represents only about 70 percent of the total aperture area of the 1.33:1 aspect ratio of the film. You can see why it is so easy for critical action to be cut off in films viewed on television.

One other method is to take the videotape and put it through a process developed by Film-Look Inc., Burbank, California, that makes it look more "film-like." There are producers who have used the system and like the effect. But my questions is, why not shoot it on film in the first place? There is a TV serics called "JAG" that uses clips from films and video. This process is very useful in this case. It averages the looks, so they seem to match.

Lighting Considerations

The inevitable conflict between the lighting needs of recording media and the obligation to the live audience who paid good money to see the concert is always a tough fight. The normal concert lighting look has to be broadened for these other media. A compromise must be reached, or the recorded product will suffer. Your job as lighting designer is to enhance the artist's image. If the tape or film is bad because you would not compromise your concert lighting, the artist is the loser.

When I first started doing rock video in 1972 as the lighting director for Don Kirshner's "Rock Concert" series, I had already logged six years of concert tour lighting. The concert lighting director is, in fact, the concert director. We direct the audience where to look; we produce the visual picture.

In video or film, the concert lighting director becomes subservient to the director, who chooses the image, framing, and other shots to be recorded. The concert lighting must be broadened to facilitate these needs, something the live show usually avoids. The video lighting director has to use a broader brush stroke when lighting.

How can we best handle the live show so that video or film and live audiences are equally happy? I find that a concert does not have to be relit. Balance is the key. The best video cameras have a contrast ratio of 32:1; film has a much wider latitude (from 64:1 to 128:1). Video gives you five f stops, as opposed to film, which gives you eight or more. As a result, video lighting ratios should not exceed 3:1 in the overall picture balance. Digital cameras have changed the game somewhat, but the 2:1 ratio is still used to teach video lighting. Concert lighting normally exceeds any of these guidelines, which, especially in heavy metal concerts, helps give the lighting that raw-edge quality. The area in which digital cameras have improved is the acceptable light levels needed for an image. Now it is not uncommon to see situation comedies shot at 35 to 50 fc with these video cameras.

What the Camera Sees

The best way to check how the camera will "see" the stage is to purchase a contrast filter for about 20 dollars. The Tiffen Company's model, which is widely used in film production, works well in video if you get it with a 2.0 neutral density filter. Hold the glass to your eye and watch a live concert to see how much of the detail will be missed by the video camera's reproduction system. The same procedure can be used with film once the film stock and its properties are determined. A different filter, with the appropriate higher contrast, helps accomplish the same thing for film.

Another part of balance is color. The contrast filter shows you how some color combinations are lost when recorded with the camera. Although most video cameras used by professionals are digital models now, a large number of tube cameras are still in use, so I will explain their problems. The video camera has definite limitations, and one of these is *saturation*. In the three-tube Plumbicon or Saticon camera, a beam-splitter breaks the light received through the camera lens into red, blue, and green signals. The green channel sees more light in the visible spectrum. The red channel is almost half as sensitive and cannot produce enough beam voltage to eliminate residual image retention. That residual image, or comet tailing, can generally be corrected by means of reducing the saturation of the color. *Lag* means the tube is not receiving enough light energy for it to provide a sufficient signal to the receiver. It gives you a ghostlike image and noise. Too much of any one color causes tearing, which looks much like lag but is caused by color saturation.

The newer video cameras are all digital. That means that they do not have tubes any longer and are not subject to lag or comet tailing. Saturation problems have been virtually eliminated. The cameras are smaller and lighter and much more portable. All cameras can now be electronic news gathering (ENG) style, which means they can have onboard recording and playback systems built into the camera, or they can be cabled back to a control master station. Each camera is more flexible both physically and in terms of image.

One thing has not been totally eliminated. Because of unequal color sensitivity and the reduced contrast properties of video cameras, color shades do not always reproduce exactly as we see them. Blue-green can turn out green because the pixels are more sensitive to green. Oranges and some magentas appear red, and lavenders turn blue on the television receiver because the home viewer's television is not as sensitive as the camera or the recording medium. When watching a playback monitor remember that the monitor in the control room probably costs $4,000 and the one the video controller is using costs $10,000. They got their money's worth: better resolution and color telemetry. The video controller can influence this to some degree, but the camera's electronics are the final controlling factor. You have to experiment to understand this problem.

If you have film or slides in the live show they probably will not be bright enough to be recorded on the tape. Slides and film are best added electronically during post-production through effects processes. Remember, you are lighting for a broader view of the show, and what the eye sees is not what the camera sees with its very limited contrast ratio. Lighting on scenic pieces generally must be increased in intensity if the pieces are to be read. There are ways of compensating for this in video through the efforts of the video controller. The controller watches and controls, among other things, the iris of the video camera. However, you should not count solely on this ability to boost the level electronically to make the light intensity acceptable.

Cutaways

The often repeated example of why cutaways are important is the five-minute guitar solo that goes over splendidly with the live audience but is dull when transposed to film or tape. Television viewers have very short attention spans and must be kept interested with visual images that add to the enjoyment of the music. Extensive studies have been made on how often to change images if you want to keep a television viewer's attention. The director must use cutaways such as the live audience's reaction to the solo or other band members' reactions during the solo.

Key light is generally considered a film term. The key light is the primary source of illumination from the direction from which the camera views the scene most of the time. It is this source that often has the lowest footcandle reading on the concert set. In television it often is the brightest. In concert lighting, the back light is usually the brightest. Because follow spots are usually the concert designer's only front light and because they cannot be trained on all the musicians all the time, it is unlikely that the camera has enough illumination for other shots, or cutaways, on the drummer, keyboard player, or other individual band members.

The lighting problem on cutaways can be solved in three ways. First, add follow spots. This is not always an artistically justified solution, I know, but it will do when no additional fixed lighting can be added. Second, add an even bank of front white light that produces at least 50 to 75 fc. The video controller will be thrilled, but it takes away from the audience's interest in what is happening on stage. Third, try placing white light specials from the front on the drummer and keyboards and backup singers. They can be dimmed up only as required. This causes the least change in the live look while satisfying the video controller's and the director's needs.

Audience Lighting

Audience lighting for taping or filming a live show is a must. Without it, the show might as well be shot on a sound stage where camera placement and lighting are optimal. What makes the performance live is the audience's reaction to the band. The producer and director need that reaction on tape. A talk with the director yields definite ideas on how to handle audience lighting. Generally, the discussion focuses on four questions:

1. Should the light be colored or white?
2. Is the audience light to be on all the time or only between songs?
3. Does the director want front, side, back light or a combination on the audience?
4. How much time and money can be spent to mount additional lighting for the audience?

I do not like to light an audience from the onstage angle because it puts light in their eyes constantly and makes it difficult for them to concentrate on the stage performance. Back light is great for showing the size of the audience on a wide shot, and side light picks up enough faces to satisfy most directors without annoying the whole crowd. You see many audiences lit with colored pools of front light, especially in the back of the auditorium or arena. It looks great on camera but is very distracting to the audience.

Just accept the fact that whatever you do, it is a no-win situation, and make the best of it. The audience hates being distracted no matter what you do, so you might as well give the video or film what it needs with as much consideration to the audience as possible. I recommend side light as being best and only turned on between songs and during a few fast numbers. Remember the reactions can be cut in anywhere, so the specific song being performed makes no difference as long as there is no reference to the stage in the shot.

Accommodation

Whatever the lighting director does to accommodate video or film on a live concert has adverse effects on the artist and the road crew's normal operation of the tour, so try to understand the crew's problems and the pressure they are feeling from the artist. If you go into this with an open mind and a willingness to cooperate, much can be accomplished, and an exciting show can be recorded that satisfies everyone.

23

Postscript: Looking Back

The first edition of this book offered a look at concert lighting techniques. This edition expands on that body of material, yet cannot reflect everything anyone has ever done in the field. While I hoped someone else would come along and add to what I started eight years ago, that has not happened. So, again, I must say that there is so much to be learned from every experience. Every attempt to push the use of this equipment and these techniques to a wider creative horizon adds to our game book. Use every opportunity to try to launch new uses for what I have presented in these pages. As the old saying goes, "The wise man knows when to keep the good things he sees and discard the things that are not useful to him." Nothing that is tried is useless or bad. The collective learned experience is what makes ideas grow and become perfected.

The actual designs shown in this book by me and others represent only a very small sample of what wonderful, creative solutions designers have come up with to make their designs work. Every concert I see brings new uses and ideas, new combinations of styles. It all just goes to bolster my firm belief that we are not even close to seeing the ultimate use of concert lighting techniques. It is up to you to do that someday.

What I said eight years ago about the field of concert lighting having moved well beyond the narrow label of Rock and Roll lighting is now a given. Methods originally developed for tour lighting continue to find a place in the everyday workings of dance, regional theatre, Broadway, bus and truck companies, location television, opera, and film. Architecture is the newest field to use these techniques to enhance physical designs and attract people to the building.

The use of moving light fixtures, trusses, and other innovative ideas that sprang from the minds of creative people working in the concert touring industry are now firmly ensconced in virtually every business that has a need for creative lighting solutions.

Early concert-style Rock and Roll performances on television were accepted by the viewing public so well that the television people took notice even if they did not jump in with both feet. I introduced the use of color projected on people rather than limited to the cyclorama on the "Don Kirshner Rock Concert" series in 1973. Now the PAR-64 fixture finds wide use on location video and even in network lighting. It is becoming rare to find a television studio in which a few dozen PAR-64s are not in use.

I am not advocating the ouster of the venerable Fresnel, but I am an advocate for continued change. Change happens in two ways: through new inventions and, probably more realistic for theatre and all its sister media, through the borrowing of techniques and equipment. Lighting has never been a heavily financed area of research in the theatrical arts, and therefore we must take what we can from other sources.

Concert designers and their equipment suppliers have taken found space and created theatre. When people are able to reach beyond the Rock and Roll label, they can see what real advances have been made, both in design potential and in the high-tech electronic explosion spearheaded with the intelligent luminaire.

I do not like all Rock and Roll music, just as I do not like all opera, but it is time we investigated the art of this media without being hampered by our own prejudices against the music itself. Take the good elements and discard the bad; improve techniques and adapt them to other areas. This is the essential character of theatre, the great adapter.

This book reveals only a small part of what concert tour lighting has to offer. The Bibliography gives the names of magazines that regularly print articles about concert lighting. For those who need to broaden their basic knowledge of lighting, there is a list of books I feel are essential to making use of the full potential of the material in this book. I hope you will obtain these books and use them to broaden your knowledge.

To Be or Not to Be on the Internet?

I am not sure this is the right place for this, but it just doesn't seem to fit into any other chapter. I want to talk about two parts of what can be called the *designer's workbox*. First is a discussion of whether a designer needs a computer.

Whether you see it as a invaluable tool, a wise investment or a handy helper, a computer is now part of most people's lives. Should it be a part of the designer's tools? The main argument is not whether you can use one to make your work more efficient. It is the problem of rapidly changing technology. The cash investment you make will not be a long-term one. The field is leaping ahead almost every day. Do you go IBM compatible or Macintosh? What compatibility of operating systems, size of hard drives, RAM, CD drive capability, built-in modems with higher and higher speeds, and so on, are questions the salesperson will ask. Because it is a pretty hefty cash outlay, do you lease or buy? To help make up your mind, let's discuss what a computer does for you as a designer.

On small club tours, especially if you are using a local lighting supplier almost every night, there are probably no pressing needs other than a nifty toy for killing time on the bus or for keeping in touch with friends on the Internet. E-mail is quickly becoming the choice for communicating among touring and theatre industry professionals. It allows rapid communication and data transfer to remote locations quickly and efficiently. Because you can use a computer to send a message or files instantaneously and reply even more quickly than fax, people now call the U.S. Postal Service "snail mail." By the way, it is possible to send a fax via the Internet if the person on the receiving end does not have E-mail service. Europe and most of South America are not totally on line. This is because of old phone systems that do not have the capability of transmitting clean data signals.

Obtaining E-mail service is easy and inexpensive. Many servers, as they are called, offer E-mail access only. You get your own E-mail name and address. Or you can use one of the generic, broad-based systems such as Prodigy or America On-Line, which provide access to the World Wide Web, weather, news, and stock reports as well as E-mail service. It appears that you will someday need this type of service to exist in any business, not only ours.

The larger the tour, the more necessary a computer may become. Depending on the lighting console, it may be possible to back up different versions of the show to a portable computer's hard drive and make off-line changes while on the bus between venues. Even designers of small shows who require the local promoter to simply rent 12 Intellabeam or Cyberlights fixtures can carry their own program disk to save time at the venue. Using one of the programs mentioned in chapter 10, you can write a program or make changes off line. Some manufacturers such as Whole Hog and E.T.C. allow users to download the latest version of their console software via their Internet site.

Keeping your paperwork up to date, printing cue sheets, drawing truck packs, making crew lists, writing and sending invoices, setting airplane reservations, and updating the light plot are all things you can use a computer to do while you are traveling. The mobile office is something that is a reality for many owners of small businesses and salespeople. With a laptop computer you can be in touch with your suppliers, clients, or accountant at any hour of the day or night.

I have already discussed producing a light plot with a computer, so I will not revisit that point. If you do use a computer to make a light plot, make sure of the amount of hard drive you will need and the type of memory the laptop has to be sure that the programs you want to run do so efficiently.

With the technology of both Macintosh and IBM or compatible PCs coming closer together, it is impossible to recommend one system over the other. It is generally believed that Macintosh is a more user friendly system, and most advanced graphics programs use Macintosh operating systems. But Macintosh has suffered in the past few years, and its share of the market is decreasing, making it likely that sheer volume will bury it eventually whether the system is better or not. In my office we are split down the middle. All the computer-assisted drafting machines are PC based, and my two partners, Jeff and Dawn, use Mac systems. This does cause some problems, but the comfort factor each of us has with our own systems makes it necessary to bring all these into play. There is software that allows Mac users to read PC files and configure their files to operate the PC-based printers and plotters in the office. But we are coming to the point at which we need to move beyond the personal computer to a network system. That is an issue that has to be addressed one day but not at the time of your first computer purchase. It is not for this book.

It is likely that someone in the production office or on the tour will have a printer, so the question of lugging one around with you versus the initial cost of purchase gives you some options. Because files can be saved to be printed at any time, it may not be necessary to have your own printer on the road. You can also go to a 24-hour printing and copy store that allows you to print on their machines for a small charge. Some can even print your light plot on C or D size paper.

Whatever your feeling about entering the computer age, be fully aware that your competitor is in the same boat. Spend the money or not? Take the time to learn how to operate it? Is it worth either or both? That decision is yours, but the weight falls heavier and heavier on the side of technology every day. Don't be caught unprepared to meet the future.

The Designer's Workbox

When you leave for the road, you *will* forget something! The best thing you can do is to keep a running list of what you will need the next time you work on the road. Some designers keep a workbox or plastic storage box just for the road filled with many of the items on the following list. The list contains some of the things that many designers I know want to have when they hit the road.

1. Computer and modem, printer, and printer interface cable If you choose not to go with a laptop, you can save space by not taking a monitor if you know that the lighting console has one. It may be possible to connect your PC to it.

2. Diskettes! Don't count on your lighting console coming with them. Most newer systems use readily available high density (HD) disks, but should you be using an older-model lighting console, you might need a low-density diskette, and they are becoming harder to find. You'll want at least three copies of the current show.

3. Paper! Lest we forget, the computer does not save paper, it is a paper eating machine—mostly because it is easy to print a hard copy, make changes, and print another. We actually increase our paper use, so carry a lot of paper, at least a ream . . . or two!

4. Production book You'll need something to keep your notes together. This is the catch-all of previous shows' cues, songs not on the current list, copies of letters, faxes, receipts, itineraries, photos, venue notes and names, reviews, everything you may need to refer to as you go forward with a later tour by the same artist. On larger tours this book can grow to three or four inches, so use a large binder with front inside pockets.

5. Running book This is a smaller book with your cue sheets in the current order you'll use to run the show. Try different arrangements to produce a book that works for you. You might try inserting dividers for every song to allow quick reference should the artist suddenly change the show order. Diskette holders allow you to keep show disks in the book. A trip to the office supply store yields many options. Clear plastic page holders are good for cue pages to protect them from rain, spilled drinks, and humidity.

6. Portable cassette deck with search and external speakers for programming with rehearsal tapes The speakers allow other operators to follow along for programming without the artist onstage. I also like to have earphones for extended listening on planes. Bring blank cassettes and coax your audio engineer to run tapes of rehearsals. Guard them as if they were gold. They are necessary for your work, but a lost rehearsal tape can be the end of your job. Bootlegged tapes bring big money on the underground market. If they are traced back to you, the mistake *will* cost you your job!

7. Console tape and fine-point "Sharpies" Artist's tape is best because the adhesive allows it to be taken up without sticking to the console. White electrical tape also is popular but doesn't hold up to bright sunlight. "Sharpies" are non-smear, fine-point pens, which are excellent for marking the artist's tape.

8. Small lamp with stand or task light It's best to own one, but if you do not, ask your lighting supplier to bring them. A music stand is great for holding the running book, and it needs good light. The lights built into the console rarely work for this purpose, and you need them to illuminate the console.

9. Headset This is something to consider if you'll be doing a lot of touring. Using our own assures comfort and hygiene. You'll probably want a double-muff headset to block out excessive noise.

10. Ear plugs Speaking of noise, many Rock and Roll technicians, road crew, and musicians have hearing problems caused by high decibel levels. You also are susceptible to feedback during setup and sound check, which can damage your ears when you are close to the sound cabinets during load-in. You can buy disposable earplugs at FBOs (fixed base operations) at small private airfields or shooters' earplugs at gun shops. Another way to go is to find a hearing-aid store that will custom mold an earpiece that can fit in your ear. A set can be designed as a headset earpiece that is very comfortable or as a sound baffle to keep out high-frequency sound while allowing you to hear the normal human voice.

11. Scale rule, scissors, pads of paper, pencils and sharpener, small flashlight with extra batteries, and a multitool, such as a Leatherman® You may not want to look like a Boy Scout, but it is far better to be prepared than to keep running out for small items. By the way, I use a cheap, disposable mechanical pencil made by Paper-Mate, Inc., since it saves me from carrying a pencil sharpener.

12. Extra copies of the light plot You never have enough!

13. Camera Take photos of the rig as it goes together as well as wider shots that show the entire system in place. They go a long way toward explaining what you will be doing during load-in. A picture *is* worth a thousand words. Of course, production photos are a necessity for your own portfolio. The question of videotaping arises. If you have a video camera by all means shoot the load-in. Assuming you can get permission from the band (in writing is best), you may even tape the performance. It's the greatest tool to refresh your memory of a two-year-old tour that needs remounting. Also, check early on with the venue about union rules for payment. Even your home movies can be considered a saleable recording that would require payment under some contracts to the musicians and crew. Be very careful with this one.

14. Finally, look around your own studio What do you use most? What would you miss if you were away from your studio for a few weeks or months? How you deal with life on the road has a lot to do with your comfort zone. Make sure you have the things with you that make your work and life tolerable, or you will not succeed on the road.

Final Comments

A life in any of the entertainment arts is exciting. But the challenges are exceeded only by the disappointments. People who make the climb to success in this field tend to be those who have little need, in their younger years, for heavy personal attachments: family, pets, physical property. As for a singer, dancer, or actor, the road for a designer is filled with potholes, rejection, and disappointments. Can you keep your eye on the prize? Do you have the drive to keep butting your head against a seemingly solid brick wall? Only time will tell. I do not want to appear to be saying don't try. Do try. You'll never know if you don't. And who knows, along the way you may find some off-shoot of this career for which you are better suited or are more comfortable in. Anyway, success should be judged only on your own value system, not on that of others.

Bibliography

There is currently only one other book on the basic subject of this one. *Concert Sound and Lighting Systems* was published in 1988, also by Focal Press. I keep hearing that there are several books in the works, including one dedicated to moving lights, but nothing has surfaced at this time. Your best sources continue to be articles appearing in technical and professional periodicals. The list that follows is given as supplemental reading on concert lighting and other lighting techniques. Reprints or back issues can be obtained directly from the publishers.

The books listed are given to help readers broaden their knowledge of the other design media discussed in this book. Cross-over use of techniques is constantly being tried in other media, so an understanding of all media is necessary to compete in the lighting world today.

Periodicals

Cue
Twynam Publishing, Ltd.
Kitemore, Faringdon
Oxfordshire SN7 8HR England

Light and Sound International
John Offord Publications, Ltd.
12 The Avenue
Eastbourne
East Sussex BN21 3YA England

Lighting Design and Application
The Illuminating Engineering
    Society of North America
345 East 47th St.
New York, NY 10017

Lighting Dimensions
Lighting Dimensions Associates
135 Fifth Ave.
New York, NY 10010-7193

On Stage
On-Stage Publishing
6464 Sunset Blvd.
Suite 570
Hollywood, CA 90028

Pro Light & Sound
Mountain Lion Publications
5302 Vineland Ave.
North Hollywood, CA 91601

Strandlight
Strand Lighting, Ltd.
P.O. Box 51
Great West Road
Brentford
Middlesex TW8 9HR England

Tabs (*out of publication*)
Rank Strand Electric
P.O. Box 70
Great West Road
Brentford
Middlesex IW8 9HR England

Theatre Crafts
Theatre Crafts Associates
135 Fifth Ave.
New York, NY 10010-7193

Books

The Beauty of Light
Bova, Ben
John Wiley & Sons, Inc.
New York, New York
1988

Cinema Workshop
Wilson, Anton
A.S.C. Holding Co.
Hollywood, California
1983

*Concert Sound and Lighting
Systems*
Vasey, John
Focal Press
Boston, Massachusetts
1988

Electronic Cinematography
Mathias, Harry, and Richard
   Patterson
Wadsworth Publishing
   Company,
Belmont, California
1985

The Lighting Art
Palmer, Richard H.
Prentice-Hall Inc.,
Englewood Cliffs, New Jersey
1985

TV Lighting Methods
Millerson, Gerald
Focal Press
Boston, Massachusetts
1982

Lighting the Stage
Bellman, Willard F.
Harper & Row Publishers
New York, New York
1967

Stage Rigging Handbook
Glerum, Jay
Southern Illinois University Press
Carbondale, Illinois
1987

*The Techniques of Lighting for
Television and Motion Pictures*
Millerson, Gerald
Focal Press
Boston, Massachusetts
1982

Theatre Words
Luterkort, Ingrid, editor
Nordic Theatre Union
Solna, Sweden
1980

Glossary

Accent   A design technique in concert lighting that concentrates the illumination at strategic points on the stage to punctuate the music with heavy color or intensity.

ACL (aircraft landing light)   A PAR-64 design with a very narrow beam pattern that operates at 28 volts. It was originated for jet aircraft and adapted for Rock and Roll.

Air light   The use of light beams to create patterns and design elements. The patterns may or may not be focused on the artist.

Aircraft cable (wire rope)   A cable made of stranded stainless steel wire of high tensile strength used for hanging trusses, sound, and scenic elements when house pipes are not available. Theatrical rigging usually requires $^3/_8$-inch or $^1/_2$-inch diameter cable.

Back light   Illumination of a subject from the rear to produce a highlight along its edge.

Box truss   Structure built of aluminum, steel, or chrome-moly, designed as a portable support for lighting fixtures but sometimes used for support of drapery, scenery, or sound equipment.

Bridle   In rigging, a system for using more than one hanging point to distribute the load.

CAD   Computer-aided design.

Carnet   U.S. Customs document listing products and parts taken from country of origin but to be returned. Not used for items to be sold outside the country.

Chain hoist   Electrically operated lifting device usually of chain; often referred to as *chain climber.*

Chase   To sequence channels of dimming in a timed, programmed manner.

Chip camera   A video camera that uses computer technology, not vacuum tubes, to produce an image.

Color temperature   The color quality of light, measured in degrees Kelvin, that relates its spectral distribution to that of a standard black-body radiator.

Contract rider   A supplementary agreement between promoter and artist that has its basis in the original contract and is incorporated by reference to the original contract. It usually contains specific physical requirements of the artist's current show, such as stage size, power, dressing room needs, and food.

Contrast range   The brightness ratio between the lightest and darkest tones in a scene.

Cyclorama A vertical surface used to form a background. It usually is monochromatic and is made of either hardwood finish with a fabric covering or heavy cloth, often muslin, stretched vertically and horizontally to produce a smooth surface.

Depth of field The zone or range that shows clarity closest to and farthest from a lens at sharpest focus. The zone increases as the lens aperture is reduced (often accomplished by means of increasing light level) or the lens angle is widened.

End stage The placement of a portable stage in an open, flat-floor building centered on the short end to give maximum seating capacity.

Equipment manager Professional term for the person who sets up and maintains the band equipment.

Exposure The selective control of reproduced tonal values within a system's limits. *Overexposure* results when reflected light exceeds the camera's limits. *Underexposure* results when a surface is insufficiently bright to be clearly discerned in the picture.

Fall hazard Any situation in which a worker loses balance and can fall to a lower level and be injured.

Fill light The supplementary illumination used to reduce shadow or contrast range.

F stop A measure of the light-transmissive ability of a camera or projection lens.

Flash button On a lighting console, a momentary contact switch that allows a control channel to bypass the fader and instantly bring the circuit to 100 percent output. Found on consoles designed for Rock and Roll applications.

Follow spot A high-power, narrow beam light suited for long throws (typically 100 to 300 feet), generally with an iris, shutters, and color changer. It is designed for hand operation to follow the movements of performers.

Found space Any space used for theatre, concerts, or television productions not specifically designed as a performance area.

Full body harness A harness that has an attachment point above the shoulders, so the person falling cannot become inverted and fall out of the rig.

Glycol An alcohol with a molecular structure that has two hydroxyl groups.

Gobo A pattern or breakup placed in front of a hard-edged light designed to cast a specific design or modeling onto a surface.

Grand tour A tour taken by a star, usually with only a piano, to perform excerpts of famous opera and classical works.

Ground man A term used for a rigger stationed on the ground who sets up and attaches what the "high man" needs.

Groupies People who are so devoted to a popular recording artist that they collect memorabilia, join fan clubs, and go out of their way to be everywhere the artist is.

Hang time The length of time that fog stays in the air without dissipating.

Hanging point The point on the truss from which the attachments are made for rigging.

Haze An accumulation in the atmosphere of very fine, widely dispersed, solid liquid particles giving the air an opalescent appearance.

High man A term used for a rigger who works high on a structure to attach rigging for support of flown materials such as trusses.

High-density dimming The use of advanced engineering and microprocessors to miniaturize an electronic dimmer.

HMI Metal halide lamp (mercury/argon additives) in tubular, double-ended form at 5,600 degrees Kelvin.

Hod A number of individually jacketed cables, usually three 12-gauge wires, taped together for easy transport and layout on a lighting pipe.

HTI Metal halide short-arc lamp at 5,600 degrees Kelvin.

Hybrid Console Lighting consoles designed to operate both conventional as well as DMX compatible moving lights.

IATSE The International Alliance of Theatrical Stage Employees. The international bargaining unit for stagehands such as property managers, audio technicians, carpenters, riggers, electricians, wardrobe managers, and other backstage employees.

Iso Abbreviation for *isolated*. In television it denotes the switching of a camera onto a tape reel other than the master tape.

Kelvin temperature The unit of temperature used to designate the color temperature of a light source.

Key light A motivating source of illumination that establishes the character and mood of the picture.

Key word A method of calling cues that does not rely on visual or mechanical signaling devices. A word such as *go* or *out* prompts someone to react in a planned manner.

Lag A persistent or smearing afterimage on a television screen that follows the path of a moving object.

Layering The use of color to create depth and separation by means of different shades or saturations of a single color.

Letter of agreement A legal agreement generally written in plain language based on a business letter form rather than a legal form.

Light show A mixture of theatrical lighting, projections, film, and black light images used to create an environment for the audience (popular in the 1960s).

Looks Planned patterns of light, and often color combinations, programmed and used one or more times in a concert.

Lumen A unit of (light) flux.

Lumen per watt The number of lumens produced by a light source for each watt of electrical power supplied to the filament.

Luminaire The word now being used by several manufacturers to describe their moving light fixtures.

Luminance The true measured brightness of a surface.

Matrix, pin matrix A device used to group channels to one or more master controllers, often employing a small pin or patch placed on the console.

Middle-of-the-road (MOR) Music that is marketed between easy listening and Rock and Roll, such as the music of Barry Manilow, Air Supply, and John Denver.

Moving lights (see Luminaire)   Computer controlled lights that move by means of motor drives. They may remotely allow for color changes, focus, and pattern insertion.

Multi-cable   More than one complete electrical circuit housed in the same flexible protective jacketing.

Off-line editing   Preliminary editing of videotapes with copies of the original tapes; usually performed on a low-cost $^3/_4$-inch editing system. Allows a director to conduct editing experiments before making final decisions without expensive editing bay and editor costs (often called a *work tape*).

On-line editing   Final editing of videotapes using the original master tapes to produce a finished program.

Package dimming   The grouping of typically 6 or 12 dimmers in a single integrated enclosure, often used for portable work.

PAR-64   A parabolic aluminum reflector light used with a quartz lamp sealed behind one of a group of lens configurations. The *64* designates the diameter of the lens in eighths of an inch.

Patching   Interconnection of dimmer output to loads via a patch panel, a system that usually uses a plug and jack on the line side of the load only.

Per diem   A daily allowance paid by an employer to the crew and cast while they are away from home, used to cover nonreimbursed expenses such as food and laundry.

Pickup point   The point of attachment to the building's load-bearing structure used for rigging.

Pigtails   Short 3-foot to 5-foot cables, usually 2/0 or 4/0 welding cable, used to connect to the house power panel.

Pin matrix   See Matrix.

Pink contract   An agreement issued by the IATSE to qualified members who want to travel outside their local jurisdiction.

Prep   The time devoted to organizing and packaging materials such as lighting or sound before the rehearsal or tour, usually in a location other than the first venue.

Programming   The real-time mixing of multiple video camera shots or taped feeds onto one master tape or into a live line transmission.

Proscenium   An arch placed so as to separate the audience from the acting or performance space.

Psychovisual   Relating to the psychological use of color to effect emotional response in the viewer.

Punch light   A lighting fixture with a highly concentrated beam that allows long throws.

Ray light   A reflector with a separate 120-volt lamp, usually of 600 watts, that fits into a PAR-64 housing. This unit creates a very narrow beam of light; the same as an ACL but without the 28-volt problem of matching to 120-volt dimming.

Rigging   The process of installing lines or motors to support trusses, scenery, and other elements in their needed positions.

Road company   The authorized production of a play or musical that is produced in one city and is then performed in multiple cities for limited engagements around the country.

Roadies   An early term used for the people who traveled with popular bands to take care of the musical equipment.

Root mean square (RMS) A method of averaging a sine wave to arrive at a mean average.

Saturation The purity of a color; the extent to which a color has been diluted.

SCR (silicon-controlled rectifier) dimmer A solid-state electronic device used to control lamp brightness by cutting off part of the cycle or the alternating current supply in a specific type of dimmer.

Scrim A gauze-like curtain that when illuminated from the front appears opaque but becomes transparent when light is brought up behind it.

Scroller A color changer that uses a string of colors, from 6 to 24, that is remotely controlled.

Set 1. The order of songs to be performed, generally used for musical performances in which no dialogue or scripted words are recited. 2. The stage design of a production.

Side light The source used to rim faces and model profile shots, often at or near head height.

Six foot rule If a worker is exposed to the possibility of falling six feet or more, fall protection must be provided and used.

Smoke Small, solid particles dispersed in air that reduce visibility and reflect light.

Soft patch An electronic means of assigning dimmers to control channels without physical wiring of jumpers on a terminal board or patch panel.

Span set A circle made of nylon web strands encased in a nylon covering that is wrapped around areas of load-bearing structures to prevent chafing.

Streaking The well-defined light or dark horizontal stripes superimposed across a picture that result from an area of extremely high tonal contrast in the picture.

Theatrical smoke Smoke created either through a chemical reaction or combustion (often caused by heating an oil-based liquid until it vaporizes).

Thyristor Opto-isolated solid state relay used to control high voltage in a controlled manner.

Torm A slang word for *tormentors*, which are the side curtains that hang next to the proscenium opening. These curtains can be adjusted to alter the width of the performance area.

Trade usage A custom or widely used practice common to a business that is unwritten but believed to be generally understood.

Truss A metal structure designed to support a horizontal load over an extended span. In theater and concert work, it is the term applied to the structure that normally supports the lighting over a 40 to 60 foot clear span.

Tungsten-halogen lamp (quartz) A lamp design that achieves an almost constant output and color temperature with a high lumen output throughout the working life of the lamp. This results from the halogen vapor (or bromine or iodine) that facilitates a chemical recycling action, preventing the blackening of the bulb wall with filament particles.

Turnaround In music, a point in the tune when the melody is broken up by another musical idea, after which the original melody is repeated.

United Scenic Artists (USA)   A national trade union that represents theatrical designers such as set designers, lighting directors, scenic artists, and model makers.

Venue   The location of a gathering; often used in legal contracts to designate the location of the concert.

Violent failure   The term most often used to describe the explosion of a lamp.

Wire rope   Similar to aircraft cable but generally with less tensile strength.

Xenon   A compact source discharge lamp that contains xenon gas in a pressurized lamp housing.

Yellow card   A term used by the IATSE to designate shows in which all the technicians are members of the union working under a signed agreement for wages and working conditions sanctioned by the international office.

Index

Index